ACPL ITEM
DISCARDED

DO NOT REMOVE
CARDS FROM POCKET

ALLEN COUNTY PUBLIC LIBRARY

FORT WAYNE, INDIANA 46802

You may return this book to any agency, branch,
or bookmobile of the Allen County Public Library.

DEMCO

CITY WOMEN

CITY WOMEN

Work, Jobs, Occupations, Careers

VOLUME 1: AMERICA

Helena Znaniecka Lopata

with
Cheryl Allyn Miller
and
Debra Barnewolt

PRAEGER SPECIAL STUDIES • PRAEGER SCIENTIFIC

New York • Philadelphia • Eastbourne, UK
Toronto • Hong Kong • Tokyo • Sydney

Library of Congress Cataloging in Publication Data

Lopata, Helena Znaniecka, 1925-
    City women.

    Bibliography: p.
    Includes index.
    Contents: v. 1. America—
        1. Urban women—Employment—United States.
I. Miller, Cheryl. II. Barnewolt, Debra. III. Title.
HD6095.L67 1984 331.4'09173'2 84-15933
ISBN O-03-069246-6 (alk. paper)

Published in 1984 by Praeger Publishers
CBS Educational and Professional Publishing
a Division of CBS Inc.
521 Fifth Avenue, New York, NY 10175 USA
© 1984 by Helena Z. Lopata

456789 052 987654321

Printed in the United States of America
on acid-free paper

Dedicated
to
Richard Lopata

Preface

The study upon which *City Women: Work, Jobs, Occupations, Careers* is based has a long history. The senior author founded the Center for the Comparative Study of Social Roles at Loyola University of Chicago in 1972 and was busy writing the results of a study entitled "Support Systems Involving Widows in Non-Agricultural Areas," when several of us, female faculty and graduate students, decided to study the changing commitments of American urban women, with special attention to jobs and family roles. The first proposal, co-authored with Kathleen Norr, then in Loyola's Sociology Department, was submitted to the newly formed National Institute on Education, where it did not get over the final hurdle. Our sample for that study was to be limited to college educated women. The Social Security Administration, represented by Dr. Henry Brehm, saw the proposal and expressed an interest in our submitting a revised version that would include women of all educational levels. The Social Security Administration's interest in women's changing commitments is not surprising, because it is concerned with the effect upon contributions to the system, and long term benefits from the system which accompany involvement in the labor force. Its in-house researchers, who are mainly economists, were also interested in knowing how different kinds of women perceive its programs. The revised proposal, titled "The Changing Commitments to Work and Family Roles among American Women and their Future Consequences for Social Security" went through various reviews and was funded for the years 1975-79. Dr. Brehm, Chief of Research Grants, Office of Research and Statistics of the SSA, became our project officer and was of tremendous help in all stages of research and analysis. We also obtained ideas from other members of the Office of Research and Statistics, including Patience Lauriat, Lucy Mallan, Lola Ireland, Wayne Finegar, Virginia Reno, and Gayle Thompson. The preliminary report, coauthored by Helena Lopata and Kathleen Norr, was forwarded to SSA in 1978, the final report in 1979.

vii

The research plan, about which more details are included in the Introduction and Volume II, called for interviews with a sample of women aged 25 to 54 who reside in the Chicago Consolidated Area. The interviews were conducted and the data reduced by the Survey Research Laboratory of the University of Illinois, Circle Campus, under the direction of Ron Czaja, although we at the center developed the interview and helped train the all-female staff of interviewers. Members of the Survey Research Laboratory whom we wish to thank, in addition to Ron, are Beth Eastman, Andy Montgomery, Richard Warnecke, and David Shoemaker.

The staff of the Center for the Comparative Study of Social Roles then consisted of Helena Lopata, principal investigator, Kathleen Norr, deputy director, Monica Velasco, Deb Barnewolt, and Jenny Ettling. Monica, Deb, and Jenny performed the difficult task of co-ordinating the research and administration of the project, as well as typing countless drafts of the interviews and reports with efficiency and good humor. Kathy taught all of us, including the graduate assistants, the fundamentals of statistics and programming. Without her the reports could not have been completed and the knowledge she provided was carried with us to Volume II of this work. Deb Barnewolt, Marlene Simon, Sue Meyering, and Cheryl Miller, the project research assistants, contributed to interview development, computer operations, and reports. Steve Brusko assisted in the initial literature review and Ron Szoc provided invaluable advice on data analyses and computer programming. The project was fortunate to have extensive support from Loyola University of Chicago. Special thanks are due Dr. Thomas M. Gannon, S.J., then chair of the Department of Sociology, Dr. Ronald E. Walker, Dean of the College of Arts and Sciences, Dr. Thomas Bennett, Director of Research Services, William Oswald, General Counsel, and John Ward, Director of Grants Accounting with his entire staff. Our colleagues in the department listened to various ideas and problems, drawing on their own work for suggestions. They include Judith Wittner, Kathleen McCourt, Kirsten Gronbjerg, Phil Nyden, Robert McNamara, and Peter Whalley. Karole Heyrman was tapped for her insights on the occupational role of nurse.

In the meantime, three of us who were still connected with the center after the reports were finished became increasingly interested in the occupational differences among the women in our sample, including: variations in paths followed to their current job, perceptions of the complexity and other characteristics of the job and the self, and the role cluster within which the job is located. We decided to return to the data and try a completely different analytic approach than was used in the reports, but with them as a foundation. The reports pointed not only to change, especially among the youngest age cohort, but also to great heterogeneity and decrystallization of life patterns and constructed reality. We now wanted to examine in more detail not only the mobility paths but the background, histories, self and job definitions, and role clusters of women in the same occupational category, within the same occupation, and even in allegedly similar jobs. Helena Lopata decided to review the literature on different occupations, historically and in modern America. This became Volume I of our study. Cheryl Miller was especially interested in the life patterns of role involvements, having written her dissertation titled "Life Course Patterns of Chicago Area Women: a Cohort Analysis of the Sequencing and Timing of Related Roles through the Middle Years" (Loyola, 1981). Cheryl's focus in our work was on the background characteristics, schooling and job training, employment and occupational histories of our seven major and 26 sub-category occupational groups for Volume II. The segment she wrote is then followed by Helena Lopata's analysis of the construction of reality, especially as it refers to the job and the self-concept of the women in our sample. Deb, who was interested in the composition and structure of women's role clusters, contributed to the examination of the relation between the role of employee, wife, mother, and homemaker within the resources available to women. Her dissertation focuses on the interrelation of roles in women's lives and the role "packages" that women create.

We had planned a single volume book, but by the time we covered all these factors for each occupational category of service—blue-collar, clerical, sales, homemaker (as managers of households), manager, and professional and technical workers—we had amassed an enormous amount of material. Luckily, Lynda Sharp of Praeger shares our excitement over the book and agreed to publish it in two volumes. Volume I contains background material relating to the history and current situation of American women in the various occupational categories and many of the occupations in which our respondents are situated. It provides knowledge generated by other social scientists and demographers yet remains almost exclusively the work of Helena Lopata. However, assistance was called for in the chapter on the professionals. Cheryl Miller contributed to the section on public school teachers, having served in that role in a junior high school before turning to sociology. Deb's interest in medical occupations enabled her to contribute to the sub-section on nurses.

Volume II, which contains our analyses of the Chicago area interviews, is a shared venture. Cheryl focused on the background and histories, Helena on the construction of reality as far as the job and the self are concerned, and Deb on the role cluster. More detail on the content of Volume II and the people who contributed to our understanding of the Chicago scene is contained in its Preface and Introduction. Throughout our work, Cheryl, Deb, and Helena have exchanged material for editorial, content, and reference suggestions.

Helena Lopata's work on Volume I was greatly facilitated by several groups and people. The recipient of a research award from the Murray Center of Radcliffe College in the Spring of 1982, she wishes to thank Ann Kolby, Patricia King, and the staffs of Murray Center and the Schlesinger Library for help in using the resources of this institution. Loyola University provided a research leave in the Fall of 1983 to enable her to finish this overview and to "pull it all together." Richard Lopata provided knowledge of the world of work and suggestions as to sources, as well as ideas.

Contents

Contents

TABLES

FIGURES

1

ORGANIZING CONCEPTS

This book is devoted to an examination of the work carried out by city women in modern America, and the way this work is organized into jobs falling into occupational categories and individual careers.

THE CONCEPTS: WORK, JOBS, OCCUPATIONS, CAREERS

Sociologists and other observers of human behavior have difficulty defining the concept of work. Some, like Udy (1970), have limited their discussion to "any purposive human effort to modify man's physical environment." Others define it as "an effort or exertion done typically to make a living or keep a house," as did de Grazia (1964: 223). The last quotation satisfies modern feminists who object to the usual tendency of Americans to limit the meaning of work to paid labor, as if the many tasks carried out in the roles of housewife, wife, or mother, as well as in voluntary community activity were not work. Oakley (1974a) attributes such limitation, and the consequent disregard of housework as real work, to sexism: "It has treated housework merely as an aspect of the feminine role in the family—as part of the women's role in marriage, or as a dimension of child-rearing—not as a work role." Many definitions of work focus on paid effort.

Since this book is focused on the work of women, we are using the female pronoun for the general case. We will be using the male pronoun when men are specifically indicated.

1

Using housework as an example, we can see the absurdity of defining work as 'paid employment.' A housewife, according to this definition,
does not work. But if a husband must replace her services—with a housekeeper, cook, baby sitter—these replacements become workers, and the
husband has added to the Gross National Product the many thousands
of dollars the replacements are paid. It is, therefore, an inconsistency of
our definition of work that leads us to say that a woman who cares for
her own children is not working, but if she takes a job looking after the
children of others, she is working.

Viewing work in terms of pay alone has also produced a synony-
mity of 'pay' and 'worth,' so that higher-paid individuals are thought by
many to have greater personal worth than those receiving less pay (Special Task Force to the Secretary of HEW, 1973: 2-3).

Hall's (1975: 4) definition of work as "an activity that produces something of value for other people" also contains inherent difficulties, although it does incorporate the Marxist view of labor long ignored by
occupational sociologists. It places into question any work producing
something of value to the worker alone and brings forth the problem
of defining value. The large dictionaries such as those published by
Oxford or Random House offer columns of definitions. Other texts,
such as Gallagher and Palazzolo's (1977) edition *The Social World of
Occupations*, or Ritzer's (1977) *Working*, do not even list it in the index and contain no definitions. In *The Random House Dictionary of
the English Language* (1966: 1644), we find 53 definitions of work,
including:

1. Exertion or effort directed to produce or accomplish something;
   labor, toil
2. That on which exertion or labor is expended; something to be made
   or done; a task or undertaking
3. Productive or operative activity
4. Employment, as in some form of industry, especially as a means of
   earning one's livelihood; to be without work, to look for work

We have selected the first of these definitions for the purpose of this
book. Work, according to this definition, is effort directed toward a
goal, be it a song, a rapidly eaten meal, or a more durable contribution
to the ideas, norms, or material objects of a culture. The fact that the
goal is not always reached does not preclude the effort from being defined as work. Most work consists of a variety of interrelated tasks,
with more or less flexible boundaries of start, duration, and end. In
addition, the work of one person is usually related to the work of another person or a larger social unit. This means that it is usually woven

into social roles, defined as sets of interdependent social relations between a social person and a social circle involving duties and rights (Znaniecki, 1965). The work of a mother is incorporated into the social role of mother, containing relations with everyone to whom she has duties and from whom she receives rights because she is a mother.

A division of labor that makes possible the continued existence and reproduction of a social group is a universal human phenomenon, but only recently have the social roles within which a major segment of work is contained been turned into jobs. Jobs are social roles containing work and other aspects of social relations with all members of a social circle. An additional characteristic of jobs, lacking in most other social roles, is evident in the fourth definition of work quoted from *The Random House Dictionary*: "employment, as in some form of industry, especially as a means of earning one's livelihood." It is important that the idea of "earn one's livelihood" be specified. This phrase usually brings to mind a salary or wage, that is, money received in return for doing one's job. However, earning a living can be accomplished through exchanges of services, or indirectly, as in the case of the homemaker who is the unpaid member of a two-person career or job (Papanek, 1973). Her full-time work at home makes it possible for another member of the family, usually the husband, to earn the money which she transforms into direct sources of livelihood for herself and the children (Lopata and Brehm, forthcoming). "The housewife, for example, does not receive pay for her work. Her work does, however, have important indirect yields, particularly if part of her husband's career depends upon her success in the housewife's role" (Hall, 1975: 6).

> The clear fact is that keeping house and raising children is work—work that is, on the average, as difficult to do well and as useful to the larger society as almost any paid job involving the production of goods or services. The difficulty is not that most people don't believe this or accept it [we pay lip service to it all the time] but that, whatever our private and informal belief systems, we have not, as a society, acknowledged this fact in our public system of values and rewards (Special Task Force to the Secretary of HEW, 1973: 179).

Thus, although work is part of the "normal flow of life" (O'Kelly, 1980; Ryan, 1979), not all work has been converted into jobs in modern society, defined as work-focused social roles, and not all social roles are jobs. These definitions make it possible to include the process of preparing a meal for an income-producing husband, of performing the duties of a doctor, or reading a textbook in preparation for teaching a class as both work and part of jobs. This frees us from rejection of work which does not modify the physical environment forced on us by Udy's (1970) definition, or concern about value to others to which Hall's (1975) definition limits us.

Jobs have other characteristics, some of which are common to other types of social roles. The work is organized into what the organizers assume to be logical sets of tasks. They have specific criteria for entrance and stages of involvement; relations with others are bureaucratized or formalized along authority and communication lines of the system within which they are contained. Of course, many jobs remain charismatically pulled together and informally carried out, but modern American society tries to develop jobs along lines enabling predictability of behavior because of the size and complexity of the system.

Jobs are performed in modern capitalistic or socialistic societies within organized social groups or in more loosely bound social circles, with the work being divided into sets of interlocking and complementary social roles. Although jobs are thus situationally located, their work and social relations are usually duplicated in other locations and in other groups, with a generalized cultural label, or occupational title, applied to them (Udy, 1970). Udy (1979: 5-6) makes a strong argument in favor of separating the concepts of job and occupation.

> A *job* may be thought of as a role ordinarily performed primarily for the purpose of earning a livelihood in a commercial economy. It is a component of social structure. More often than not it is a specific role in a particular organization, involving a specified range of activities, particular modes of interaction with others, a given degree of authority and control, and a specified amount of pay. An *occupation*, on the other hand, emerges as a more or less publicly recognized cultural category, into which certain people are both popularly and officially classified because they all hold, or in some cases, at one time have held jobs exhibiting that particular set of characteristics which constitute the criteria for inclusion in that particular occupational category. Occupations are thus culturally defined by certain selected aspects of jobs that many jobs have in common.

> Occupations are aggregations of jobs, grouped on the basis of their similarity in content—similarity in the tasks they involve, the duties and responsibilities they entail, and the conditions under which they are performed. *The DOT* (*Dictionary of Occupational Titles* of the U.S. Department of Labor) maps the several million jobs held by the 100 million members of the U.S. labor force into 12,099 occupations (Cain and Treiman, 1981: 254) (see also Whalley, 1982).

When a woman becomes identified with a certain occupation, be it a waitress or professor of sociology, she can, with luck, obtain a job with any of several employers. Of course, there are occupations for which there is only one job, such as that of President of the United States. The point being made here is that the job is a situated occupation, specific to a definite social circle and that many jobs, which are more or less similar in makeup, fall into an occupation. Thus, the label "nurse" is applied to, and identified with, many social persons who have met specific qualifications for licensing. In addition, there are many jobs open to nurses, depending on whether they want to work in a private hospital, public health clinic, the Veteran's Administration, a school, or in private duty. The occupational title is already a summary label, covering many jobs and variations of content, duties, and conditions. The proliferation of occupations in a society, including American society, has necessitated even greater aggregation of occupations into a few categories. The chapters of this book are organized by these occupational categories, such as service or professional and technical workers. The reader must keep in mind, however, that these categories lump together many occupations which are quite varied and often bear little similarity to one another.

THE JOB AS A SOCIAL ROLE

The tendency of Americans to consider only tasks when describing jobs, especially if they involve manipulation of data or things, necessitates a fuller development of the idea of a job as a social role. As mentioned, social roles contain four basic components: the social person, the social circle, the duties of the person, and the rights making the performance of these duties possible (Znaniecki, 1965). The circle consists of everyone with whom the person interacts in order to carry forth the role. Social roles have cultural foundations most participants know well enough to enter their relations or which they can gain in "on the job training." The goals or purposes toward which the role aims can often be carried out in a variety of ways, but each social circle, and the group or society in which it is lodged, develops variations on the themes. Even new roles, such as that of astronaut, are built on similar existing roles and are modified by the requirements of the new goals or technology and the characteristics of the persons and the circles. Most social roles have existing social circles whose members enter and exit flexibly, and which precede a new incumbent or social person. Thus, most of the ongoing life of a society is organized into social roles within the major institutions and simply requires the replacement of a social person or circle member. The new participants may introduce varying degrees of change in the relations because of their characteristics, including the ability to carry forth the duties or preferences associated with the social role. However, the basic purposes for which the roles were created tend to remain stable or to change slowly. Doctors still diagnose and treat in an effort to save patients, although their training has been greatly modified over the centuries and laboratory technicians, X-ray specialists, and complex hospital staffs have been added to their social circles. The social person of doctor varies in personal characteristics such as gender from society to society (Sokolowska, 1965) but the purpose of the role remains relatively stable.

Not all social roles entered into by a social person have already established social circles. Women starting in private practice as doctors must pull together their own circle of patients, colleagues, complementary specialists, X-ray and other diagnostic laboratories, hospitals, and so forth. Women entering the role of homemaker or housewife must do the same, forming their own social circle of co-residents in the home, suppliers of services or goods, neighbors with whom to exchange supports, and societal resources as needed, such as the police in case of burglary, firefighters in case of fire, and a variety of other services in case of domestic emergencies (Lopata, 1966, 1971). Such roles as doctor in private practice or homemaker are indeterminate and entrepreneurial, although each society provides role models and resources for their performance (Mack, 1956). The size and complexity of the social circle and the rights and duties involved in each role vary considerably in such a society as ours, by social class, income, involvement in other social roles, basic goals and values (Kohn, 1977; Lopata, 1969).

A major point being made here is that a social role is a set of relations, people doing things which can be observed and whose results can be studied, rather than a set of expectations or cultural ideals. The life of society is carried out through the patterned interaction between social persons and social circles. A social person in a social role consists of a package of human characteristics which is tested for admission into the role and which is actually used in the performance of the role's duties or the receipt of its rights. Not all aspects or characteristics of an individual are involved in each role, and roles vary considerably in how much of the total self becomes involved. The social person of customer requires only the ability to communicate with the seller by entering a store, telephoning, or writing and presenting oneself in an acceptable manner followed by payment for the objects or services received (Goffman, 1959). Although the social circle of the customer may include a variety of people who manufacture the object, transmit the request for it, and so forth, direct communication may be limited to only a few individuals. The immediate layer of the social circle consists of everyone who interacts with the person in order to enable her to carry out in the normatively prescribed manner the role that is to be fulfilled. The rights granted the social person of customer include provision of safety, space, time, polite manner on the part of the service personnel, honesty in the representation of the object, and so forth (Znaniecki, 1965). The duties vary by the complexity of the social circle, since each member must be interacted with, directly or through an intermediary, if only to transmit instructions on how to best serve the main beneficiary of the role—the client/customer/student/patient. The more people the doctor surrounds herself with in order to diagnose and treat a patient, the more people she has to interact with. On the other hand, such assistants or auxiliary personnel shorten the time required for the treatment of any one patient and, allegedly, improve the quality of results through specialized knowledge. Thus, the work involved in the diagnosis and treatment can be carried out mainly by the doctor, or divided among a variety of specialists, while the doctor retains the function of coordinating the information and transmitting the results to the patient with prescriptions for treatment, often from pharmacists the doctor does not even know.

As mentioned before, most work in modern, urban America is carried out in large and complex settings and involves relations with large and complex social circles. These social circles usually contain categories of people whose presence can be diagrammed.

We can take the social role of a nurse in a pediatric department of a city hospital to illustrate our concepts. The client part of the social circle would be the child patient. The child's parents could also be treated as clients or as part of the work group assisting the nurse, depending on their relation to the staff and their involvement with the child's treatment. Other nurses perform that role simultaneously or on different shifts from the nurse in question, making possible the functioning of the hospital. Other members of the work team would involve the pediatrician and any personnel provided by the hospital to assist the nurse, such as the pharmacist, physical therapist, practical nurse, social worker, and so forth. Administrators consist of the nursing supervisor, head nurse, and the hospital's director, the staff in the accounting and admission offices, and so forth. Other workers include the maintenance crew, other physicians and nurses in other wards, purchasing agents, the dietician and kitchen staff, laboratory technicians, and pathologists. Suppliers who usually have more direct contact with the administration than with the nurse are people who bring in medications, linen, food, and all items needed in the care of patients and for the functioning of the hospital. The community includes the neighborhood in which the hospital is located, the police, fire department, and others who bring in patients. The "cosmopolitan" world involves the nursing associations and other institutions and representatives which influence the duties and rights of nurses. Presenting the segments in the form of a circle rather than as a "role set," à la Merton (1968) is advantageous because we are able to indicate the interaction among those involved in the role. The pediatrician, active in the circle of the nurse, also interacts with the child, the parents, the administrators, and others because they form part of her own social circle of pediatrician.

Of course, most social persons do not have all the characteristics the cultural norms considered ideal for doctors, housewives, or incumbents of any social role in the society. Likewise, these social circles do not contain the ideal clients, assistants, suppliers, or managers. For example, schools train secretaries to type rapidly and accurately, be familiar with spelling and proper forms of data presentation, take dictation, handle difficult situations with visitors, and so forth. However, many firms can not afford a secretary of this quality and must settle for one who is far from perfect.

Not all brilliant new PhDs can get jobs in the top ten universities, so they join colleagues and students in less ideal settings. As we shall see in the following chapters, settings make a great deal of difference in the type of characteristics demanded of the social person before entrance into a social role is allowed, as well as in the duties and rights involved in the exchanges. Even in such indeterminate roles as that of homemaker, there are limitations to what a woman can do and whom she can pull into the circle (Lopata, 1971; Mack, 1956). Money and access to services are needed. It is hard to avoid in-laws and their demands for meals during visits. The addition of infants to the household activates the role of mother, definitely changing the role of housewife or homemaker. So does the removal of a member through divorce. A woman in a farm household has different resources available to her in the role of homemaker than does the penthouse urbanite or the slum dweller. There are many ways of being a secretary, and

Figure 1.1   The Social Role of a Worker

Note: The size of the segment in the circle indicates the relative importance of the duties of the social person to that segment.

it makes a great deal of difference whether one manages an office or a fast food restaurant.

ROLE STRAIN

The fact that a person prepares for an occupation, applies for a job, and is accepted by an existing social circle, does not mean that all problems are anticipated or solved. Often the training is inadequate or inappropriate. Each work setting has its own norms or rules. Each relation must be developed and maintained separately, then woven into the other relations of the role (Brim and Wheeler, 1966). Each segment of the social circle is likely to have different ideas about what the social person should do and demand that its expectations be met and met first, before duties to other segments are performed (Goode, 1960). According to Goode (1960), and as developed by Ritzer (1977), *role strain* can arise from a variety of sources. *Role overload* occurs when the person is expected to meet too many demands from too many sources, even when the demands are not "onerous, difficult or displeasing" (Goode, 1960: 485). *Inter-sender* strain occurs when contradictory demands are made by different people in the circle, *intra-sender* strain when the same person or circle segment makes contradictory demands. *Role ambiguity* results from inadequate definitions of the rights or duties associated with a social role or when social circle members do not hold the same role expectations as the social person. Problems arise when resources are inadequate for meeting the role's duties or when the role's rights are not honored by others. Many employees, educated or trained to expect the cooperation of certain segments of the circle responsible for assisting the performance of the job, join companies lacking such services. Many heads of state of countries which send their bright young women and men for training in such roles as medical doctor to the United States complain that the products of such an education are not competent to perform that role in a homeland which lacks complex laboratories, equipment, and other specialists.

Difficulties in the lives of people can arise out of the fact that each social role has its own code of ethics and value systems which may conflict with those the person learned elsewhere or has internalized in different roles. This *role-person strain* often occurs when students are given an idealized image of the occupation they are about to enter, only to find that the organization which hired them considers nothing more important than profits and has a policy of "let the buyer beware" (caveat emptor). Reality shock often results in "burn-out" in nurses, social workers, and teachers.

People handle the problems connected with role strain in a variety of ways: compartmentalization, delegation of duties, elimination of the role relationship, exiting a role, extension and creation of barriers against intrusion to "prevent others from initiation or even continuing role relationships" (Goode, 1960: 487). Merton (1968) and Gouldner (1957, 1958) pointed out that people develop hierarchies of importance of roles or role segments. For example, people who are involved in a stress-creating role can focus on the demands of a local reference group, or on a cosmopolitan one in deciding which duties to carry forth first and which values are the most important (Gouldner, 1957). University students can decide that the judgment of a professor in a class in which they are enrolled and from which they expect credit to be more important than that of peers.

While discussing social roles, we need to clarify our stand on the frequently used concept of "sex roles" (Lopata, 1980; Lopata and Thorne, 1978). Accepting the definition of social role as a set of functionally interdependent social relations, we can question the existence of sex roles in modern America on two counts. In the first place, what is involved in social interaction and self awareness is really gender identity, not sexual identity. There is a whole set of actions and sentiments involved in gender behavior and inaction. Babies at birth are defined as either male or female by sexual characteristics and are treated differently if one rather than the other identification is determined. Gradually, with direct socialization and in response to the "looking glass" self perceived in the eyes and manner of significant others, gender identification becomes a pervasive gender identity, a social phenomenon. In the second place, we question the existence of a separate gender role, whose duties and rights have as their only function the maintenance of status differences between males and females, independent of other social roles. What is true of the social world is that men and women relate to each other in a variety of defined social roles, as lovers, husbands and wives, parents, friends, co-workers and so forth. Awareness of similarities or differences in gender identity is present, with more or less strength, in social encounters, but only part of the social person enters into sets of relations. Other characteristics of appearance (Stone, 1962) or demeanor (Goffman, 1956, 1959) influence the relation, but social roles have a purpose or goal other than the maintenance of such distinction and involve more than two people. American society is especially geared toward functional roles, rather than status relations. It appears that the status or identity distinctions between men and women are thus always included in social roles, but are not themselves social roles. At least, we shall so treat them in this book.

ROLE CLUSTERS AND ROLE CONFLICT

Human beings are never participants in only one social role. In order to be the social person of one role there must be at least two members in the social circle. They, in turn, are members of the social circles of others. In addition, modern life requires human beings to bring together several different roles into their *role cluster*. Some roles are more closely related, falling into the same institutional domain than are others. For example, American society has traditionally tied the roles of wife, mother, and homemaker together for women in certain age categories. Men are expected to combine the roles of husband and father together with that of employee, not only for economic maintenance of the other two roles, but also to take part in the economic life of the society. Some persons build multi-dimentional life spaces by choosing roles in several institutional spheres; other restrict themselves, or are restricted by others, into a very narrow set of roles within limited social circles (Coser, 1975). Previous research has indicated the tremendous importance of formal education in preparation for complex social engagement by women, traditionally trained to be passive vis-a-vis the world outside the family institution, but now living in a society which demands volunteeristic engagement (Lopata, 1973, 1979, 1981a).

The presence of several social roles in a person's role cluster creates many opportunities for *role conflict* when demands of one role interfere with the demands of another. If the demands are of a contradictory nature, they can overburden the person, create problems of assigning priorities, and cause a great deal of emotional drain. The most difficult situations of role conflict occur when there is no clear-cut hierarchy of importance assigned and agreed to by the members of the different social circles. Each role's social circle may consider the duties toward it more important than those to other roles. An excellent example of almost built-in role conflict occurs in the lives of modern American women who combine the roles of job holder, wife, and mother. Recent changes have removed the role of homemaker from strong and direct competition with the "big three," but all evidence, not only from our study but from numerous other research, points to problems in women juggling these roles. We shall return to these when discussing each occupational category. (Lopata, 1969, 1971; Lopata and Norr, 1979, 1980). On the other hand, some roles demand high levels of commitment and do not tolerate excuses along role conflict lines (Mortimer, Hall, and Hill, 1978). Coser (1974) calls these "greedy institutions."

The relationship between social roles within one person's cluster, or at least between some of them, can be illustrated with the following figure. Roles which fall into the family institution allegedly share the same value system and are supposedly easier to balance than roles crossing institutions. However, personal relations frequently compete

Figure 1.2 Generalized Composition of the Social Circles of Four Major Social Roles of American Women.

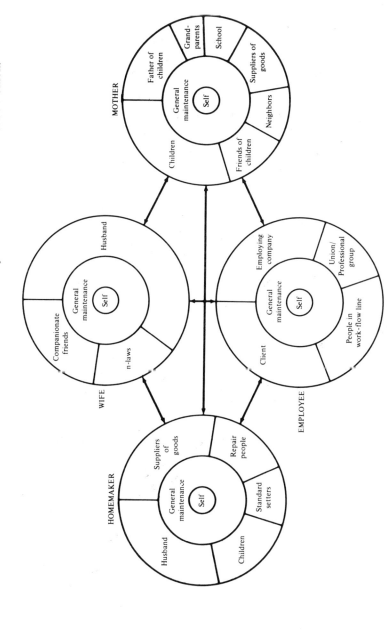

Note: The arrows do not designate segments of interconnected social roles, only the interconnection among them.

13

against each other, as young husbands report jealousy over the time their wives devote to newborn infants (Dyer, 1963; Hobbs, 1965; Le Masters, 1957; Rossi, 1968). Friendship can be seen as competing with companionate marriage (Lopata, 1981b). Each close associate of a total human being expects to be "primary" in the heart of that being. Things get further complicated when a man is both a husband in the circle of a woman's role as wife and the father in the circle of a woman's role as mother.

CAREER: AS DEFINED BY SOCIOLOGISTS AND BY WOMEN

Finally, when speaking or work, organized into jobs, contained in occupations, and summarized in occupational categories, we can also look at a person from the vantage point of a career by sociologists and as we rapidly found out, by women. The women in our Chicago area sample had very different ideas as to what constitutes a career than what even disagreeing sociologists have in mind. Sociologists usually look at the career of a person either in retrospect or a projected future if they discern some pattern to the succession of jobs the woman has followed. Thus social scientists studying professionals and business managers refer to a career as a sequence of jobs which involve upward mobility, in terms of increases of responsibility, authority, prestige, and pay (Hall, 1975; Ritzer, 1977). Others refer to a career in terms of stages of involvement, including preparatory, initial, trial, stable, and retirement (Miller and Form, 1980). Ritzer (1977: 69) summarized Stebbins's explanation of three aspects of individual careers which could refer to either a series of jobs or stages of involvement in one occupation:

> The career pattern is the consensually recognized series of stages associated with a given occupation. In a sense, this is an 'ideal' pattern of occupational movement and few individuals ever follow it totally. Because of this gap between the ideal and the actual, we need the concept of individual objective career. This is the series of stages through which an individual actually traverses during his or her worklife . . . Finally, there is the concept of subjective career or the individual's personal recognition and interpretation of his individual objective career in light of the career pattern associated with his occupation.

The main definitions of "career" by people studying the world of work contain the assumption of a continuous involvement in an occupation or a series of interrelated jobs with a strong feeling of commitment and dedication (Ritzer, 1977). However, as Wilensky (1961) pointed out many years ago, most people do not have orderly careers.

This is true of many blue-collar male workers, and it is especially true for female workers. We were curious as to whether women defined themselves as having or planning a career. Answers varied according to occupation. Luckily, we also decided to ask our respondents for a definition of a career and obtained some very interesting answers, some of which are reproduced below. What do you think of as a career?

> A job that utilizes my interest, knowledge and training. I am not in one now [works in retail sales] because I can't follow my plan [married at age 26, now 28]. Only one of us can afford to continue an education. *Best job* will be as head of a medical research laboratory, coordinating all the research and performing various research experiments. It's challenging, it's a job that I can continually learn from and grow with and that is most important to me.

> Something that answers my needs; it fulfills me. I feel I'm utilizing all my abilities in a career [trained as a nurse; worked as a staff nurse in a hospital, in surgery assisting the surgeon and preparing the patient for surgery; became a nursing supervisor setting policies and procedures, evaluating employees]. I am supervising in areas where I have expertise. I'm knowledgeable. I'm capable of performing the job. I have confidence with what I'm doing.

> A career to me would be someone who has learned a specific trade or developed a specific skill through formal education and experience or practice and doing this the better part of their lives.

As we shall discuss in Volume II, we finally decided to use the concept of career as understood by the women in our Chicago area sample. Thus, we refer to their employment and occupational histories, rather than trying to arbitrarily decide which have followed a succession of interconnected and upwardly mobile jobs, and we refer to career commitment. The latter concept refers to the woman's own identification of the self as a "career woman" and her statement that she has followed a career in the past, is in one now, or plans for one in the future.

The methods used in Volume I are the standard ones of literature review, organized according to the sociological concepts discussed above and the occupations of the women in our Chicago area sample. Unfortunately, the literature is not evenly developed on all occupations in which women work.

REFERENCES

Brim, Orville, and Stanton Wheeler. 1966. *Socialization After Childhood*. New York: John Wiley.

Cain, Pamela S., and Donald J. Treiman. 1981. *The DOT* as a source of occupational data. *American Sociological Review* 46 (June): 253-78.

Coser, Lewis A. 1974. *Greedy Institutions: Patterns of Undivided Commitment.* New York: The Free Press.

Coser, Rose Laub. 1975. The Complexity of Roles as a Seedbed of Individual Autonomy. In *The Idea of Social Structure: Papers in Honor of Robert K. Merton*, edited by Lewis A. Coser, pp. 237-63. New York: Harcourt, Brace Jovanovich.

Dyer, Everett D. 1963. Parenthood as crisis: A re-study. *Marriage and Family Living* 25 (May): 196-201.

Gallagher, Bernard J. III, and Charles S. Palazzolo, eds. 1977. *The Social World of Occupations.* Dubuque, Iowa: Kendall/Hunt.

Goffman, Erving. 1959. *The Presentation of Self in Everyday Life.* Garden City, New York: Doubleday Anchor.

_____. 1956. The nature of deference and demeanor. *American Anthropologist* 58 (June): 473-502.

Goode, William. 1960. A theory of role strain. *American Sociological Review* 25 (August): 483-96.

Gouldner, Alvin K. 1958. Cosmopolitans and locals. *Administrative Science Quarterly* (March): 444-80.

_____. 1957. Cosmopolitans and locals. *Administrative Science Quarterly* (December): 281-306.

de Grazia, Sebastian. 1964. *Of Time, Work and Leisure.* Garden City, New York: Doubleday Anchor.

Hall, Richard. 1975. *Occupations and Social Structure.* Englewood Cliffs, New Jersey: Prentice-Hall.

Hobbs, Daniel F., Jr. 1965. Parenthood as crisis: A third study. *Journal of Marriage and the Family* 27 (March): 367-72.

Kohn, Melvin L. 1977. *Class and Conformity: A Study in Values.* Chicago: University of Chicago Press.

LeMasters, E. E. 1957. Parenthood as crisis. *Marriage and Family Living* 19: 352-55.

Lopata, Helena Z. 1981c. American women: Education and the construction of reality. *Quarterly Journal of Ideology*, special issue, Judith R. Blau, editor 5 (3, Fall): 11-24.

_____. 1981b. Friendship: Historical and Theoretical Perspectives. In *Research on the Interweave of Social Roles: Friendship*, edited by Helena Z. Lopata and D. Maines, pp. 1-19. Greenwich, Connecticut: JAI Press.

_____. 1981a. Polish-American Families. In *Ethnic Families in America: Patterns and Variation*, edited by Charles H. Mindel and Robert W. Habenstein. pp. 17-42. New York: Elsevier, 2nd. edition.

_____. 1980. The Chicago woman: A study of patterns of mobility and transportation. *Signs*, special issue on *Women and the American City*. 5 (Spring, 3):S161-S169.

_____. 1980. "Self Images and the structure of the self-concept: American urban women." Paper presented at the annual meetings of the American Sociological Association.

_____. 1979. *Women as Widows: Support Systems*. New York: Elsevier-North Holland.

_____. 1975. Couple-companionate Relationships in Marriage and Widowhood. In *Old Families/New Families*, edited by N. Glazer-Malbin, pp. 119-49. New York: D. Van Nostrand.

_____. 1973. *Widowhood in an American City*. Cambridge, Massachussetts: Schenkman, General Learning Press.

_____. 1971. *Occupation: Housewife*. New York: Oxford University Press.

_____. 1969. Social psychological aspects of role involvement. *Sociology and Social Research* 53 (April): 285-98.

_____. 1966. The life cycle of the social role of housewife. *Sociology and Social Research* 53 (April): 5-22.

Lopata, Helena and Henry P. Brehm, forthcoming, *Dependent Wives and Widows: From Social Problem to Federal Program*. New York: Praeger.

Lopata, Helena Z. and Kathleen Norr. 1980. Changing commitments of American women to work and family roles. *Social Security Bulletin* 43 (June): 3-14.

_____. 1979. Changing Commitments of American Women to Work and Family Roles and Their Future Consequences for Social Security. Final report to the Social Security Administration.

Lopata, Helena Z. and Barrie Thorne. 1978. On the term "sex roles." *Signs* 3 (3): 718-21.

Mack, Raymond. 1956. Occupational determinateness: A problem and hypotheses in role theory. *Social Forces* 35 (October): 20-34.

Merton, Robert. 1968. *Social Theory and Social Structure*. New York: Free Press.

Miller, Delbert C. and William H. Form. 1980. *Industrial Sociology Work in Organizational Life*. New York: Harper and Row.

Mortimer, Jeylan, Richard Hall, and Robert Hill. 1978. Husband's occupational attitudes as constraints on wives' employment. *Sociology of Work and Occupations* 5 (August): 285-313.

Newsweek, 1963. Convention Wives—Help or Hindrance (May 13): 82-83.

Newsweek, 1957. Sizing Up Executives' Wives (May 13): 93-95.

Oakley, Ann. 1974b. *The Sociology of Housework*. Bath, England: Pitman Press.

_____. 1974a. *Women's Work: A History of the Housewife*. New York: Pantheon Books.

O'Kelly, Charlotte G. 1980. *Women and Men in Society*. New York: D. Van Nostrand.

The Oxford Universal Dictionary. 1955. Oxford: Clarendon Press.

Papanek, Hanna. 1973. Men, women and work: Reflections on the two-person career. *American Journal of Sociology* 78 (January): 852-72.

Random House Dictionary of the English Language. 1966. New York: Random House.

Reese, Albert. 1973. *The Economics of Work and Pay*. New York: Harper & Row.

Ritzer, George. 1977. *Working: Conflict and Change*. Englewood Cliffs, New Jersey: Prentice-Hall.

Rossi, Alice. 1968. Transition to parenthood. *Journal of Marriage and the Family* 30 (Feb.): 26-39.

Ryan, Mary P. 1979. *Womanhood in America: From Colonial Times to the Present*. New York: New Viewpoints.

Sokolowska, Magdalena. 1965. Some reflections on the different attitudes of men and women toward work. *International Labor Review*. 92 (July): 35-50.

Special Task Force to Secretary of Health, Education, and Welfare. 1970. *Work in America*. Cambridge, Massachussetts: The MIT Press.

Stone, Gregory, P. 1962. Appearance and the Self. In *Human Behavior and Social Process*, edited by A. Rose, pp. 88-117. Boston: Houghton Mifflin.

Udy, Stanley H. 1979. "The configuration of occupational structure." Paper presented at the annual meeting of the American Sociological Association.
————. 1970. *Work in Traditional and Modern Societies*. Englewood Cliffs, New Jersey: Prentice Hall.

Whalley, R. Peter. 1982. "The Social Production of Technical Work: The Case of British Engineers." Unpublished Ph.D. dissertation, Columbia University.

Wilensky, Harold L. 1961. Orderly careers and social participation: The impact of work history on social integration in the middle mass. *American Sociological Review* 26 (August): 521-39.

Znaniecki, Florian W. 1965. *Social Relations and Social Roles*. San Francisco: Chandler.

2

WOMEN'S WORK:
HISTORICAL PERSPECTIVES

The history of women's work and the ways in which it has been organized into social roles is obviously part of the history of work in general. The latter chronicle is, in turn, closely related to the organization of the society or community within which the work is carried out, the ideology through which it is perceived, explained, and evaluated, and the technology that is utilized in its performance. Some societies have organized tasks such as paid child care or the catering of foods into jobs, while others leave the duties involved in cooking for the family or "playing with" children as part of the normal flow of unpaid work or do not even consider them as work per se. The value system surrounding work can come from religion, political ideologies, or the economic institution itself. Even the leisure institution can provide the rationale for paying actors and sports figures higher salaries than waitresses and teachers or even doctors (Stone, 1973). Villages organized around hunting or fishing may honor the work of men specializing in such activities more than those of food gatherers or farmers, even if the majority of the foodstuff comes from their efforts. In some communities barter and market activity provide the trader with many advantages, including knowledge of what is going on away from the home, contact with others, and feelings of solidarity. In turn these advantages are often translatable into increased power within the community and the home (Boserup, 1970; Touba, 1980). On the other hand, this combination of tasks may result in overwork and role strain, preventing capitalization upon such advantages (Huntington, 1975).

As far as we know, division of labor by age and sex is universal, but the distribution of tasks and relations varies considerably (O'Kelly, 1980; Ryan, 1979). In more complex societies, the work done by any particular member also varies by social class, the role cluster, and personal resources for the acquisition of skills and knowledge necessary for entrance and retention of the job. But whatever the division of labor and the accompanying value system, work throughout the majority of human history has been a cooperative venture, both in hunting and gathering societies and in agricultural civilizations (Miller, 1981; O'Kelly, 1980).

In family production for subsistence, the general rule for the division of labor is for each sex to specialize in a particular process or product. The adult person who is responsible for the production is usually helped by children or young persons of the same sex (Boserup, 1970; 140). Few fishermen went to sea alone; most formed tightly knit units for the dangerous forays (Norr and Norr, 1974). Nomadic groups were also closely integrated, with a flexible division of labor as needs arose. Work was interwoven with leisure and the family was closely tied to the economic institution (Boulding, 1976; Mead, 1949/ 1970*; O'Kelly, 1980).

There is much disagreement among anthropologists and social scientists as to the position of women in premodern societies, mainly because their status has varied to such an extent. However, the importance of cooperative work and exchange between the sexes is acknowledged by all. Many factors have contributed to the ebb and flow of the status and related rights of women, but the primary emphasis has been on the evaluation given their reproductive activity and how that affects their work (Boserup, 1970; Glazer, 1976, 1980). For example, Boserup (1970) documented that:

> European settlers, colonial administrators and technical advisers are largely responsible for the deterioration in the status of women in the agricultural sectors of developing countries. It was they who neglected the female agricultural labour force when they helped to introduce modern commercial agriculture to the overseas world and promoted the productivity of male labour (Boserup, 1970: 53-54).

---

*Throughout this volume, in cases where there is an important time gap between dates, the date of the first publication of the work will be given first, followed by the date of the edition being used here so that the reader will know the setting in which the author is writing.

Historians and others following Engels (1884/1972) have claimed that with the emergence of private property, women lost political rights and the contributions of their work to the social unit were devalued. In an earlier period, the clan held more fluid rights to property. Members were dependent on it to maintain themselves until their death or until they were unable to work for other reasons (Boulding, 1976; Hartmann, 1976; Sacks, 1974).

> Engels presents a historical dynamic by which women were transformed from free and equal productive members of society to subordinate and dependent wives and wards . . . In the early stages of society, productive resources were owned communally by the tribe or clan . . . The creation of private property made its owner the ruler of the household. Women and other property-less dependents worked to maintain and augment the household head's property, for he was now engaged in competitive production and exchange with other heads of households (Sacks, 1974: 200-211).

Of course, this explanation does not answer the question of why men, rather than women, acquired rights over private property. The pre-existing tendency toward patriarchy, however, does explain it (Hartmann, 1976). In early Roman times, married women were considered part of the "chattel" or movable property of the husband (Boulding, 1976; Kiefer, 1934/1971; Murstein, 1974). They could not inherit property and under the principle of *manus*, the property they brought with them to the marriage belonged to the husband. Only later, as the power of the state increased, did the husband lose some of his rights over the wife. Still, the father retained his "patria potestas" rights over his children, even married daughters (Kiefer, 1934/1971).

The concept of property rights covers a complex of norms. Block (1964) pointed out that property rights of the type known today did not evolve in Europe until late feudal times. Before that, sets of obligations and rights of land use were exchanged for a portion of goods produced from it. Such license of use was a result of a formal arrangement between the manor lord and the vassal and was not inherited. The rights of the land reverted to the manor lord for new assignment with the death of the vassal. "It is very rare, during the whole of the feudal era, for anyone to speak of ownership either of an estate or of an office" (Block, 1964: 115). At the same time, the manor lords, kings, and other members of the upper classes had control over real property. Women's rights to inheritance or even control over the goods they brought with them to marriage varied considerably (Burke,

1978; Kamen, 1971). It must be remembered that the vast majority, 80 to 90 percent, of the people of Europe were peasants or serfs until the late Middle Ages and did not acquire land as property to be passed on to offspring. When inheritance became the norm in France, Germany, Burgundy, and Italy, and the fief became subject to private ownership, it went only to sons. This was because women could not bear arms and so could not fulfill the major obligation binding the vassal and the lord to each other—going to war.

> Nothing appeared more contrary to the nature of the fief than to allow it to be inherited by women. Not that the Middle Ages had ever deemed them incapable of exercising authority . . . No one was disturbed by the spectacle of the great lady presiding over the baronial court when her husband was away. But women were held incapable of bearing arms (Block, 1964: 200) . . . The primary duty [of the vassal] was, by definition, military service (220).

As the Middle Ages waned and then moved on into preindustrial times, the evaluation of the status of women in European societies depends on the class of women being considered and whether the focus is on rights of ownership or management. Thus, Stuard (1976: 9-10) concluded that the rights and status of women decreased as the Middle Ages progressed because of a

> lessening of the public activity of women, a lower place in ecclesiastical opinion, fewer roles in guild organizations and less agricultural administration if not less agricultural labor . . . The late eleventh and twelfth centuries stand in many ways as a watershed between the greater opportunity of women in early medieval times and the more confining circumstances of life in the later Middle Ages (Stuard, 1976: 10).

On the other hand, Tuchman (1978) found women quite active in the economic sphere of life during the fourteenth century. In addition, Aries (1962), Laslett (1971), and Oakley (1974a) concluded that they were economically quite productive as late as the seventeenth century.

> In everyday life, women of noble as well as non-noble class found equality of function, if not of status, thrust on them by circumstances. Peasant women could hold tenancies and in that capacity rendered the same kinds of service for their holdings as men, although they earned less for the same work. Peasant households depended on their earnings. In the guilds, women had monopolies of certain trades, usually spinning and ale-making and some of the food and textile trades. Certain crafts excluded females except for a member's wife or daughter; in others they worked equally with men. Management of a merchant's household—of

his town house, his country estate, his business when he was absent—in addition to maternal duties gave his wife anything but a leisured life (Tuchman, 1978: 216).

Herlihy (1976: 24) found that women in medieval times could manage land, sell surpluses, collect rents, and

> be active in various community functions. We must first note, in general terms, that the women during the Middle Ages everywhere always had some importance in the management of the household economy. The wife characteristically supervised the household's 'inner economy,' those activities carried on in or near the house, cooking, brewing, spinning and weaving, usually too, the garden and the raising and care of yard animals . . .

In addition, according to many historians, women managed households, farms, and businesses when their husbands were absent because of wars, crusades, or exploratory or trade related travel (Herlihy, 1976). In *The Merchant of Prato*, Origo (1957) detailed his wife's management of their business affairs during his numerous trips in the late fourteenth century, showing that she was able to conduct financial arrangements with a variety of persons. On the other hand, in societies such as England or the United States, where the official or common laws held women to be minors, the ability of the wife to conduct business affairs was hampered. In such countries they could not hold title to property, testify in court, or sign papers as witnesses (Chafe, 1972: 2).

WORK AND LIFE IN PRE-INDUSTRIAL WESTERN EUROPE

By the seventeenth century, much of the work of Europeans had already been converted into jobs. People were hired for these jobs and were expected to perform more or less clearly defined, goal directed tasks in relation to other workers and employers. This does not mean that family production for subsistence did not continue (Boserup, 1970). Clark (1919/1968) drew a distinction between three types of productive work:

   a. Domestic industry is the form of production in which the goods produced are for the exclusive use of the family and are not therefore subject to an exchange or money value;
   b. family industry is the form in which the family becomes the unit for the production of goods to be sold or exchanged;
   c. capitalistic industry or industrialism is the system by which production is controlled by the owners of capital and the labourers or producers, men, women, and children receive individual wages.

Domestic industry involved a variety of activities:

> Brewing, dairy-work, care of poultry and pigs, production of vegetables and fruit, spinning flax and wool, nursing and doctoring, all formed part of domestic industry (Clark, 1919/1968: 5).

The self-sufficient family involved only in domestic industry gradually became the exception. History tells us that some specialization in the form of family industry developed even in villages, but especially in towns and the rapidly expanding cities. Crafts and produce were exchanged or sold to others in the same community or within a limited area, in return for goods or other specialities.

> At this stage, women often continue to be independent producers and to train younger women in the craft. At a somewhat later stage, though still at the village level, whole families may, as a full-time occupation, specialize in the production for sale of some commodity or in the performance of some service for the general public (Boserup, 1970: 140-41).

Of course, on the basis of existing evidence, it is often impossible to determine the extent to which any single producer of objects for sale works alone at home or has the direct cooperation of the whole family (Lopata, Barnewolt and Norr, 1980). In addition, when the activities and products are similar, it is difficult to separate work carried out for the benefit of the family in domestic industry from that which brings in supplies or income. Domestic industry can be considered family or capitalistic industry when it becomes organized into a job with a definite social circle that integrates tasks with the social relations.

One way in which work was organized into jobs in the pre-industrial era was through the system of apprenticeship and servitude. Such people initially lived with the family and shared all the work, both in the domestic and family industries. Servants were numerous in Western Europe. Laslett (1971: 13) reported that almost a third of the homes in English communities had servants and/or apprentices living with them during that era. These servants tended to be either young girls or boys from poorer families who could not be supported at home or young people sent to equal status families in order to be "properly trained." The English especially feared too much leniency in the socialization of their own children and sending them out to service was considered one way to insure good habits and "strength of character" (Laslett, 1971; Laslett and Wall, 1972; Oakley, 1974a; Tilly and Scott, 1978).

In the seventeenth century, in an English parish studied by Macfarlane, two-thirds of the boys and three-quarters of the girls between puberty and marriage were living away from home, and some began leaving at age 10 (Gordon, 1978: 58).

The work of women in pre-industrial England varied by location. Women farmers had "an active share in the management of the household" (Pinchbeck, 1930/1969: 3), but in later decades the wealthier farmers obtained servants and did less of the physical work themselves. Dairy work was deemed especially difficult. Finally this led to specialization in the care of cows, milking, and cheese-making, and the hiring of "dairywomen" (Pinchbeck, 1930/1969: 12). Many families supported themselves through the use of village common lands and the right to glean harvest lands and gather wood from estates. These women, known as cottagers, led a difficult life, especially because they were expected to support themselves and their children until the latter were old enough to contribute work themselves. "In the seventeenth century the idea is seldom encountered that a man supports his wife; husband and wife were then mutually dependent and together supported their children" (Clark, 1919/1968: 12). Wage earners who had insufficient property to maintain themselves and the people dependent on them hired themselves out; however, they received individual wages because employers assumed that their families supported themselves through other means (Clark, 1919/1968: 12).

Support through a variety of activities was made even more difficult in England after the enclosure of common land in the early sixteenth century, resulting in great poverty and displacement.

> During the closing years of the fifteenth century, the emergence of the wool industry in England began to transform the economic and social arrangements governing agriculture. As sheep raising became more profitable, much land was converted from tillage to pasture, and large numbers of peasants were displaced by the emerging entrepreneurial gentry which either bought their land or cheated them out of it (Piven and Cloward, 1971: 12).

Thus, there developed a large population of English people who had few sources of maintenance and who needed paid work. They worked for wealthy farmers, in the beginning cottage industries, or performed services or other entrepreneurial activity for pay. Many became dependent upon charity. The Elizabethan Poor Laws, formulated first in the early seventeenth century, were witness to the extent of this poverty. The agrarian revolution led to the appearance of women day-laborers and the development of the gang system of workers who moved from farm to farm (Pinchbeck, 1930/1969: 85). The traveling was exhausting, especially in conjunction with heavy work. Small children were often carried by the mothers to the field and kept quiet with the help of opiates (Hewitt, 1958; Pinchbeck, 1930/1969).

The nonagricultural work of women, as described by Clark (1919/ 1968), Hewitt (1958), Hill (1896), Oakley (1974a), and Pinchbeck (1930/1968), included commerce and trade, services such as alemaking and midwifery, and the manufacture of clothing such as lace collars or gloves, or materials such as linen, cotton, and even wool. Mayhew (1861) described many women among the "street people" in his *London Labor and The London Poor*. It was the textile industries, however, which drew the largest number of women as wage earners. They usually worked at home with their children and husbands, with the husbands serving as the family representative in contacts with the provider of the raw material and the purchaser of the finished goods. Home or cottage industry started as early as the fourteenth century and lasted in some areas of England well into the eighteenth century. The hours were long and children as young as three or four years of age contributed to the work. People worked, ate, and slept in the same room, one that often lacked adequate space, light, and ventilation. Since most of the workers did not grow their own flax or wool but "worked up" material provided by the employer, much time was wasted in obtaining the material and delivering the product (Pinchbeck, 1930/1969: 134).

As mentioned before, women also worked in crafts or businesses with their husbands, sometimes acquiring rights to guild membership in widowhood. Since the widow was usually given only part of the inheritance, which restricted her ability to buy out the other heirs, problems arose at the death of the husband if there were several family members who could inherit the enterprise. In some cases, the widow is known to have retained the establishment with the help of an apprentice who later even married her (Laslett, 1971). Widows could carry forth transactions even though married women did not have legal rights to conduct business and their husbands had to sign all contracts. The combined nutritional and hygienic deficiencies of life in premodern times aged people early and widowhood was frequent, especially since men tended to marry women younger than themselves (Lutz, 1973). A man in his forties was already considered old, and Lutz (1973) estimated that husbands and wives lived together only about 12 years. Because of this, families contained many widows, widowers, orphans and, because of remarriage, stepparents and stepchildren. Few people lived long enough to see the marriage of their youngest child and very few were alive when their grandchildren were born. When the father died, male guardians were assigned to children, even if the mother was still alive (Walker, 1976).

The presence of servants and apprentices, as well as the very nature of life in pre-eighteenth century Western Europe, made it very public. The concepts of privacy, family boundaries, and age stratification were foreign to these societies. Aries (1962) described this public life as focused in three locations: the manor home, the village, and the urban neighborhood. Other historians have developed this theme even further (Laslett, 1971; Shorter, 1975). The management of manor home by both the husband and the wife involved them in interaction with a broad circle of the gentry, the princely court, and later the nation. The dwelling contained numerous people who worked, ate, slept, and in general, lived in large central halls and were visited day and night by others conducting business and political intrigue. Births and deaths were public events and the boundaries between the family and the rest of the household were not clearly drawn (Aries, 1962, 1981).

The second locus of life was the village. Residents met on their way to and from their fields, in church, and while engaged in games and other leisure time activities involving people of all ages, both sexes, and often several classes or subclasses. Privacy as known in modern urban centers was not important in the lives of villagers (see also Reymont, 1925). Although village life involved a duplication of effort within each farm and household, much of this labor was public. Because fields consisted of strips of land communication among people planting, weeding, hoeing, or caring for animals was possible throughout the day (Miller, 1981).

The third location of social interaction was the urban household and neighborhood. Apprentices and servants shared work and the round of life with family members, and people congregated in the streets to observe all kinds of public activity. Laslett (1971) described the household of a family of bakers, one which involved all the residents in cooperative work.

EARLY INDUSTRIALIZATION IN WESTERN EUROPE

Despite the literature chronicling the relatively minimal rights of women in pre-industrial Europe, most feminist authors agree with Hartmann (1976), Rosaldo and Lamphere (1974), and Sicherman

(1975) that women's status declined when productive work moved out of the home and away from family control into factories and management control. The removal of productive work from the home and its organization into occupations and specific jobs in large organizations involved several stages and had numerous consequences on the work, life spaces, and life-styles of women and men. The first step toward industrialization was the putting-out system of cottage industry (proto-industrialization, Brownlee and Brownlee, 1976; Hesse, 1979; Marglin, 1974). It was an intermediate step between home production of goods for use and factory production of goods for sale and profit to the owner. The distinction between paid and unpaid work became refined with the movement of production to factories.

The second step of industrialization, the creation of factories, developed gradually both in England and the United States.

> The emergence of the factory systems was by no means dramatic; New England's textile mills gained sustained competence only in the 1820s, when they capitalized on lessons learned from the fierce British competition that followed the War of 1812. For many of the young women in the initial factory labor force, industrialization meant a relatively smooth passage from market-oriented, household spinning or weaving to small-scale factory textile production (Brownlee and Brownlee, 1976: 13).

Again, however, this step represented a significant change in the work lives of men and women who went to the factories to work. The factory system removed the workplace from the home: "In the new order, work was separated from family life; an activity performed away from the home for its monetary return and not for itself" (Oakley, 1974a: 33). Secondly, this step put control of the production process into the hands of capitalists. With the move from the home to the factory, their control extended to control over the labor process as well as control over the product of that labor (Marglin, 1974). Later management became separated from ownership with the creation of the corporation (Hertzler, 1961).

After the introduction of the factory and the centralization of capital and power, domestic and family industry diminished in importance to the society. New technology made this shift possible. The system was considered a great improvement over cottage industries because the product was standardized, the owners of the means of production had increased control over the workers, and there was less time "wasted" in the distribution of materials and products.

The factory won its victory by outproducing the working family, taking away the market for the products of hand labour and cutting prices to the point where the craftsman had either to starve or take a job under factory discipline himself (Laslett, 1971: 18).

In spite of the use of the male pronoun by Laslett in the above quotation, most of the early factory workers were women and children (Shorter, 1975). Oakley (1974a: 37) found that 46 percent of the factory workers in 1835 were women aged 13 and older and 15 percent were children of both sexes under the age of 13. In earlier years, and especially in the textile industries, the proportion of women and children was even higher. However, especially in England, men became increasingly interested in factory work as the capacity for self-maintenance through agriculture decreased. Oakley (1974a) documented the separation of most productive work from the family and how it affected women's work as men entered industry. From the start of industrialization this process has continued for two centuries, involving three time periods:

1. From 1750 until the early 1840s, when the family was increasingly displaced by the factory as the place of production, but women followed their traditional work out of the home.
2. From the 1840s until 1914, when a decline in the employment of married women outside the home was associated with the rising popularity of a belief in women's natural domesticity.
3. From 1914 until the 1950s, when there is a discernible, though uneven, tendency toward the growing employment of women, coupled with a retention of housewifery as the primary role expected of all women (Oakley, 1974a: 34).

There is considerable debate among social scientists as to the situation of women workers during the era of early industrialization. Pinchbeck (1930/1969) considered factory work to be an improvement over cottage industry:

It has been generally admitted that women gained greatly by the transference of manufacture from home to the factory . . . Now that the home was no longer a workshop, many women were able, for the first time in the history of industrial classes, to devote their energies to the business of homemaking and the care of their children, who stood to benefit greatly by the changed home conditions . . . As scattered domestic workers women had had few opportunities for any interchange of ideas among themselves and still less for any form of cooperation in their common interests (307-08).

In her *Wives and Mothers in Victorian Industry*, Hewitt (1958), however, supported the image of difficult work conditions in new factories. For example, in 1849 women worked a 13½ hour day, five days a week with 1½ hours off for meals; in addition, they worked a half day on Saturday. At the same time, they were not freed from homemaking and husband and child-care work when they returned home. Infants were sent to wet nurses in a "baby farming" system or were cared for by older siblings.

Marx (see Bottomore, 1956; Braverman, 1974; Marglin, 1974) contrasted factory work with a somewhat idealized notion of craft work. He maintained that factory work was less advantageous than craft work for the workers because they were tightly supervised, unable to see the product of their work, and especially because they lacked control over the rhythm and organization of their behavior. Shorter (1973: 18), in tracing the history of *Work and Community in the West*, was very negative in his evaluation of the factory.

> Three elements of the work situation essential to guild solidarity had been lost in the dark, satanic mill: workers' independence, small industrial scale and labor force stability.

In general, one's judgment of the condition of work in factories depends upon the criteria chosen and the sources of contrast available to them. Many observers point out that the contrast with guild work was unfair because, in fact, most workers did not have these advantages. Instead they worked hard and long on the land, as servants, or in the cottage industries (Kamen, 1971; Pinchbeck, 1930/1969).

Oakley's (1974a) second stage of industrialization is interesting and involves several sub-movements. One such sub-movement was the purposeful squeezing out of women from factories, guilds, and many occupations such as midwifery with the help of "protective" legislation. The second was the development of an ideology of "true womanhood" or "women's natural domesticity." The third sub-movement was the "creation of childhood." When the child was placed into the center of the family stage, motherhood took on different meaning and importance (Aries, 1962; Rothman, 1978). Knowledge of these changes is important to the understanding of the paid and unpaid work of women in modern times.

English society allowed mothers and small children to eke out a living in any way possible, including factory labor, because it was disturbed by growing poverty and the increasing number of people supported by charity. These conditions were a result of convolutions in social structure, increased population, the enclosure acts, and the consequences of industrialization. However, the society began to worry about the effects of such work involvement. Reformers such as the Webbs (Abbott, 1929) and novelists such as Charles Dickens portrayed the working mother and the child in sorrowful terms. Engels's *The Condition of the Working Class in England*, published in 1844, contained a highly negative picture of women working outside of the home (Oakley, 1974a: 45-46).

Descriptions of working conditions in coal mines, and other places that were deemed unhealthy, raised the consciousness of both the British public and the newly developing American society (Hewitt, 1958). The press and speakers in public meetings increasingly called for special legislation that would regularize the places and times of women's work and limit the age at which children could be hired. Horton and Leslie (1960: 5) explained that the new movement for protective legislation reflected a change in the definition of the situation:

> Child labor was no social problem as long as most people thought child labor was acceptable. Only when a considerable number of people decided that child labor was harmful and began saying 'isn't it awful'— only then did child labor become a social problem.

Although child labor was originally seen as an economic necessity, or even a desirable means of teaching children good habits, paid work became redefined as harmful to their health and education. The redefinition was slow in crystallizing, as we shall see when discussing American history, and it was fought in the public sphere by employers who wanted cheap labor and by some charitable organizations who felt that children should be kept busy in "worthwhile" activity (Oakley, 1974a; de Mause, 1974a).

The Mines Act of 1842, the first protective legislation aimed at women in England, "excluded women from colliery employment" (Oakley, 1974a: 44).

> Two years later, the 1844 Factory Act took the radical and unprecedented step of classing women of all ages with children as "protected persons." Their hours of labour were restricted to twelve a day in the textile trades. In 1847, a further Act limited labour to fifty-eight hours a week for women and young people over thirteen and an Act of 1850 made the ten-hour day for "protected persons" effective by abolishing the shift or relay system. Much later, in 1891, an Act was passed pro-

hibiting the employment of women four weeks before and four weeks after childbirth, and the 1895 Factories and Workshops Act prohibited overtime for women (Oakley, 1974a: 44).

The Infant Life Protection Society worked, in the meantime, on a Factory Amendment Bill in 1873 and the Factory and Workshop Bill of 1891 mentioned by Oakley (Hewitt, 1958: 170-77).

The introduction of "protective legislation" had the effect of decreasing the number of occupations open to women (Abbott, 1929; Oakley, 1974a). As men became more involved in paid employment away from agriculture, the guilds increased their pressure to remove existing females and to keep out any new women workers. The legislation made women even less attractive to employers who were faced with an increasing labor supply of men, who were already preferred for a variety of reasons, including their allegedly steadier employment. The apprenticeship system contributed to this gradual "exclusion of women from many of the occupations they had in the fifteenth century" (Pinchbeck, 1930/1969: 125). Because they were limited by irregular training, wives and daughters were less able to continue the work of a deceased husband or father. In addition:

> When the home was separated from business premises, women ceased to take an active share in their husbands' affairs and so lost the experience they would otherwise have gained. At the same time, the development of large scale business and the need for greater capital made it increasingly difficult for women, even in their own trades, to set up in business on their own account (Pinchbeck, 1930/1969: 280).

Gradually, the patriarchal and patrilineal systems consolidated male control over public life, which included most occupations and specific jobs (Hartmann, 1976; Lipman-Blumen, 1976; Sanday, 1974). This move was assisted by the continued absence of legal rights under common law. Although they never had the right to their own earnings by that law, the knowledge of their contribution resulted in greater power in the family than was true when they produced for domestic use only. Thus, their removal from paid employment created a situation of total economic dependence upon the breadwinner, husband, or father.

> The shift from domestic to industrial production in the nineteenth century increased women's dependence on men, not only in economic terms, but in the psychological subtleties of their relationships (Meacham, 1977: 64).
>
> Capitalism and industrial revolution with mass production, wages and money to buy services, liberated the man from kin control and the

family as a work group. Before, man needed a wife and children; now he can get a divorce and buy services. [Women's situation is] opposite— [she] went into economic dependence upon the husband since domestic industry broke down and [she] has little opportunity to earn money (Clark, 1919/1968: 1).

The attempt to get women out of the factories, which, according to Oakley (1974a: 44-45), was motivated "largely by the anxiety of men whose own situation had been radically transformed by the change to factory production," was accompanied by an ideological shift. The redefinition of the roles of women, and even of their health and personality, emerged in Victorian England and spread to the United States. This process has been labeled the movement of "the cult of true womanhood" or the theory of "spheres" (Douglas, 1977). According to this social ideology, the world is divided into two spheres, the domestic one dominated by the woman and the public one domi- nated by the man (Sicherman, 1975; Welter, 1966).

> Any review of the now familiar evolution of the "woman's sphere" must start with the decline of economic production in the home and the transformation of domestic work into an activity with no commer- cial value. This trend was first visible in affluent middle-class families where women supported by their husbands could afford to stay home and devote themselves to the primary care of their families . . . By the middle of the nineteenth century the vast majority of working-class mothers apparently were no longer gainfully employed (Bloch, 1978: 246).

The ideology condemned female employment on a number of fronts: It was immoral; it was too physically taxing; it contributed to the neglect of families; and it interrupted the natural division of labor between the sexes (Oakley, 1974a; Pinchbeck, 1930/1969; Rothman, 1978). The "cult of true womanhood" was accompanied by the "cult of true motherhood" and, according to Aries (1962) and Shorter (1975), the creation of childhood as a definite stage of life requiring specialized care. Before the eighteenth century, children were treated as miniature adults whose high mortality rates in infancy and child- hood discouraged strong emotional involvement in them by parents (Aries, 1962; Kamen, 1971; de Mause, 1974a, 1974b; Shorter, 1975). Middle-class women of England and France often sent newborn infants to wet nurses in villages, in spite of the knowledge that such condi- tions resulted in even higher death rates than home care. Sussman (1977) reported the continuation of the "wet nursing business" in France as late as World War I, while Coleman (1976), Kamen (1971), and de Mause (1974a, 1974b), and others documented infanticide and neglect throughout the *History of Childhood* (de Mause, 1974a) until recent decades (see also Illick, 1974).

According to Aries (1965), around the turn of the eighteenth century, childhood became defined as an important stage of life that required protective care and freedom from work. It also became firmly established with the organization of the school system. At about the same time, motherhood was redefined as a role with important child maintenance and socialization functions (Shorter, 1975). This romantization of both childhood and motherhood had important consequences for the lives of women, especially for those living above the poverty level in Western Europe and America (Oakley, 1974a). It was accompanied by other major social changes: the scientific revolution, the invention of such instruments as the telescope and microscope, and new theories explaining the world in scientific rather than religious terms; the commercial revolution, bringing not only new objects but also knowledge of different ways of life; wars of centralization creating large political states; and relatively rapid industrialization and urbanization. The turmoil created by all these changes has been modifying women's lives dramatically since the seventeenth century. The newly created states, having to rely on the loyalty of members through nationalistic identification rather than on the control of serfs by manor lords, turned to mass education of children. Emerging nationalism, as well as the evolution of democratic political ideologies, meant that societies became more interested in a general population that was literate rather than limiting education to the upper classes as had been done in the past (Aries, 1962; Znaniecki, 1952). Aries (1962) attributed the "creation of childhood" partially to the school system which separated children by age group from the normal flow of life and from children of other ages. Increasingly protected by new laws and ideologies, children were no longer able or forced to work in home industry or in the factory. Instead, they were enrolled in school during the day and taken care of at home before and after school by full-time mothers who were completely devoted to parental, marital, and homemaking roles (Rothman, 1978).

Even though they were discouraged from working and actually pushed out of paid employment, women did not withdraw from jobs completely. Those who worked outside of the home stayed in some of the factories and other workplaces or developed such entrepreneurial activities as trading. Mayhew (1861) listed a variety of street sellers in London, who were peddling such things as fish, vegetables, fruits, flowers and roots, edibles, drinkables, stationery, songs, newspapers, literature, manufactured articles, second-hand articles, live animals, "mineral productions," and curiosities. The streets also contained performers and artists. Women worked as innkeepers and brewers. Finally, many professions remained open to women, although the army, church, and law were closed. Teaching, nursing, and midwifery continued to draw women, and those of higher classes but without economic support went out to work as governesses or companions (Clark, 1919/1968; Hill, 1896). Toward the second half of the nineteenth century, banks, telegraph offices, post-offices, insurance companies, railway offices, and other establishments using clerks began hiring women. Finally, servants included not only young people, but also women of all ages who were generally unmarried (McBride, 1976). McBride (1976: 11-15) found an enormous expansion of servants in England and France with urbanization and modernization. Accompanying this growth, the occupation was gradually feminized as men withdrew and rural, untrained women became employed in households. Of course, cloisters and the homes of a variety of religious organizations housed many women and provided work and livelihood for them (Bernard, 1981; Boulding, 1976; Rothman, 1978).

UNIQUE FEATURES OF WOMEN'S WORK IN AMERICA

The social status of women and the organization and evaluation of their work in American society have received mixed reports from historians and social scientists (Brownlee and Brownlee, 1976; Carr and Walsh, 1978; Chafe, 1972; Dulles, 1965; Martineau, 1934/1962; Ryan, 1979; Smuts, 1959/1971; Tilly and Scott, 1978; de Tocqueville, 1835/1966). Some historians maintain that women had independence and high status in America, in spite of legal restrictions imposed by the common law imported from England, mainly because there were relatively few women and because during the western push there was an imperative demand for their labor (Carr and Walsh, 1978). Although America adopted many values and behavioral patterns from Britain, for a variety of reasons it could not duplicate the total social structure or culture. It was impossible to transplant sufficient segments of the mother country to create a replica of it in the New World. The life that English immigrants could create on this side of the ocean was of necessity very different from that into which they had been socialized back home. Many characteristics of the new land—especially its size and natural resources, as well as the absence of a rigidified class structure and feudal history—removed many constraints but simultaneously forced new behavior. People left the homeland desiring new experiences. All these and many more factors resulted in a slow build-up of political and economic systems based upon landowning families and small communities. Families worked together to clear and plant the land, moving westward to conquer new territory while the eastern belt built up cities and industries. Although initially limited to domestic production, with some barter and the purchase of imported goods, the farmers were soon able to feed the growing urban population that was expanding through continued immigration and a high birth rate (Bell, 1972). The immigrants were mainly young men, but venturesome women also came across the ocean without families, often as indentured servants. Some men brought families over and communities continued to expand. However, the shortage of women was a reality for many decades, as was the hard work.

Thus, while the new nation could draw upon its European heritage, it was freed from the "hampering drag of centuries-old social and cultural habits and attitudes to impede its advances" (Davidson, 1951/1974: ix; see also Lipset, 1979). Its dependence upon English culture decreased through the influence of its revolutionary and democratic ideology, emphasis on individualism, insistence on freedom from tradition when it interfered with the economic institution, laissez-faire policies, and states' rights (Brinker, 1968). Democracy as an ideology, however, did not include a concern with the civil rights of women, children, Indians, or black slaves (Leiby, 1978). As the economic institution became the focal one, even the religious foundations of the new nation were pushed into the background in comparison. The emerging values combined with Puritanism in a new way, resulting in a rigid curtailment of leisure, high regard for hard work, and admiration of economic success as its visible product even more than in other Protestant countries (Weber, 1905/1958; Leiby, 1978). According to Leiby (1978:7), American culture consolidated its focus on democracy and individualism during the 45 or so years of isolation from England following the Revolutionary War. Because the society could no longer depend on England for its manufactured goods, new forms of working and producing also evolved during this period. Unwillingness by England to allow local manufacture had stymied industrialization efforts in the Colonies. Several inventions following the War of Independence and later the Civil War enabled large scale industry to develop and the nation to absorb millions of immigrants into the factories and mines, many of whom were unskilled, unlettered, and unable to understand the English language.

Women in America were strongly controlled by the British common law which treated them as minors (Chapman and Gates, 1977; Demos, 1970; Riegel, 1975; Ryan, 1979).

> At marriage, common law made the wife legally incapable and laid on the husband the duty of supplying her with what the lawyers called "necessities," that is, with those things that seemed essential for her existence and such other things as accorded with the standard of life he was able to maintain . . . The custody of the child belonged, with his earnings, to the father (Abbott, 1938: 600).

The patriarchal nature of the system prevented women from holding titles to property, forced them to bear the husband's name, and until very recently, defined their domicile:

> . . . when a women marries, she loses her domicile and acquires that of her husband, no matter where she resides or what she believes or intends . . . As of 1974, only four states allowed married women to have separate domiciles from their husbands for all purposes; another 15 allowed women to have separate domiciles for voting, six for election to public office, five for jury service, seven for taxation and five for probate (Babcock, et al., 1975: 575-76).

Ramey (1977: 350) summarized the legal situation of women in America as follows:

> The majority of American women live their lives without ever being recognized by law as legal persons. In most jurisdictions until recently, a woman was a minor until age 21. Most women marry at about age 21, and since man and wife are one in the eyes of the law, and that one is the man, the woman may never become a legal person.

The fact that there was a real demand for women and their work in pioneer and colonial America is evident in the following description of the work involved in the running of a Kansas farm:

> On a typical Kansas farm, in short, the work of women provided almost all that was necessary for keeping house, feeding, clothing, and otherwise sustaining the family. This meant that the income from the cash crops could be used to develop the farm, purchase machinery, improve stock, replace dugouts and sod huts with frame houses and outbuildings, put up fences, and still keep up with the mortgage payments in years of drought, grasshoppers, or low prices. Without this division of work, few farmers could have survived the years of learning to cope with the unfamiliar soil and climate of the West (Smuts, 1959/1971: 8-9).

In Marxist terms, the woman's work at that time was mainly used to create products of "use value" while men's work increasingly created products with "exchange value." Of course, seasonal variations in agricultural work necessitated cooperative labor. Interestingly, this division created a distinction between paid and unpaid work that was expanded through capitalism and industrialization.

Norton (1979: 335) and others have recently questioned the effectiveness of equating the need for women's work in colonial times with high social status:

> It has often been asserted that colonial women, especially those who lived in the seventeenth century, had a "high" status relative to their sisters in England and their descendants in the United States. Because females were relatively few in number [and therefore presumably in demand as marital partners] and because their labor was vital to the survival and maintenance of the household, it has been believed that colonial women probably wielded power within the home and that they were valued members of society. Current scholarship describes a more complex picture.

Ryan (1979) pointed out that many of the women who entered the United States as unmarried migrants were indentured servants and thus did not raise the status of their gender. Sicherman (1975) explained that the need for a person's labor does not necessarily translate itself into status and power, as evidenced in the situation of slaves or of unskilled workers. In fact, Sicherman (1975) devoted her review essay on American history and the status of women to the presentation of the complexities of past and current interpretations of this history.

As in the rest of Western Europe and other modern countries, the trend of converting men's work into paid employment while women's home-based work was limited to family use resulted in the creation of the concept and status of "private dependent" (Eichler, 1973; see also Nilson, 1978). Wives who were discouraged from employment, children who were judged legally of school age, and any other relative who was unable to work, either because the person was disabled or retired without an income, were thus converted into private dependents. They were automatically dependent on the male breadwinner or, in his absence, on the parish or the state (Glazer, 1976, 1980; Lopata and Brehm, 1985).

> The actual economic dependency of a homemaker is not inequitable in itself but is made so by the law. The refusal to value homemaking services in economic terms unfairly brands her as a socially nonproductive person. The supposed right to be supported by the husband without regard to her contributions to the family categorizes her as a parasite . . .

Having chosen dependency [through marriage], the traditional legal
rules serve to keep the wife dependent (Krauskopf, 1977: 105-6).

Since colonial times, the economic dependency of wives has been reinforced through industrialization, mass immigration, urbanization,
and all the components of American modernization. The exclusion
of economically productive labor from the home helped create an
employee rather than an entrepreneurial work structure (Mills, 1951).
Although "two-thirds of the nation's population still lived in rural
areas in 1890, and nearly half of its families still made their living from
the soil" (Smuts, 1959/1971: 4), the northeastern part of the country
experienced major occupational changes much earlier than that. This
was accompanied by a demographic change in the composition of the
family as women decreased their fertility.

As we have seen, working women in America were in a variety of
occupations during the seventeenth, eighteenth, and nineteenth centuries in spite of the emerging theory of "true womanhood." Their
jobs, however, were increasingly sex segregated (Brownlee and Brownlee, 1976). Although most nonfarm-employed women worked in the
textile industry, as they did in England, they were gradually pushed
out by immigrant males as technology changed, in a chicken-and-egg
mutual influence between the type of worker and the technology
(Baker, 1964). Women leaving old occupations moved into teaching,
nursing, and employment in shops, offices, and the slowly expanding
nondomestic service sector. The "Civil War period seems to have been
the turning point for women in textiles" (Baker, 1964: 23). In the
so-called sweat shops they worked with the newly invented sewing
machines, making such nondurable goods as ready-to-wear clothing,
collars, and cuffs or buttonholes and buttons for men's shirts, gloves,
and so forth. They also specialized in making hats and caps and the
tops of boots and shoes (Abbott, 1913; Sumner, et al., 1910). The
tobacco industry hired them, in spite of protests by men who had a
monopoly in the field. Women were also involved in printing and publishing. They were often used as strikebreakers as the union tried to
keep them out of the industry. Food and other nondurable items
such as candy were also prepared or manufactured by them. They
participated in the production of watches and clocks. Thus, Harriet
Martineau's (1934/1962) observation that in the nineteenth century
women could be employed in America in only six occupations was
incorrect if the presence of women in the occupation was considered
as opposed to their concentration. Historian Baker (1964: 51) concluded that "by 1890 only nine out of 369 general groups into which

the country's industries had been assigned did not employ women." She found women who were farm employees, domestics, service workers in the hotel and restaurant business, teachers after the Civil War, nurses, saleswomen, telephone and telegraph workers. Slave women worked in the fields or homes of their masters, while the white mistresses organized and supervised complex households and sometimes whole plantations in the absence of a husband. The invention of the typewriter brought more women into offices, with manufacturers such as Remington and organizations such as the YMCA training them to use these machines as early as the 1870s (Baker, 1964; Rothman, 1978). Other women worked as bookkeepers, receptionists, and switchboard operators.

The situation of servants has an interesting history in America. Early in the life of this country indentured servants worked alongside family members, spinning, weaving, or farming. They contributed also through sewing, baking, soap making, brewing, and canning (Wertheimer, 1977). Domestic service gradually lost its status. Initially it had a relatively high standing among women's occupations because families sent daughters and sons to the homes of others to learn skills and discipline. The loss of status was partly due to the decrease of productive work in the home, a change which simplified the level of skill required of the servant.

> As factory work offered working-class women options, domestic service continued to lose standing. The freedom to come and go, to have even a few hours a day to call one's own, seemed preferable to the virtual slavery of household service (Wertheimer, 1977).

Newly arriving immigrant women took over domestic service, but usually, having few skills for working in urban homes, they had to be taught the rudiments of house maintenance. Their presence helped again to lower the standing of this occupation. Bernard (1981) asked: "Why were native born women shying away from domestic service, accepting lower paying jobs instead?" The answer to this query was the fact that such jobs lacked a chance for promotion and were characterized by

> . . . mechanical repetitive work; lack of organization; irregularity of hours; limitation on free time; competition with foreign-born and blacks; interference by those less skilled; [and] . . . low social status (Bernard, 1981: 260, quoting Salmon, 1897).

According to Salmon, even the term "servant" was pejorative in America.

Salmon sees five factors leading to the abandonment of the term in the first decades of the Republic: the practice of indenturing servants, creating the redemptioneers; the use of the term for slaves; the leveling tendencies of a new country; a literal interpretation of the Declaration of Independence; and the influence of French philosophical ideas on social and political theories (Bernard, 1981: 263, quoting Salmon, 1897).

Social class distances developed in household relations when servants were defined as "help" and no longer considered part of the family. Evidence of this was found in the use of titles and uniforms, contributing to the unwillingness of American-born women to take on the role of servant, even though the wages were comparatively good. McBride (1976) found the same trends in England and France up until World War I, although most explanations for the low status of domestic employment in America refer to the unique characteristics of the new nation.

Some of the causes of the servants' alienation from their work are the now familiar conditions of long hours, miserable housing, virtual loss of freedom, and an often degrading master-servant relationship (99).

Nevertheless, domestic work did provide housing and food for new immigrants or migrants to the city.

Although women in America did occupy a variety of jobs, only 20 to 25 percent of them were in the paid labor force during the years of 1900 to 1914 (Kessler-Harris, 1981). Married women and widows also maintained a home and were thus part of the unpaid labor force. Even after the cottage industry turned into factory work, the vast majority of women worked in the home without pay or in addition to entrepreneurial activity. Women canned, took in washing, sewed, and sold these products. They also took care of children or ran boarding and rooming houses. Because immigration and internal migration to cities meant that these urban areas were expanding, renting rooms and providing cooked meals was a frequent source of earnings for women (Davis, 1971; Lopata, 1976, 1980, 1981). The rapid expansion of American cities, especially in the nineteenth century when land became scarce and industrial jobs beckoned, led to a constant shortage of inexpensive housing (Lopata, 1976, 1981; Lopata and Norr, 1979, 1980). Immigrants and people who were unattached because of personal crisis or community actions needed housing and food. This demand was met by boarding lodges that were often run by women. This was one of the few remaining home-based income producing sources that existed as industry moved into the factories (Smuts, 1959/1971:

14). Morgan and Golden (1979: 64-65), for example, described the household composition of Mount Holyoke families of 1880:

> Just over one-third of all households included non-related persons—boarders, domestic servants, or other resident employees of the household head—but few households included more than one of these. The presence of domestic servants was the most frequent in households with native-born heads, probably reflecting their higher occupational status, while households with Canadian-born heads were most likely to include a boarder. The prevalence of boarding, and particularly the widespread tendency for private households to contain boarders appears to be characteristic of towns during the early industrial period of both Western Europe and North America, and probably represents a short-term response to the housing shortage created by rapid population growth and migration into town.

Calhoun (1917/1945: 181-88) claimed that the proliferation of hotels, restaurants and private clubs, as well as boarding and lodging homes, was brought about by the American "addiction to hotel and boarding-house life." He attributed this "addiction" to the "servant problem," the instability of employment, youth at marriage, and a dislike for housework. In the case of the immigrants, however, such living arrangments were temporary; the boarders were often relatives of the family who owned the house or persons from the same region or same village in the Old Country (Lopata, 1976, 1981).

We thus find an interesting situation for women in America during the nineteenth century. Some women worked for pay; immigrants tried by every means possible to earn money so that they could return to their home country or purchase their own home in this land. Jobs were available, but ethnic norms often forbade daughters and wives from entering either paid employment in general or certain types of jobs in specified organizations (Golab, 1977; Lopata, 1976, 1981). The "cult of domesticity" ideologically supported the desire to restrict the paid activity of women. Protective legislation, which controlled the hours and type of work that women and children could perform, made them less attractive to employers. Unions actively tried to keep women out of many occupations and to remove them if they were already participants. Ware (1977: 12) documented the change in female labor force participation and occupational distribution, attributing the trends to the union movement:

> The basic demand of the unions, led by the Western Federation of Miners, was for a living wage, which could enable a man to support his family in comfort and decency . . . They shared the perception of man-

hood and womanhood which had become popular during the nineteenth century when industrialization had destroyed the household as a productive unit based on shared activity and substituted the dichotomized world of work which was the domain of men and the home now defined as woman's "natural" sphere.

THE CULT OF TRUE WOMANHOOD: AMERICAN VERSION

In combination with leadership from religious ministers, the "cult of domesticity" developed unique American features. It was embellished with the help of the romanticized ideals of motherhood and "high culture." Welter (1966) agreed with the English commentators such as Oakley (1974a) that the cult was perpetuated in order to keep women out of paid employment. Its American variation had far reaching repercussions. One of the first effects was the accompanying redefinition of the personalities of women and men in their own spheres. The difficulty of conditions in the new land, requiring highly competitive action, following cooperative efforts during settlement times helped crystallize the theory in a way impossible in Victorian England. The men's sphere of life was defined as physically dangerous, competitive, and harsh. The men living in it were considered to lack an interest in, and the chance to acquire "culture," because they were limited to an amoral struggle for survival (Douglas, 1977). The world of the home and hearth was supervised by the true woman who was redefined as warm, pure, and delicate, but economically dependent, submissive, physically in need of protection, and not involved in society (Cott, 1977; Dulles, 1965; Hartman and Banner, 1974; Rosaldo and Lamphere, 1974; Sicherman, 1975; Welter, 1966). Although it was originally based on the Victorian romantization of the upper-class woman as economically unproductive, delicate to the point of fainting, but devoted to the arts and literature as "high culture," true womanhood became the ideal in America for all women who could afford such a life, as an illustration of both higher morality and vicarious leisure (Veblen, 1899/1953). It was particularly popular among the East Coast cities and in nonfrontier and nonagricultural homes. Although early suffragettes fought the stereotype of women as fragile, passive, lacking in mental ability and stamina, nervous and hysterical (Bird, 1976; Smith-Rosenberg, 1972), the weight of the image, reinforced by Darwinism and Freudianism, retained its hold on American culture well into the 1950s in the form of the "feminine mystique" (Friedan, 1963; Harris, 1979; LaPierre, 1959). The rigors of pioneer life and the existence of slaves and immigrant women working hard to help the family survive in the strange land were neglected in this image of true womanhood restricted to home and the family (Cott, 1977).

> The attributes of True Womanhood, by which a woman judged herself and was judged by her husband, her neighbors, and society could be divided into four cardinal virtues—piety, purity, submissiveness, and domesticity. Put them all together and they spelled mother, daughter, sister, wife—woman. Without them, no matter whether there was fame, achievement, or wealth, all was ashes. With them she was promised happiness and power (Welter, 1966: 151).

Jessie Bernard (1981) summarized the American variation of the women's sphere ideology:

> Women's sphere was an ideological construct for explaining and rationalizing the sexually separatist system that had by now crystallized in the United States. The ideology had several components: (1) a belief that although women were not intrinsically inferior to men, their sphere still had to be subordinated to that of men in the interest of national welfare; (2) a belief that women's sphere had its own contribution to make in the form of running the household competently and taking care of all its members, a female profession to be prepared for and taken as seriously as any other; (3) a belief that women's sphere was a place for emotional sustenance and for healing the hurt inflicted by the outside world; (4) a belief that women's sphere had a duty and responsibility to uphold and transmit the moral standards of society; and (5) a belief that the home, extended to include related moral and charitable activities, was the natural, normal, and only concern of women's sphere (91).

The consequences of the division of the world into the two spheres, public and private, had repercussions upon the life of the society (Laslett, 1973). These were evident to de Tocqueville (1835/1966) in the 1870s:

> In America, more than anywhere else in the world, care has been taken constantly to trace clearly distinct spheres of action for the two sexes, and both are required to keep in step, but along paths that are never the same. You will never find American women in charge of the external affairs of the family, managing a business, or interfering in politics; but they are also never obliged to undertake rough laborer's work or any task requiring hard physical exertions (601) . . . they seem to take pride in the free relinquishment of their will, and it is their boast to bear the yoke themselves rather than to escape from it . . . In America a woman loses her independence forever in the bonds of matrimony. While there is less constraint on girls, there more than anywhere else, a wife submits to stricter obligations (599).

Dulles (1965) also reported that European observers were surprised at the absence of women in American public life, including recreation, as well as at the absence of street life in general.

Bernard (1981) and others, however, felt that the "spheres" ideology had positive consequences upon the lives of women, because it enabled them to create their own world of friendship, with its own culture and values (see also Douglas, 1977; Smith-Rosenberg, 1978). While men's interests remained fixed on the economic institution as the focal one in their lives, the idealization of the home and motherhood increased the work of women, especially after the discovery of the germ theory of illness (Rothman, 1978). Ehrenreich and English (1979) observed the changes in ideas about homemaking with the advent of "domestic science." Numerous social scientists have documented the fact that the role of housewife or homemaker in modern American society can be performed at a variety of levels at its expanding circle and full-house plateau stages (Lopata, 1969, 1971). The heterogeneity of ways by which it was carried forth was of course traditionally affected by social class and personal resources, but new health and psychological knowledge in the nineteenth century led to a general expansion in the role.

Ehrenreich and English (1979) dubbed the last 100 years of American life as "the century of the child." The growth of this movement was assisted by numerous experts and a push toward "educated motherhood." Observers of this society find this thrust much stronger than what was ever experienced in Europe, where traditional child-rearing and child defining norms still operate even after the "discovery of childhood" on that continent (Aries, 1962; Ehrenreich and English, 1979; Rothman, 1978). Child-rearing guides, originally written for American fathers, now directed their attention to mothers. The harsh discipline of Puritan years, when parents were taught the importance of "breaking the wills" of children, was replaced with sentimental and "developmental" mothering (Demos, 1970; Lantz, et al., 1968, 1973, 1975; de Mause, 1974a, 1974b; Sicherman, 1975).

In addition to redefining the personalities of women and men, providing an atmosphere conducive to female friendship, increasing the complexity of the role of homemaker, and contributing to the importance assigned the role of mother, the "cult of domesticity" had the long-range effect of *The Feminization of American Culture* (Douglas, 1977). Middle-class women, who were increasingly educated and affluent and had time to devote to cultural activities, combined forces with Protestant clergy, who had been gradually losing status and influence over the society. Together, they developed a campaign of reform and dissemination.

Between 1820 and 1875, the Protestant church in this country was gradually transformed from a traditional institution which claimed with certain real justification to be a guide and leader to the American nation to an influential ad hoc organization which obtained its power largely be taking cues from the nonecclesiastical culture on which it was dependent (Douglas, 1977: 25).

This movement spread those aspects of the culture which fell in the women's province. Women who no longer needed to "feed, clothe and equip the nation" (Douglas, 1977: 57) turned their attention by the 1830s to a monopolization of "high culture" and the dissemination of its values and attitudes.

The movement to "reform" American society became the goal of this coalition of middle-class women dependent upon their husbands and the clergy and included removal of many of the characteristics identified with the male world, such as drinking alcohol and the accompanying tavern life, "the vices," and "exploitation" of workers, particularly women and children. Both were the creators and the consumers of very sentimentalized popular culture which was disseminated through all the popular press. Feminine influence on culture was represented as a moral one, designed to soften the harshness of public life with the help of the value system emerging from the private sphere of life. Not surprisingly, this definition of the situation and the goal of feminizing social life were often resented by men, thus increasing the schism between men and women in America.

To summarize, the situation of the married woman in America was unique—the society was new and was building rapidly with a certain competitive harshness to its public life. At the same time the private sphere developed its own sub-culture (Cott, 1977; Douglas, 1977). Toward the middle of the nineteenth and the beginning of the twentieth century, middle-class women, who had become private dependents in what is now called two-person career marriages, turned their attention toward "reforming" or "feminizing" the societal life and culture (Papanek, 1973). Some of their efforts were directed toward the removal of children from paid work and the expansion of the school system. Other efforts were directed toward protective legislation limiting the kinds of work and the conditions of employment of those women who had to have jobs outside the home. At the same time, a quarter of American women of all ages were employed and both women and children contributed to the family income through a variety of entrepreneurial activities. Family maintenance was also made possible through work activities of women who were not rewarded directly with money, the main source of livelihood and status in the American society. In most cases the husbands earned the money which women converted into a variety of life-styles (Cott, 1977).

THE SPECIAL CASE OF THE HUSBANDLESS WOMAN

Although employment of married women outside of the home was frowned upon in post-colonial America, unmarried girls who had finished their limited schooling were expected to work helping their mothers in the home or on the farm. Later they worked for pay which was turned over to the head of the household (Pleck, 1979). Unmarried girls were the first factory workers in mill towns, towns that were specially organized around their needs for housing and the "protection of their virtue" (Pleck, 1979). Hareven and Langenbach (1978) described the work of such girls in *Amoskeag: Life and Work in an American Factory City*, developed in 1837. Similar communities, the most famous of them Lowell, Massachusetts, arose up and down the Connecticut Valley (Easton, 1976; Hareven, 1977; Hareven and Vinovskis, 1978). In "The Lady and the Mill Girl: Changes in the Status of Women in the Age of Jackson," Lerner (1969) explained that life for the mill girls was very different from that of the emerging middle-class wife. The numbers of such young women, and their proportion in the female population of nineteenth-century America, could be quite large. For example, between 36 and 38 percent of the women aged 15 or older living in New York State in the years 1855, 1865, and 1875 were single (Vinovskis, 1978: 53). Whether living in specially constructed dormitories with chaperones or as boarders with town families, these young women contributed their wages after expenses to their families' total income and were thus regarded as an economic asset that enabled their mothers to stay home and take care of the family even if the father was not able to earn a steady income (Abbott, 1913). Because of the instability of business life, seasonal fluctuations, and the policies of employers, the economic situation of many families during the early industrialization period in America was precarious. The earnings of each member were needed and parents even allowed very young children to work in factories or otherwise earn money. The other main source of income for unmarried women was domestic service, which was usually rewarded with low wages but which insured housing and food, as well as training in homemaking skills. This was often the only occupation allowed or available to young immigrant or second generation women (Lopata, 1976, 1981).

An entirely different life faced women who had been married but whose husbands had died, but historians do not agree on the social status of widows in pre-industrial America. Until fairly recently it was assumed that their status was high:

> Widows were quite popular, even those with children. One reason was their economic status. The European custom of leaving the major portion of an estate to the eldest son did not survive in the colonies. In the typical family, the widow, guaranteed at least one-third of her husband's estate, was the main beneficiary. Her second husband automatically acquired the product of these lands during her lifetime. Further, since children were a definite economic asset in the largely agrarian society, her proven fertility was no detriment to remarriage. Benjamin Franklin aptly noted that "a rich widow is the only kind of second-hand goods that will always see a prime cost" (Murstein, 1974: 300).

The last statement of the above quotation certainly does not reflect high personal status of widows. Sicherman (1975: 466) reported on a study by Keyssar (1974) which questioned the assumption that many colonial American widows were rich. His study of widows in a town in Massachusetts found their inheritance to be smaller than the income of the town's average family. They were often unable to maintain a farm or business, either because they did not inherit it whole, or because they lacked sufficient funds to hire workers. The going rate of labor, in short supply, was quite high (see also Sussman, et al., 1970). Keyssar's (1974) conclusion was that widows were "relatively poor, dependent and lacking other options" (121) because so few occupations and ways of earning a living were open to women.

Kleinberg (1973) studied the life situation of working-class women in Pittsburgh, in the period between 1800 and 1890, and found widows frequently beset by problems. They often lived in the older part of town:

> The older section of the city had one of the highest percentages in the city of household heads who were widows [19 to citywide 14] ... Their widowhood was not a result of the natural aging processes but of the hazards of the mills and mill neighborhoods ... As difficult as it was for women generally to find work, the widows in the mill area were isolated in parts of the city which had no jobs for them at all. The proportion of residents in these areas who might require their services as seamstresses, washerwomen or servants was low since these were precisely the areas which had few middle or upper class residents ... Instead they depended upon meager savings, the labor of their children or handouts from charitable agencies [49-50] ... Forty percent of all widows' sons

were working at ages ten to fourteen [205] , 27 percent of the widows' daughters worked [206] . . . If women worked at all, they did so as an interlude between childhood and marriage or after the death or desertion of their husbands [227] .

Other descriptions of life in nineteenth century America make references to various activities for money or barter carried out by women, specifying that they were widows. Abbott (1913: 13) found them (1) keeping taverns and "ordinaries," (2) shopkeeping, (3) running businesses, (4) in trade, (5) running dame schools, (6) in service where they spent most of their time in manufacturing, i.e., as spinners or seamstresses, (7) printing, (8) as bakers and wine makers, and (9) knitting, spinning, and weaving in household industry.

TRENDS IN WOMEN'S PAID EMPLOYMENT AND OCCUPATIONS IN AMERICA

A main problem in tracing trends in the employment and occupational involvement of American women, or anyone else for that matter in any country, lies in the methods by which such data are obtained. Generally speaking, we must depend upon the census of populations for such information. Unfortunately, every method of trying to reach and record each person in a large and complex society has its drawbacks, and an additional problem for social scientists lies in the attempts by governments to offset these difficulties by changing procedures or instructions given to enumerators. This is particularly true of census data on the occupations of women. Hill (1929), who summarized information on *Women in Gainful Occupations 1870 to 1920* for the United States Department of Commerce's Bureau of the Census, pointed to examples of such changes:

> While an attempt was made in 1820 and again in 1840 to classify the population by main divisions of industry, distinguishing agriculture, manufactures, and commerce, the first complete census of occupations was taken in 1850, when for the first time the name of each person enumerated was recorded on the census schedule, together with sex, age, and other personal data including occupation . . . The 1850 occupation inquiry was restricted to adult males . . . in 1870 it applied to each person, male or female, without limitation as to age.
>
> As regards the home housekeeper, in 1870 and again in 1880 the enumerators were instructed that 'women keeping house for their own families or for themselves without any other gainful occupation' were to be entered on the schedules as 'keeping house,' and grown daughters assisting them were to be reported as without occupation, the term

'housekeeper' being reserved for such persons as received wages or salaries for their services (Hill, 1929: 3).

Hill (1929: 1-6) continued listing variations in the method of obtaining and tabulating data on women in later censuses.

The fact that married American women refrained from working in jobs outside of the home until rather recently can be documented statistically, as illustrated by Table 2.1. In 1890, only 4.6 percent of married women were officially listed as in the civilian labor force. The percentage of married women in paid employment, or at least in jobs, remained low until the last few decades, although it moved up gradually until it hit the 40 percent level in 1970. Interestingly enough, for several reasons it did not drop during the Depression (Milkman, 1979). In the first place, the sex segregation of jobs had solidified by the 1930s and the labor market continued to expand in the female-dominated sector even during the depression years (Bell, 1972; Oppenheimer, 1977). In addition, because women cost employers less, they were less apt to be fired "during a period of worsening business conditions" (Milkman, 1979: 511). Women were already underemployed; therefore, the figures for that period were not very different from those of the preceding or following times. Finally, many women were pushed into the labor force by the unemployment of their husbands. Milkman (1979) noted, however, that it was the work of women in the home which was altered most during the Depression because they had fewer resources for the purchase of commodities produced outside of the home.

World War II involved women in paid employment much more than before, because men were drafted into the armed services, leaving their jobs behind. Women were thus employed in jobs previously identified as male, but always with an understanding that such employment would last "for the duration" only and that the return of the men from the war would require the firing of the women.

> Sixty percent of the women who entered the labor market between 1940 and 1944 were 35 years old or more, and more than half of them were or had been married (Milkman, 1979: 529).

The society made every effort to accommodate the needs of working mothers. Factories even set up nurseries nearby, all of which closed with the end of the war.

The post-World War II years were accompanied by an extensive campaign to get women back into full-time homemaking, a campaign based on what Betty Friedan (1963) labeled "the feminine mystique."

Table 2.1 Marital Status of Women in the Civilian Labor Force: 1940 to 1982

Year	Female Labor Force (1,000)					Percent Distribution Female Labor Force			Female Labor Force As Percent Of Female Population				
	Total	Single	Married total[1]	Married, husband present	Widowed or divorced	Single	Married[1]	Widowed or divorced	Total	Single	Married total[1]	Married, husband present	Widowed or divorced
1940	13,840	6,710	5,040	4,200[2]	2,090	48.5	36.4	15.1	27.4	48.1	16.7	14.7	32.0
1944[2]	18,449	7,542	8,433	6,226	2,474	40.9	45.7	13.4	35.0	58.6	25.6	21.7	35.7
1947[2]	16,323	6,181	7,545	6,676	2,597	37.9	46.2	15.9	29.8	51.2	21.4	20.0	34.6
1950	17,795	5,621	9,273	8,550	2,901	31.6	52.1	16.3	31.4	50.5	24.8	23.8	36.0
1955[2]	20,154	5,087	11,839	10,423	3,227	25.2	58.7	16.0	33.5	46.4	29.4	27.7	36.0
1960	22,516	5,401	13,485	12,253	3,629	24.0	59.9	16.1	34.8	44.1	31.7	30.5	37.1
1965	25,952	5,912	16,154	14,708	3,886	22.8	62.2	15.0	36.7	40.5	35.7	34.7	35.7
1968	28,778	6,357	18,234	16,821	4,187	22.1	63.4	14.6	40.7	51.3	39.1	38.3	35.8
1969	29,898	6,501	19,100	17,595	4,297	21.7	63.9	14.4	41.6	51.2	40.4	39.6	35.8
1970	31,233	6,965	19,799	18,377	4,469	22.3	63.4	14.3	42.6	53.0	41.4	40.8	36.2
1971	31,778	7,220	20,034	18,573	4,524	22.7	63.0	14.2	42.5	52.8	41.4	40.8	35.7
1972	33,132	7,543	20,845	19,336	4,744	22.8	62.9	14.3	43.7	55.0	42.2	41.5	37.2
1973	34,195	7,838	21,487	19,951	4,870	22.9	62.8	14.2	44.2	55.9	42.8	42.2	36.7
1974	35,708	8,362	22,202	20,541	5,144	23.4	62.2	14.4	45.3	57.4	43.8	43.1	37.8
1975	36,981	8,599	23,037	21,360	5,345	23.2	62.3	14.5	46.0	57.0	45.1	44.4	37.7
1976	38,399	9,282	23,643	21,814	5,474	24.2	61.6	14.3	46.8	59.2	45.8	45.1	37.3
1977	40,053	9,702	24,429	22,681	5,922	24.2	61.0	14.8	48.0	59.2	47.2	46.6	39.0
1978	41,747	10,487	24,976	23,136	6,284	25.1	59.8	15.1	49.2	60.7	48.1	47.5	39.9
1979	43,844	11,304	26,073	24,223	6,467	25.8	59.5	14.8	50.8	62.9	49.9	49.3	40.0
1980	44,934	11,242	26,828	24,900	6,864	25.0	59.7	15.3	51.1	61.5	50.7	50.1	41.0
1981	46,415	11,628	27,536	25,460	7,251	25.0	59.3	15.6	52.0	62.3	51.7	51.0	41.9
1982	47,095	11,801	27,843	25,756	7,451	25.1	59.1	15.8	52.1	62.2	51.8	51.2	42.1

[1]Includes married, spouse absent.

[2]As of April.

Source: U.S. Bureau of the Census, 1983. Statistical Abstract of the United States. 1984 (104th Edition). Washington, D.C., p. 413.

Note: Persons 14 years old and over through 1965: 16 years old and over thereafter. As of March, except as indicated. Prior to 1960, excludes Alaska and Hawaii. Figures for 1940 based on complete census revised for comparability with intercensal series. Later data based on Current Population Survey; see text, p. 2 and Appendix III. See also *Historical Statistics, Colonial Times to 1970*, series D 49-62.

Table 2.2 Married Women (husband present) in the Labor Force, by Age and Presence of Children: 1948 to 1970 (As of March, except as noted)

Year	Number in labor force (1,000)						Labor force participation rate[1]					
				With children under 6 years						With children under 6 years		
	Total	With no children under 18 years	With children 6 to 17 years only	Total	No children 6 to 17 years	Also children 6 to 17 years	Total	With no children under 18 years	With children 6 to 17 years only	Total	No children 6 to 17 years	Also children 6 to 17 years
1981*	25,460	11,426	8,432	5,603	–	–	51.0	46.3	62.5	47.8	–	–
1970	18,377	8,174	6,289	3,914	1,874	2,040	40.8	42.2	49.2	30.3	30.2	30.5
1969	17,595	7,853	6,146	3,596	1,756	1,840	39.6	41.0	48.6	28.5	29.3	27.8
1968	16,821	7,564	5,693	3,564	1,641	1,923	38.3	40.1	46.9	27.6	27.8	27.4
1967	15,908	7,158	5,269	3,480	1,629	1,851	36.8	38.9	45.0	26.5	26.9	26.2
1966	15,178	7,043	4,949	3,186	1,431	1,755	35.4	38.4	43.7	24.2	24.0	24.3
1965	14,708	6,755	4,836	3,117	1,408	1,709	34.7	38.3	42.7	23.3	23.8	22.8
1964	14,461	6,545	4,866	3,050	1,408	1,642	34.4	37.8	43.0	22.7	23.6	21.9
1963	14,061	6,366	4,689	3,006	1,346	1,660	33.7	37.4	41.5	22.5	22.4	22.5
1962	13,485	6,156	4,445	2,884	1,282	1,602	32.7	36.1	41.8	21.3	21.1	21.5
1961	13,266	6,186	4,419	2,661	1,178	1,483	32.7	37.3	41.7	20.0	19.6	20.3

Year												
1960†	12,253	5,692	4,087	2,474	1,123	1,351	30.5	34.7	39.0	18.6	18.2	18.9
1959	12,205	5,679	4,055	2,471	1,118	1,353	30.9	35.2	39.8	18.7	18.3	19.0
1958	11,826	5,713	3,714	2,399	1,122	1,277	30.2	35.4	37.6	18.2	18.4	18.1
1957	11,529	5,805	3,517	2,208	961	1,247	29.6	35.6	36.6	17.0	15.9	17.9
1956	11,126	5,694	3,384	2,048	971	1,077	29.0	35.3	36.4	15.9	15.6	16.1
1955[2]	10,423	5,227	3,183	2,012	927	1,086	27.7	32.7	34.7	16.2	15.1	17.3
1954[2]	9,923	5,096	3,019	1,808	883	925	26.6	31.6	33.2	14.9	14.3	15.5
1953[2]	9,763	5,130	2,749	1,884	1,047	837	26.3	31.2	32.2	15.5	15.8	15.2
1952[2]	9,222	5,042	2,492	1,688	916	772	25.3	30.9	31.1	13.9	13.7	14.1
1951[2]	9,086	5,016	2,400	1,670	886	784	25.2	31.0	30.3	14.0	13.6	14.6
1950	8,550	4,946	2,205	1,399	748	651	23.8	30.3	28.3	11.9	11.2	12.6
1949[2]	7,959	4,544	2,130	1,285	654	631	22.5	28.7	27.3	11.0	10.0	12.2
1948[2]	7,553	4,400	1,927	1,226	594	632	22.0	28.4	26.0	10.8	9.2	12.7

*U.S. Department of Labor: Bureau of Labor Statistics, 1983. *Marital and Family Patterns of Workers: An Update*. Bulletin 2163. (May)

†Denotes first year for which figures include Alaska and Hawaii.

[1]Married women in the labor force as percent of married women in the population.

[2]As of April.

Source: U.S. Bureau of the Census. *Historical Statistics of the United States: Colonial Times to 1970, Bicentennial Edition, Part II.* Washington, D.C.: U.S. Government Printing Office, 1975:134.

Reminiscent of the "true womanhood" ideology, the mystique identified all women with homemaking, wifehood, and motherhood and
discouraged any thoughts of, or commitment to, occupations and
careers outside of these roles. The strength of the campaign, which
capitalized on work of such psychiatrists as Freud (see Friedan, 1963;
La Pierre, 1959), Helene Deutsch (1944), or Lundberg and Farnham's
(1947) *Modern Woman: The Lost Sex*, and utilized print as well as
film (see *Lady in the Dark*), is documented elsewhere and appears to
have been effective (Lopata, 1971). By 1950, only 22 percent of married women with husbands present in the home were gainfully employed, a percentage about the same as in 1920 (see Table 2.2). However, there is no agreement among the social scientists as to the nature
of the ebb and flow of women in the world of work. Friedan (1963)
claimed that movement away from commitment to the public, especially the occupational world, occurred in the late 1940s and 1950s,
after reaching a peak in the 1920s. Bernard (1964) dated the redirec-
tion of attention by women who had taken up the feminist banner
away from higher education and professions to a period of disillusion-
ment in the 1920s. Stricker (1979), on the other hand, claimed that
there never was a decrease in the total number of women so oriented,
only a relative decrease in the proportion of women among those
achieving higher degrees and involvement in professions due to the
upsurge in the number of men so involved.

Whichever argument is accepted, the fact remains that the numbers
and proportions of women oriented toward careers outside of the
home have been very small until recent years. Those who were so committed to these goals had to renounce marriage and motherhood because the American society was unwilling to provide public resources
that made dual or triple role commitment possible, and because men
were generally unwilling to marry highly educated career women (Komarovsky, 1953). Figures in Table 2.2 indicate that even when marriage decreased its negative influence on the paid employment of
women, motherhood did not. In 1948, for example, only 9 percent
of mothers who had at least one child under six years of age were in
jobs outside of the home.

The expansion of female labor force participation was accompanied by the expansion of jobs in service and clerical sectors (see
Tables 2.1 and 2.3).

A service economy is largely a female-dominate economy—if one
considers clerical, sales, teaching, health technicians and similar occupations. In 1960, 80 percent of all workers in the goods-producing area

Table 2.3 Occupational Distribution of Employed Women, Annual Averages, Selected Years 1900-1979

Occupation	Percentage of Employed Women									Percentage of All Workers 1979[3]
	1900[1]	1910[2]	1920[2]	1930[2]	1940[1]	1950[3]	1960[3]	1970[3]	1979[3]	
Professional-technical	8.2	9.8	11.7	13.8	13.6	12.5	12.4	14.5	16.1	43.3
Managerial-administrative, officials, proprietors (nonfarm)	1.4	2.0	2.2	2.7	3.6	4.4	5.0	4.5	6.4	24.6
Sales	4.3	5.1	6.3	6.8	7.3	8.7	7.7	7.0	6.9	45.1
Clerical	4.0	9.2	18.7	20.9	21.6	27.8	30.3	34.5	35.0	80.3
Craft, foremen	1.4	1.4	1.2	1.0	1.0	1.5	1.0	1.1	1.8	5.7
Operatives (including transportation)	23.7	22.9	20.2	17.4	18.5	19.6	15.2	14.5	11.3	32.0
Nonfarm laborers	2.6	1.4	2.3	1.5	0.9	0.8	0.4	0.5	1.3	11.3
Service, private	28.7	24.0	15.7	17.8	18.0	12.4	14.8	16.5	17.2	97.6
Service, nonprivate	6.7	8.4	8.1	9.7	11.2	8.7	8.9	5.1	2.6	59.1
Farm workers	19.0	15.7	13.5	8.4	4.3	3.6	4.4	1.8	1.2	18.0

Sources: [1] Gordon, Margaret. "Women and Work: Priorities for the Future." In C. Kerr and J. M. Rosow (eds.) *Work in America: The Decade Ahead.* New York: D. Van Nostrand, 1979: 117.
[2] U.S. Bureau of the Census. *Historical Statistics of the United States: Colonial Times to 1970, Bicentennial Edition, Part II.* Washington, D.C.: U.S. Government Printing Office, 1975: Table D182-232, p. 140.
[3] U.S. Department of Labor. *Perspectives on Working Women: A Databook, Bulletin 2080.* Washington, D.C.: U.S. Government Printing Office, 1980: Table 10, p. 9 (includes 14 and 15 year olds).

were men, and 20 percent women; conversely, in the service sectors only 54 percent of all workers were men and 46 percent women. Looked at along a different axis, 27 percent of all employed females worked in the goods-producing sector, while 73 percent of all women worked in the service sector (Bell, 1972: 179).

These trends, both in the expansion of these sectors and in the concentration of women in them, continue.

> The large increase in the number of women professional workers may be attributed to a variety of social and economic developments. The school-age population expanded greatly, resulting in the employment of a rising number of women as teachers, other educational personnel, and librarians. The concern for the health of the American population, and especially of older persons, resulted in enlarged medical facilities and expanded health programs which provided increasing numbers of jobs for women as nurses, therapists, dieticians, pharmacists, clinical laboratory technologists and technicians, and other professional and technical health workers. The growth of business and industry and of governmental operations provided opportunities for many more women as accountants and computer specialists. The sharp growth in social welfare and recreation programs contributed to an increase in the number of women as professional, social and recreation workers (U.S. Department of Labor, 1975: 95).

Other theories concerning the increase of women in the labor force abound. Smith (1979a) summarized four explanations. One is given by economists who posit that the ratio of costs and benefits associated with employment outside the home has changed. If real wages increase and the returns on housework do not, then the net benefits for working outside of the home grow and more women decide to look for employment. This model assumes that the "income effect" (the decrease in the "push" into the labor force by women as family income increases) will be outweighed by the "pull" of growing real wages. Oppenheimer (1970) offered a second explanation in terms of the expansion of sex-specific jobs. Demographic explanations focus on the effect of later marriages, rising divorce rates, and falling birth rates. Lastly, Smith (1979b) and Gordon (1978) saw changes in the attitudes toward women and their "proper" place as contributing to the increasing female labor force participation rates.

> In sum, during most of the period since World War II, all the factors discussed here—improvement in job opportunities, demographic change, and the liberalization in attitudes—have contributed to the expansion of the female labor force (Smith, 1979b: 7).

Not only are more women now in paid employment, but the profile of the female labor force has also changed. The greatest increase has been in the number and percentage of married women and mothers who are employed outside the home (Smith, 1979b). As Gordon (1978) asserted, if this trend continues, as it is expected to, (Smith, 1979a, 1979b), there are widespread implications for both family and market structures in the future. As more married women of child-bearing age and more mothers of preschool children work outside of the home, the age, marital, and mothering characteristics of the female labor force more closely approximate the profile of the total female population (Blau, 1978). This means that the female labor force is increasingly diversified as to its personal characteristics so that assumptions as to the "type" of woman who is employed are no longer valid.

As women from all marital and socioeconomic backgrounds have entered the labor force, the feminist movement has been working to achieve equality in career opportunities and job compensation. Nevertheless, despite these movements (i.e., an increased number of women in the labor force and increasing attention to the ideals of equality), the wage gap between men and women is growing wider rather than narrower. In 1955, the average female employee earned 64 percent of the wages paid to a similarly employed man. This percentage dropped to 59 percent by 1970 (Special Task Force to the Secretary of HEW, 1973) and by 1974 the median income for women was only 57 percent of the median for men (Howe, 1977). This wage gap has not narrowed in the last several years and is causing widespread concern among employed women. The legislation against wage discrimination (the Equal Pay Act of 1963) does little to alleviate this problem because discrimination against women most often takes the form of job segregation rather than unequal pay for the same job. Recently, the call for equal pay for work of comparable value has proven to be a rallying cry for organized employed women.

OCCUPATIONAL SEGREGATION AND SCHEDULE INFLEXIBILITY IN AMERICA

Although Bird (1979) called the influx of married women into the labor force a "revolution," there are two aspects of the change which have not yet been fully developed. Women are still, even more than years ago, segregated in a relatively few female dominated occupations with easy entrance and exit boundaries, but low pay and restricted mobility opportunities (Lopata and Norr, 1979, 1980; Oppenheimer, 1970).

> . . . in 1975 more than two-fifths of all women workers were em-
> ployed in ten occupations—secretary, retail trade salesworker, book-
> keeper, private household worker, elementary school teacher, waitress,
> typist, cashier, sewer and stitcher, and registered nurse. Each of these
> occupations employed over 800,000 women . . . There were 57 occupa-
> tions in which at least 100,000 women were employed in 17 of the [57]
> occupations, women accounting for 90 percent or more of all employees.
> In more than half of the occupations [31 out of 57], women made up
> 75 percent of all employees . . . Male employment showed much less
> occupational concentration (U.S. Department of Labor, 1975: 91-92).

The second lag in the American working situation is the failure of the
system to make adjustments in the rhythm of work, in terms of time
and career lines, to accommodate women, or men for that matter, who
face role conflict arising from needs of children or other persons in
their lives. The economic institution is still focused upon itself, demanding that people adjust their lives to its schedule without flexibility.

There are many explanations for the concentration of women in
female-dominated occupations. Blau (1978) pointed to a historical
explanation. It contended that the influx and absorption of women
into the labor force has occurred in three ways: the expansion of the
traditional female occupations, the rise of new occupations which are
defined as female, and a shift in the sexual composition of some occupations from male to female. However, we still do not know why
occupations become so labeled, or why the composition changes. An
examination of both occupations and industries shows women drawn
to jobs in the fastest growing industries, where they are concentrated
at the lower levels and seldom move into supervisory, managerial, or
technical positions.

Baker (1964) explained the distribution of women in occupations
in terms of technology. The technological structure of the work in
many jobs has helped women move in or out of particular occupations, as was the case of the textile mills when looms were introduced.
However, the social role characteristics of jobs have also influenced
whether women are allowed entrance into them or consider them as
viable alternatives. Early textile mills were specifically organized to
attract the unmarried daughters of farmers. With an influx of immigrants and the increased willingness of native men to enter factories,
other ways of organizing the job became possible. One of the reasons
American business and industry have failed to provide, or to encourage the government to provide, adequate arrangements for maternity
leaves or day care centers is that this society still does not really

approve of paid employment outside of the home for mothers. While American society was pushing women to stay home, countries such as Poland, which lost a high proportion of men during World War II (one-sixth of the total population), went out of their way to attract, train, and retain women not only in female-oriented occupations, but also in previously masculine occupations (Lobodzinska, 1970, 1974; Lopata, 1976; Piotrowski, 1963; Roby, 1973; Szczepanski, 1970). The majority of doctors, dentists, lawyers, and engineers in Poland, as well as in the Soviet Union, are women, unlike what exists in the United States (Sokolowska, 1965). Creches and nursery schools are provided in countries that encourage women to be in the labor force; maternity and paternity leaves, as well as time off to care for an ill child have been instituted in several countries (Kahn and Kamerman, 1975; Kamerman and Kahn, 1978; Lipman-Blumen and Bernard, 1979).

One of the theories attempting to explain the occupational segregation of women refers to them as a "reserve army," pulled into the labor force as needs arise. Milkman (1979) documented the weakness of this theory by showing that women were less affected by the Depression than men were. Hartmann (1976) argued that the transition to capitalism did not begin the sexual segregation of jobs, but simply expanded the already established patriarchal system, one which Lipman-Blumen (1976) called the "homosocial" control of public life. It is Hartmann's thesis that the better organized male workers maintained their domination through sex-ordered job segregation; "capitalism grew on top of patriarchy" (Hartmann, 1976: 168). With the separation of work from the home during the industrial revolution, women grew more dependent on men economically as they were increasingly excluded from industry and job training. And, as capitalism developed to its more advanced stages, men enforced the segregation in the labor market *and* strengthened the domestic division of labor.

A combination of historical and sociological approaches to the analysis of occupational segregation by sex in the United States was undertaken by Gross (1968). Using an index of segregation (the percentage of females who would have to change their occupation so that the distribution of sexes in occupations would be the same) for each census year from 1900 to 1960, he found no significant difference in sexual segregation over the years. There has been some "reduction in segregation, which seems to be accomplished by men entering female occupations, rather than the reverse" (1968: 208), but this is masked by the fact that the occupations that are more segregated have been growing faster than those which are less segregated. Oppenheimer (1970) cautioned the social scientist against conceiving of *the* labor market and *the* demand for labor, rather than positing a multiplicity of labor markets, some of which are competitive with each other, while others are not competitive at all. She discussed six factors which work to keep certain jobs female dominated. First, there is the availability of female labor, permitting certain occupations to be monopolized by women. Second, they are a cheap but educated labor force, leading to reliance on them in certain occupations. Third, belief in sex-linked characteristics are held by employers, unions, and instruction programs which train women for jobs. Fourth, the power of tradition has led to a labeling of some jobs, and this has led to an unwillingness of women to even try entry. Finally, difficulties in work relations, assumed or real, in mixed groups or ones in which women supervise men, lead employers to discriminate. Other problems of past or current work limitations of women, such as lack of geographical mobility, career interruptions, educational specialization, etc. contribute to images of women and men workers that lead to occupational selection (Laws, 1976; Suelzle, 1973).

Economists offer numerous explanations of the sex segregation of occupations, focused mainly on the characteristics of the labor force. The overcrowding, employer "tastes," and "human capital" approaches fall outside of the province of this book, and are only mentioned in case the reader wishes a deeper analysis of the situation (see Blau and Jusenius, 1976; Sokoloff, 1980; Stevenson, 1978). Among others, Doeringer and Piore (1971) have observed the evolution of a "primary" and "secondary" labor market dichotomy. Their explanation is that most women work in the secondary market, which is less structured, has multiple channels of entry with short promotion ladders (or nonexistent ones), low wages, and less job stability. The primary market, on the other hand, is highly developed, entry is restricted to high level jobs with long promotion ladders, and work stability is encouraged through high wages and provisions for job security. (For more information on dual labor market theory see Bibb and Form, 1977; Edwards, 1980; Edwards, Reich and Gordon, 1975; Kalleberg and Sorensen, 1979; Piore, 1975; Stevensen, 1975.) Blau and Jesenius (1976) are critical of the dual labor market analysis because it does not explain the further sex segregation within each sector, the differentiation within the female sector, or the differential treatment accorded to women and men within the primary sector.

In conclusion, there are numerous theories which attempt to explain the very striking sex segregation of occupations and industrial sectors in the United States, though none do so too successfully. The most segregated occupation, of course, is that of homemaking. Very few men enter this occupation at the present time although there is much media coverage of the few couples who are involved in "role reversal." Another obvious characteristic of this type of job is the fact that it does not draw direct pay. Glazer-Malbin (1976), in reviewing the literature on housework, pointed to the fact that its monetary value to the family and to the economy of the nation (often referred to as the market cost approach) has never been determined (see also Barker and Allen, 1976 and Malos, 1980 for mainly Marxist explanations of the politics of housework). Time allocation studies of housework have documented that there has been no drop in the average work week of the full-time housewife over the past 50 years (Vanek, 1974, 1978) and that employed married women still perform the bulk of domestic work (Berk and Berk, 1979; Epstein, 1970; Lopata, Barnewolt and Norr, 1980; Oakley, 1974a, 1974b; Walker, 1969, 1970). Glazer (1980) identified four characteristics of domestic work which she feels impinge on women's paid work: state trivialization of domestic work, the fact that domestic work has undergone more apparent than real changes, the additional fact that household labor-saving technology has not reduced the work of full-time homemakers, and finally that mothering has become even more time consuming than before. Glazer's (1980) argument is founded on the thesis that housewifery is ascribed on the basis of sex because other social relations in society assume that women are responsible for housework and child care. Thus, the paid work that women are channeled into is limited by "occupational compatibility"—work that is compatible with their domestic responsibilities. The sex-labeling of jobs and women's discontinuous involvement in the labor force are tied to women's domestic labor. The history of women's work as wage laborers, first in the textile industry and later on in other factory systems, was defined by their domestic labor. Glazer's efforts in trying to explicitly state how women's domestic responsibilities in the family have affected women's activities outside the family show how women's paid labor force participation is organized around the assumption that domestic labor is women's primary concern. (For another discussion of the link between female work and family roles and how that can be conceptualized as a sex-segregated, dual market mechanism see Pleck, 1977.)

We can expect the contradiction between work and family roles to continue as a problem as the proportion of women in the paid labor force grows. In addition, as women become increasingly aware of this contradiction and the division of labor within the home is broken down, it will become a problem for more and more men as well. One way of dealing with the issue has been to restructure the work schedules of women and men who are employed outside the home. It is probable that the number of alternatives to full-time work will increase in the future as it has in the recent past. The temporary employment industry, for instance, has grown faster than any other segment of the work force (Tepperman, 1976). This type of employment offers flexibility in both scheduling of hours and number of hours worked per week, but it does not pay well or offer other financial benefits.

In addition, a number of experiments concerning flexible work hours and shortened work weeks have been conducted in the U.S. and Europe. These experiments began in 1967 in the research and development department of a German aerospace company, Messerschmitt-Bolkow-Blohm. Flex-time was adopted at the plant to deal with problems involving traffic jams and tardiness, but it proved to have a whole host of accompanying effects on the work force. The use of flexible schedules proliferated in Europe during the 1970s; by 1975 about 6,000 European firms had adopted such schedules. The adoption of such alternative work schedules has been much slower in the U.S., but it seems to be accelerating in the last half of this decade. Until recently flexible work schedule programs in America were found in smaller nonunionized organizations, but this too is changing (Polit, 1979). The current administration has cut back on governmental use of flex-time.

Part-time employment, which is not a new phenomenon, is also increasing as an alternative to full-time work. In the last 20 years the degree of part-time employment has increased at a remarkable rate, nearly twice that of the increase in female employment. Most of the workers who are employed part-time are women (80 percent). In 1974, 31 percent of the working wives in the U.S. were employed part-time (Hayghe, 1976; Polit, 1979). Among the 30.2 million women working in nonagricultural occupations in 1974, 21.7 million (almost 72 percent) were on full-time schedules and 8.5 million worked part-time. Of those women who worked part-time, 7.4 million did so for voluntary reasons and 1.1 million worked part-time due to economic slowdown (U.S. Department of Labor, 1975). Part-time work is particularly common in occupations in the education and service industries. In 1973 approximately 60 percent of the women who worked in sales, transport operation, and farm labor did so on a part-time basis. In addition, two out of three private household workers were on a part-time schedule. (U.S. Department of Labor, 1975).

Women are most affected by the growth of alternatives in work scheduling. Traditionally, women, the elderly, young people, and the disabled have been the workers most concentrated in this "marginal" work force participation.

> Those who are represented by the part-time work movement include women who are reentering the workplace but do not wish to work full-time, dual career couples who are faced with an increasingly difficult time finding two full-time jobs [that is, in the same university or even in the same town]; persons with cardiac and other medical problems who are instructed to return to work but on a part-time basis; and persons ideologically committed to maximizing time for private nonwork-related interests (Arkin and Dobrofsky, 1979: 161-62).

Not all part-time work is undertaken voluntarily, however. "Involuntary part-time work, including short work weeks, layoffs for a day or two, and the like, greatly exceeds 20 percent; like recent rates for employment, these figures run considerably higher among women workers than men" (Bell, 1973: 80). *Worksharing* is also on the rise. Under such arrangements weekly hours, as well as pay, are reduced so that all workers may retain their jobs, even at a lower salary. Advocates of such plans argue that their implementation spreads the impact of a recession and fosters a higher degree of job attachment, keeps employment skills fresh, and allows workers to retain fringe benefits. Critics maintain, however, that such plans interfere with seniority privileges, and when subsidized by the government may discourage firms from adapting to technological and organizational changes (Bednarzk, 1980; Best and Mattesich, 1980). Demographically, blacks and women were disproportionately more likely to be on involuntarily shortened schedules because of decreased demand for their labor.

When female part-time workers are compared to male part-time workers, it becomes apparent that many of the inequities faced by female full-time workers are also faced by part-timers. Especially telling is the continuation of sexual segregation in part-time jobs. Seventy percent of all female part-time workers were in sales, clerical, and nondomestic service occupations as compared to 45 percent of the men who were employed part-time. It is interesting to note that part-time pay rates for men are about on par with rates for women. This probably reflects the fact that male part-time workers are minorities and are either younger or older than average (68 percent of male part-timers are either younger than 22 years old or over 55 compared to 42 percent of the women) (Barrett, 1979).

Part-time jobs usually pay lower rates than comparable full-time work and fringe benefits arc scanty if they are included at all. Representative of this reality, Smith (1979c) found part-time employment to be heavily concentrated in low wage occupations. In addition, the wage rates of women part-timers are usually lower than those of women full-time workers in the same occupation. Tuckman and Vogler (1979) found that there was a substantial gap in basic insurance coverage for those with part-time academic jobs. Less than half of the part-timers surveyed were covered by social security at their academic job, less than 20 percent had an institutional retirement plan, only 6 percent received life insurance coverage, and about 11 percent were eligible for workers' compensation. As reported by Polit (1979) the 1972 Wage Survey in four urban areas found part-time employees receiving a prorated portion of the paid holidays and vacations in only about half the cases. Less than one-fourth of the part-time workers were able to participate in pension plans and life and health insurance were "generally not provided." In addition to these drawbacks, part-time jobs are frequently "dead-end" positions with few career opportunities. Polit (1979: 202) found that "most women working part-time in well-paying, challenging jobs appear to have obtained their positions by first demonstrating their competency as full-time employees." However, in spite of the low pay, lack of fringe benefits, and general lack of promotional opportunity, the demand for part-time work may outstrip the supply of part-time jobs.

SUMMARY

The organization of work and its allocation to different kinds of societal members provides a fascinating subject for sociological and historical analysis. So does the connection between work as a set of tasks and various social roles, such as those of employee, wife, or mother. A third subject of interest to social scientists is social status, which is reflected in the complex of rights surrounding a person and is derived from identities, social roles, and positions vis-a-vis others in the family, community, and society. These topics are, however, complex and the examination of the work, social roles, and status of women over time provides alternate evaluations and explanations. The safe generalization is that there has always been a division of labor, although the distribution of tasks beyond the bearing and nursing of children has varied enormously. Simply taking the last three centuries of Western European history (English and French for the most part) and variations on the themes which developed in America as *The New Nation* (Lipset, 1979), we find that an important change in the work of women has been the removal and modification of their traditional work into jobs in organizations outside of the home. The work of men underwent a similar process but with resulting higher status and greater innovation. Agriculture changed so dramatically during modernization that large groups of dependent assistants were no longer necessary.

The organization of traditional work into jobs and the introduction of new jobs within broad occupational categories accompanied the introduction of personal property as a means of exchanging work and products for money. The transformation of only part of women's work into jobs made them economically dependent upon men whenever the social system or cultural ideologies prevented their self-support. Men were freed of their dependence upon clans, families, and communities when their work became "public," that is, evaluated in terms of its contribution to the gross national product (Eichler, 1973; Engels, 1884/1972; Hartmann, 1976; Hill, 1929).

Ideologies that affect the work women do, as well as its organization and position in the prestige hierarchy, include not only the definition of the importance of work roles but also definitions of "women," "men," and "children." A major change in such definitions occurred in the English-French form of Western European history and in America with the introduction of "true womanhood," public and private "domains" or "spheres," "childhood," and so forth. The ideologies, forcefully elaborated upon in America, discouraged women from involvement in the public sphere of life if they could afford to do so. However, the process of keeping women at home produced consequences which resulted in a backlash. More educated middle-class women combined with the male Protestant clergy to feminize and "moralize" the society. The welfare and protective activities had their own backlash, restricting the earning power of those women who wanted to be employed outside of the home and increasing male hostility to women's employment activity. Although this argument sounds very much like the tendency to "blame the victim" of discrimination in the job market, it has been argued that this movement contributed to continued and even increased occupational sex segregation.

Whatever the historical, structural, and perhaps, to some extent, psychological, reasons for the distribution of women in paid and unpaid work, the recent "revolution" so touted in mass media and social science has only partially changed the female world of work. It has, in fact, increased the disorganization and dissonance in the lives of American women. Women, particularly married ones, and more surprisingly (in view of the ideological history of the United States) mothers of young children, are now working for pay, in addition to their work as homemakers, wives, and mothers. However, they are still working mainly in female-dominated jobs, at 60 percent of what men earn in their jobs, and with short promotional ladders. Sixteen years ago Gross's (1968) analysis suggested that many women and men will have to change their occupations and work locus before the second stage of the "revolution" in women's employment takes place. In addition, the presence of women in the labor force has not yet affected the organization of work in occupational and career terms. According to Kahn and Kamerman (1975) and numerous others involved in comparative research (Roby, 1973), the economic and political sectors in America are not willing to modify work scheduling in recognition of the fact that the job is not the only role in which women and men are involved, and that there is a need to facilitate other roles over the life course.

This chapter has mainly documented some of the trends which have led American society to its current division of labor and the policies affecting the work that women do. It is the purpose of this book to examine how women in different occupational categories reach their current employment status and occupation, what they do on the job, and how they combine their jobs with their other social roles.

REFERENCES

Abbott, Edith. 1913. *Women in Industry: A Study in American Economic History*. New York: D. Appleton.

––––––. 1929. The Webbs on the English Poor Law. *Social Service Review* 3: 252-69.

Abbott, Grace. 1938. *The Child and the State, Volume II: The Dependent and Delinquent Child*. Chicago: University of Chicago Press.

Arkin, William, and Lynne R. Dobrofsky. 1979. Job Sharing Couples. In *Working Women and Families*, edited by K. W. Feinstein, pp. 159-76. Beverly Hills, California: Sage Publications.

Aries, Philippe. 1962. *Centuries of Childhood: A Social History of Family Life*. New York: Vantage Books.

––––––. 1981. *The Hour of Our Death*. New York: Alfred A. Knopf.

Babcock, Barbara Allen, Ann Freedman, Eleanor Holmes Norton, and Susan C. Ross. 1975. *Sex Discrimination and the Law: Causes and Remedies*. Boston: Little, Brown.

Baker, Elizabeth Faulkner. 1964. *Technology and Woman's Work*. New York: Columbia University Press.

Barker, Diana Leonard, and Sheila Allen (eds.). 1976. *Dependence and Exploitation in Work and Marriage*. New York: Longman.

Barrett, Nancy. 1979. Women in the Job Market: On Employment and Work Schedules. In *The Subtle Revolution: Women at Work*, edited by R. E. Smith, pp. 63-98. Washington, D.C.: The Urban Institute.

Bednarzik, Robert W. 1980. Worksharing in the U.S.: Its prevalence and duration. *Monthly Labor Review* 103 (July): 3-12.

Bell, Daniel. 1972. Labor in the Post-industrial Society. In *The World of the Blue-Collar Worker*, edited by I. Howe, pp. 159-97. New York: Quandrangle Books.

Bell, Carolyn Shaw. 1973. Age, sex, marriage and jobs. *The Public Interest* (Winter): 75-89.

Berk, Sarah Fenstermaker (ed.). 1980. *Women and Household Labor*. Beverly Hills, California: Sage Publications.

Berk, Richard, and Sarah Fenstermaker Berk. 1979. *Labor and Leisure at Home: Content and Organization of the Household Day*. Beverly Hills, California: Sage Publications.

Bernard, Jessie. 1964. *Academic Women*. University Park, Pennsylvania: Pennsylvania State University Press.

————. 1981. *The Female World*. New York: The Free Press.

Best, Fred, and James Mattesich. 1980. Short-time compensation systems in California and Europe. *Monthly Labor Review* 103 (July): 13-22.

Bibb, Robert, and William H. Form. 1977. The effects of industrial, occupational, and sex stratification on wages in blue-collar markets. *Social Forces* 55 (4): 974-96.

Bird, Caroline. 1976. *Enterprising Women*. New York: New American Library.

————. 1979. *The Two-Paycheck Marriage: How Women at Work are Changing Life in America*. New York: Rawson, Wade Publishers.

Blau, Francine D. 1978. The Data on Women Workers, Past, Present and Future. In *Women Working*, edited by A. H. Stromberg and S. Harkess, pp. 29-62. Palo Alto, California: Mayfield Publishing Company.

Blau, Francine D., and Carol L. Jusenius. 1976. Economists' Approaches to Sex Segregation in the Labor Market: An Appraisal. In *Women and the Workplace*, edited by M. Blaxall and B. Reagan, pp. 181-200. Chicago: University of Chicago Press.

Bloch, Ruth H. 1978. Untangling the roots of modern sex roles: A survey of four centuries of change. *Signs* 4 (Winter): 237-52.

Block, Marc. 1964. *Feudal Society*. A. Manyon (trans.). Chicago: University of Chicago Press.

Boserup, Ester. 1970. *Woman's Role in Economic Development*. New York: St. Martin's Press.

Bottomore, T. B. (trans.). 1956. *Karl Marx: Selected Writings in Sociology and Social Philosophy*. New York: McGraw-Hill.

Boulding, Elise. 1976. Familial constraints on women's work roles. *Signs* 1 (Autumn): 95-117.

Braverman, Harry. 1974. *Labor and Monopoly Capital*. New York: Monthly Review Press.

Brinker, Paul A. 1968. *Economic Insecurity and Social Security*. New York: Appleton-Century-Crofts.

Brownlee, W. Elliot, and Mary M. Brownlee. 1976. *Women in the American Economy: A Documentary History, 1675 to 1929*. New Haven, Connecticut: Yale University Press.

Burke, Peter. 1978. *Popular Culture in Early Modern Europe*. New York: New York University Press.

Calhoun, Arthur. 1917/1945. *A Social History of the American Family from Colonial Times to the Present*. New York: Barnes and Noble.

Carr, Lois Green, and Lorena S. Walsh. 1978. The Planter's Wife: The Experience of White Women in Seventeenth Century Maryland. In *The American Family in Social-Historical Perspective*, edited by Michael Gordon, pp. 263-288. New York: St. Martin's Press.

Chafe, William H. 1972. *The American Woman: Her Changing Social, Economic and Political Roles, 1920-1970*. New York: Oxford University Press.

Chapman, Jane Roberts, and Margaret Gates (eds.). 1977. *Women Into Wives: The Legal and Economic Impact of Marriage*. Beverly Hills, California: Sage Publications.

Clark, Alice. 1919/1968. *Working Life of Women in the Seventeenth Century*. New York: Augustus M. Kelley, Reprints of Economic Classics.

Coleman, Emily. 1976. Infanticide in the Early Middle Ages. In *Women in Medieval Society*, edited by S. M. Stuart, pp. 47-70. Philadelphia: University of Pennsylvania Press.

Cott, Nancy F. 1977. *The Bonds of Womanhood: Women's Sphere in New England, 1780-1885*. New Haven, Connecticut: Yale University Press.

Davidson, Marshall. 1951/1974. *Life in America*. Bicenntenial edition. Boston: Houghton Mifflin.

Davis, Michael M. Jr. 1971. *Immigration, Health and the Community—1921*. Montclair, New Jersey: Patterson, Smith.

Demos, John. 1970. *A Little Commonwealth, Family Life in Plymouth Colony*. New York: Oxford University Press.

Deutsch, Helene. 1944. *The Psychology of Women*. New York: Grune and Stratton.

Doeringer, Peter B., and Michael J. Piore. 1971. *Internal Labor Markets and Manpower Analysis*. Lexington, Massachusetts: D.C. Heath and Company.

Douglas, Ann. 1977. *The Feminization of American Culture*. New York: Avon Books.

Dulles, Foster Rhea. 1965. *A History of Recreation: America Learns to Play*. New York: Appleton-Century-Crofts.

Easton, Barbara L. 1976. Industrialization and femininity: A case study of nineteenth century New England. *Social Problems* 23 (April): 389-401.

Edwards, Richard C. 1980. *Contested Terrain*. New York: Basic Books.

Edwards, Richard C., David M. Gordon, and Michael Reich (eds.). 1975. *Labor Market Segmentation*. Lexington, Massachusetts: D.C. Heath and Company.

Ehrenreich, Barbara, and Deidre English. 1979. *For Her Own Good: 150 Years of the Experts' Advice to Women*. Garden City, New York: Anchor Press.

Eichler, Margrit. 1973. Women as Personal Dependents. In *Women in Canada*, edited by M. Stephenson, pp. 36-55. Toronto: New Press.

Engels, Frederick. 1884/1972. *The Origin of the Family, Private Property and the State*. New York: International Publishers.

Epstein, Cynthia F. 1970. *Woman's Place: Options and Limits on Professional Careers*. Berkeley, California: University of California Press.

Freidan, Betty. 1963. *The Feminine Mystique*. New York: Norton.

Glazer, Nona. 1976. Housework. *Signs* 1 (Summer): 905-22.

———. 1980. Everyone Needs Three Hands: Doing Unpaid and Paid Work. In *Women and Household Labor*, edited by S. F. Berk, pp. 249-73. Beverly Hills, California: Sage Publications.

Golab, Caroline. 1977. *Immigrant Destinations*. Philadelphia: Temple University Press.

Gordon, Michael. 1978. *The American Family: Past, Present and Future*. New York: Random House.

Gross, Edward. 1968. Plus ca change: The sexual structure of occupations over time. *Social Problems* 16 (2): 198-208.

Hareven, Tamara K. 1977. Family time and historical time. *Daedalus* 106 (Spring): 57-70.

Hareven, Tamara K., and Randolph Langenbach. 1978. *Amoskeag: Life and Work in an American Factory City*. New York: Pantheon Books.

Hareven, Tamara K., and Maris A. Vinovskis (eds.). 1978. *Family and Population in Nineteenth-Century America*. Princeton, New Jersey: Princeton University Press.

Harris, Barbara. 1979. Careers, Conflict and Children: The Legacy of the Cult of Domesticity. In *Career and Motherhood: Struggles for a New Identity*, edited by A. Roland and B. Harris, pp. 55-86. New York: Human Sciences Press.

Hartman, Mary S., and Lois Banner (eds.). 1974. *Clio's Consciousness Raised: New Perspectives on the History of Women*. New York: Harper and Row.

Hartmann, Heidi. 1976. Capitalism, patriarchy and job segregation by sex. *Signs* 18 (Spring special supplement): 137-169.

Hayghe, H. 1976. Families and the rise of working wives—An overview. *Monthly Labor Review* 99 (May): 3-17.

Herlihy, David. 1976. Land, Family and Women in Continental Europe. In *Women in Medieval Society*, edited by S. M. Stuart, pp. 13-45. Philadelphia: University of Pennsynlania Press.

Hertzler, J. A. 1961. *American Social Institutions*. Boston: Allyn and Bacon.

Hesse, Sharlene J. 1979. Women Working: Historical Trends. In *Working Women and Families*, edited by K. W. Feinstein, pp. 35-62. Beverly Hills, California: Sage Publications.

Hewitt, Margaret. 1958. *Wives and Mothers in Victorian Industry*. Westport, Connecticut: Greenwood Press.

Hill, Georgiana. 1896. *Women in English Life: From Medieval to Modern Times*. London: Richard Bentley and Sons.

Hill, Joseph A. 1929. *Women in Gainful Occupations 1870-1920*. Washington, D.C.: U.S. Government Printing Office.

Horton, Paul, and Gerald Leslie. 1960. *The Sociology of Social Problems*. New York: Appleton-Century-Crofts.

Howe, Louise Kapp. 1977. *Pink Collar Workers: Inside the World of Women's Work*. New York: G.P. Putnam's Sons.

Huntington, Suellen. 1975. Issues in women's role in economic development: Critique and alternatives. *Journal of Marriage and the Family* 37 (November): 1001-1012.

Illick, Joseph. 1974. Child-rearing in Seventeenth-century England and America. In *The History of Childhood*, edited by Lloyd de Mause, pp. 303-50. New York: Psychohistory Press.

Kahn, Alfred J., and Sheila B. Kamerman. 1975. *Not for the Poor Alone: European Social Services*. New York: Harper Colophon Books.

Kalleberg, Arne L., and Aage B. Sorenson. 1979. The sociology of labor markets. *Annual Review of Sociology* 5: 351-79.

Kamen, Henry. 1971. *The Iron Century: Social Change in Europe 1550-1660*. New York: Praeger.

Kamerman, Shelia B., and Alfred J. Kahn. 1978. *Family Policy: Government and Families in Fourteen Countries*. New York: Columbia University Press.

Kessler-Harris, Alice. 1981. *Women Have Always Worked: A Historical Overview*. Old Westbury, New York: The Feminist Press.

Keyssar, Alexander. 1974. Widowhood in eighteenth-century Massachusetts: A problem in the history of the family. *Perspectives in American History* 8: 83-119.

Keifer, Otto. 1934/1971. *Sexual Life in Ancient Rome*. London: Abbey Library.

Kleinberg, Susan. 1975. "Technology's stepdaughters, the impact of industrialization upon working class women, Pittsburgh, 1865-1890." Unpublished Ph.D. dissertation, University of Pittsburgh.

Komarovsky, Mirra. 1953. *Women in the Modern World: Their Education and Their Dilemmas*. Boston: Little, Brown.

Krauskopf, Joan M. 1977. Partnership Marriage: Legal Reform Needed. In *Women Into Wives: The Legal and Economic Impact of Marriage*, edited by J. R. Chapman and M. Gates, pp. 93-121. Beverly Hills, California: Sage Publications.

Lantz, Herman R., M. Britton, Ray L. Schmitt, and E. D. Snyder. 1968. Preindustrial pattern in the colonial family in America: A content analysis of colonial magazines. *American Sociological Review* 33 (June): 413-26.

Lantz, Herman R., Jane Keyes, and Martin Schultz. 1975. The American family in the preindustrial period: From baselines in history to change. *American Sociological Review* 40 (February): 21-38.

Lantz, Herman R., Ray L. Schmitt, and Richard Herman. 1973. The preindustrial family in America: A further examination of early magazines. *American Journal of Sociology* 79 (November): 566-89.

La Pierre, Richard. 1959. *The Freudian Ethic*. New York: Duell, Sloan, and Pearce.

Laslett, Barbara. 1973. The family as a public and private institution: A historical perspective. *Journal of Marriage and the Family* 35 (August): 480-92.

Laslett, Peter. 1971. *The World We have Lost*. New York: Charles Scribner Sons.

Laslett, Peter, and Richard Wall (eds.). 1972. *Household and Family in Past Time*. Cambridge, England: Cambridge University Press.

Laws, Judith Long. 1976. Work aspirations of women: False leads and new starts. *Signs* 3 (Spring): 33-50.

Leiby, James. 1978. *History of Social Welfare and Social Work in the United States*. New York: Columbia University Press.

Lerner, Gerda. 1969. The lady and the mill girl: Changes in the status of women in the age of Jackson. *American Studies Journal* 10 (Spring): 5-15.

Lipman-Blumen, Jean. 1976. Toward a Homosocial Theory of Sex Roles: An Explanation of the Sex-Segregation of Social Institutions. In *Women and the Workplace*, edited by M. Blaxall and B. Reagan, pp. 15-31. Chicago: University of Chicago Press.

Lipman-Blumen, Jean, and Jessie Bernard (eds.). 1979. *Sex Roles and Social Policy*. Beverly Hills, California: Sage Studies in International Sociology.

Lipset, Seymour Martin. 1979. *The First New Nation: The United States in Historical and Comparative Perspective*. New York: W.W. Norton.

Lobodzinska, Barbara. 1970. *Malzenstwo w Miescie*. Warszawa: Panstwowe Wydawnictwo Naukowe.

————. 1974. *Rodzina w Polsce*. Warszawa: Widawnictwo Interpress.

Lopata, Helena Z. 1969. Social psychological aspects of role involvement. *Sociology and Social Research* 53 (April): 285-98.

————. 1971. *Occupation: Housewife*. New York: Oxford University Press.

————. 1976. *Polish Americans: Status Competition in an Ethnic Community*. Englewood Cliffs, New Jersey: Prentice-Hall.

————. 1980. Euro-ethnic Families and Housing in Urban America. In *Civil Rights of Euro-Ethnic Americans in the United States*, U.S. Commission on

Civil Rights, (eds.), pp. 165-92. Washington, D.C.: U.S. Civil Rights Commission.

_____. 1981. The Polish American Family. In *Ethnic Families in America*: *Patterns and Variations*, edited by C. H. Mindel and R. W. Habenstein, pp. 15-20. New York: Elsevier.

Lopata, Helena Z., Debra Barnewolt, and Kathleen Norr. 1980. Spouses Contributions to Each Other's Roles. In *Dual Career Couples*, edited by F. Pepitone-Rockwell, pp. 111-41. Beverly Hills, California: Sage Publications.

Lopata, Helena Z., and Kathleen Norr. 1979. "Changing commitments of American women to work and family roles and their future consequences for social security." Final report to the Social Security Administration.

_____. 1980. Changing commitments of American women to work and family roles. *Social Security Bulletin* 43 (June): 3-14.

Lundberg, Ferdinand, and Marynia F. Farnham. 1947. *Modern Women: The Lost Sex*. New York: Harper and Brothers.

Lutz, K. Berkner. 1973. Recent research on the history of the family in Western Europe. *Journal of Marriage and the Family* 35 (August): 395-405.

Malos, Ellen (ed.). 1980. *The Politics of Housework*. London: Allison and Busby.

Marglin, Stephen. 1974. "What do bosses do? The origins and functions of hierarchy in capitalist production." *Review of Radical Political Economics* 4: 60-112.

Martineau, Harriet. 1935/1962. *Society in America*. S. M. Lipset (ed.). Garden City, New York: Doubleday Anchor.

de Mause, Lloyd (ed.). 1974a. *The History of Childhood*. New York: The Psychohistory Press.

_____. 1974b. The Evolution of Childhood. In *The History of Childhood*, edited by Lloyd de Mause, pp. 1-73. New York: The Psychohistory Press.

Mayhew, Henry. 1861. *London Labor and the London Poor*. London: Charles Griffin and Company.

McBride, Theresa. 1976. *The Domestic Revolution: The Modernization of Household Service in England and France 1820-1920*. New York: Holmes and Meier.

Meacham, Standish. 1977. *A Life Apart: The English Working Class, 1890-1914*. Cambridge, Massachusetts: Harvard University Press.

Mead, Margaret. 1949/1970. *Male and Female: A Study of the Sexes in a Changing World*. New York: Dell Publishing Company.

Meyerson, Abraham. 1927. *The Nervous Housewife*. Boston: Little, Brown.

Milkman, Ruth. 1979. Women's Work and the Economic Crisis: Some Lessons From the Great Depression. In *A Heritage of Her Own: Toward a New Social History of American Women*, edited by N. F. Cott and E. H. Pleck, New York: Simon and Schuster.

Miller, Gale. 1981. *It's a Living: Work in Modern Society*. New York: St. Martin's Press.

Mills, C. Wright. 1956. *White Collar*. New York: Oxford University Press.

Morgan, Myfanwy, and Hilda H. Golden. 1979. Immigrant families in an industrial city: A study of households in Holyoak. *Journal of Family History* 4 (Spring): 59-68.

Murstein, William I. 1974. *Love, Sex and Marriage Through the Ages*. New York: Springer Publishing Company.

Nilson, Linda Burzotta. 1978. The social standing of housewife. *Journal of Marriage and the Family* 40 (August): 541-48.

Norr, Kathleen L., and James L. Norr. 1974. Environmental and technical factors influencing power in work organizations: Ocean fishing in peasant societies. *Sociology of Work and Occupations* 1 (May): 219-51.

Norton, Mary Beth. 1979. American history: Review essay. *Signs* 5 (Winter): 324-33.

Oakley, Ann. 1974a. *Women's Work: A History of the Housewife*. New York: Pantheon Books.

————. 1974b. *The Sociology of Housework*. Bath, England: Pitman Press.

O'Kelley, Charlotte G. 1980. *Women and Men in Society*. New York: D. Van Nostrand.

Oppenheimer, Valerie K. 1970. *The Female Labor Force in the United States*. Westport, Connecticut: Greenwood.

————. 1977. The female labor force in the United States: Demographic and economic factors governing its growth and changing composition. In *Population Monograph Series*, No. 5. Berkeley, California: University of California.

Origo, Iris. 1957. *The Merchant of Prato, Francesco di Marco Datini: 1335-1410*. New York: Alfred A. Knopf.

Papanek, Hanna. 1973. Men, Women and Work: Reflections of the Two-person Career. In *Changing Women in a Changing Society*, edited by J. Huber, pp. 90-110. Chicago: University of Chicago Press.

Pinchbeck, Ivy. 1930/1969. *Women Workers and the Industrial Revolution, 1750-1850*. London: Bass.

Piore, Michael J. 1975. Notes for a Theory of Labor Market Stratification. In *Labor Market Segmentation*, edited by R. C. Edwards, M. Reich, and D. M. Gordon, pp. 125-50. Lexington, Massachusetts: D.C. Heath.

Piotrowski, Jerzy. 1963. *Praca Zadowowa Kobiety a Rodzina*. Warszawa: Ksiazka i Wiedza.

Piven, Frances Fox, and Richard A. Cloward. 1971. *Regulating the Poor: The Functions of Public Welfare*. New York: Pantheon Books.

Pleck, Elizabeth H. 1979. A Mother's Wage: Income Earning Among Married Italian and Black Women, 1896-1911. In *A Heritage of Her Own: Toward a New Social History of American Women*, edited by N. F. Cott and E. H. Pleck, pp. 367-92. New York: Simon and Schuster.

Pleck, Joseph. 1977. The work-family role system. *Social Problems* 23 (April): 417-27.

Polit, Denise F. 1979. Nontraditional Work Schedules for Women. In *Working Women and Families*, edited by K. W. Feinstein, pp. 195-210. Beverly Hills, California: Sage Publications.

Ramey, James W. 1977. Legal regulation of personal and family life styles. *The Family Coordinator* 6 (October): 349-60.

Reymont, Ladislas. 1925. *The Peasants: Fall, Winter, Spring, Summer.* New York: Knopf.

Riegel, Robert E. 1975. *A Story of Social Change.* Madison, Wisconsin: Fairleigh, Dickenson University Press.

Roby, Pamela (ed.). 1973. *Child Care—Who Cares? Foreign and Domestic Infant and Early Childhood Development Policies.* New York: Basic Books.

Rosaldo, Michelle Zimbalist, and Louise Lamphere (eds.). 1974. *Women, Culture and Society.* Stanford, California: Stanford University Press.

Rothman, Sheila M. 1978. *Woman's Proper Place: A History of Changing Ideals and Practices.* New York: Basic Books.

Ryan, Mary. 1979. *Womanhood in America: From Colonial Times to the Present.* New York: New Viewpoints.

Sacks, Karen. 1974. Engels Revisited: Women, the Organization of Production and Private Property. In *Women, Culture and Society*, edited by M. Z. Rosaldo and L. Lamphere, pp. 205-22. Stanford, California: Stanford University Press.

Salmon, Lucy Maynard. 1897. *Domestic Service.* New York: Macmillan.

Sanday, Peggy R. 1974. Female status in the Public Domain. In *Women, Culture and Society*, edited by M. Z. Rosaldo and L. Lamphere, pp. 189-205. Stanford, California: Stanford University Press.

Shorter, Edward. 1973. *Work and Community in the West.* New York: Harper and Row.

_____. 1975. *The Making of the Modern Family.* New York: Basic Books.

Sicherman, Barbara. 1975. Review essay: American history. *Signs* 1 (Winter): 461-85.

Smith, Ralph E. 1979a. The Movement of Women Into the Labor Force. In *The Subtle Revolution: Women at Work*, edited by R. E. Smith, pp. 1-29. Washington, D.C.: The Urban Institute.

_____. 1979b. *Women in the Labor Force in 1990.* Washington, D.C.: The Urban Institute.

_____. 1979c. Hours Rigidity: Effects on the Labor-market Status of Women. In *Working Women and Families*, edited by K. W. Feinstein, pp. 211-22. Beverly Hills, California: Sage Publications.

Smith-Rosenberg, Carroll. 1972. The hysterical woman: Sex Roles in nineteenth century America. *Social Research* 39 (Winter): 652-78.

_____. 1978. The Female World of Love and Ritual: Relations Between Women in Nineteenth Century America. In *The American Family in Social-Historical Perspective*, edited by M. Gordon, pp. 334-58. New York: St. Martin's Press.

Smuts, Robert W. 1959/1971. *Women and Work in America.* New York: Schocken Books.

Sokoloff, Natalie. 1980. *Between Money and Love: The Dialetics of Women's Home and Market Work.* New York: Praeger.

Sokolowska, Magdalena. 1965. Some reflections on the different attitudes of men and women toward work. *International Labor Review* 92 (July).

Special Task Force to the Secretary of Health, Education and Welfare. 1973. *Work in America.* Cambridge, Massachusetts: The MIT Press.

Stevenson, Mary Huff. 1975. Women's Wages and Job Segregation. In *Labor Market Segmentation*, edited by R. C. Edwards, M. Reich, and D. M. Gordon, pp. 243-56. Lexington, Massachusetts: D.C. Heath.

——. 1978. Wage Differences Between Men and Women: Economic Theories. In *Women Working*, edited by A. H. Stromberg and S. Harkess, pp. 89-107. Palo Alto, California: Mayfield Publishing Company.

Stone, Gregory R. (ed.). 1973. *Sports, Games and Power.* New Brunswick, New Jersey: E.P. Dutton.

Stricker, Frank. 1979. Cookbooks and Law Books: The Hidden History of Career Women in Twentieth Century America. In *A Heritage of Her Own: Toward a New Social History of American Women*, edited by N. F. Cott and E. H. Pleck, pp. 476-98. New York: Simon and Schuster.

Stuard, Susan Mosher (ed.). 1976. *Women in Medieval Society.* Philadelphia: University of Pennsylvania Press.

Suelzle, Marijean. 1973. Women in Labor. In *Marriages and Families*, edited by H. Z. Lopata, pp. 325-34. New York: D. Van Nostrand.

Sumner, Helen L., et al. 1910. *History of Women in Industry in the United States: Report on the Condition of Women and Child Wage-Earners in the United States, Volume IX.* Washington, D.C.: U.S. Government Printing Office.

Sussman, George D. 1977. The end of the wet-nursing business in France, 1874-1914. *Journal of Family History* 2 (Summer): 237-58.

Sussman, Marvin B., Judith N. Cates and David T. Smith. 1970. *The Family and Inheritance.* New York: Russell Sage Foundation.

Szczepanski, Jan. 1970. *Polish Society.* New York: Random House.

Tepperman, Jean. 1976. *Not Servants, Not Machines: Office Workers Speak Out.* Boston: Beacon Press.

Tilly, Louise A., and Joan W. Scott. 1978. *Women, Work and Family.* New York: Holt, Rinehart and Winston.

de Tocqueville, Alexis. 1835/1966. *Deomocracy in America.* J. P. Mayer (ed.). Garden City, New York: Doubleday Anchor.

Touba, Jacquiline Rudolph. 1980. Sex Segregation and the Woman's Role in the Economic System: The Case of Iran. In *Research in the Interweave of Social Roles: Women and Men*, edited by H. Z. Lopata, pp. 51-98. Greenwich, Connecticut: JAI Press.

Tuchman, Barbara W. 1978. *A Distant Mirror: A Calamitous Fourteenth Century.* New York: Alfred A. Knopf.

Tuckman, Howard P., and William D. Vogler. 1979. The fringes of a fringe group: Part-timers in academe. *Monthly Labor Review* 102 (November): 46-49.

U.S. Bureau of the Census. 1975. *Historical Statistics of the United States.* Washington, D.C.: U.S. Government Printing Office.

U.S. Department of Labor. 1975. *Handbook on Women Workers*. Washington, D.C.: U.S. Government Printing Office.

Vanek, Joann. 1974. Time spent in housework. *Scientific American* 231 (November): 116-20.

_____. 1978. Housewives as Workers. In *Women Working*, edited by A. H. Stromberg and S. Harkess, pp. 492-516. Palo Alto, California: Mayfield Publishing Company.

Veblen, Thorstein. 1899/1953. *The Theory of the Leisure Class*. New York: Macmillan.

Vinovskis, Maris A. 1978. Marriage patterns in mid-nineteenth century New York State: A multivariate analysis. *Journal of Family History* 3 (Spring): 51-61.

Walker, Kathryn E. 1969. Time spent in household work by homemakers. *Family Economic Review* 3: 5-6.

_____. 1970. Time spent by husbands in household work. *Family Economic Review* 4: 8-11.

Walker, Sue Sheridan. 1976. Widow and Ward: The Feudal Law of Child Custody in Medieval England. In *Women in Medieval Society*, edited by S. M. Stuard, pp. 159-72. Philadelphia: University of Pennsylvania Press.

Ward, Barbara (ed.). 1963. *Women of New Asia*. Paris. UNESCO.

Ware, Caroline. 1977. Introduction. In *Class, Sex and the Woman Worker*, edited by M. Cantor and B. Laurie, pp. 3-19. Westport, Connecticut: Greenwood Press.

Weber, Max. 1905/1958. *The Protestant Ethic and the Spirit of Capitalism*. T. Parsons (trans.). New York: Scribner.

Welter, Barbara. 1966. The cult of true womanhood: 1820-1869. *American Quarterly* 18 (Summer): 151-60.

Wertheimer, Barbara Mayer. 1977. *We Were There: The Study of Working Women in America*. New York: Pantheon Books.

Wilensky, Harold. 1975. *The Welfare State and Equality*. Berkeley, California: University of California Press.

Zand, Helen Sankiewicz. 1956. Polish family folkways in the United States. *Polish American Studies* 13 (July-December): 77-88.

Znaniecki, Florian. 1952. *Modern Nationalities*. Urbana, Illinois: University of Illinois Press.

3

SERVICE WORKERS

This country is pioneering in a new state of economic development. We are now in a "service economy"—that is, we are the first nation in the history of the world in which more than half of the employed population is not involved in the production of food, clothing, houses, automobiles and other tangible goods (Fuchs, 1965: 1).

THE SERVICE SECTOR AND SERVICE WORKERS

The revolutionary aspect of the shift of the American economy to the service sector is the rapidity with which it has taken place. Most of human history involved agricultural work. As late as 1820, 73 percent of American workers were engaged in that sector of the economy (Hall, 1975: 18). By 1960 the percentage had dropped to 6.3. The industrial sector took over in extractive industries and the production of basic necessities such as clothing and shelter, then increasingly tools and objects defined as necessary for the building and maintenance of complex societies and life-styles (Braude, 1975). The service sector, the third major division of the economy, has become the largest in very recent years and is projected to become typical of most jobs and interactions in the world of work in what Bell (1973) has called "the post-industrial society." This service sector contains within it a wide range of activities, organized into diverse and hierarchically differentiated sets of occupations and jobs.

... the service sector has been defined to include wholesale and retail trade, finance, insurance and real estate, general government (including the military in most instances) and the services traditionally so designated, including professional, personal, business and repair services (Fuchs, 1968: 16).

To better understand the service related occupations which we will be examining under the rubric of "service workers," we must first look more closely at some internal distinctions made by economists and other social scientists in their attempt to order and classify social systems. One of these distinctions is between "goods" and "services" (Fuchs, 1965; Greenfield, 1966; Stanback, 1979). Although outwardly obvious in separating process for a consumer from product, these areas do not have clear-cut boundaries and relations.

There exists no authoritative consensus on either the boundaries or the classification of the service industries (Fuchs, 1968: 14, quoting Springler, 1956).

One of the problems of separating productive labor from that defined as service labor is that some aspects of both are often involved in a particular job. Bakers produce *goods*, but the process of selling them falls into the occupation of *sales*person, and the wrapping of items is a *service*. The work of a dentist is a *service*, although it may result in the addition of a *good*, in the form of a false tooth (Fuchs, 1968: 15). A woman hiring a seamstress is buying a *service*; one purchasing a ready-to-wear outfit is classified as acquiring a *good*. In other words, some of the labor which people perform for themselves or for others has been converted and identified as production or manufacturing, with an emphasis on the end product. Other labor is defined as a service, even if a tangible product is involved. Nevertheless, the distinction is useful as a gross classification system.

Another separation made by economists and other social scientists is between producer goods and services and consumer goods and services. Just as industrialization removed much of production from the home, creating jobs in complex organizations for the manufacture of goods to be sold to other producers and to private consumers, so demands by producers and consumers have created the expanded service industry. Consumer services, like consumer goods, have developed side by side with producer services and goods (Greenfield, 1966). A family can buy bread in a store or have a newspaper delivered at its door and obtain haircuts in barber or beauty shops. Larger economic units, too, use services and goods within their territory or outside of it. Both consumer and producer goods and services have multiplied in number and variety over the years. Greenfield (1966: 11) defined these for us as follows:

[Producer services are] those services which business firms, non-profit institutions and governments provide and usually sell to the producer rather than to the consumer. Consumer goods are defined as those satisfying a final demand, and producer goods as those entering into the further production of output. It follows therefore that producer services are in the nature of intermediate and not final outputs.

Many of the services which producers require are similar to those requested by consumers. For our purposes, we can divide them into building maintaining services, people maintaining services, or organization maintaining services. With the need for homes and other buildings to be maintained, there has emerged a proliferation of services for cleaning walls, floors, and furniture, washing laundry and windows, repairing almost anything, softening water, removing garbage, decorating interiors and landscaping exteriors, protecting against harm, delivering, and removing goods. When we define the homemaker as a manager of her home, we can compare her use of services to that of larger consumer or producer units. We can also show how the job of a self-employed domestic cleaner differs from that of women cleaning offices in the employ of a janitorial service. People maintaining services are also widely varied and encompass medical, legal, physical, and mental care: all the services a government provides so that people can travel, feel safe, and live a relatively ordered life; the services that make people look "good" by the standards of their culture; eat and drink thanks to the help of other people's work, and so forth.

Another type of service, which we labeled organization maintaining, benefits mainly producers rather than private consumers, although we can not ignore such activities as catering food for voluntary associations. Greenfield (1966) and Fuchs (1965, 1968) detailed such services and Stanback (1979) developed a functional classification which includes policy-making services (banking, legal, personnel, system analysis, consulting, economic and market research and testing) and administrative services (advertising, equipment rental, duplicating and stenography, public relations, data processing and so forth).

The range of services listed in the preceding discussion indicates the need for further distinctions among jobs within the service sector of the economy. These jobs vary considerably in the amount of education and training they require, in how much prestige and other rewards they command, and in the importance of their contribution to the unit they influence (as well as the importance of that unit in the society). They certainly vary in the composition and complexity of their social circles and the duties and rights they involve. Stanback (1979) hypothesized an emerging dichotomy among these jobs based on the variation of these characteristics:

> It is entirely possible, though the case is by no means proven, that we are moving toward a sharply dichotomized service work force offering, on the one hand, the skilled, responsible and relatively well-paying jobs of certain professionals, trained technicians or artists, but on the other (sic), the unskilled and undemanding and poorly paid jobs of salespersons, service workers or laborers (Stanback, 1979: 106).

When we look at the occupations involved in the service sector, however, we find this process of dichotomy too simple. This sector, and the industrial one as well, contains occupations on all six levels of the structure, ranging from service workers to manual, clerical, sales, managerial, and professional employees. Since we are interested in the jobs in which women are involved, we will focus on these occupations regardless of the sector or industry and refer to others only when they are influential in how the job is carried forth. In this chapter, we limit ourselves to service workers, the vast majority of whom work in the service sector of the economy. Only 18 percent of the service workers in nonservice industries are women, while women's share of jobs in the service sector is still at a high of 67 percent (Stanback, 1979: 54; see also Waldman and McEaddy, 1974).

Thus, the final distinction among occupations in the service sector of the economy is between occupations disproportionally dominated by women and those dominated by men, a cleavage discussed in Chapter 2. Women tend to be heavily concentrated in the lower level occupations in the service industry, with the exception, of course, of nurses and teachers.

> It becomes clear that the exceptionally high ratios of professionals in the business and professional service industries are primarily due to the presence of male workers (Greenfield, 1966: 77).

It is interesting to note that even the U.S. Department of Labor (1973: 10) contributed to this phenomenon as late as 1973 by listing only the following service occupations in its *Careers for Women in the 70's*: cosmotologist, hospital attendant, licensed practical nurse, state police officer, and stewardess or flight attendant. Women are also found primarily in the consumer segment of the service industry, which tends to pay less than the producer segment (Greenfield, 1966). They are in jobs of easy entrance and exit, with opportunities for part-time work. These jobs are assigned low prestige in our society. In spite of this, Fuchs (1965, 1968) concluded that these employees should be less alienated than are industrial workers because they have a chance to relate personally with clients or customers.

The continued concentration of women in a limited number of service sector occupations is slowly being offset by a new trend, albeit still limited in numbers, toward dispersal. Women are entering the jobs of janitory or maintenance management of buildings other than their own homes, of bartender, and police officer. They have expanded their participation in "business and repair" services from 11 percent of the total of such workers in 1940 to 31 percent in 1970 and have moved from 12 to 20 percent in the postal services (Waldman and McEaddy, 1974: 4).

We will now look in greater detail at four types of services in which our Chicago area women are involved: building maintenance, food, nonprofessional health-related, and personal and protective services.

Building Maintenance Services

During the last century, American society has witnessed a dramatic decrease in domestic workers, both in numbers and in relation to the number of households (Grossman, 1980). At the same time, there has been an increase in the size of the work force involved in maintaining public buildings, usually under the auspices of property management or janitorial service firms.

We discussed the main reasons for the increased unpopularity of domestic work in Chapter 2. Basically these were:

> The extremely low status, the personalized mistress/servant relationship, the atomization of work, the designation 'servant,' and the servility and deference required led nearly all who could afford to to avoid it (Katzman, 1978a: 268).

In addition, at a time when most occupations were gaining fringe benefits and social security for disability and retirement, domestic workers were left out. Having no power through organization and usually minimally educated and hired by private employers not oriented toward benefits, domestic workers were highly dependent and deprived of rights other workers were beginning to enjoy (Christensen, 1971: 48-49). In addition, as Bernard (1981) and Katzman (1978b) have pointed out, the ideology of democracy and egalitarianism, combined with the lack of socialization of the newly middle-class mistress into traditional "servant management," removed much of the ritual which protected employer/employee relations from strain (see also McBride, 1976). The removal of many productive activities from the home, the simplification and shrinkage of this household, and the alleged technological improvements in home maintenance decreased the need for many domestic workers.

> Part of the relative decline in importance of household labor within the women's occupational structure was due to the transfer of household tasks to the commercial or industrial sector (Katzman, 1978a: 54).

The making of soap, baking of breads and cakes, canning of foods, and making and cleaning of clothes were decreasingly carried forth at home. However, the "servant problem"—meaning the shortage of trained help—so frequently discussed by observers of the American scene, indicates that it was the servant supply, not the demand, which shrank (Christensen, 1971; Katzman, 1978a). The daughters of native-born farmers were replaced by foreign-speaking immigrant women. As immigration decreased, the main source for domestic workers became black, middle-aged, relatively uneducated women who could not find other types of jobs and whose husbands were often unemployed, underemployed, or absent (Christensen, 1971; Grossman, 1980). A study conducted in 1968 found "1.7 million women employed as private household workers, including babysitters" (Christensen, 1971: 48). Most of the domestics lived in the urban areas of the South, were black, older than the average female workers, and received few fringe benefits and little in the line of wages.

The second major change in domestic work, in addition to the decrease in the number of such workers, has been the tendency for such workers to live out of rather than in the homes in which they are employed. In 1968, only 11 percent of domestic workers lived in and those tended to be imported from other countries or were "old timers" (Christensen, 1971: 51). Lack of privacy, continuous availability to meet the demands of the employer, and the lack of a social life are disadvantages which apparently bother domestics who live in the home of the employer more than they offset the advantages of housing and food. An exception is for new immigrants or people who come over temporarily to earn money illegally and return to the home country (Lopata, 1976a, 1981). Most women who have remained in the occupation of domestic servant choose to come to work daily, returning home after they finish their chores. Employers also often do not need or can not afford full-time help. The dinner hour then becomes a problem with day domestics because upper- and middle-class families who can afford cooks and similar employees often eat late in the evening. This requires servants to spend long hours serving and cleaning up. Compromises are sometimes negotiated and the relation becomes less intensive and superordinate-subordinate. If this is achieved the independence of the worker increases. Most day workers, however, do not work for one family, coming on only specified days and going to other homes the rest of the time. In addition, domestics often do not work a 40-hour week. Two studies carried out in 1967 and 1968 found that:

> More than four out of 10 [service employees] worked 26 weeks or less; just under two out of 10 worked between 27 and 49 weeks; only four out of 10 worked 50 to 52 weeks . . .
>
> In 1968, 62 percent of the women private household workers worked part-time [less than 35 hours a week]. Of the full-time workers, 64 percent worked between 35 and 40 hours a week. The remaining 36 percent worked longer hours (Christensen, 1971: 47-52).

One reason women prefer to live outside of the employer's house is that so many have families of their own and are even heads of households. These family responsibilities require that they be home nights in many cases.

The shortage of domestic workers in the face of a higher demand and high unemployment in an economy demanding more educated employees has motivated many governmental and private agencies to attempt to remove some of the disadvantages of this occupation. Programs include unionization of workers, development of training programs for both employers and employees, rationalization and standardization of tasks and relations. Agencies have sprung up which serve as intermediaries—arranging wages and work, providing transportation to the homes of the employers or nearby locations, and guaranteeing the honesty and competence of the employee while protecting her from exploitation. Certain tasks, such as cleaning of windows, cooking, caring for children, or hard physical labor have been redefined as outside the province of domestic workers.

The most aggressive attempts at "restructuring" this occupation have been proposed by the National Committee on Household Employment, incorporated in 1965, and the National Household Employment Trade Association, organized in the mid-1970s at the stimulation of the Women's Bureau of the U.S. Department of Labor (Christensen, 1971: 51-52). Elizabeth Koontz (quoted by Christensen, 1971: 51), director of the bureau, recommended three "revolutions" in the industry:

> We must change workers; we must change the condition of the industry itself; and we must change the attitudes of the employers.

The job of domestic worker varies by the size, composition, and complexity of the household, the presence of other workers and services, resources and restrictions, and the types of relations she develops with all members of her social circle. Some live-in domestics still exist in the Chicago area and some households employ cooks, child-care helpers, and general maids, though few contain the quantity and specialization of servants presented in the television series *Upstairs/ Downstairs*.

Building service workers live on a different schedule. Public buildings are filled with people carrying forth the activities for which the unit is set up, being vacated only evenings and nights. Because the workers are not responsible for cleaning up their own, or shared areas, their abandonment of the territory leaves it in a condition which must be changed before they can return to their jobs. The need for such building maintenance on more than an individual basis is a recognized feature of modern industrial life. Each office worker or legal firm does not hire a cleaning person. Rather, janitorial services of all types have emerged, as stated before, and they hire cleaning people. Most of the cleaning staff of such services are women who come in during the late afternoon or night and clean, polish, and do whatever the contract calls for. Some of these women also work days, others share earning duties with their husbands or other people and divide the childcare into different segments of the 24-hour day. They usually work in teams under supervision. Generally speaking, they have much less independence and autonomy in selecting jobs, rhythm of work, and level of specialization than do the household maintenance workers. The cleaning staffs of hotels where people sleep and meet tend to be hired individually by such establishments, unless serviced by janitorial firms.

Food Services

A vast number and range of people are involved in the processes of preparing, serving, and cleaning up after the food that Americans consume. Employment in the industry doubled between 1958 and 1976, especially in the latter years (Carnes and Brand, 1977: 10). During the same period, the average number of hours per week that the nonsupervisory employee worked dropped from 35.6 to 27.0. The industry has a very high turnover rate and many of the establishments do not operate year-round. As a result of both sets of factors, only 22 percent of the workers were employed full time and year-round in 1976. Women form 64 percent of the workers in the industry, a much higher proportion than is true of other areas of employment (Carnes and Brand, 1977: 11). One of the dramatic shifts in the industry has been from "full-service restaurants to fast food establishments" (Carnes and Brand, 1977: 10). Multi-unit establishments and restaurant chains have introduced principles of industrial engineering to food dispersal, including off-premise preparation of food, which cuts down on the need for chefs and others with culinary skills, simplication of work processes, and innovations in food preservation methods (Carnes and Brand, 1977: 12).

In recent years there are many reasons why Americans have created a demand for eating and drinking establishments and, in turn, responded to the increased supply of these services. Economic prosperity and the increasing participation of women in the labor force have provided both the means and the incentive for eating out. With servants no longer in the home to prepare meals, women as well as men are unwilling to spend many hours a day in the kitchen (Social Research, Inc., 1972). In terms of food service employees, we find a proliferation of cooks and kitchen helpers, hostesses, waitresses and bartenders, cafeteria line workers, people who deliver food already organized on trays to patients in hospitals and nursing homes, busboys and busgirls, dishwashers, and others involved in cleaning up after people eat. This does not include agricultural occupations in which food is grown or jobs connected with the manufacture and processing of foods in factories, discussed in Chapter 4. Caterers and food delivery people bring food in various degrees of preparation to the home. Many other workers contribute to the food service industry, often as drivers between locations. Garbage removal trucks take away the remnants, which usually amount to one-third of the total food brought into a household. Such drivers are not part of the service occupations. Food buyers insure that stores and restaurants maintain a steady supply of necessary items, demonstrators show people how to use new products, and checkers add up purchases in stores. Each of the occupations connected with food service contains subdivisions; the variety of roles is dependent upon numerous factors, including the traditional, often ritualistic, ways the work is divided and people relate to each other. Food establishments vary from posh restaurants to stand-up counters, from epicurean food "emporiums" through vast supermarkets, to "ma and pa" neighborhood stores and "deli" restaurants. Although the person in a store who wraps a food purchase can be considered as performing a service in this industry, our chapter will focus on people carrying forth a food or drink related service as the major part of their duties. In our sample of Chicago area women, this includes mainly cooks and kitchen helpers, hostesses, waitresses, and bartenders.

Cooking

The *Dictionary of Occupational Titles* (1977) devotes pages to the description of various categories of cooks by type of food, such as "Chinese-style"; type of meal, such as short order; type of dish, such as pizza; the process used, such as frying; or main utensil, such as wok. The location of the cooking varies by type and situs of restaurant and, according to the other uses to which the building is devoted. Schools, hospitals, government office buildings, department stores may provide prepared food for workers or "clients" such as school children or patients. Distinctions are also made in the type of food and service by time of day, such as night or morning. The *Dictionary of Occupational Titles* provides descriptions for very specialized jobs such as "cook, apprentice, pastry" or "prep (preparing for line) cook." Passenger ships and trains prepare food and flight attendants warm up food prepared elsewhere for airline passengers. Private household cooks are listed separately.

Cooks come from a variety of backgrounds with a wide range of training and experience. Except for those working in high status places, cooks tend to change jobs fairly frequently, as do waitresses. In spite of the old adage that only men can be chefs, newspapers and magazines more and more frequently run stories on female chefs. Generally, however, the traditional bias against women keeps them from being able to get the training and experience necessary for jobs in the more prestigious establishments (Howe, 1977).

The job of cook varies by the size of the establishment, the presence of other categories of workers in the cook's social circle, the type of food and clientele in which it specializes, and even the atmosphere which influences the division of labor and cooperation among circle members. In relatively small restaurants a woman may not only take the order, but also prepare the food, take it to the customer, and clean up after the customer has paid her and gone. Slow times in a restaurant may result in a decrease of staff so that the remaining cook must carry forth all the steps necessary to provide food service. If the preparation is not too complex, that is, if it does not require specialized knowledge and time, fast food establishments such as hamburger stands and fried chicken places do not require extensive experience or training for their cooks, and the kitchen is often run by very young part-time or summer employees.

On the other hand, complex restaurants may have great worker specialization with a profusion of assistants, usually known as kitchen helpers. Since there is so much overlap in activities required in the kitchen, the title of a job does not of itself define what the person has to do. Of course, this is true of most occupational titles, as we shall see (see Miller, et al., 1979).

Cooks usually do not come into direct contact with customers, unless of course, their work is designed to be public, as in Japanese restaurants. Customers sit around tables which have cooking surfaces on top, with cooks making a ritual of preparing the food in front of the diners. The description of "waiter, formal" (U.S. Department of Labor, 1965) included the task of preparing certain dishes in front of the patron, but few women are in jobs in which the waitress becomes the cook for show purposes. Some of the fast food or ultra-modern restaurants have created an open space between the cook and the customer so that the preparation can be observed, but most cooks work in kitchens closed from view to anyone but the restaurant staff. Whyte (1946, 1949) diagrammed and discussed the social consequences of the physical arrangements of a restaurant in terms of the relations between cooks and waitresses. It is the waitress who mediates the relation between cooks and customers, although she does not have the power to directly modify the behavior of either (see also Howe, 1977). The same, of course, is true in relations between waitresses and bartenders (Spradley and Mann, 1975; Whyte, 1949).

Waitressing

The 1965 *Dictionary of Occupational Titles* listed 24 different types of waiters but only eight types of waitresses. There are two reasons for this discrepancy: first, the positions open to each sex are specialized and second, the early editions of the *Dictionary of Occupational Titles* had an alleged sex bias built into their job descriptions (Witt and Naherny, 1975). There were seven hotel and restaurant waitressing jobs, and one position in all kinds of camps. These waitress jobs are listed as follows: informal, banquet, buffet, cafeteria, cocktail, head, and take out. Men were also listed as assistant, head banquet, bar, buffet, captain, club, counter, waiter-entertainer, formal, room service, and outside delivery waiters. As described by the *Dictionary of Occupational Titles* (1965), a formal waiter:

> Serves meals to patrons according to established rules of etiquette, working in a formal setting. Presents menu to diner suggesting dinner courses, appropriate wines and answering questions regarding food preparation: Writes order on check or memorizes it. Relays orders to kitchen and serves courses from kitchen and service bars. Garnishes and decorates dishes preparatory to serving. Serves patrons from chafing dish at table. Observes diners to fulfill any additional request and to perceive when meal has been completed. Totals bill and accepts payment or refers patron to Cashier II [clerical]. May carve meats, bone fish and fowl, and prepare flaming dishes and desserts at patron's table. When serving at banquets, may be designated waiter or waitress banquet.

Howe (1977) also discussed the hierarchical structure of food serving, in which men dominate the positions in better restaurants. Banquet service is very different from that of ordinary serving. Waiters were also listed as working in "water transportation," as stewards in dining rooms, cabin, economy, first, second, third, and tourist classes of ships, and in dining cars of railroads. Only men were listed as combining the job of waiter with that of entertainer, although there were, even then, restaurants in which women carried forth both activities. A woman can work, according to the 1965 *Dictionary of Occupational Titles*, as a waitress in a camp, where she:

> ... sets table and serves family-style meals to members of construction or industrial camps. Refills containers as they are emptied. Removes soiled dishes from table. Cleans and resets table after each meal. In small camps, may be required to perform other duties such as peeling potatoes, washing dishes and cleaning floors, walls and windows.

Interestingly enough, children's camps, which draw large numbers of workers during the season, are not listed.

The 1977 *Dictionary of Occupational Titles'* (225-26) job titles have been desexed and reorganized, although many of the descriptions remain the same. Waiter/waitress appears in all 18 titles bearing the same and similar names. In addition hosts/hostesses and stewards/stewardesses (except ship) have been added. All people serving food or drink during ship, train, and airplane trips are listed separately. The listing thus focuses on the type of place and service. For example, room service, take out, canteen, raw shellfish preparer (who also serves these, mainly in bars), wine and bath steward/stewardess are all listed separately. One of the better known changes in title was from airline stewardess to flight attendant.

Butler and Skipper (1980, 1981) and Whyte (1946, 1949) detailed the differences among restaurants and the consequences of these differences upon the role of waitress. Some establishments draw people who intend to spend considerable time and money and demand extensive services, because of the reputation, price, decor, or location of the restaurant. Such establishments employ staffs with many layers of personnel and divide the labor and contact with customers with specificity. The maitre ds (hotel, restaurant) take reservations and seat people or call them when the tables are ready, escort them there, and usually provide the menu. Hostesses sometimes fill this position, but are not regarded as of equivalent stature. Wine somaliers advise on the selection from their "cellars," cocktail waitresses take beverage orders and bring back the refreshments while busboys fill water glasses. Waitresses take food orders, occasionally also providing "tips" as to what is "especially good" or listing specials of the day. Few waitresses, as stated above, work in places where there is an extensive support staff (Howe, 1977: 94).

A very important segment of the social circle of the waitress as described by Howe (1977), Spradley and Mann (1975), and Whyte (1946, 1949), are those who prepare the food or drink she must serve the customers, the cooks and the bartenders. The negotiation process with these people is a constant of the job, as are the relations with other members of the support team. If the busboy does not clear the table quickly, the waitress receives pressure from the hostess and serves fewer customers, thereby cutting down on her opportunity for tips, approximately 20 percent of which she has to share with the busboys anyway (O'Connor, 1971). Some restaurants frown on having waitresses clear the tables, even if they have the time to do so.

The short-order or fast food restaurant provides its own sources of role strain, in the form of impatient customers and role overload as many people demand attention at the same time (Whyte, 1946, 1949). The type of clientele and their orders vary also by the time of day and can range from rough and sexually aggressive men as occasionally portrayed in the television shows *Alice* and *Making a Living* to the women and men described by Howe (1977) who demand attention and constantly change orders. Rowdy teenagers in fast food establishments can also be a source of strain for the waitress, especially when the restaurant becomes a "hang-out." Each waitress has her own "client classificatory system" (Lopata, 1976b) which leads to predictions of behavior from initial encounters or even a first glance and sometimes turns into a self-fulfilling prophecy. Howe (1977: 102-3) reported a seven-fold system developed by one of the waitresses she studied:

1. I-want-service-now-or-else attitude
2. The male customers who look you straight in the breasts
3. Women with women
4. One man sitting alone
5. A man and a woman together
6. The pickers
7. The customers who understand

A frequent source of strain for waitresses is the failure of cooks to prepare dishes listed on the menu, irritating customers when told that they cannot have a specialty they have decided upon. This is particularly true of American patrons; those of other nations tend to be more understanding of shortages.

Characteristics of the restaurant other than the behavior of co-workers or the clientele also affect the role of waitresses. Howe's (1977) description of the waitresses in one New York restaurant stressed the importance of the physical arrangements of the establishment, not only in terms of its location in the city but also in terms of spatial distribution and assignments. For example, the presence of stairs which must be traversed up and down all day long contributes to fatigue and resentment over assignment to inconvenient stations. Personal, or "back region," space inaccessible to customers where waitresses can change clothes or sit and relax and eat is very important to the women (Goffman, 1959; Howe, 1977). Control over space is a means of control over people. One of the bartenders in *The Cocktail Waitress* (Spradley and Mann, 1975) was able to demand, and receive, services from the women which did not fall in the province of their jobs because he convinced everyone that the bar was a "man's world." Both waitresses and bartenders can use space to manipulate the behavior of customers, especially if they expect them to offend other patrons (Gusfield, Kotarba and Rasmussen, 1981).

Although some states forbid waitresses from mixing drinks, many work in establishments in which they must go behind the bar in the absence of the bartender (Cavan, 1966). In fact, some of the respondents have worked as bartenders, specializing in mixing drinks and serving them only to people who sat at the bar itself, and filling orders of waiters or waitresses.

One of the more unusual forms of waitressing is now called "flight attendant." The role is actually complex and requires extensive training because of the possibility of air crashes, hijacking, misbehavior, or sudden illness on the part of the passengers. In addition, concerted efforts have been made to portray this job as glamorous and exciting due to extensive travel and high standards of personal appearance which must be met (Murdy, et al., 1973). Variation in the standards have occurred in recent years, married women, mothers, minority group members, and men having made the personnel less homogenized (Givens and Garbin, 1977). There is debate, because of the variety of services performed, whether the "flight attendant" should even be classified under service occupations. However, part of the job is definitely the serving of drinks and food and most of the contact with passengers revolves around this activity. Most of the time the work is routine and involves merely the offering or selling of drinks, the heating of prepared meals, and their distribution to passengers wishing this service. Flight attendants also provide refreshments to the crew. The glamour of the job, placing the status above that of restaurant waitress, is contained in the opportunity to meet a variety of people and to travel, both on assignment and with the help of free passes. One of the women who participated in the exploratory stage of our study explained that she had sufficient seniority to work in the first class section. She preferred this location because she did not have to rush so much and got to know her passengers. It is, however, hard work, especially on short flights since all passengers must be serviced. Special requests can complicate the standard routine. The activity is highly public, with a small "back region" subject to view of passengers who walk into it and sometimes to ones sitting in nearby seats (Goffman, 1959). There are passengers who are drunk, belligerent, or sexually harassing, who are hard to deal with, especially in view of the image stewardesses have acquired as sexually permissive. The interaction, however, is public and other passengers as well as the rest of the crew can assist any individual stewardess having problems with a passenger. There is less need to constantly negotiate with members of the social circle than is true of restaurants or cocktail lounges because of the various persons and status protective devices built into the role.

Another interesting variation on the role of waitress is the carhop. Such waitresses come to cars parked in the restaurant's lot to take orders from the drivers and passengers. Food served in drive-in restaurants is usually mass-prepared and considered "fast food." The carhop returns to a restaurant window, places the order, then takes the prepared food arranged on a tray by the cooks or intermediaries and carries it out to the car. The customers remain in their own territory while the carhop transports the food between the restaurant and their car. She is thus more exposed to the possibility of unpleasant encounters than if she worked in the restaurant itself in view of other employees. Drive-in restaurants usually provide protective mechanisms to avoid trouble. Of course, an increasing number of restaurants of this type have recently eliminated the carhop; instead drivers order from one side of the "drive-thru" by calling their choice through an intercom and pick up the completed order, as well as pay for it, at the other side of the building. This service is accomplished with minimum personal contact between the customer, cook, and food server.

As mentioned before, some establishments catering to customers provide only drinks, occasionally accompanied by simple snacks (Cavan, 1966; Gusfield, Kotarba and Rasmussen, 1981; Spradley and Mann, 1975). Again, the division of labor within such places depends on the number of customers, the complexity of drinks they order, and the physical distribution of the bar and the customers. Women originally did not work as bartenders in America, being limited to taking orders and serving the drinks prepared by male bartenders. This situation has changed in some locations and more and more bartenders are now women.

There are some establishments in American cities, as well as elsewhere, in which the role of waitress has special variations of behavior or relation with others. "Gaslight" private clubs hire waitresses who also have musical talent and training and who take turns performing on the stage while others take their place serving customers. Hugh Heffner has outfitted the waitresses at the Playboy Clubs in "bunny" costumes which reveal their legs and buttocks and artificially uplift their breasts. Many of these club rooms have entertainment on the stage, while the bunnies, who seldom are involved in the show, serve patrons dinner and drinks during the performances.

Because of the costumes and general atmosphere of the places, as well as the presence of alcohol, cocktail waitresses, especially the "bunnies," often face unpleasant encounters with male customers involving sexual undertones or advances. The waitresses in such situations function as a team, often with the help of the maitre d' or bartender, to control behavior without offending the paying customer.

Nonprofessional Health Services

As mentioned in the Introduction, the service sector of the American economy involves many layers of workers. In the food related industries it includes the dietitian in a hospital or school, which is a professional occupation. Medical treatment, which also includes prevention and diagnosis, is a service which is especially prone to heirarchical and vertical proliferation of occupations. Doctors are considered to be professionals, nurses semi-professionals (we shall discuss these distinctions in Chapter 9), and hospital administrators managers. Status hierarchies, with definite boundaries, exist within hospitals between each category of worker: administrators, doctors, nurses, and nursing assistants. Because status gaps also exist in private practice, private medical offices usually require, in addition to the doctors, nurses and a secretary-receptionist.

Licensed practical nurse and nurse aide fall into the category of health service jobs. The expansion of medical care to a high proportion of the American population and the alleged shortage of registered nurses have led in recent years to the creation of these jobs to take over some of the more routine tasks for which extensive training is unnecessary. It is estimated that there are over two million nursing assistants in the United States at the present time, most of whom are women employed in nursing homes and related establishments (Diamond, 1981). The nurse aide appears to be lowest in status in this hierarchy, although attempts are now under way to unionize and increase both pay and status. The *Dictionary of Occupational Titles* (1977) describes the nurse aide as being restricted to maintenance rather than health intervention tasks.

> *Nurse Aide*: Assists in care of hospital patients, under direction of nursing and medical staff; answers signal lights and bells to determine patients' needs. Bathes, dresses and undresses patients. Serves and collects food trays and feeds patients requiring help. Transports patients... Dusts and cleans patients' rooms. Changes bed linens, runs errands, directs visitors, and answers telephone. Takes and records temperature, pulse and respiration rates and food and liquid intake and output, as directed... (*Dictionary of Occupational Titles*, 1977: 241).

The licensed practical nurse is responsible for more of the patient's medical treatment while the nurse aide is mainly limited to temperature taking and other simple routines.

Nurse, licensed, practical: Care for all, injured, convalescent and handicapped persons in hospitals, clinics, private homes, sanitariums, and similar institutions. Takes and records temperature, blood pressure, and pulse and respiration rate. Dresses wounds, gives enemas, douches, alcohol rubs and massages. Applies compresses, ice bags and hot water bottles. Observes patients and reports adverse reactions [medical personnel in charge . . .] (*Dictionary of Occupational Titles*, 1977: 65).

Thus this job calls for more intensive physical or medical care of the patient than is required of the nurse aide, but has less responsibility for complex treatment than is assigned the R.N.

The role of nurse aide, or nurse assistant, as now redefined, contains many sources of strain, mainly because of its newness within the hospital structure. It was created to relieve the nurse of some of the more onerous and time consuming care of the patient, activated by an alleged acute shortage of nurses. As in cases of all new roles, it needs to be fitted into the system in terms of defining relations (Kotelchuck, 1976).

Personal Maintenance and Protective Services

Just as buildings need maintenance and protection against harm, so do people. In an affluent society some of this care can be turned over to specialists. In this section of the chapter we are focusing on such personal maintenance services as that of beautician, i.e., hairdressers, electrolysists and manicurists, and protective services such as those of school crossing guards or police officer.

The beauty field is an extensive one in American society, though it fluctuates as a source of employment in response to both the economic situation of the country and especially of the community, and to fashion. The service is labor intensive and typically performed in small, neighborhood shops. Most shops offer similar services: haircuts, permanent waves, hair coloring, washing and setting, as well as manicures. "Class" shops provide extensive and expensive hair, face, and body care and draw from a wide geographical but narrow socioeconomic belt of relatively wealthy customers (Allison, 1976; Givens and Garbin, 1977). According to Fuchs (1968), change within the beauty business is often introduced by technological innovation, such as permanent wave machines, cold-wave processes, coloring improvements. The recent tendency of American women toward informal hairstyles has decreased the business of shops specializing in hair setting but has resulted in mushroom growth of establishments devoted to cutting and coloring of hair. The job of beautician requires specialized training, can be performed part-time, and experiences frequent turnover. The dream of many beauticians is ownership of a salon, but lack of business training frequently results in the closing of the shop (Yukl and Kanuk, 1979).

The complexity of modern society, the size and anonymity of communities, the mobility of the population, and the danger associated with crime and the automobile, plus a variety of other reasons dealt with by criminologists, result in the development of a complex protective system. Guards protect buildings that are vacated by regular workers or to which access is limited for security reasons. Guards protect people who must cross dangerous intersections or those who are incarcerated to protect the public. Police officers attempt to protect people in their jurisdiction and to bring offenders against person or property to justice. In only a few of these public or private protective jobs can women be found. An exception is the female-dominated occupation of school crossing guard, who appears when children are on their way to or from school. It is not, however, a full-time job, and it does not pay well. Police jobs and those involving alleged danger from criminals have traditionally been male dominated. The very idea that women should be so endangered or should be forced to kill or injure another human being has gone against the Victorian ideology of "true womanhood," neglecting thus the images of the frontier woman and the female defender against enemy (even Allied) troups. The determined refusal of Americans to allow women into the armed forces until recent years and their assignment and treatment in the units when allowed to join reflect this ideology. So has the limitation and treatment of women in police forces such as those of New York City or Chicago (Fry and Greenfield, 1980). However, civil rights demands for equality of opportunity have resulted in a grudging admission of women into the protective services other than those of school crossing guards. Our sample contains a few policewomen, correction officers, and even a security guard in a male prison.

THE CHICAGO AREA SERVICE WORKERS

A total of 236 women out of 1,877 in our sample held a service job as the last one in which they were involved, and 142 are still in such occupations. A high proportion work in the food industry, as waitresses and cooks. There are more nonwhites in this category than in any of the other occupational sets. The cleaners are both day household workers and night office staffs, with some school janitors. More than half of the health allied workers are nonwhite and only 32 percent of the cleaning women are white. The level of education tends to be low, as is the socioeconomic background of the parents. Interestingly enough, the food workers, especially the waitresses, are fairly well educated, a number having gone to college. For these workers this tends to be a stop-gap job, often taken on a part-time basis. The beauticians and policewomen consider themselves "professional," mainly due to the training they have received. Job changes are frequent in most of these occupations among Chicago area women, as they are nationally.

SUMMARY AND CONCLUSIONS

The service jobs that we have examined are extremely varied, ranging from cleaning women, waitresses and cooks, nurse assistants and beauticians to policewomen. These are the less prestigious jobs in the service sector of the economy, although several of these occupations are making a valiant try at being redefined as "professionals"— often to contrast themselves with amateurs rather than to pattern themselves after the established professionals. Beauticians and police officers point to their specialized training, unique body of knowledge, and importance to the public. Some occupations in this broad category have easy entrance and exit points, others witness turnover in the jobs by people who nevertheless remain involved in the occupation. Some, such as that of police officer require greater commitment and usually involve longer employment. There are fewer employment agencies where jobs are available, after all. Women dominate the building maintenance area, both in private and in public cleaning jobs. Agencies are increasingly active as intermediaries between the user and the worker, even in domestic service. Team division of labor does away with the isolation of these jobs, especially if performed at night, in counterbalance to the normal flow of life (Becker, 1969). Others who work as "outsiders" to this flow include building guards and police officers on night shifts.

Food service workers have histories of numerous job shifts. Women even move from one occupational category to another as childcare and other sets of relations make this type of job at least temporarily attractive. On the other hand, there appear to be many job changers who stick to waitressing or cooking. The more prestigious food establishments are more able to retain their workers, since the rewards are greater and the prestige rubs off on all but the lowest status worker.

The allied health field has grown enormously and is predicted to continue expanding in the future, mainly in occupations now dominated by women. This is particularly true of the service level jobs which are relatively new. Role strain exists in relations with nurses who tend to look down on the nurse aides and nurse assistants as well as with the "nonmedical staff." With lines of demarkation unclear, the new layer of health workers is attempting to gain status vis-a-vis the hierarchy, with little success thus far in spite of an emphasis on training. Service jobs vary considerably in the extent to which they are unionized and to which women are involved and benefit from such organization.

REFERENCES

Allison, Elizabeth K. 1976. Sex-linked earning differential in the beauty industry. *Journal of Human Resources* 11 (Summer): 383-90.

Becker, Howard S. 1963. *Outsiders.* New York: Free Press.

Bell, Daniel. 1973. *The Coming of the Post-Industrial Society.* New York: Basic Books.

Bernard, Jessie. 1981. *The Female World.* New York: The Free Press.

_____. 1974. *The Future of Motherhood.* New York: The Dial Press.

Braude, Lee. 1975. *Work and Workers: A Sociological Analysis.* New York: Praeger.

Butler, Suellen, and James K. Skipper, Jr. 1981. Working for tips: An examination of trust and reciprocity in a secondary relationship of the restaurant organization. *The Sociological Quarterly* 22 (Winter): 15-27.

_____. 1980. Waitressing, vulnerability and job autonomy. *Sociology of Work and Occupations* 7 (November): 487-502.

Carnes, Richard B., and Horst Brand. 1977. Productivity and new technology in eating and drinking places. *Monthly Labor Review* 100 (September): 9-15.

Cavan, Sherri. 1966. *Liquor License.* Chicago: Aldine.

Christensen, Ethlyn. 1971. Household employment: Restructuring the occupation. *Issues in Industrial Society* 2 (Spring): 47-51.

Diamond, Timothy. 1981. "Some applications of feminist theory to changes in the nursing labor force." Paper given at a conference on women and work.

Fry, Louis W., and Sue Greenfield. 1980. An examination of attitudinal differences between policewomen and policemen. *Journal of Applied Psychology* 65 (January): 123-26.

Fuchs, Victor R. 1968. *The Service Economy.* New York: National Bureau of Economic Research.

_____. 1965. "The growing importance of the service industries." New York: National Bureau of Economic Research, occasional paper 96.

Givens, H. Lytle, and Albeno P. Garbin. 1977. Social-personal characteristics and occupational choice processes of female flight attendants. *The Vocational Guidance Quarterly* (December): 116-24.

Goffman, Erving. 1959. *The Presentation of Self in Everyday Life*. Garden City, New York: Doubleday, Anchor Books.

Greenfield, Harry I. 1966. *Manpower and the Growth of Producer Services*. New York: Columbia University Press.

Grossman, Allyson Sherman. 1980. Women in domestic work: Yesterday and today. *Monthly Labor Review* 103 (August): 17-21.

Gusfield, Joseph, Joseph Kotarba, and Paul Rassmussen. 1981. The Public Society of Intimates: Friends, Wives, Lovers and Others in Drinking-Driving Drama. In *Research in the Interweave of Social Roles: Friendship*, edited by H. Z. Lopata and D. Maines, pp. 237-57. Greenwich, Connecticut: JAI Press.

Hall, Richard. 1975. *Occupations and Social Structure*. Englewood Cliffs, New Jersey: Prentice-Hall.

Howe, Louise Kapp. 1977. *Pink Collar Workers: Inside the World of Women's Work*. New York: G. P. Putnam's Sons.

Katzman, David M. 1978a. *Seven Days a Week*. New York: Oxford University Press.

_____. 1978b. Domestic Service: Woman's Work. In *Women Working*, edited by A. H. Stromberg and S. Harkess, pp. 377-91. Palo Alto, California: Mayfield.

Kotelchuck, David (ed.). 1976. *Prognosis Negative: Crisis in the Health Care System*. New York: Vintage Books.

Lopata, Helena Z. 1981. The Polish American Family. In *Ethnic Families in America: Patterns and Variations*, edited by C. H. Mindel and R. W. Habenstein, pp. 15-20. New York: Elsevier.

_____. 1976a. *Polish Americans: Status Competition in an Ethnic Community*. Englewood Cliffs, New Jersey: Prentice-Hall.

_____. 1976b. The expertization of everyone and the revolt of the client. *The Sociological Quarterly* 17 (Autumn): 435-47.

McBride, Theresa. 1976. *The Domestic Revolution: The Modernization of Household Service in England and France, 1820-1920*. New York: Holmes and Meier.

Miller, Joanne, Carmi Schooler, Melvin L. Kohn, and Karen A. Miller. 1979. Women and work: The psychological effects of occupational conditions. *American Journal of Sociology* 85 (July): 66-94.

Murdy, Lee B., S. B. Sells, James F. Gavin, and David L. Toole. 1973. Validity of personality and interest inventories for stewardesses. *Personnel Psychology* 26: 273-78.

O'Connor, Charles M. 1971. Wages and tips in restaurants and hotels. *Monthly Labor Review* 94 (July): 47-50.

Ritzer, George. 1977. *Working: Conflict and Change*. Englewood Cliffs, New Jersey: Prentice-Hall.

Roby, Pamela. 1981. *Women in the Workplace: Proposals for Research and Policy Concerning the Conditions of Women in Industrial and Service Jobs*. Cambridge, Massachusetts: Schenkman.

Social Research, Inc. 1972. *The Changing Perception of Food in Modern Life.* Chicago, Illinois.

Spradley, James, and Brenda Mann. 1975. *The Cocktail Waitress: Women's Work in a Man's World.* New York: John Wiley and Sons.

Stanback, Thomas M., Jr. 1979. *Understanding the Service Economy: Employment, Productivity, Location.* Baltimore, Maryland: The Johns Hopkins University Press.

U.S. Department of Labor. 1977. *Dictionary of Occupational Titles.* Washington, D.C.: U.S. Government Printing Office, fourth edition.

————. 1965. *Dictionary of Occupational Titles.* Washington, D.C.: U.S. Government Printing Office, third edition.

U.S. Department of Labor, Women's Bureau. 1973. *Careers for Women in the 70s.* Washington, D.C.: U.S. Government Printing Office.

Waldman, Elizabeth, and Beverly J. McEaddy. 1974. Where women work: An analysis by industry and occupation. *Monthly Labor Review* 97 (May): 3-13.

Whyte, William F. 1949. The social structure of the restaurant. *American Journal of Sociology* 54 (April): 302-10.

————. 1946. When Workers and Customers Meet. In *Industry and Society*, edited by W. F. Whyte, pp. 123-47. New York: McGraw-Hill.

Witt, Mary, and Patricia K. Naherny. 1975. *Women's Work: Up from .878.* Madison, Wisconsin: University of Wisconsin Extension.

Yukl, Gary A., and Leslie Kanuk. 1979. Leadership behavior and effectiveness of beauty salon managers. *Personnel Psychology* 32: 663-75.

4

BLUE-COLLAR WORKERS

The Equal Pay Act passed by Congress in 1963 and administered by the Wage and Hour Division of the Department of Labor states that men and women who perform 'equal work' must receive equal wages. Enforced by the Equal Employment Opportunity Commission (EEOC), Title VII of the Civil Rights Act of 1964 prohibits sex discrimination in the hiring, promotion, training, layoff, and discharge policies of employers, employment agencies, union, and hiring halls with fifteen or more employees. Order 11246, issued by President Lyndon B. Johnson in 1965 and amended in 1967 by Executive Order 11375, forbids discrimination against women in companies contracted with the federal government; this order is administered by the Office of Federal Contract Compliance of the Department of Labor (Roby, 1981: 31).

One area in which the above quoted federal acts and orders could help American working women is in blue-collar occupations. Women have traditionally worked in industries and jobs which are the least skilled and lowest paid. In their attempt to move into a broader spectrum of the industrial manufacturing and construction fields, they have been fought not only by employers, but also by most unions. Recently, thanks to the activity of groups alert to discrimination, women have been making strides into nontraditional for them or male intensive fields, often at great costs. The political atmosphere influences tremendously the ease with which change is introduced. For example, the Reagan administration is attempting to loosen the influence of anti-discrimination legislation by changing the breadth of coverage of the contracts order to apply to only those segments of an employer's establishment which are directly benefitting from government funds.

BLUE-COLLAR WORK

The concept "blue-collar worker" is seldom defined, even in books devoted to this segment of the population (Komarovsky, 1964; Shostak, 1969). Levinson (1975: 20) points to the usual division of occupation into "blue collar or white collar; working class or middle class."

> In terms of occupation, the division is basically between manual, essentially physical or menial labor, and managerial or intellectual work. Blue-collar workers mean people who work with their hands, not with their minds.

The label "blue collar" thus refers to manual jobs, which are traditionally performed in work clothes other than those with "white collar" shirt and tie of male managerial and professional workers. Levinson (1975) and others contributing to the literature often blur the distinction between "blue-collar workers" and "working class." The first concept refers to a set of occupations, the second to socioeconomic status and life-style. Several observers of the American scene note that many jobs classified as "white collar" are really not very different from those of the "blue collar" label, but that social class life-styles vary considerably (Levinson, 1975; Braverman, 1974). Glenn and Feldberg (1977) write of the "proletarianization" of clerical work. So does Braverman (1974), who simultaneously examines in great detail the changes in nonagricultural, manual work brought about, he argues, by capitalism and the desire of management to control workers. He contends that capitalism, with the help of "scientific management," has reduced most work into simplistic, tightly supervised, and unskilled packages.

The level of skill involved in manual work varies considerably, however, and the job itself consists of more than the set of tasks. We will deal in this chapter with women who are in manual jobs, accepting with protest the terminology separating these jobs from "white collar" ones. The protest springs from the sexist nature of the terminology describing work clothes because it neglects clothing worn by women to their work in corporations, law firms, restaurants, and other locales.

Most of the literature focusing on women in blue-collar jobs deals with one or more of the following topics: their distribution in sex segregated jobs and recent movement to nontraditional ones, sexual harassment on such jobs, protective legislation, union membership, and the usual concern with alienation typical of social science judgments of manual work.

Distribution

Blue-collar jobs of all levels of skill have decreased in proportion to other types of jobs in American society since the turn of the century (Braverman, 1974). Many new occupations resembling them have been classified as "white collar," often as a means of attracting workers (Levinson, 1975). However, they still make up a substantial segment of the job market. Women are often found in them, mainly in sex-segregated industries, occupations, and locations (Baker, 1978; Davis, 1980; Howe, 1977; Oppenheimer, 1970; Stevenson, 1973; Waldman and McEaddy, 1974).

> Most of the labor force in 1900 worked at manual occupations. In fact, 30 percent of the 1900 labor force was unskilled labor (Braude, 1975: 41) . . . Over half of all women at work in 1910 were employed in operative and service occupations; today over half of all women at work are found in the clerical and professional sectors (Braude, 1975: 45).

Although women operatives formed 15 percent of the female labor force in 1974, they made up 52.6 percent of the workers in the production of durable goods and 63.9 percent of workers in nondurable goods, especially foods and apparel (Waldman and McEaddy, 1974: Table 3).

> In both 1940 and 1970, approximately nine out of ten women working in the manufacturing industry held semiskilled operative or white collar clerical jobs. Nearly three-fifths were engaged in the production of nondurable goods. In this sector, most women work in the production end as operatives [for example, assemblers], as checkers, examiners and inspectors, and as sewers and stitchers. About 11 percent of all professionals in nondurable goods were women (Waldman and McEaddy, 1974: 8).

The 1975 Handbook on Women Workers: (1975: 99) also documents this concentration of urban women in only a few types of jobs and industries. Only 4.1 percent of all craft workers are women; they are underrepresented in mining, construction, and manufacture of fabricated metal products, machinery (except electrical) and transportation equipment (*1975 Handbook on Women Workers* (1975: 99). They are overrepresented in the manufacture of electrical equipment and supplies, instruments, and related products (Waldman and McEaddy, 1974: 6). The reason usually given for their presence in these two manufacturing specialties is that they have "small hands." For example, in Chicago a disproportionately large number of female manual workers are employed by companies making radio and television equipment (Equal Employment Opportunity Commission, 1976).

However, the number of women entering nontraditional manual jobs, meaning male intensive ones, is increasing, according to several observers (see Davis, 1980; Gruber and Bjorn, 1982; Harlan and O'Farrell, 1982; Hedges and Bemis, 1974; Lyle and Ross, 1973; McIlwee, 1982; O'Farrell, 1980; O'Farrell and Harlan, 1982). According to Hedges and Bemis (1974: 14), the trend toward dispersal of women into male-dominated manual jobs was given impetus by the Equal Opportunity Act of 1964 and an agreement between "American Telephone and Telegraph on behalf of Bell Systems companies and the U.S. Department of Labor and Equal Employment Opportunity Commission" in 1973 to end discrimination of women in skill trades and management. The act was used effectively by many women and groups to open up jobs and occupations previously closed to them. Hedges and Bemis (1974: 14) report great changes in the distribution of women between 1960 and 1974:

> Of roughly 80 trades listed in the census, most showed rates of increase for women that exceeded the rate of increase for men; some exceeded the numerical increase as well. Even in many trades in which employment of men remained stable or declined, the number of women increased. As late as 1960, women were such a tiny minority in nine trades that the census reported them filled entirely by men. A decade later, no trade was so dominated by men (Hedges and Bemis, 1974: 14).

Reubens and Reubens (1979: 108) also document the increasing tendency of women to enter nontraditional jobs between the years of 1960 and 1970:

> Women in male intensive occupations constituted a small minority, 13.5 percent, of all women workers. They also accounted for only about seven percent of total employment in the male intensive occupations at a time when women comprised 33 percent of all workers. Ten years later the 1970 census showed just over four million women in the male intensive occupations . . . Women in male intensive occupations constituted 15 percent of all women workers, only a little above the 1960 share. Similarly, women accounted for 10 percent of all workers in male intensive occupations while they were 38 percent of the total employment.

Hedges and Bemis (1974) offer several reasons, in addition to the Equal Opportunity Act, for the increase of women in craft and related jobs, including the narrowing of the educational gap between men and women in skilled occupations, the women's movement, federal support for equal employment opportunities, the push for equal pay for equal work, and changes in women's interest in such jobs and in employment in general (see also Reubens and Reubens, 1979).

Several recent books have concentrated on women "pioneers" who are entering manual work previously in the province of men. Those include Mary Walshok's (1981) *Blue-Collar Women: Pioneers on the Male Frontier*, Jerolyn Lyle and Jane Ross's (1973) *Women in Industry: Employment Patterns in Corporate America*, and Phillis Wallace's (1980) *Women in the Workplace*. Brigid O'Farrell, Sharon Harlan, and Mary Walshok have especially contributed to our knowledge of blue-collar women workers. The latter found that many women who became pioneers in male-dominated occupations as welders, carpenters, mechanics, plumbers, electricians, and so forth had very independent childhoods and strong mothers but were also influenced in adulthood by "turning points."

> Turning points are key experiences, relationships or events that usually have the following three qualities: (1) they represent opportunities or demands for new sets of behaviors and perspectives; (2) they involve having to make often difficult or conflicting choices, and then acting on those choices, and (3) they often involve shifts in responsibility for oneself or for others (Walshok, 1981: 99).

Once working, the pioneers gradually developed a stabilized work identity, although most had actually stumbled into the occupation without career planning. All who withstood the sexual harassment experienced on the job remained and became successful, were active learners and "carried their weight" without asking for help in heavy tasks from co-workers (see also Brodsky, 1976; Mackie and Pattullo, 1977). Establishing rapport with the men and gaining their respect was an absolute necessity because so much of the success on the job was dependent upon informal information exchanges. Walshok (1981) identifies ten characteristics of the successful pioneer in male-dominated skilled manual jobs:

1. Identifies herself as a worker from an early age;
2. is more task-oriented than interpersonally oriented;
3. is preoccupied with puzzles and problem solving;
4. gives non-ideological interpretation of own and colleague behavior;

5. has skills resulting from some advanced education;
6. knows how to seek out information and opportunities necessary for mastering tasks;
7. is in a network of competent, savvy peers;
8. receives support from friends and family for risk taking;
9. wants good compensation and benefits for her labor;
10. is secure about her employment prospects in skilled trades.

Books about women in nontraditional blue-collar jobs, defined by Reubens and Reubens (1979: 106) as those in which women form a considerably smaller proportion of the work force than their current share of the total employed population, are supplemented by numerous mass communication articles and stories about women truck drivers, construction workers, miners, telephone installers and repairers, and automobile mechanics (see also Riemer, 1979).

The initial excitement among sociologists over the women "pioneers" in male intensive jobs has given way recently to a more careful examination of their life on the job, especially of sexual harassment and discrimination preventing mobility (see Gruber and Bjorn, 1982; Harlan and O'Farrell, 1982; McIlwee, 1982; O'Farrell and Harlan, 1982). Gruber and Bjorn (1982) studied the sexual harassment of women auto workers, and O'Farrell and Harlan (1982) reported on "Craftworkers and clerks: The effect of male co-worker hostility on women's satisfaction with nontraditional blue-collar jobs." Harlan and O'Farrell (1982) found that the pioneers they had previously studied perceived few opportunities for job advancement. Reubens and Reubens (1979: 116) state that:

> . . . the continued increase of females in the labor category while men show a sharp decrease, and the disproportionate female increase in the factory operatives group, confirm our earlier point concerning the creation of new female ghettos in occupations and jobs which men are leaving, voluntary (sic) or involuntarily . . . men have continued to dominate the upward mobility channels.

The fact remains, however, that few women are in nontraditional manual jobs and that there are many barriers to their trying to obtain them (Oppenheimer, 1968, 1970; Reubens and Reubens, 1979; Roby, 1981). O'Farrell (1980) discusses some of these barriers in her overview of the situation of women vis-a-vis nontraditional blue-collar jobs. Teenage girls are not socialized for the world of work as a major life commitment, let alone to prepare themselves for nontraditional jobs. This cultural lag exists in spite of the fact that women are apt to spend at least 25 years in the labor force (see also Gordon, 1979;

Roby, 1981: 68). Women often lack knowledge about such jobs. They have not experienced a stint in the armed service where training in high skill jobs is now available and from which educational and occupational advantages accrue (but see Rustad's 1983 *Women in Khaki* for a description of the problems faced by women trained in "men's fields" in the volunteer armed services). Another reason women face barriers to entrance in male intensive jobs is the tendency for the entry point to these occupations to be an apprenticeship program (Harlan and O'Farrell, 1982). This avenue is often closed to women, at least informally. Employers are unwilling to invest in training women because of the assumption that they will not stay in the labor force for long or consistently and will not return to the job after a child-bearing break. One of the methods of keeping them out is to set the age limit of entrance at 25; this is the age at which women planning families are unwilling to devote several years to an intensive training program and full-time work (see also Lefkowitz, 1970).

According to O'Farrell (1980: 147), another reason that women shy away from nontraditional jobs is a lack of confidence in their ability to learn work so "foreign" to their gender and for which they lack role models. McIlwee (1982: 330-1) found that women pioneers who left such jobs within two years lacked self-confidence, felt their training had been insufficient, had task-performance problems and difficulties with co-workers and/or supervisors who denied them "access to work related information." Fear of sexual harassment keeps many women from trying to enter male intensive jobs. Companies also fail to transfer women from clerical to manual jobs when openings occur and women themselves hesitate over losing seniority and the comfort of an established position which they know well. They are aware that they are the last-hired workers in jobs that are new to them and are therefore also less secure in terms of "layoff and bumping rights." These privileges allow higher status workers to take over the job of a lower status person when their own job is threatened. Reubens and Reubens (1979: 120) argue that:

> There is considerable evidence, especially for women whose choice of male intensive occupations would be limited to nonoffice work, that many women prefer female intensive jobs and would rather strive for closing the earnings gap than changing their occupations.

Thus, the combination of reasons, structural or individual, as well as the total lack of experience by employers, supervisors, co-workers, and employees of having women work outside of the traditional female intensive jobs decrease the probability that attempts to disperse the labor force into gender unspecified occupations will take place quickly. Many women do not try to enter nontraditional jobs, employers produce long lists of justifications for their failure to hire and train women in them, unions have maintained a sexist stand or been uninvolved, and so forth (Laws, 1976, 1980; Lyle and Ross, 1973; Mackie and Pattullo, 1977; Oppenheimer, 1968; Suelzle, 1973).

Protective Legislation

Protective legislation, limiting the ages that children are allowed to work for pay, and the conditions of work for women has been a subject of many-sided debates over the years (Steinberg, 1982). The legislation concerning women is almost inevitably directed toward their work in blue-collar jobs. Beginnings of such legislation date back to the turn of the twentieth century in response to social pressures for the correction of what became defined as gross exploitation of workers. It dealt mainly with wages, hours (length and time within the day), time within the pregnancy and post-partum cycle, and physical characteristics of the work. The right of the federal government to regulate the working conditions of employees in economic organizations through laws was won slowly, with the help of social reformers and unions. This right defines workers as first and foremost members of the society whose obligation is to protect their health and welfare. However, the limitation of protective legislation to women, once children were officially eliminated from the labor force, has created problems, providing justification for the exclusion of women from jobs with better pay and longer career lines. Although this legislation was formulated with the help of many women leaders to prevent exploitation and harmful working conditions, it has tended to limit women's occupational choice.

Chavkin (1979) has examined some of the logic behind this protective legislation. The basic argument against hiring women for certain jobs was concern for the "future generations" which might be affected by women performing heavy work or being in unhealthy environments. However, as she points out, women have, and continue to perform heavy work inside and outside of the home. Chavkin (1979: 316) summarizes Stellman's (1977) statement in *Women's Work, Women's Health: Myths and Realities*:

> Stellman describes collusion on the part of manufacturers to support protective legislation designed to exclude women from certain jobs rather than have to improve working conditions for all.

Chavkin (1979: 312-13) then concludes from her review of the literature that:

> First, it is important to stress that hazards to reproduction in the workplace are real . . . Second, protecting only women from these embryotoxic, mutagenic, and teratogenic agents that infest the contemporary workplace achieves only part of the goal of 'safeguarding the species' . . . Third, it is striking that concern for the fetus is primarily voiced in those high-paying industries where women have only recently gotten their feet in the door.

Thus, according to Chavkin (1979), protective legislation focused on the higher paying jobs of blue-collar men rather than on the lower paying jobs of women. Furthermore, Bell (1979) points to the failure to "implement safety and health regulations for women in the workplace" because manufacturers were unwilling to improve standards or hire more expensive workers, and because the Occupational Safety and Health Administration, the Environmental Protection Agency, and the Equal Employment Opportunity Commission could not police all work situations. Thus, the legislation has served in many instances as an excuse for not hiring women in higher paying blue-collar jobs, at the same time it was failing to protect them in lower paying jobs.

Union Membership

Only 11 percent of working women belonged to unions in 1976 for a variety of reasons (Roby, 1981: 91). In contrast, 29 percent of men wage and salary workers were union members that year, which helps explain, at least partially, the wage gap between the sexes (Antos, Chandler and Mellow, 1980). The first unions drew craft workers together and were opposed to industry-wide organization. Men, rather than women, tend to be in this type of job as well as in the higher paying occupations and industries which unions are more apt to organize (Raphael, 1974: 28). "Or, to put it another way, an industry is more likely to be unionized if most of its workers are men" (Raphael, 1974: 28). The occupations in which women are concentrated are often not organized. Women tend to be members of unions less frequently than men in mixed occupations. Thus, it is the combination of job, industry and person which contributes to the low level of unionization of women.

Many unions have historically expressed hostility toward women workers and tried to push them out of higher paid jobs when organizing older occupations, even trying to prevent their entrance into new occupations, in spite of federal norms for equal opportunity (Raphael, 1974). Both Hartmann (1976) and Sicherman (1975) document this hostility of union organizers:

> The difficulty of organizing women workers has usually been attributed to rapid turnover, the large proportions of young workers, and the heavy double burden on married women. But ... male union leaders, fearful of competition and lowered wages, did little to support women's organizing efforts in the garment industry and opposed the creation of separate unions as well (Sicherman, 1975: 477-78).

Hartman (1976) presents an even more complicated picture of the process by which women were limited to sex-segregated occupations and kept out of unions:

> Historically, male workers have been instrumental in limiting the participation of women in the labor market. Male unions have carried out the policies and attitudes of the earliest guilds, and they have continued to reap benefits for male workers. Capitalists inherited job segregation by sex, but they have quite often been able to use it to their own advantage. If they can supersede experienced men with cheaper women, so much the better; if they can weaken labor by threatening to do so, that's good, too; or, if failing that, they can use those status differences to reward men, and buy their allegiance to capitalism with patriarchal benefits, that's okay too (Hartmann, 1976: 166).

Unions which are predominantly female-intensive, such as the International Ladies' Garment Workers Union, the Amalgamated Clothing Workers, and the Textile Workers have not actively fought discrimination in other unions (Raphael, 1974: 32). Also, even when women are members of unions, they are seldom in high status offices (Bergquist, 1974; Dewey, 1971; Raphael, 1974).

Obstacles to union participation on the part of blue-collar women include the following, reported from Bergquist (1974: 5) from a study by the New York State School of Industrial and Labor Relations:

> (1) Personal-cultural—including extensive home responsibilities and a lack of personal self-confidence; (2) job related—including discrimination by employers against union employees; and (3) union related—including unfamiliarity with union procedures and a need for encouragement to participate.

The reasons listed above tend to "blame the victim" and are based on the assumption that there are unions to join and a willingness of existing members to accept women. Another reason often given to explain why women are so seldom unionized is the frequency with which they work part-time and thus are not considered for membership or are unwilling to invest money in dues out of their small earnings. The presence of "home responsibilities" are real, as all observers have noted. Full-time women employees must rush home after work and do not have the time to participate actively in the organizational life of unions. The timing of meetings tends to be synchronized with men's rather than women's life schedules. Union halls are often located in places where women feel uncomfortable, such as the back rooms of the neighborhood taverns or adjacent to a men's organization like the Veterans of Foreign Wars or the Elks. The combination of all these factors results in not just low membership by women, but also their unwillingness to turn to unions rather than to the Equal Employment Opportunity Commission with grievances about sexual harassment, exploitation, or unfair treatment of any kind (Dewey, 1971: 47; Raphael, 1974: 30).

Alienation

The fourth major topic in the literature devoted to manual or blue-collar workers is alienation, its causes and consequences. The topic has its origin with Marx, who abandoned it and related concepts later because he felt it "had turned into ideological prattle in the mouths of petty bourgeois authors" (see Braverman, 1974: 27). Marxists have defined much of modern work as meaningless. They blame capitalism for making workers estranged from work and themselves through job simplification along "scientific management" lines or because of the wish by management to control workers (Braverman, 1974; Form, 1980). Blauner (1964), Braverman (1974), Garson (1975), and the Special Task Force (1973) which produced *Work in America* are among those who focus on the "degradation" or "demeaning" nature of jobs in modern industrial United States (see also Chinoy, 1955; Glenn and Feldberg, 1977; Walker and Guest, 1952). Form (1980), however, cautions against the idealization of work in the past and the assumption of alienation of the worker in the present; Simpson, Kaplan, and Ritzer (1975: 187) find *Work in America* highly biased in the portrayal of work and "a grotesquely one-dimensional man."

Blauner (1964) found many reasons for alienation among assembly line workers, including powerlessness due to the inability to control the speed or pace of the conveyor belt or line, or the supervisors (see also Ritzer, 1977). Garson (1975) and Cavendish (1982) show

how women are able to devise games to offset these controls. The same system was found to exist in the Hawthorne Works, made famous by Roethlisberger and Dickson (1939) through their studies. The importance of the social circle in unskilled and semi-skilled jobs is evident only when the authors describe the day by day life of manual workers, as did Garson (1975), Cavendish (1982), Coyle (1982), and Armstrong (1982). Schrank (1980) did a similar study of men workers.

One of the problems Marxists, insistent on the presence of alienation among many workers and on blaming it on capitalism, have in observing the scene is the frequency with which workers report job satisfaction. Women are especially bound to be defined as in simplistic jobs and their satisfaction is defined not by the failure of the observer to understand the complexity of the social role but by "false consciousness" or that women are uninterested in demanding work (see Andrisani, 1978; Quinn, Staines and McCullough, 1974; and Wild, 1979 for documentation of job satisfaction).

The fact that the tasks of many blue-collar jobs have been highly simplified under the influence of "scientific management" and the scientific-technical revolution, including automation and the separation of planning from execution, cannot be denied (Braverman, 1974; Chinoy, 1955; Toffler, 1980; Walker and Guest, 1952). However, the tasks of jobs vary considerably in the extent of their complexity. Analysts sent by the U.S. Department of Labor to evaluate such complexity in relation to work with data, people, and things were able to provide hierarchical judgments used for the various editions of The *Dictionary of Occupational Titles* (1939, 1949, 1965, 1977). The scores given manual jobs in the *DOT* will be used in this chapter as a means of organizing the jobs of blue-collar Chicago area women. Since Kohn and Schooler (1973, 1978, 1982) and Miller et. al. (1980) have demonstrated the relation between work complexity and intellectual, as well as psychological functioning of the worker, we expect to find differences among the women not only in their perceptions of their jobs, but also in other aspects of their life-style and constructions of reality and associations among these variables. However, several problems that must be kept in mind exist in our dependence upon the *DOT* scores in this analysis.

In the first place, as several social scientists have commented, the *DOT* judgments of the complexity of jobs have been biased in favor of men. Female-dominated occupations or those resembling home and family work have been evaluated below those dealing with things in male dominated jobs (Miller, et al., 1980; Witt and Naherny, 1975).

A research team analyzing the fourth edition of the *DOT* (1977) found it much less biased against women's jobs than was true of the prior editions, but they still reported problems, often created by the scarcity of observations of workers (Miller, et al., 1980; see also Cain and Treiman, 1981).

Another problem with the complexity scores in The *Dictionary of Occupational Titles* from the point of view of sociologists is the tendency of the analysts of each occupation to look mainly at the tasks involved; workers usually see their jobs as social roles, or sets of relations. These two ways of looking at the situation of workers are highly divergent. A day-care worker was classified at the same level of complexity as a groom of horses in the 1965 edition (Witt and Naherny, 1975). She, on the other hand, may view herself as developing human beings, in spite of obstacles of inadequate resources, too many children, and so forth. Because we as sociologists are interested in the world in which people live and work, we must consider the worker's own evaluations, or constructions of reality. People employed in different sectors of the American economy use divergent standards against which they judge their jobs, and it is our obligation to learn their definitions of these jobs, seen as social roles, rather than accepting only the definitions others make of them.

CHICAGO AREA BLUE-COLLAR WORKERS

A total of 263 women in our sample held a blue-collar job the last time they worked outside of the home and 143 remain in such an occupation, the others having withdrawn from the labor force to become full-time homemakers: In other words, only 46 percent are still working for pay, the smallest proportion of all our employees. Fifty percent of the clericals are still in such jobs, 60 percent of the service, 61 percent of the sales, 63 percent of the professionals, and an extremely high 87 percent of the management workers are still employed. This may say something about the unattractiveness of the jobs they held, since their family income is not so high as to justify withdrawal from the labor force. They are also the oldest group in our sample, averaging 38 years (the sample contains only women aged 25 to 54).

The Chicago area women are located on four levels of complexity in dealing with things if they are in blue-collar jobs. The simplest of these is *Handling*. The *Dictionary of Occupational Titles* (U.S. Department of Labor, 1965: 650) defines these jobs as follows:

Handling: Using body members, handtools, and/or special devices to work, move, or carry objects or materials. Involves little or no latitude for judgment with regard to attainment of standards or in selecting appropriate tool, object, or material (see also the 1977 *DOT* and Miller et al., 1980: 22).

The second level of complexity in the blue-collar jobs our women hold is defined by the *DOT* as *Tending and Feeding* Machine and Equipment. Actually, these are two separate levels, but we combined them because of the small size of workers in each division:

Tending: Starting, stopping and observing the functioning of machines or controls. . .Little judgment is involved in making these adjustments.
Feeding-Offbearing: Inserting, throwing, dumping or placing materials in or removing them from machines or equipment which are automatic or tended or operated by other workers.

The next higher level of blue-collar occupations is called *Manipulating* and consists of the following activities;

Manipulating: Using body members, tools or special devices to work, move, guide, or place objects or materials. Involves some latitude for judgment with regard to precision attained and selecting appropriate tool, object, or material, although this is readily manifest.

We have no women in our sample working in jobs defined by the *Dictionary of Occupational Titles* (1965: 650) as being of the highest level of complexity in relation to "things," and we had to combine the next three levels to obtain our "high complexity" category. The levels are described by the *DOT* as follows:

Precision working: Using body members and/or tools or work aids to work, move, guide, or place objects or materials in situations where ultimate responsibility for the attainment of standards occurs and selection of appropriate tools, objects, or materials, and the adjustment of tool to the task require exercise of considerable judgment.
Operating-Controlling: Starting, stopping, controlling and adjusting the process of machines or equipment designated to fabricate and/or process objects or materials. Operating machines involves setting up the machine and adjusting the machine or material as the work progresses. Controlling equipment involves observing gauges, dials, etc. and turning valves and other devices to control such factors as temperature, pressure, flow of liquids, speed of pumps, and reactions of materials. Set-up involves several variables and adjustment is more frequent than tending.
Driving-Operating: Starting, stopping, and controlling the actions of machines or equipment for which a course must be steered, or which must be guided, in order to fabricate, process, and/or move things or people.

Thus, the "high complexity" category of manual jobs which we have is not at the highest levels of the *DOT*, simply because few women have the training and experience to reach such levels. Much of the literature dealing with women in nontraditional blue-collar jobs does not apply to them, as will be evident in Chapter 4, Volume II. More than half of them are working at the bottom levels of complexity in the tasks associated with "things." Their work is best described in Garson (1975), Cavendish (1982), Coyle (1982), and Armstrong (1982).

SUMMARY AND CONCLUSIONS

Although most women in blue-collar jobs are no longer working in "sweatshops", these places have not by any means vanished:

> Basically. . ., what had come to be called sweating in the nineteenth century was related to the arbitrary nature of demand, liability to rush orders and sudden gluts of production which provided manufacturers with no incentive to stockpile. Low wages, low rent and above all reliance on vulnerable female labour, especially that of immigrants, reduced overheads and permitted manufacturers to hire and fire at any sign of expansion or contraction of the business (Hoel, 1982: 80).

Machines, including those contributing to automation, have physically lightened much of the manual labor available to women (see Chapter 2). Sexual segregation in industries and workplaces still abounds, with resultant lower pay and management assumptions about the need for simplicity in jobs allocated to female workers. Pioneers are moving into the better paying jobs which were traditionally, at least within the last century's definition of tradition, in the province of men, but most women remain in the layers of jobs which are defined by the *Dictionary of Occupational Titles* at the lower levels of complexity in the manipulation of things. When seen as social roles, these jobs are found to have greater complexity, especially in the attempts to manipulate not just the things, but especially the other people involved in the social circles. Job satisfaction comes from simply having employment (Seifer, 1973) but also from the games which can be played and the informal relations at work. Women workers are not as frequently unionized as men, due to a variety of factors, including the unwillingness of men to help them to organize or to allow them in the male-dominated unions. Time constraints and the location of union meetings in places where women feel uncomfortable have contributed to a lack of active involvement even where unions exist. Protective legislation is being fought by women because its main effect has been to limit them to less profitable occupations. Legislation has opened up new avenues to new jobs, but these are affected, however, by the economy. The problem of apprenticeship remains, since jobs which use this as the only avenue of entrance have age restrictions or similar devices which form barriers to women.

REFERENCES

Andrisani, Paul J. 1978. Job satisfaction among working women. *Signs* 3: 588-607.

Antos, Joseph R., Mark Chandler, and Wesley Mellow. 1980. Sex differences in union membership. *Industrial and Labor Relations Review* 33, No. 2 (January): 162-69.

Armstrong, Peter. 1982. If It's Only Women It Doesn't Matter So Much. In *Work, Women and the Labor Market*, edited by Jackie West, pp. 27-43. London: Routledge & Kagan Paul.

Baker, Sally Hillsman. 1978. Women in Blue-collar and Service Occupation. In *Women Working, Theories and Facts in Perspective*, edited by Ann H. Stromberg and Shirley Harkess, pp. 339-76. Palo Alto, California: Mayfield.

Bell, Carolyn. 1979. Implementing safety and health regulations for women in the workplace. *Feminist Studies* 5, No. 2 (Summer): 286-301.

Bergquist, Virginia A. 1974. Women's participation in labor unions. *Monthly Labor Review* 97, No. 10 (October): 3-9.

Blauner, Robert. 1964. *Alienation and Freedom*. Chicago: University of Chicago Press.

Braude, Lee. 1975. *Work and Workers, A Sociological Analysis*. New York: Praeger.

Braverman, Harry. 1974. *Labor and Monopoly Capital*. New York: Monthly Review Press.

Brodsky, Carroll. 1976. *The Harassed Worker*. Lexington, Massachusetts: Lexington Books.

Cain, Pamela S., and Donald J. Treiman. 1981. The dictionary of occupational titles as a source of occupational data. *American Sociological Review* 46 (June): 253-78.

Cavendish, Ruth. 1982. *Women on the Line*. London: Routledge & Kegan Paul.

Chavkin, Wendy. 1979. Occupational hazards to reproduction: a review essay and annotated bibliography. *Feminist Studies* 5, No. 2: 310-25.

Chinoy, Ely. 1955. *Automobile Workers and the American Dream*. Boston: Beacon Press.

Coyle, Angela. 1982. Sex and Skill in the Organization of the Clothing Industry. In *Work, Women and the Labor Market*, edited by Jackie West, pp. 10-26. London: Routledge & Kagan Paul.

Davis, Howard. 1980. Employment gains of women by industry, 1968-1978. *Monthly Labor Review* (June): 3-9.

Dewey, Lucretia M. 1971. Women in labor unions. *Monthly Labor Review* 92, No. 2 (February): 42-48.

Dubin, Robert. 1956. Industrial workers' worlds. *Social Problems* 3: 131-42.

Equal Employment Opportunity Commission. 1976. *Employment profiles of women and minorities in 23 metropolitan areas.* Research Report No. 49. Washington, D.C.

Form, William. 1980. Ideological Issues on the Division of Labor. In *Sociological Theory and Research, A Critical Appraisal*, edited by Hubert M. Blalock, Jr., pp. 140-55. New York: The Free Press.

Garson, Barbara. 1975. *All the Livelong Day: The Meaning and Demeaning of Routine Work.* New York: Doubleday.

Glenn, Evelyn N., and Roselyn L. Feldberg. 1977. Degraded and deskilled: the proletarianization of clerical work. *Social Problems* 25, No. 1 (October): 53-64.

Gordon, Margaret. 1979. Women and Work: Priorities for the Future. In *Work in America: The Decade Ahead*, edited by Clark Kerr and Jerome M. Rosow, pp. 111-37. New York: D. Van Nostrand.

Gruber, James E., and Lars Bjorn. 1982. Blue-collar blues: the sexual harassment of women auto workers. *Work and Occupations* 9, No. 3 (August): 271-98.

Harlan, Sharon, and Brigid O'Farrell. 1982. After the pioneers: prospects for women in nontraditional blue-collar jobs. *Work and Occupations* 9, No. 3 (August): 363-86.

Hartmann, Heidi. 1976. Capitalism, patriarchy and job segregation by sex. *Signs* 18, No. 4 (Special Supplement, Spring): 137-69.

Hedges, Janice N., and Stephen E. Bemis. 1974. Sex stereotyping: its decline in skilled trades. *Monthly Labor Review* (May): 14-22.

Hoel, Barbro. 1982. Contemporary Clothing 'Sweatshops,' Asian Female Labour and Collective Organization. In *Work, Women and the Labor Market*, edited by Jackie West, pp. 80-98. London: Routledge and Kagan Paul.

Howe, Irving (ed.). 1972. *The World of the Blue-Collar Worker.* New York: Quadrangle Books.

Howe, Louise K. 1977. *Pink Collar Workers.* New York: Avon.

Kohn, Melvin L., and Carmi Schooler. 1982. Job conditions and personality: a longitudinal assessment of their reciprocal effects. *American Journal of Sociology* 87, No. 6 (May): 1257-1286.

————. 1978. The reciprocal effects of substantive complexity of work and intellectual flexibility: a longitudinal assessment. *American Journal of Sociology* 84: 24-52.

————. 1973. Occupational experience and psychological functioning: an assessment of reciprocal effects. *American Sociological Review* 38: 97-113.

Komarovsky. 1964. *Blue Collar Marriage.* New York: Vintage.

Laws, Judith L. 1980. *The Second Sex: Sex Role and Social Role.* New York: Elsevier.

————. 1976. Work Aspirations of Women: False Leads and New Starts. In *Women and the Workplace: The Implications of Occupational Segregation*, edited by Martha Blaxall and Barbara Reagen, pp. 33-49. Chicago: University of Chicago Press.

Lefkowitz, Joel. 1970. Effects of training on the productivity and tenure of sewing machine operators. *Journal of Applied Psychology* 54, No. 1: 81-86.

Levinson, Andrew. 1975. *The Working-Class Majority*. New York: Penguin Books.

Lyle, Jerolyn R., and Jane L. Ross. 1973. *Women in Industry: Employment Patterns of Women in Corporate America*. Lexington, Massachusetts: Lexington Books.

Mackie, Lindsay, and Polly Pattullo. 1977. *Women at Work*. London: Tavistock.

McIlwee, Judith S. 1982. Work satisfaction among women in nontraditional occupations. *Work and Occupations* 9, No. 3 (August): 299-35.

Miller, Ann R. et al. (eds.). 1980. *Work, Jobs and Occupations*. Washington, D.C.: National Academy Press.

Miller, Gale. 1981. *It's a Living: Work in Modern Society*. New York: St. Martin's Press.

O'Farrell, Brigid. 1980. Women and Nontraditional Blue-collar Jobs in the 1980s: An Overview. In *Women in the Workplace*, edited by Phillis A. Wallace, pp. 135-65. Boston: Auburn House.

O'Farrell, Brigid, and Sharon Harlan. 1982. Craftworkers and clerks: the effect of male co-worker hostility on women's satisfaction with non-traditional blue-collar jobs. *Social Problems* 29 (February): 252-65.

Oppenheimer, Valerie K. 1970. *The Female Labor Force in the United States*. Westport, Connecticut: Greenwood Press.

_____. 1968. The sex-labelling of jobs. *Industrial Relations* (May): 219-34.

Quinn, Robert P., Graham L. Staines, and Margaret R. McCullough. 1974. *Job Satisfaction: Is There a Trend?* Washington, D.C.: United States Department of Labor.

Raphael, Edna. 1974. Working women and their membership in labor unions. *Monthly Labor Review* 97, No. 5 (May): 27-33.

Reubens, Beatrice G., and Edwin P. Reubens. 1979. Women Workers, Nontraditional Occupations and Full Employment. In *Women in the U.S. Labor Force*, edited by Ann F. Cahn, pp. 102-26. New York: Praeger.

Riemer, Jeffrey W. 1979. *Hard Hats, The Work World of Construction Workers*. Beverly Hills, California: Sage.

Ritzer, George. 1977. *Working: Conflict and Change*. 2nd ed. Englewood Cliffs, New Jersey: Prentice Hall.

Roby, Pamela. 1981. *Women in the Workplace: Proposals for Research and Policy Concerning the Conditions of Women in Industrial and Service Jobs*. Cambridge, Massachusetts: Schenkman.

Roethisberger, F. J., and W. J. Dickson. 1939. *Management and the Worker*. Cambridge, Massachusetts: Harvard University Press.

Rustad, Michael. 1983. *Women in Khaki: A Study of American Enlisted Women*. New York: Praeger.

Schrank, Robert. 1980. *Ten Thousand Working Days*. Cambridge, Massachusetts: The MIT Press.

Seifer, Nancy. 1973. *Absent from the Majority: Working Class Women in America*. New York: National Project on Ethnic America.

Shostak, Arthur B. 1969. *Blue-Collar Life*. New York: Random House.

Sicherman, Barbara. 1975. Review essay: American history. *Signs: Journal of Women in Culture and Society* 1, No. 2 (Winter): 461-85.

Simpson, Richard L., H. Roy Kapland, and George Ritzer. 1975. Review symposium on work in America. *Sociology of Work and Occupations* 2, No. 2 (May): 182-98.

Special Task Force of the Department of Health, Education and Welfare. 1973. *Work in America*. Cambridge, Massachusetts: MIT Press.

Steinberg, Ronnie. 1982. *Wages and Hours: Labor and Reform in Twentieth-Century America*. New Brunswick, New Jersey: Rutgers University Press.

Stellman, Jeanne M. 1977. *Women's Work, Women's Health: Myths and Realities*. New York: Pantheon Books.

Stevenson, Mary. 1973. Women's wages and job segregation. *Politics and Society* (Fall): 83-96.

Suelzle, Marijean. 1973. Women in Labor. In *Marriages and Families*, edited by Helena Z. Lopata, pp. 325-34. New York: D. Van Nostrand.

Toffler, Alvin. 1980. *The Third Wave*. New York: William Morrow.

U.S. Department of Labor, Women's Bureau. n.d. *Steps to Opening the Skilled Trades to Women*. Washington, D.C.: U.S. Government Printing Office.

U.S. Department of Labor. 1977. *Dictionary of Occupational Titles*. Washington, D.C.: U.S. Government Printing Office.

_____. 1965. *Dictionary of Occupational Titles*. Washington, D.C.: U.S. Government Printing Office.

_____. 1945. *Dictionary of Occupational Titles*. Washington, D.C.: U.S. Government Printing Office.

_____. 1939. *Dictionary of Occupational Titles*. Washington, D.C.: U.S. Government Printing Office.

U.S. Department of Labor. 1975. *1975 Handbook on Women Workers*. Women's Bureau. Washington, D.C.: Bulletin 297.

Waldman, Elizabeth, and Beverly J. McEaddy. 1974. Where women work: an analysis by industry and occupation. *Monthly Labor Review* 97: 3-13.

Walker, Charles R., and Robert Guest. 1952. *Man on the Assembly Line*. Cambridge, Massachusetts: Harvard University Press.

Wallace, Phillis (ed). 1980. *Women in the Workplace*. Boston: Auburn House.

Walshok, Mary L. 1981. *Blue Collar Women*. Garden City, New York: Anchor Books, Doubleday.

_____. 1978a. Occupational values and family roles: a descriptive study of women working in blue-collar and service occupations. *The Urban and Social Change Review* 11, Nos. 1, 2: 12-20.

_____. 1978b. The integration of work and family roles among women in blue collar occupations. *The Urban and Social Change Review*.

Wild, Ray. 1979. Job needs, job satisfaction, and job behavior of women manual workers. *Journal of Applied Psychology* 54, No. 2: 157-162.

Witt, Mary, and Patricia K. Naherny. 1975. *Women's Work: Up from .878*. Madison, Wisconsin: University of Wisconsin Extension.

5

CLERICAL WORKERS

C. Wright Mills called an office "the enormous file:"

> As skyscrapers replace rows of small shops, so offices replace free markets. Each office within the skyscraper is a segment of the enormous file, a part of the symbol factory that produces the billion slips of paper that gear modern society into its daily shape (Mills, 1956: 189).

The paper which is finally filed away by office clerks has usually gone through many hands and may again be pulled out for reference. It consists of reports from one branch of an organization to another or from external sources to relevant receivers in a firm. It can be a letter dictated by a "boss" to his secretary or to a dictaphone, then typed by the secretary and mailed out, or a memo for internal use. Receptionists greet guests or patients and direct them to the person they came to see, or act as gatekeeper preventing admission. Switchboard operators connect callers or take messages. Thus, the "billion slips of paper," processed individually or in bunches must be handled by a variety of white-collar workers, lumped together under the title of clerical workers.

CLERICAL WORK: THE LITERATURE

The Research Institute of America recently published a *Personal Report for the Professional Secretary* (Murtaugh n.d.) and advertised it with a letter summarizing the questions which it allegedly answers:

1. Tell-tale signs of an upcoming promotion—what do you look for?
2. Is there a way to help the executive with a social problem?

3. Does socializing with other secretaries help—or hurt?
4. When do you contribute to the office grapevine—when do you resist it?
5. How do you handle a verbal confrontation with another employee?
6. Is there a quicker way to move into the higher ranks?
7. Can you set things up so that you always have respect from fellow employees?
8. What do you do when someone insults you in view of others?
9. Is the professional secretary with an aggressive attitude better off?
10. At what point do you put your foot down?

These questions are preceded by the following paragraph:

... today's successful professional secretaries—no matter how they feel about social changes—must from a standpoint of interaction with executives, employees and customers ... and other duties, such as communications, hiring practices and the like, at least be cognizant of today's new social climate (Murtaugh, no date: 1-2).

The questions and the paragraph above are interesting, both in their patronizing manner and in their assumption that social changes are occuring which could be disliked by the secretary. There is the implication that a pitfall in interacting with co-workers could lead to social isolation. The combination of questions and suggestions portrays a very complex world—of the secretary—and suggests a hierarchical structure of the office. This hierarchy is evident in the jobs reported by our respondents whose jobs vary from those of executive secretaries down to filing clerks.

Several themes run through the literature on clerical workers, the first being the proliferation of such jobs in recent decades. A second theme, alluded to above, is that of change, summarized by Glenn and Feldberg (1977: 52) as "degraded and deskilled: the proletarianization of clerical work." A third subject is similar to the one discussed in connection with our analysis of manual workers, sex-segregation into *The Secretarial Ghetto* (Benet, 1972). Finally, there is frequent reference to job satisfaction, attachment to work, and the failure of women office workers to unionize.

Proliferation of Clerical Work

All observers of American economic life and occupational structure stress the rapid and extensive expansion of "the enormous file" (Mills, 1956) and the clerical workers needed to receive, organize, file, and send out the reams of paper involved in communications among the multiplicity of organizations (Braverman, 1974; Crozier, 1971;

Feldberg and Glenn, forthcoming; McNally, 1979; Seidman, 1978). Glenn and Feldberg (1979) document the expansion of clerical workers as well as the domination of this occupational category by women in Table 5.1. Sixteen million clerical workers are a vast number of people located in a very specialized set of occupations. Braverman (1974) associates this expansion to the need for record keeping in each corporation but also to distrust of the people with whom it communicates and exchanges commodities so that all action involves double-entry bookkeeping. Glenn and Feldberg (1979: 315) point out that "The increased size and complexity of organizations mean that internal control, coordination, and communications become increasingly critical for organizational survival." In addition to internal communication, each organization is involved with other organizations and/or individuals who are their clients or customers or providers of supplies and services. Government regulations and documentation for tax purposes increase the need for record keeping. We saw the need of organizations for maintenance services in Chapter 3. That was only a small segment of the social circle of organizations, if we can carry over the concept of social role to organizational life. Braverman (1974: 295-96) himself documents the great variety of occupations involved in the clerical category, after giving figures of their expansion:

> It must be emphasized, for the sake of avoiding confusion with the common but absolutely meaningless term 'white-collar worker,' that the clerical classification to which these figures refer and which is discussed in this section includes only such occupations as bookkeeper, secretary, stenographer, cashier, bank teller, file clerk, telephone operator, office machine operator, payroll and timekeeping clerk, postal clerk, receptionist, stock clerk, typist and the like—and it includes these clerical workers no matter where they are employed, in private or in governmental offices, in manufacturing, trade, banking, insurance, etc.

The Secretarial Ghetto

Closely connected with the topic of the expansion of clerical work and proliferation of clerical workers is the discussion of the shift from a male intensive to a female intensive occupation. This subject is usually covered through a historical overview and what appears to be an idealization of the nineteenth century male clerk's job. Much of this literature implied a close relation with the employer, complex responsibility, and upward mobility. Braverman (1974: 298) states that "clerical work in its earlier stages has been likened to a craft."

Table 5.1 Growth of the Clerical Forces 1870-1977 (in thousands)

	1870	1880	1890	1900	1910	1920	1930	1940	1950	1960	1970	1977
Total clerical workers	91	186	490	770	1,885	3,311	4,274	4,847	7,635	9,783	13,714	16,106
As Percent of employed persons	.7	1.1	2.1	2.6	5.1	8.0	9.0	9.1	12.8	14.7	17.4	17.8
Female clerical workers	2	8	83	204	677	1,601	2,223	2,549	4,597	6,629	10,233	12,715
As Percent of all clerical	2.4	4.3	16.9	26.5	35.9	48.4	52.0	52.6	60.2	67.8	74.6	78.9

Note: Figures are not strictly comparable due to minor reclassifications of occupational categories.

Sources: For the years 1870-1940, total clerical workers and female clerical workers, compiled from Janet M. Hooks, *Women's Occupations Through Seven Decades,* U.S. Department of Labor, Women's Bureau. Bulletin No. 218, Washington, D.C., 1947. Table 11A Occupations of Women Workers, 1870-1940; Table 11B: Occupations of All Workers, 1870-1940. For years 1870-1940, employed persons from U.S. Bureau of the Census, *Historical Statistics, Abstracts of the U.S.,* Series D57-71. For the years 1950-1970, from U.S. Bureau of the Census, *Statistical Abstract for the U.S.,* 1972; Table 366: "Employed Persons, by Major Occupation Group and Sex: 1950-1972." For 1977, U.S. Department of Labor, Bureau of Labor Statistics, *Employment and Earnings,* 25 (January, 1978); Table 21: "Employed Persons by Occupation, Sex, and Age."

From Evelyn Nakano Glenn and Roslyn L. Feldberg, Clerical Work: The Female Occupation, in Jo Freeman, ed. *Women: A Feminist Perspective.* Palo Alto: Mayfield, 2nd ed. 1979, p. 319. Reprinted with permission.

However, Braverman does caution that:

> This picture of the clerk as assistant manager, retainer, confidant, management trainee, and prospective son-in-law can of course be overdrawn (294).

Mills (1956) also warns that the "idealized portrait of the craftsman" cannot be compared to a real description of most factory and white-collar work. Much of the literature which uses historical data to better understand the current situation of clerical workers attempts to explain the processes by which the male clerk, idealized or not, lost ground and was replaced by women, and the consequences of this change. Economic and organizational changes, most claim, increased the demand for clerical workers from 1880 on to such an extent that there were not enough men with a high school education not already engaged in better paying jobs and employers turned to women (Braverman, 1974; Davies, 1974; Feldberg and Glenn, forthcoming; Miller, 1981; Mills, 1956). The invention of the typewriter introduced the first revolution in office work, and this machine became the province of women who were considered more dexterous with their fingers than were men. The fact that the Remington company in the 1880s chose them rather than men to train in the use of the machine notably hastened the trend. Although it took some time before the field of clerical work became fully dominated by women, the proportion had risen to 72 percent by 1960 (Davies, 1975: 284). During the process of feminization men were further discouraged from entering these occupations by the depressed wages they offered. Three of the great attractions of clerical work for women were its abundance, the cleanliness of surroundings as contrasted to factory or farm work, and social status. Employers originally treated the women clerical workers "politely" and justified the low earnings by voicing expectations of high turnover because most of the employees were unmarried young women.

Married women were held back from employment by the cult of "true womanhood" and immigrant or otherwise economically destitute women were insufficiently educated in general or to American culture to qualify (Davies, 1975; Kessler-Harris, 1982). Actually, the wages were inferior to those of men but superior to those most women could earn elsewhere (Davies, 1975: 286). In addition, white-collar, even clerical, occupations provided higher status than most female intensive jobs (Davies, 1975; Mills, 1956). Thus the feminization of clerical occupations involved action from three sets of persons: the men who did not swarm to clerical jobs as they expanded, the women who did, and the employers who hired women and reorganized the jobs into simpler sets of tasks in anticipation of the need for frequent replacement of workers. In addition, personal services to the employer were added as the role became identified as that of "office wife." By the end of the nineteenth century middle-class women occupied the offices in subordinate positions as men began moving up to managerial ones.

Proletarianization of Clerical Work

C. Wright Mills (1956) foresaw negative changes in the role of the clerical workers as a result of the introduction of machines. It is he who first introduced the concept of proletarianization to the analysis of clerical work:

> In the definitions we have used, however, proletarianization might refer to shifts of middle-class occupations toward wage-workers in terms of income, property, skill, prestige or power (Mills, 1956: 295).

Braverman (1974) blamed capitalism for lowering the skill level of clerical work, but Feldberg and Glenn (forthcoming), in analyzing the processes by which the office changed between the 1880s and the post-World War II period, consider these changes to be an inevitable consequence of the increase in size, need for standardization, and the introduction of scientific management. Feldberg and Glenn (forthcoming) summarize the concept of proletarianization as developed by Braverman.

> Proletarianization results from breaking down of work into a series of fragmented, repetitive steps, each of which is assigned to 'detail' workers, thereby separating the 'conception' from 'execution.' This growth proletarianization involves several elements: the reorganization of work to achieve greater rationalization and managerial control over the work process; the application of new technology, computers and electronic communication, which imposes standardized ways of handling and processing information; the downgrading of clerical jobs so that they require less skill and worker discretion (Feldberg and Glenn, forthcoming, 4).

The key idea is that clerical work is becoming more like manual, blue-collar work than like the semi-managerial and independent work of the nineteenth century male clerk. However, it has become much more efficient and it is doubtful if the clerk of bygone years really had such an interesting job copying everything by hand. The intro-

duction of the typewriter certainly changed the writing process, duplicating machines modified and facilitated copying, and the word processor and computer are now revolutionizing clerical work. Many observers find the combination of scientific management techniques for
examining and restructuring the office and of machines doing much
of the work having degrading consequences for the workers (Braverman, 1974; Ellul, 1954/1967; Glenn and Feldberg, 1977; Howe, 1977;
Tepperman, 1976). On the other hand, the revolution is not yet over.
Many of the changes are transitional and some people, like Toffler
(1980), see the introduction of computers as individualizing and lib-
erating forces. It was the "second wave" of industrialization, according to him, which created work in factories and offices which

> steadily grew more repetitive, specialized and time-pressured and em-
> ployers wanted workers who were obedient, punctual and willing to
> perform rote tasks (Toffler, 1980: 384).

The new "third wave" of change is reducing the mass characteristics
of work, media, and the rest of social life. The producer and consumer
will merge into a "prosumer" who designs what s/he wants, instructs
the computer, which then automates machines to make individuated
objects for consumption. Community and home life will be revitalized
as the need for a central office to which people must commute van-
ishes or at least decreases considerably.

Whatever the future holds, most offices remain at various levels
of "rationalization" and complexity of organization. The larger the
need for paperwork and the unwillingness of management to reor-
ganize jobs along the most "efficient" lines, the more complex and
hierarchically deep the social system but the simpler the individual
job at the bottom levels. Crozier (1971) and others after him have
presented classifications of office workers. Crozier's (1971) includes
secretaries, miscellaneous clerks, typists, supervisors, and administrative assistants. Feldberg and Glenn (forthcoming, Chapter III) found the
following four types of workers, organized by "degree of rationalization, scope of activities, types of controls and relation to technology":

> *Data entry* represents the most rationalized, standardized and closely
> controlled variety, with the narrowest range of activity . . . It is also one
> of the most sex-segregated occupations (24) . . . They work separately,
> each at her own machine, a small console which looks like an oversize
> typewriter with an attached electronic screen (17).
>
> *Coding jobs* are slightly less rationalized, in part because they are
> less tied to machines and in part because the material they work from,

the information which comes into the organization, is not already standardized (24) . . .

   The all-round clerks . . . are relatively unstandardized and encompass
a wide range of activities.

   . . . *secretarial* work is least rationalized, despite the possibility of
greater rationalization in the near future (24).

According to Feldberg and Glenn (forthcoming) the specialized word
processing typewriters may relieve the secretary of most of the typing
tasks, leaving her free for administrative work and direct services for
the boss. Secretaries for a single or a very limited number of bosses
are the traditional type of clerical worker about which novels were
being written early in this century (Mills, 1956). Kanter (1977) vividly
describes the private secretaries in a corporation, differentiating them
from pool secretaries who are called to perform specific tasks for different managers. The status and role of the secretary is dependent
upon the status of her boss and the relationship is personal and patriarchal. The role is arbitrarily confined or open, depending on the
boss's boundaries. Loyalty to the boss is an extremely important
element of the role, the flow of work of secondary importance. A
number of writers refer to the secretary as the "office wife" not only
because of the personal nature of the relationship but also because
the woman was expected to perform duties similar to those performed
at home by the wife (Benet, 1972; Kanter, 1977: 89). McNally (1979:
55-59) outlines the qualities of "the perfect secretary":

   The perfect secretary is expected to combine in herself a mixture
   of abilities and qualities in much the same way as the perfect wife. Not
   only must she be capable of certain minimal speeds on the typewriter
   and when taking dictation, just as wives must display a certain bare
   level of competence with a frying pan, but she must also 'understand'
   her boss, much as a wife must be sensitive to her husband's whims and
   moods (55-56) . . . One survey discovered that 80 percent were willing
   to run errands, and 74 percent were willing to do the shopping for their
   bosses and their families (57).

Bloomfield (1973) considers the use of private secretaries to be inefficient. Observing a sample of such workers, he concluded that they
spent 22 percent of their time typing, 55 percent in administrative
work, 5 percent waiting for work, and 18 percent away from the desk
(see also Howe, 1977). He considers it much more efficient to divide
the work of the secretary into two jobs:

One is that of a correspondence secretary who performs all the tasks associated with typing (transcription, proofreading, editing), and the other is that of administrative secretary who performs the nontyping tasks (795).

The support system for these two types of secretaries includes messengers who eliminate the need to leave the desk and "word processing and administrative support groups, each with its own management structure" (795). His system would eliminate peaks and valleys of work load due to the uneven nature of executive rhythms with the aid of pooling within each group and "reasonable rules . . . adhered to with a supervised back-up." The new system would also insure consistent use of the expensive office equipment, a concern of all efficiency-prone managers.

What Mr. Bloomfield (1973), who is executive vice president of Office Management Systems Corporation, suggests is exactly what other authors, especially Marxists, decry as the tragedy of capitalism. With reduced skills, work becomes meaningless and the worker, under close supervision, loses independence and becomes alienated from the self (Braverman, 1974; Ellul, 1954/1967; Glenn and Feldberg, 1977; Mills, 1956).

Attachment to Work and Unionization

Union organizers who have found it hard to unionize office workers explain the difficulty by saying that these are women who are either focused mainly on their families or who identify too strongly with management (Blum, 1971; Tepperman, 1976). The descriptions of the ideal secretary and of the private secretary in the corporation would confirm the second explanation (Kanter, 1977; McNally, 1979). Since upward mobility out of secretarial into management positions was almost universally impossible, status improvement for the private secretary came from the mobility of her boss, who usually took her along as he moved up the ladder (Kanter, 1977). However, "rationalization" of the office removed such personal ties from the roles of most clerical workers. Some were removed even from human contact, being placed in separate rooms in front of computers or word processors. Pool secretaries had each other but the attachment to management still remained in the subculture and provided its own form of status (Dubin, et al., 1976). Class consciousness seems not to be strong among clerical workers (Crozier, 1971; Feldberg and Glenn, 1977; Mills, 1956).

Feldberg and Glenn (1979) criticize occupational sociologists for using a job-model of influence on men and a gender-model of influence on women. What they mean is that sociologists such as Blauner assume that women will not be as motivated to work or as influenced by their job as men because of their sex and implied family concerns. Thus the location of women in the occupational structure and their reported job satisfaction are attributed to personal characteristics and not the structure of the local labor market. These assumptions concerning women are very evident in clerical work environments. Williamson and Karras (1970) repeated a study of job satisfaction originally conducted among college students and female clerical workers to determine if they were more influenced by "motivators" or "hygiene" factors. The "hygiene" factors included having a good boss, good physical working conditions, good salary, job security, and liberal fringe benefits. "Motivators" included challenge to ability, high responsibility, importance of job, opportunities for advancement, and voice in decision-making. These authors concluded that

> ... female clerical workers tend to rank hygienes as more important than female college students ... the higher the job status, ... the more likely the respondent was to indicate a preference for motivators over hygienes ... length of service [also important] (Williamson and Karras, 1970: 346).

Other observers of women workers who contrast them to men state that women are more interested in the social aspects of the job, men in the instrumental. However, recent literature directing men and women on how to get power, how to move up in the organization, and how to win friends and influence people stress the social aspects of their roles (see Chapter 8). Those that focus on the instrumental aspects of the jobs are very likely to be looking for signs of alienation (see Chapter 4). It would not be surprising to find clerical workers stressing social aspects of their roles, not just because of socialization but because these jobs have become so simplified and routinized, so influenced by machines and deprived of challenge and mobility that the instrumental features can not draw attachment and commitment (Dubin, et al., 1976). Finally, it is the social or relational aspects of the roles which make the difference in providing an atmosphere congenial or alienating to the worker. Many a man or woman have left a job because of the relational rather than instrumental features. Dubin (1956) found few workers attached to their jobs as "central life interests." Attachments come from payoffs for working such as are money, perquisites, power, authority, status, and career (Dubin et al., 1976: 304-10). Few of these payoffs accrue to women clerical workers.

Howe (1977), Seifer (1976), and Tepperman (1976) discuss efforts at unionization of clerical workers, stressing the importance of developing class consciousness, pulling them away from the identification with management, and decreasing fear of losing the job if they join. Tepperman (1976) even lists the commonly held myths that are part of the clerical subculture and which glamorize or at least positively evaluate the office and management. On the other hand, McNally (1979) discusses all the sources of dissatisfaction of female clerical workers and suggests that one solution is a change of jobs. One of the problems of job change is that a simple interview can not really tell the job seeker much about the milieu of the office. It takes several days or even months for an employee to learn whether or not she will be satisfied with the new position. She suggests that one solution to this problem is temporary work or joining a firm which is called when an office needs a short term replacement because someone left, is sick, on vacation, or in other emergency situations. "Urban nomads," as Olesen and Katsuranis (1978) call them, experience the environment for a short period of time and often use this method of finding a more permanent job. Others like the flexibility of the situation, especially if they have children, since they can refuse a job when home needs make going out difficult. The advantages include variety not only of tasks but also of social relations and environments and the expanding employer need for such workers. The disadvantages are the uncertainty of employment, the need to constantly learn new patterns of work, having often to catch up with a great deal of unfinished business, and loneliness because the temporary is usually not allowed involvement in the cliques of the office. In fact, she is often resented by the permanent staff if she is replacing someone they like and they fear that she might take the job as her steady employment.

THE CHICAGO AREA CLERICAL WORKERS

Clerical workers are the most numerous of all American employed women, due to the combination of the structure of the economy and its division of labor and the socialization and training of women in this society. Our Chicago sample, however, negates some of the conclusions of prior researchers concerning women in clerical jobs. Rather than remaining in them throughout their working lives, a very large number of the women have gone in and out of clerical jobs in the past, often ending up in managerial, sales agent, and even professional or technical occupations. Until very recent years young women have not made long-range plans for career involvement, especially in male-dominated occupations. High schools and short-term job training make it possible for women to learn secretarial skills. Some jobs, such as that of file clerk, do not even require off-the-job training. This does not mean, however, that a first, or even a long-term job in the clerical arena cuts off other avenues, although mobility within a large corporation may be closed, as Kanter (1977) found at INDSCO. Observing the world of work and the mass communication media can broaden a young woman's horizons toward other occupational opportunities. A vast array of school and job training resources have been made available in urban centers. In addition, women who leave clerical jobs to become homemakers can re-enter the labor force at a later date in a different industry or type of employment.

Thus, 21 percent of the women in our sample whose last job (or current one) was professional or technical had done clerical work in their first job or the one longest held. Such an occupational history is true of 59 percent of the managers, 54 percent of the sales workers, 13 percent of the manual, and 30 percent of service workers. On the other hand, 21 percent of the women now in clerical jobs were previously in other occupational categories. The jobs that were included in our historical overview had to have been worked at least 15 hours a week and held at least six months a year. Looking at the drop-out from the last job to the current situation, we find that only 52 percent of the 698 women are still working as clericals, the remainder having become full-time homemakers or are working so few hours a week that we consider them as homemakers. This means that only 19 percent of the total sample are currently working as office clerks, receptionists, secretaries, or high-level clericals such as administrative assistants. A peak of 82 percent of the women who last held a clerical job have worked intermittently since first entering the labor force, having dropped out at least once. One thing that intrigues sociologists is the third or so of clerical workers who were able to move to higher status jobs.

The four categories into which the clerical jobs of the Chicago area women fall, clerks, receptionists, secretaries, and high complexity office support workers, a logical division evident elsewhere in modern America, indicate the diversity of positions available in the area. Most of the literature on the proletarianization of clerical work refers to the tasks assigned to the relatively unskilled clerk (Braverman, 1974; Howe, 1977; Mills, 1956). Howe (1977) describes the daily round of activities of a typical office worker who moves paper and utilizes the services of specialty office sections. Much of this description deals with the personal relations and negotiations required in order to achieve the allegedly simple duties. Social relations are a central part of the job of receptionist who does not even need secretarial skills in a large office. It is her function to serve as an intermediary between people coming in from the outside and the local workers. Switch-board operators have a similar purpose, exept that they do not deal with incoming calls on a face-to-face basis. Secretaries perform the standard functions for an entire office, or for a limited number of middle management staff. Few are assigned the position of servicing only one "boss"; the shortage of trained secretaries made such assign-ments economically inefficient. Executive secretaries, those special-izing in medical or legal work, or "assistants to...." form the high complexity segment of our sample, having more authority and flex-ibility and not being part of a general office force.

SUMMARY AND CONCLUSIONS

The early office workers were men, and most of their work re-quired copying documents by longhand, a far cry from the idealized picture often drawn when contrasting current clerical jobs with those of an earlier period. The introduction of the typewriter and the deci-sion by the manufacturers to train women, rather than men, into its use, in addition to several other changes in the American society re-sulted in the virtual domination of the office by women. Although much of the literature focuses on the proletarianization of clerical work i.e., its reduction to the level of manual labor, requiring little decision-making or autonomous action, a careful examination of the clerical occupations shows a great range of jobs. All the paper work required in running a private business or a public agency can not be produced with the use of machines and "automated" workers. Deci-sion-making is still required in most jobs. The anti-female bias is evident in many descriptions of secretarial jobs, although they often resemble those of male lower and middle management. Recently formed unions and voluntary organizations of office workers, such as the Boston initiated "9 to 5," have pushed for better pay and increas-ing autonomy and "dignity" for office workers. This movement sup-ports the literature in terms of current moves to deskill and degrade

(Glenn and Feldberg, 1977) much clerical work, offsetting the argument that secretaries can not be unionized because of their identification with management and, especially, with their "boss."

REFERENCES

Benet, Mary Kathleen. 1972. *The Secretarial Ghetto*. New York: McGraw-Hill.
Bloomfield, Robert M. 1973. The Changing world of the secretary. *Personnel Journal* (September): 793-98.
Blum, Albert A. 1971. The Office Employee. In *White-Collar Workers*, edited by Albert A. Blum, Marten Estey, James W. Kuhn, Wesley A. Wildman, and Leo Troy, pp. 3-45. New York: Random House.
Braverman, Harry. 1974. *Labor and Monopoly Capital*. New York: Monthly Review Press.
Crozier, M. 1971. *The World of the Office Worker*. Chicago: University of Chicago Press.
Davies, Margery. 1975. Woman's Place is at the Typewriter: The Feminization of the Clerical Labor Force. In *Labor Market Segmentation*, edited by Richard C. Edwards, Michael Reich, and David M. Gordon, pp. 279-96. Lexington, Massachusetts: D.C. Heath.
Dubin, Robert. 1956. Industrial workers' world: a study of the central life interests of industrial workers. *Social Problems* 3: 131-42.
Dubin, Robert, R., Alan Hedley, and Thomas C. Taveggia. 1976. Attachment to Work. In *Handbook of Work, Organization and Society*, edited by Robert Dubin, pp. 281-341. Chicago: Rand McNally.
Ellul, Jacques. 1954/1967. *The Technological Society*. New York: Vantage Press.
Feldberg, Roslyn, and Evelyn Glenn. *White Collar Ghetto: Clerical Work in Bureaucratic Enterprises*. Forthcoming.
_____. 1980. "Technology and work degradation: re-examining the impacts of office automation." Unpublished paper.
_____. 1979. Male and Female: Job versus gender models in the sociology of work. *Social Problems* 26 (5 June): 524-38.
_____. 1977. "Category of collectivity? The consciousness of clerical workers." Unpublished paper.
Glenn, Evelyn Nakano, and Roslyn L. Feldberg. 1979. Clerical Work: The Female Occupation. In *Women: a Feminist Perspective*, edited by Jo Freeman, pp. 313-38. Palo Alto, California: Mayfield.
_____. 1977. Degraded and deskilled: the proletarianization of clerical work. *Social Problems* 25 (1 October): 52-64.
Howe, Louise Kapp. 1977. *Pink Collar Workers: Inside the World of Women's Work*. New York: G. P. Putnam's Sons.
Kanter, Rosabeth Moss. 1977. *Men and Women of the Corporation*. New York: Basic Books.
Kessler-Harris, Alice. 1982. *Out to Work: A History of Wage-Earning Women in the United States*. New York: Oxford University Press.

Malveaux, Julianne M. 1980. Moving Forward, Standing Still: Women in White Collar Jobs. In *Women in the Workplace*, edited by Phillis Wallace, pp. 101-29. Boston: Auburn House.

McNally, Fiona. 1979. *Women for Hire: A Study of the Female Office Worker.* New York: St. Martin's Press.

Miller, Gale. 1981. *It's a Living: Work in Modern Society.* New York: St. Martin's Press.

Mills, C. Wright. 1956. *White Collar.* New York: Oxford University Press.

Murtaugh, Paul. N.D. Letter announcing *Personal Report for the Professional Secretary.* New York: Research Institute of America.

Olesen, Virginia L., and Frances Katsuranis. 1978. Urban Nomads: Women in Temporary Clerical Services. In *Women Working: Theories and Facts in Perspective*, edited by Ann H. Stromberg and Shirley Harkess, pp. 316-38, Palo Alto, California: Mayfield.

Seidman, Ann. 1978. *Working Women: A Study of Women in Paid Jobs.* Boulder, Colorado: Westview Press.

Seifer, Nancy. 1976. *Nobody Speaks for Me: Self Portraits of American Working Class Women.* New York: Simon and Schuster.

Tepperman, Jean. 1976. *Not Servants, Not Machines: Office Workers Speak Out.* Boston: Beacon.

Toffler, Alvin. 1980. *The Third Wave.* New York: Bantam Books.

Rubin, Lillian. 1979. *Women of a Certain Age: The Midlife Search for Self.* New York: Harper and Row.

Williamson, Thomas R., and Edward J. Karras. 1970. Job satisfaction variables among female clerical workers. *Journal of Applied Psychology* 54 (4):343-46.

6

SALES WORKERS

Industrialization and the mass production it enables, the multiplication of services, and the widening of markets beyond the ability of the producer or service provider to interact directly with the consumer or user have created a vast and varied array of intermediaries. The process of marketing a product or service has been a significant growth industry in the past century. Kelly (1969: 5) dates marketing of products to the growth of towns and the ability to produce goods "in anticipation of demand rather than on order." As national and international trade expanded and urban populations came to dominate life, the marketing of products became a major part of the economy.

> Today, the design and production of a good product is only one step. A producer must continually study his customer's needs and preferences. He may have to advertise his product and arrange for transportation and warehousing. And, of course, he must sell it, perhaps with the aid of wholesalers and retailers (McCarthy, 1968: 1). Almost half the consumer's dollar is spent on marketing (2) . . . Marketing is the performance of business activities which direct the flow of goods and services from producer to consumer or user in order to satisfy consumers and accomplish the company's objective (9).

SALES WORK: THE LITERATURE

The literature describing marketing stresses the need of salespersons to meet the consumer's needs, but the instructions directed toward the sales force usually emphasize the importance of "creating" needs by convincing people they must have a product or a certain type of product (Goffman, 1964; Miller, 1964). Mills (1956) was fascinated with this increasing segment of *White Collar* jobs in the "Great Salesroom":

> In the older world of the small entrepreneur there were storekeepers but few salesmen. After the Revolutionary War, there began to be traveling peddlers, whose markets were thin but widespread. By the middle of the nineteenth century the wholesaler—the then dominant type of entrepreneur—began to hire drummers or greeters, whose job it was to meet retailers and jobbers in hotels or saloons in the market center of the city. Later, these men began to travel to the local markets. Then, as manufacturers replaced wholesalers as dominant powers in the world of business, their traveling agents joined the wholesalers . . .
>
> There are still trading posts in outlying areas, and general merchandise stores. Single-line or specialty shops still numerically dominate U.S. retailing. But the department store, the chain store, the mail order house—all principally types of this century—are most in tune with the new society (Mills, 1956: 162-63).

The situation or encounter during which one (or more) person sells a good or service to one or more persons varies considerably by locale, product or service to be sold, and the characteristics of the seller, buyer, and other members of the social circles who are involved. The subculture within which the exchange takes place is also of importance with rules that are customarily observed by everyone. However, French (1963) found the most successful store salesmen to be ones who defy the peer group's informal controls concerning method of acquiring customers. Mills (1956) explains major variations in locales:

> In terms of where the sale is made, salespeople may be classified as stationary, mobile, or absentee. Stationary salespeople—now about 60 percent of the white-collar people involved in selling—sell in stores, behind the counters. Mobile salesmen—now about 38 percent—make the rounds to the houses and offices of the customers. They range from peddlers walking from door-to-door, to 'commercial travelers' who fly to the formal appointment expertly made weeks in advance. Absentee sales—ad men, now two percent of all salespeople—manage the machineries of promotion and advertising and are not personally present at the point of the sale, but act as all-pervasive adjuncts to those who are (Mills, 1956: 165).

It is interesting to note that Mills, writing in the 1950s, shifted from "salespeople" to sales*men* when talking of the mobile workers and of "absentee salesmen and admen." In so doing he reflected the reality of the selling situation in those years. Any women who were in sales worked behind counters or on floors of stores. Mobile salespersons were men, mainly because of the assumption that women would not, or should not, travel unescorted, let alone enter the domain of male business managers, purchasing agents, or owners.

The field of selling has expanded the range of roles and relations between seller and buyer considerably since Mills's (1956) time. Toffler, (1980) prophesizes in *The Third Wave* that the roles of producer and consumer will be blended into a single role of prosumer with the help of computers and robots, eliminating the salesperson entirely. Face-to-face contact between the salesperson and the buyer has rapidly decreased in frequency through the use of the telephone and the mail. In many cases, the consumer simply dials a number obtained from sound or sight advertising and gives an order and address to which an item or service is to be delivered. *Time* magazine (November 8, 1982) ran a cover story on the "Catalogue Cornucopia," the dramatic explosion of shopping through catalogues and order forms, assisted by credit card billing and involving only order clerks. Greater initiative is required of salespersons who must actively contact the potential customer over the telephone.

Face-to-face contact in places selling goods or services may not actually involve selling. Mass marketing methods, first introduced in the 1930s, such as those used in supermarkets or discount stores, depend on customer self-service, the staff simply answering questions, stocking shelves, and cashiering (Estey, 1971). McCarthy (1968), however, found much scrambled merchandizing in America, combining methods of chains, franchises, cooperatives, discount houses, and so forth. Optometrists sell frames and glasses after examining eyes, restaurants sell foods and even nonedible goods for takeout, and families temporarily turn into a sales force for "garage" and "rummage" sales.

The process by which goods and services are transferred from producer or specialist to the consumer varies considerably, not only by the locale and item, but also by the skills required of the intermediary sales force.

> In terms of skills involved, sales personnel range from the salesmen who create and satisfy new desires, through salespeople who do not create desires or customers but wait for them, to the order-fillers who merely receive payment, make change and wrap up what is bought. Some salesmen must know the technical details of complex commodities and their maintenance; others need know nothing about the simple commodities they sell (Mills, 1956: 164).

Our examination of the women of the Chicago area who are classified as sales workers found two basic categories comparable to Mills's (1956) stationary and mobile workers. These we have labeled sales clerks and agents.

Sales Clerks

Stationary salespersons can work in a variety of settings, many of which are listed by McCarthy (1968: 340-46):

1. Trading posts, variety
2. Single-line limited stores, groceries, clothing stores, etc.
3. Specialty shops with a distinct personality, catering to certain types of customers
4. Department stores, originally downtown, now with suburban branches
5. Catalogue retailers, mail order
6. Planned shopping centers

The counter or floor salespersons are responsible for a department of limited size, with customers generally being guided to them with the help of the store's advertising or reputation. They simply help the customer choose items in their area, write up the sales check, and wrap the purchase. They are considered the least prestigious of sales workers. The job involves little decision-making and is subject to close supervision. Buyers provide the merchandise and others price the items. Within retail sales, there is also a range of prestigious positions, depending on the reputation of the store and the price of the goods. Howe (1977) and Donovan (1929/1974) found sex segregation even within department stores, with women being assigned to departments with "female appropriate" goods, such as apparel, make-up, jewelry, and household items. Large and expensive items such as television sets, appliances, automobile accessories, etc. are considered more in the domain of salesmen.

In spite of the limitations of the roles of sales clerks, Mills (1956: 172-74) found a great variety in personal styles. "Salesgirls" in small towns differ, according to him, from those in metropolitan stores. The former reputedly know their customers, gain prestige from them, and are the transmitters of community gossip. The latter, on the other hand, do not really know or identify with their customers and tend to be hostile toward them. He identified several different kinds of salesgirls in big stores. Ritzer (1977: 245-46) summarizes the types, which he claims, are a "function of the nature of the salesperson, the customer, and the store":

The 'wolf' is one of the most aggressive, prowling the store and pouncing on customers, rather than waiting for them to come to her ... An even more aggressive wolf is an 'elbower', who is determined to get every customer ... The 'charmer' is the salesperson who relies on her looks and smile to make sales. The 'ingenue' is new to the job and relies on her self-effacing manner and the help of more experienced salesgirls to make sales. The 'collegiate' is a part-time college girl who relies on her 'impulsive amateurishness' to make a living. The 'drifter' is more concerned with gossiping with her colleagues than with making sales. The 'social pretender' alienates her colleagues with her 'airs' but she is attractive to wealthy customers in particular. The salesgirl who lasts to be an 'old timer' is either the 'disgruntled rebel' or a completely accommodating saleswoman. In either case, she is the backbone of the salesforce, the cornerstone around which it is built.

The department store "saleslady" or "salesgirl" is the person most often described in the literature under the general occupational category of sales when women are the focus of attention, mainly because so few members of this gender have been in personal or direct selling as agents. Donovan (1929/1974) and Howe (1977) both worked in department stores in areas dominated by women when studying the work of saleswomen. Literature describing female agents is scarce.

Sales Agents

Mobile salespersons are agents, representatives, or demonstrators of one or more manufacturer or provider of services, or intermediaries who approach customers in their own homes or places of work. They sell products, insurance, homes, and other property, advertising time or space, and all goods that are not bought by the customer coming to the seller. Competition among firms requires sales agents to be present at every level of distribution, to wholesalers, business firms, retail stores, and finally, consumers. Thus, the sales force covers all parts of the economy and competes not only in goods and services but also in availability, financing, delivery time, packaging, and so forth. In many instances, high technical knowledge is required of the personal selling agents, as well as transportation and flexibility of hours. The sales person also needs the type of demeanor and knowledge of interpersonal interaction that enables him or her to enter space controlled by others and sell goods or services the customer may not have specifically ordered or which may be already provided by competitive enterprises. Sales agents tend to be assigned territories, contacting customers and persuading them of their need for the product or service. Once a territory and accounts have been established, repeated sales draw steady commissions and established relations.

The sales field is imbued with many stereotypes of the personality requirements of successful sales agents, a typology of customers, and best procedures for different selling situations. These stereotypes have kept male and female sales workers separate until recent changes have allowed women to move into the predominantly male sales agent area. It is interesting to note how rapidly real estate, especially that which deals with private property, has been converted from a male appropriate occupation to a female domain. This shift has been accompanied by a decrease of concern with structural aspects of property and an increase of stress upon those amenities associated with the quality of "living space."

One of the areas of sales which is increasingly drawing women is that of "direct selling" to private customers. The peddler traveling the country with basic wares was the early form of direct selling in America, as both Mills (1956) and Cox (1963) point out. Vacuum cleaners and home-cleaning products have been sold door-to-door by men for many years. The field of direct sales uses four different methods (Cox, 1963: 43-45). The first method remains the same, house-to-house, although the title is often modified because of the stereotype of high pressure "foot in the door" methods. Avon cosmetics, Watkins Products such as spices and extracts, Coventry jewelry and other products are still being sold by this method, mainly, if not entirely, by women. Watkins Products has been using women "in its operation at least since the turn of the century" (Cox, 1963: 9) and Avon never had a male sales force. The seller of its main product, women's cosmetics, often needs to demonstrate its use to the customer.

The second method of direct sales is through referrals and appointments. Each time a sale is completed, the salesperson, or "demonstrator" asks the customer for names of friends, with the promise of a gift if the recommendation results in a sale. This method tries to avoid "cold" canvassing, but each new territory must be opened through some other method.

The third method of direct sales is that of party plans:

> Fun, games and business are mixed at parties at which women sell household cleaning products, cosmetics, jewelry, apparel, and plastics. ... In the party plan, a dealer enlists hostesses who invite the guests [customers] and provide the homes [salesroom] and refreshments in exchange for gifts. The dealer presides at the party, leading the games and stunts and making a sales presentation. She then takes orders for

delivery later to the hostess, who in turn distributes the merchandise to the guests (Cox, 1963: 46).

Finally, there is a "club plan" which works like a chain letter and is somewhat similar to the referral system, except that the buyer recommends a friend for "club membership." Each time the friend "joins," the recommender gets an addition to the items she has already bought. Silverware place settings and crystal are often sold in this way. In contrast to the party plan, the club plan system does not involve the "members" coming into actual contact with each other.

Direct sales requires initiative and presents many sources of strain (Evans, 1969; Ritzer, 1977). Krugman (1969) points to the strains facing insurance underwriters, most notably those created by feelings of intrusion on the privacy of the potential customer. He refers only to men in this occupation, since women entered it only recently, and recommends that companies screen candidates for sales jobs for this particular sensitivity. This is necessary according to Krugman because stress varies considerably among underwriters and can result in high turnover rates. Crane (1969) found that the main hurdling block of insurance agents is being invited into the home. To increase the probability of success such agents usually select a homogeneous set of prospects who are similar to themselves. There has been no study of women in personal selling to determine their procedures for selecting prospects, but it is quite likely that they also avoid territories and people with whom they feel uncomfortable because of class, racial, or other differences (see also Belasco, 1969). Various methods have been devised by people selling outside of their place of business to facilitate interaction with potential customers. This is because "cold" contact without prior warning often results in refusal. Prior telephoning or introduction through the mail or a mutual acquaintance are representative of such techniques. Direct sales companies often encourage their women to first send catalogues or bring free samples on a preliminary call and return later to get the order (Cox, 1963).

Because of strong competition among firms providing goods and services and the standardization of many things being sold due to increased technology, personnel directors and others hiring a sales force try to select and train people that will sell well but also remain with the company. Cox (1963: 9), writing in the 1960s, claims that a direct sales company has to recruit twice as many workers as they need each year:

> Turnover continues to plague every direct-selling company despite the granting of more and more recognition and incentive rewards with growing value.

Marketing management firms constantly remind clients with sales forces that such people are "taught not born," but there remains an assumption among the old-timers that "personality" is a major factor in success in selling. There are still sales managers who claim that "I can tell a good salesman the minute he walks in the door" (they rarely think of saleswomen). However, advertisements try to draw people with experience or college graduates in marketing, to sales training programs. All companies must familiarize the just hired sales force with their own version of selling, including the products and favored approaches to customers. Few now depend on "The School of Osmosis," and numerous books are published for sales managers on how best to train and relate to the sales force (Keesecker, 1969: 30; Robinston and Stidsen, 1967).

In spite of the allegedly rational approach to finding and training a sales force, many firms misrepresent the job or provide inadequate preparation not only in relation to the product but also in dealing with the inevitable role strains. The search procedures usually rely on advertisements at the lower levels of sales, but specialized search companies find workers for more esoteric positions. Examples of the advertisements reflect the variety of sales jobs; length of the ad often indicates unusual situations or requirements.

**SEASONAL
SALES PERSON
(Sept. - Dec.)**

Excellent opportunity to earn extra money during the Christmas season if you are not restricted by family or other weekday commitments. We have an opening in the greater Chicago area for someone who wishes to sell top-quality boxed chocolates and other specialty items to area businesses.

WE WILL TRAIN you at our own expense. Our program covers approximately 14 weeks, and the effective selling hours are between 8:30am and 4:30pm, Monday thru Friday.

Weekly salary, commission and mileage reimbursement (car required). People requiring full-time annual employment need not apply.

If you are a motivated, outgoing individual with a pleasant personality and appearance, please send a letter telling us about yourself (immediate response desired).

This ad must be directed at unemployed young, or older people, or at homemakers wanting to earn some money, since the person cannot be "restricted by family or other weekday commitments" and the job lasts only three months. The statement that "we will train you at our own expense" is evidence that the advertisement is directed at people inexperienced with the labor market because all organizations obviously must train the sales force. This training includes knowledge of their products and, in the case of direct sales (as opposed to "inside" or behind the counter and telephone sales), the best ways of approaching potential customers is an important part of orientation. An indication that the ad is aimed at housewives is the requirement that interested people "send a letter telling us about yourself." Most lower-level jobs ask the prospect to telephone. The higher status jobs require a resume of working experience, positions, and salary history. Most advertisements for sales people stress personal qualities.

STOP READING
PUBLIC RELATIONS
TRAINEE

Are you looking for a career opportunity with a fast growing major corporation? If you are willing to work and learn, neat appearing, and you can get by on $16,500 your first year while in training, there is a real chance for advancement. If you consider yourself good in dealing with people, both in person and over the phone, and have a good image, you owe it to yourself to look into this position.

Only career-minded people need call.

For appointment,
call:

000-1111

Des Plaines area.

Many of the ads are quite vague as to requirements, benefits, and duties. The August 1, 1982 *Chicago Tribune*'s help wanted ads included two which were very different, although supposedly oriented to the same type of salesperson. The one on the left is vague, aimed at the vanity of the reader with its appeal to "self-starters," indicating the impossibility of close supervision. The one on the right clearly specifies the work conditions.

The next step after hiring a sales person is training. One of the author's former students was once demonstrating a Tupperware presentation to a class in occupations and professions with such fervor that one of the other students stopped her with, "Hey, all you are selling is a plastic container, not God." She followed through on her realization that her training resembled a religious revival and wrote a prize-winning article, "The Use of Religious Revival Techniques to Indoctrinate Personnel: The Home-Party Sales Organizations" (Peven, 1968).

Home-party companies have certain characteristics which seem to require the development of a complex ideological system strongly resembling religious revival movements. These characteristics are (1) a labor force composed almost entirely of married women who have had no previous experience in the business world and (2) the fact that the women are spatially independent of a sales room, a time card, or a boss, and must spend the major portion of their working time alone (Peven, 1968:98).

Frequent meetings of the regional sales force, or even of a few women under a manager or unit leader, constant praise and recognition, opportunity to dress up and go to a party, incentive programs including trips and cars, are constantly stressed in the female intensive direct selling firms:

> Selling also gives a woman recognition and this is something that she frequently finds when she is away from her home and not while she is in her home (Cox, 1963: 195).

Peven (1968) explains at length the techniques used to build loyalty and a willingness to work hard at the "rally" or national meetings which bring hundreds of women together. These techniques are similar to those used by the Billy Graham team, with preliminary warmups of singing and rhythmic movement, followed by award and gift presentations by the president. Peven (1968: 102) quoted the last two lines of a poem written by a distributor and read to the president:

> Yes, dear God, I believe in thee,
> But now, at last, I believe in me.

Similarly, many direct sales organizations incorporate the religion or the belief in God's personal assistance into an inspirational sales meeting. Patriotism and the belief in the free enterprise system is used in a similar manner.

Although the literature often assumes that the need to indoctrinate salespersons through emotional techniques is female specific, anyone familiar with training and incentive programs knows that is not true. Not too many years ago a major food manufacturer brought the sales force together and, as part of the program, turned off the lights and played a tape allegedly recorded by a salesman during the time he waited to hear whether he had won an award for having sold the highest number of hotdogs to retail outlets and the period he went home and told his wife about it. Reportedly, there were lumps in the throats of many of the listeners. After all, in order to become efficient salesmen and saleswomen, people must be sold on the product and the company.

The literature dealing with salesmanship is full of sex stereotypes and accompanying attitudes about other alleged personality characteristics, such as the hiring of minority workers only if they are to sell to their own group. Even Cox (1963), a woman herself, perpetuates the female stereotypes:

Women fit into direct selling best because they work harder and are more dedicated than the average man. A woman is more loyal if she likes what she is doing and therefore has more respect for the company and for personalities in it. She is not necessarily working for money. Although money is important, so are other things—prestige, a sense of belonging and a feeling that her position is important (Cox, 1963: 208).

Ellman (1973), a psychologist, sent questionnaires to 500 top companies, receiving 130 responses from the personnel managers in order to write about *Managing Women in Business*. Although the survey was taken during the early 1970s, one wonders how much attitudes have changed in view of the evidence of very slow movement of women into male intensive jobs such as outside selling. Fifty-six percent of the personnel directors agreed with the statement, "Do you believe there is a need for using different techniques in training women than men?" Ninety-eight of the directors believed that there are "certain kinds of jobs at which women definitely excel," 73 percent that they are more concerned with details than men, and 74 percent that they "tend to take corrections more personally."

The Chicago Area Saleswomen

There are 132 women in our Chicago area sample who were in sales work in their last job, and 60 of them are still in sales. This is a fairly high attrition rate, but it comes mainly from sales clerks, rather than sales agents. The clerks work in retail establishments, are quite heterogenous in their background and perceptions of the job and the self and, in many cases, appear to be using the job as an intermediary one. This is especially true of the clerks who have trained, and often worked, in higher status jobs, as managers, professionals, or technicians. These women intend to get greater training and to return to such occupations. Sales agents are a very different group. Most started out as clerical workers, then returned to school or obtained training sufficient to enable them to enter the previously male dominated field of sales agents. Interestingly enough, insurance opened up to women after the Carter administration targeted banking for the enforcement of the Equality of Employment Opportunity acts. The movement of women into sales agent jobs has been dramatic. The women in our sample have a quite different profile from that of the sales clerks. They are more educated, having gone beyond high school when they first withdraw from the educational system and having returned for more schooling. They earn more than twice the money earned by clerks and consider their jobs as complex and important with many advantages to full-time employment. As we shall see in Chapter 6, Volume II, their recent movement out of clerical and into sales agent jobs is, however, causing some strain in relations with the husband.

SUMMARY AND CONCLUSIONS

The increasing division of labor experienced by modern, capitalistic, and industrialized societies has multiplied the jobs of middlemen and women who sell products and services to other producers, wholesalers, retailers, and consumers. Many of these jobs are stationary, i.e., the customer comes to a central location, such as a department or specialty store, and purchases the items displayed and stocked there. The clerk often has limited functions, stocking and organizing the merchandise, helping the customer by showing items and encouraging purchases, filling out the slips and packaging the item, if it is not to be delivered. The job obviously varies by the size of the establishment, the price of items as well as the type of goods, the complexity of the social circle, and so forth. "Salesladies" in exclusive, small shops often know their customers because there are relatively few of them and they return.

The expanding, and increasingly open field of sales agent, which includes insurance, real estate, manufacturer's representative, and direct sales organizer has a completely different set of relations. The sales agent tends to be an entrepreneur, organizing time, effort, and client contact, and visits owners or agents of businesses and other establishments, including homes. The job requires traveling, sometimes over extensive territories. A very recent sub-unit of this sales activity open to women is of the book representative of a publisher, who travels to different campuses and tries to convince faculty to use the products of her "house." Again, the duties and rights, as well as the composition of the social circle, vary among sales agent jobs.

REFERENCES

Belasco, James A. 1969. The Salesman's Role Revisited. In *Salesmanship: Selected Readings*, edited by John M. Rathmell, pp. 20-24. Homewood, Illinois: Richard D. Irwin.

Cain, Pamela S., and Donald J. Treiman. 1981. The DOT as a source of occupational data. *American Sociological Review* 46, 3 (June): 253-78.

Cox, Claire. 1963. *How Women Can Make Up to $1000 a Week in Direct Selling*. New York: D. Van Nostrand.

Crane, Lauren E. 1969. The Salesman's Role in Household Decision-making. In *Salesmanship: Selected Readings*, edited by John M. Rathmell, pp. 98-110. Homewood, Illinois: Richard D. Irwin.

Donovan, Frances R. 1929/1974. *The Saleslady*. New York: Arno Press.

Ellman, Edgar. 1973. *Managing Women in Business*. Waterford, Connecticut: Prentice Hall.

Estey, Martin. 1971. The Retail Clerks. In *White Collar Workers*, edited by Albert A. Blum, et al., pp. 46-82. New York: Random House.

Evans, F. B. 1969. A Sociological Analysis of the Selling Situation: Some Preliminary Findings. In *Salesmanship: Selected Readings*, edited by John M. Rathmell, pp. 82-87. Homewood, Illinois: Richard D. Irwin.

French, C. L. 1963. Correlates of Success in Retail Selling. In *Marketing and the Behavioral Sciences: Selected Readings*, edited by Perry Bliso, pp. 235-46. Boston: Allyn and Bacon.

Goffman, Erving. 1964. On Cooling the Mark Out: Some Aspects of Adaptation to Failure. In *Interpersonal Dynamics*, edited by W. G. Gennis, E. D. Schein, D. E. Berlew, and F. I. Steele, pp. 417-30. Homewood, Illinois: The Dorsey Press.

Howe, Louise K. 1977. *Pink Collar Workers*. New York: Avon.

Keesecker, H. C. 1969. Salesmanship—a Profession. In *Salesmanship: Selected Readings*, edited by John M. Rathmell, pp. 28-34. Homewood, Illinois: Richard D. Irwin.

Kelley, W. T. 1969. The Development of Early Thought in Marketing and Promotion. In *Salesmanship: Selected Readings*, edited by John M. Rathmell, pp. 1-8. Homewood, Illinois: Richard D. Irwin.

Kohn, Melvin L., and Carmi Schooler. 1973. Occupational experience and psychological functioning: an assessment of reciprocal effects. *American Sociological Review* 38: 97-113.

_____. 1978. The reciprocal effects of substantive complexity of work and intellectual flexibility: a longitudinal assessment. *American Journal of Sociology* 94: 24-52.

_____. 1982. Job conditions and personality: a longitudinal assessment of their reciprocal effects. *American Journal of Sociology* 87, No. 6 (May): 1257-86.

Krugman, H. E. 1969. Salesmen in Conflict: A Challenge to Marketing. In *Salesmanship: Selected Readings*, edited by John M. Rathmell, pp. 25-28. Homewood, Illinois: Richard D. Irwin.

Lopata, H. Z. 1980. "The Self-concept: Characteristics and Areas of Competence." Presented at the American Sociological Association Meetings. New York.

Lopata, H. Z., and C. Miller. 1981. "Generalized-self Characteristics and Areas of Competence." Unpublished paper.

Mason, J. L. 1969. The Low Prestige of Personal Selling. In *Salesmanship: Selected Readings*, edited by John M. Rathmell, pp. 14-24. Homewood, Illinois: Richard D. Irwin.

McCarthy, E. James. 1968. *Basic Marketing: A Managerial Approach*. 3rd ed. Homewood, Illinois: Richard D. Irwin.

Mills, C. Wright. 1956. *White Collar*. New York: Oxford University Press.

Miller, S. 1964. The social base of sales behavior. *Social Problems* 13, No. 1 (Summer): 15-24.

Oppenheimer, V. K. 1970. *The Female Labor Force in the United States*. Berkeley, California: Institute of International Studies, University of California.

————. 1977. "The female labor force in the United States: demographic and economic factors governing its growth and changing composition." Berkeley, California: University of California, Population Monograph Series, No. 5.

Peven, Dorothy. 1968. The use of religious revival techniques to indoctrinate personnel: the home-party sales organizations. *The Sociological Quarterly* 9, No. 1 (Winter): 97-106.

Ritzer, George. 1977. *Working: Conflict and Change*. Englewood Cliffs, New Jersey: Prentice-Hall.

Robinston, P. J., and B. Stidsen. 1967. *Personal Selling in a Modern Perspective*. Boston: Allyn and Bacon.

The Staff of Catalyst. 1980. *What to Do With the Rest of Your Life*. New York: Simon and Schuster.

Time. 1982. Catalogue Cornucopia. November 7, pp. 72-79.

Toffler, Alvin. 1980. *The Third Wave*. New York: Bantam Books.

Walshok, Mary. 1979. Occupational Values and Family Roles: Women in Blue-Collar and Service Occupations. In *Working Women and Family*, edited by Karen W. Feinstein, pp. 63-83. Beverly Hills, California: Sage Publications.

————. 1981. *Blue-Collar Women: Pioneers on the Male Frontier*. New York: Garden City: Doubleday Anchor.

7

HOMEMAKERS

Three political statements point the way to the liberation of housewives:
  The housewife role must be abolished.
  The family must be abolished.
  Gender roles must be abolished.
Housework is work directly opposed to the possibility of human self-actualization. . . . Housework lacks any motivating factor. . . . Because housework is not intrinsically self-actualizing, many women try to make it so. The argument that housewifery is creative homemaking stems from this motivation: they strive to elaborate the fundamental processes of housework into something bigger, better, more difficult and more rewarding (Oakley, 1974a: 222-25).

Most private households are managed by families. The main responsibility and division of labor involved in the management have varied considerably, by society, the position of the household within it, its composition, the resources and their base, the stage in the life course, and the content of the role clusters of the managers. The structure of the society, as well as its culture and subculture, influence the resources available to household managers. Also important are the assumed characteristics and areas of competence of men and women, children, and elderly. Although obviously only women can bear children, work involved in their care in the household has varied.

HISTORICAL PERSPECTIVES

In past centuries, and even at the present time in less modernized, and especially in rural areas, life in the major institutions was much more centered in the home than is true in modern times. Households provided the main personnel for educational, economic, political, recreational, and religious activities (O'Kelly, 1980; Tilly and Scott, 1978). The managers of this unit coordinated the various roles of members both in and outside of it. At subsistence levels of the economy, many other activites and relations of household members revolved around this process and the provision of basic necessities (Rosaldo and Pamphere, 1974; Tilly and Scott, 1978).

As mentioned in Chapter 2, Aries (1965) portrayed three types of households in pre-eighteenth century Europe, the peasant complex containing not only people but animals, which was also open to public village life, the manor house with as many as 200 residents performing a variety of roles and a constant flow of visitors conducting political and economic transactions, and the town house combining apprentices and servants with family members. P. Laslett (1971) detailed the public life of a household bakery in London (see also Anderson, 1971; P. Laslett and Wall, 1972). Western European and American households of the past have been known to contain a variety of people.

> While predominantly nuclear in its kinship structure, the pre-industrial and early industrial household was also likely to include others unrelated to the conjugal family unit. Among such persons were servants, boarders and lodgers, apprentices, employees, and other people's children (B. Laslett, 1973: 479).

As late as Colonial America, the household was the main producer of domestically used goods.

> Until at least the middle of the eighteenth century, there was little market for the exchange of goods, and households operated as units of production centered around the self supporting farm or the artisan shop (Kessler-Harris, 1981: 22) . . . Until the end of the eighteenth century, well over 90 percent of the population lived on the land (27).

The management of the home with so many workers and variety of tasks required for its maintenance involved a division of labor with delegation of work and authority, organization, and supervision of teamwork, as well as a system for distribution of products for consumption. Many stages of the production process were involved.

As societies grew in complexity of social structure, both horizontally and vertically, of culture and of ongoing life, variations in household location, composition, resources, and member roles mushroomed. Dwellings ranged from truncated, squatter lean-tos with members dependent upon scavanging, through the simplified nuclear urban apartment or home, to homes of heads of state run with the help of various levels of managers and large staffs. While these households were multiplying in variety of composition and structure, under the influence of changes which were discussed in Chapter 2, their functions and the roles of members were also changing. A major shift was the removal of large segments of the institutionalized spheres of life from the home and their placement outside its walls. Of course, public organizations could not displace all household functions. The unit had to retain some responsibility for educating the young, controlling behavior, producing, distributing, and consuming economic goods, transmitting belief systems and leisure activities. However, most of the members had to increasingly leave the household in order to pursue roles in organizations specializing in the various institutional functions. Public life increased in importance, especially in America, with its focus on the economic institution and the reduction of production in the home. Work was organized into jobs, as stated in Chapter 1, and people could earn their livelihood in factories and offices.

Some households continued to be public, large and complex, with activities of important segments of society flowing through them. However, most homes in modernized, industrialized, urbanized areas shrank in size and in the demands they made upon residents. With less need for servants to help with production, people became less willing to take on that job, remaining only in homes of the wealthy and contributing to the life-styles of the "leisure classes" (Veblen, 1899/1934). Apprentices began living in quarters other than the homes of masters, or worked for wages in larger producing units. The decrease of immigration and in-migration and an increase in wages and the supply of housing removed lodgers and boarders. The husband/father became the main "breadwinner" (Lopata, 1971) or "provider" (Bernard, 1981). Bernard (1981) dates the ideological changes in the lives of women and their dependence upon the man of the house to the development of the male role of "provider," which later became that of "good provider."

> The good provider as a specialized male role seems to have arisen in the transition from subsistence to market—especially money—economies that

accelerated with the industrial revolution. The good-provider role for males emerged in this country roughly, say, from the 1830s, when de Tocqueville was observing it, to the late 1970s, when the 1980 census declared that a male was not automatically to be assumed to be head of the household. This gives the role of a life span of about a century and a half (Bernard 1981: 2).

The homemaker, who often contributed more of the basic necessities for the household than did the man, became "stripped to a considerable extent of her access to cash-mediated markets" (Bernard, 1981: 2). In addition, the new American culture which stressed "achievement," "success," "making it" for the male, "escalated the provider role into the good-provider role" (Bernard, 1981: 3) and raised the importance of male roles outside of the home for which they were providing increasing affluence. Of course, this emphasis on success, discussed in Chapter 3, evidenced in part by having a full-time home-making wife, was accompanied by the development of the "cult of true womanhood" which restricted the productive activities of the wife to the personal familial realm (see Rothman, 1978; Ryan, 1979; Welter, 1966).

The combined social movements removed the husband/father from co-management of the household, since he was so seldom in it and was not expected to contribute more than the money and a few traditionally male chores to its maintenance. The management of the household fell to the woman (see also Galbraith, 1973). An interesting consequence of the ideologies surrounding these shifts is the perception of the household and the homemaker as isolated from the rest of society. As Gardiner (1979), Glazer (1980), Strasser (1978), and Weinbaum and Bridges (1979) point out, this development neglected all the unpaid work homemakers do outside of the home, and as Lopata (1971) stressed, ignored the knowledge and skills required for the utilization of societal resources in its management. The demarcation of the boundaries between the supposedly privatized home of modern America and the public sphere became exaggerated in the literature, with both feminists and those attacking them until recently under-emphasizing the strong involvement of the members of the household in society. One of the authors (Lopata, 1971) found in earlier studies that the more education a woman obtained before she became a manager of a household, the more societal resources she pulled together in order to manage it efficiently and creatively (see also Social Research, 1973). Finch (1983) has recently documented the extensiveness of the homemaker's involvement in the life of the society.

THE SOCIAL ROLE OF HOMEMAKER

The very modern American household remains the main responsibility of the wife or female household head, regardless of how many and what kinds of social roles she performs on the outside. If there is a co-manager, there is some variation in the division of responsibility and of actual work, according to a number of studies (Berk, 1980; Bernard, 1981; Bryson and Bryson, 1979; Fogarty, Rapoport and Rapoport, 1971; Lopata, Barnewolt and Norr, 1980; Pepitone-Rockwell, 1980; Pleck, 1983; Robinson, 1980; Vanek, 1979; Walker and Woods, 1976). The role of manager varies considerably, from a minimal level of complexity and work to extensive involvement with a large social circle both inside and outside of the home. One extremely important factor affecting the role of homemaker as manager is the centrality of this role in her cluster and the perceived and actual locus of control she has in its performance (Ferree, 1976; Galbraith, 1973; Hartmann, 1981; Weinbaum and Bridges, 1979). Some women are so highly dependent upon the role of the husband away from the home and as partial manager of it that their life is vicarious, not only in rewards but also in initiated activity (Lipman-Blumen and Leavitt, 1976). Whether the couple operates in a two-person career (Papanek, 1979), two-career family, or simply as a one or two-worker family makes a great deal of difference to the role of homemaker.

Previous analyses by one of the authors (see Lopata, *Occupation: Housewife*, 1971; and "The Life Cycle of the Social Role of Housewife," 1966) of the social role of homemaker examined its stages of involvement and the composition of the social circle. A series of interviews from 1956 to 1966 with both suburban and urban full-time homemakers and some urban employees women found that over half of them felt that "the modern woman is not trained for her role of homemaker." This judgment was expressed especially by the more educated suburban homemakers who saw the role as complex and requiring knowledge and skills not learned at school. Few took courses, and those who did did not pay much attention. The suburban homemakers were unlikely to feel that they learned all they needed to know from their mothers because the life they were creating was so different from the one they led as youngsters in the city (see also Gans, 1967; Riesman, et al., 1950). Many of the women turned to the mass media for solutions to problems and better ways of doing something (see also Ehrenreich and English, 1979). In addition, they turned to each other for advice and the sharing of knowledge (Lopata, 1962).

The previous research, as stated above, discovered the importance of general schooling in providing the tools for understanding the world and self-confidence in problem solving (see also Lopata, 1973). The more education a woman has, the more she is also able to see her situation in life course terms, being aware that the "expanding circle," the "peak," and the "full house plateau" (Lopata, 1966, 1971) stages of the role of homemaker last a limited number of years. She is also likely to be married to a more educated man who is able to provide a higher income with which to manage the household. In addition, she is more likely to know she can return to the labor force if she wants to and to be more aware of her options than is true of her less educated counterpart.

The role of homemaker is an indeterminate one (Mack, 1956) in that the woman has to pull together her own social circle. She generally starts doing this after marriage, although in recent years more and more women manage their own households, with others or alone, before that time. There is great variation in the utilization of resources by different women (Lopata, 1971). In order to fulfill her role as manager throughout the life course of the household, each woman must decide what she needs in the line of goods and services, assess the resources she has with which to attain them, leave the home to obtain these or have them delivered to her. She determines not only her own needs, but also those of other permanent and temporary members of the household, as well as other people who benefit from her management. Few roles allow such a broad latitude in the development of the social circle and duties and rights associated with these relations (see Lopata, 1971: 152; also Andre, 1982: 17). Some women use numerous societal resources, with knowledge of the content of goods available and ways of combining them and services. Others treat the role with minimal attention, or are so overburdened that they do not have time or energy for anything but repetitious use of a limited set of supports (Social Research, 1973; Rainwater et al., 1956; Oakley, 1974b). Restrictions in the use of resources include also money and cooperation of circle members.

At the "peak stage" of the role of homemaker, with a husband and small children in the household, the role of homemaker is influenced by the following:

1. The number and ages of the children
2. Their special needs
3. The kinds of duties undertaken by the housewife in relation to these children, because of societal, circle, or self-imposed demands

4. The kinds of duties undertaken by the housewife in relation to other members of the household (especially husband)
5. The size of the home which must be maintained
6. The number of items which must be maintained and the activities required to keep them in a desired condition
7. The number of persons helping in the performance of the duties and the type of assistance each provides
8. The number and variety of 'labor-saving' devices or 'conveniences' designed to decrease the effort or the time required to perform any of the tasks
9. The location of the household and of each task in relation to the assisting segment of the circle and to the useful objects, plus the versatility of these services as a source of shifting duties and activities (Lopata, 1966: 9-10)

Oakley (1974b) described the "full house plateau" as a very difficult one for the homemaker, and Dyer (1963), LeMasters (1957), and Rossi (1968) find transition to parenthood to be especially stressful for modern parents.

One way of understanding the variations among homemakers is to look at the literature allegedly describing or explaining them. Another is to look at the way women currently in the role of homemaker on a full-time basis describe themselves and their jobs. We shall do both in these two volumes.

HOMEMAKING: THE LITERATURE

The literature devoted to the homemaker ranges from generalized descriptions of the women in this role in a variety of societies, to the work involved in household maintenance, the division of labor, power and decision-making, class differences, and consequences for the role performer to attempts at theoretical explanations for its existence and nature. There has been an enormous proliferation of publications in social science literature on women in recent years. Wittner (1983) drew over 7,000 references in a recent library literature search. We can not cover all the areas of publications in this research and theoretical field; instead we will select only a few topics as examples of available sources which are relevant to our study of the full-time homemakers in metropolitan America.

Women as Homemakers

Although *Occupation: Housewife* (Lopata, 1971) has often been defined as the first analysis of women in this role in America, many other studies had appeared before, but under different titles and with different emphases. Riesman, Glaser, and Denney's (1950) *The Lonely Crowd* devoted much attention to how women in modern suburbia managed their homes. Mirra Komarovsky (1953, 1967) studied both educated and blue-collar women, Dingwall's (1956) *The American Woman: An Historical Study* was really an attack on homemakers/ mothers, as was Wylie's (1955) *Generation of Vipers*. More representative of sociological analyses was Rainwater, Coleman, and Handel's (1959) *Workingman's Wife* or Blood and Wolfe's (1960) *Husbands and Wives*. Friedan (1963) explained some of the *Feminine Mystique* underlying the commitment of American women to the role of home-maker to the exlusion of public roles, and Gavron's (1966) *The Captive Wife: Conflicts of Housebound Mothers* documented the problems of such women in Britain. Descriptions of the life of homemakers became increasingly negative in the 1970s, with Oakley's *Woman's Work* (1974a) and the *Sociology of Housework* (1974b). As we saw in the introduction to this chapter, Oakley concluded in the latter volume that the role should be eliminated entirely. Rubin's (1976) *Worlds of Pain* presented an unrelentingly difficult life of the working class homemaker. It was not until Andre's (1982) *Homemakers: the Forgotten Workers* that the women in this role were described through less negative prisms. As we shall see later, the most recent focus on the role of homemaker attempts to draw on several theoretical frameworks to explain, rather than describe, it.

Interestingly enough, almost all of the literature dealing with homemakers assumes that the women are married and, usually, that they have children. Otherwise, it is almost taken for granted in modern times that husbandless women who are not of retirement age are full-time employees. However, there is an increasing number of full-time homemakers in more simplified households, lacking young children and/or a husband. Ross and Sawhill (1975) first drew our attention to such women in *Time of Transition: the Growth of Families Headed by Women*. I (Lopata, 1979) have studied *Women as Widows: Support Systems*, and Kriesberg (1970) studied *Mothers in Poverty: A Study of Fatherless Families*.

Division of Labor in the Household

Much of the recent literature discussing the homemaker concentrates on the division of labor in the home and how it differs from society to society and with variations in social class, women's employment status, and the husband's occupation (Berk and Berk, 1979; Hartmann, 1981; Laws, 1979; Lopata, Barnewolt and Norr, 1980; Mainardi, 1970; Malos, 1980; Rothman, 1978; Sokoloff, 1980; Vickery, 1979; Walker and Woods, 1976). Almost all of the two-career or two-worker couple literature deals with this problem, stressing the lack of cooperation from family members in household maintenance in cases in which the former full-time homemaker takes on another occupational role, or what happens to households run in an egalitarian way when the woman ceases involvement in full-time employment on the outside. (Bird, 1979; Fogarty, Rapoport and Rapoport, 1971; Garland, 1972; Lopata, Barnewolt and Norr, 1980; Pepitone-Rockwell, 1980; Poloma, 1972; Poloma and Garland, 1970; Rapoport and Rapoport, 1976a, 1976b, 1980). Berk and Berk (1979) deal with the division of labor in their *Labor and Leisure at Home: Content and Organization of the Household Day* in great detail. S. Berk (1980) edited *Women and Household Labor*, containing many analyses of work and time problems. The amount of time spent in housework by the homemaker and husband-father has interested many a social scientist (see Nelson, 1980; Oakley, 1974b; Szalai, et al., 1972; Vanek, 1978, 1979; Walker, 1969; Walker and Woods, 1976). Pleck (1983) and Lopata, Barnewolt and Norr (1980) have studied the relationship between husbands and wives' help with family roles inside and occupational roles on the outside of the home (see also Berk and Shih, 1980).

Household Work and Consumerism

Most studies of homemakers analyze the work within the home as a system of tasks and the time involved in comparison to people in other occupations or other members of the household (see Oakley, 1974b; Berk and Berk, 1979). Recent research and theoretical analysis have expanded this approach to show how much of women's unpaid work both inside and out of the home is involved in its management, and how this work contributes to the economy of the society at large, not just the household. Glazer (1980) traces the relation between the paid and unpaid work in society, expecially that of women in both capitalist and socialist countries. Much of American society's economic life is dependent upon homemakers who drive to shopping centers, find their own goods without advice from store owners or managers, wait at home for deliveries or repair specialists, chauffeur family members to community resources which do not provide adequate transportation, and so forth (Lopata, 1980).

Galbraith (1973) is critical of a society that forces women to work without pay in order to enable its functioning:

> The conversion of women into a crypto-servant class was an economic accomplishment of the first importance . . . If it were not for this service [unpaid] all forms of household consumption would be limited by the time required to manage such consumption—to select, transport, prepare, repair, maintain, clean, service, store, protect, and otherwise perform the tasks that are associated with the consumption of goods (Galbraith, 1973: 79).

Galbraith attributes part of our high gross national product to the consumption related activity of primarily women, although it is not officially included in computing the total. One can only imagine how much time and effort go into the purchase of household consumer goods in countries in Eastern Europe, as evidenced by pictures of people waiting in lines in front of stores in Poland in the early 1980s.

Marxist analyses of housework have taken a variety of forms, with much disagreement among the theorists, but they share a common definition of domestic labor as "unpaid work that is sexually assigned" (Eisenstein, 1979: 170). There are three types of activity which female work contributes to the operation of a capitalist (and socialist) economy:

> First, reproduction of children is demanded by the need of any society to reproduce itself, and capitalist patriarchal societies need new workers. Second, production is necessary to produce material goods. In capitalist patriarchal societies commodity production is the source of both profit and wages. Third, consumption is necessary in a commodity system because that is the way one obtains the goods one needs (Eisenstein, 1979: 169).

Most of the feminist Marxists thinkers attribute the unequal division of labor not only to class power distribution of capitalism but also to the history of patriarchal dominance (Hartmann, 1976).

The argument relating to the value of women's work in the home and for the family reaches macrotheoretical proportions. Benston (1969) views the family as a feudal structure and women's work within the family as essentially nonproductive in that it produces use-value only, as opposed to market value. On the other hand, Seccombe (1973) asserts that domestic work produces exchange value in that it adds to the cost of the production of labor. He compares housework to petty commodity production because it is both individual and privatized. The wage system is seen as obscuring the relationship of domestic work to capital; it is necessary to remember that the value of house-work is part of the value of the wage package. Gardiner (1979) criti-cizes Seccombe's analysis as being ahistorical because it does not ac-count for change in domestic labor since the development of capitalism, and sees it as insensitive to feminist critiques of Marxism in that it implies intrafamily equality that simply does not exist. Her basic dis-agreement with Seccombe lies in his analogy of domestic work to petty commodity production. According to Gardiner, women are not commodity producers because they have no choice in what they produce and the value they produce does not relate to the amount of money the husband brings home. In fact, as wages decrease the value of domestic work may actually increase. She argues instead that "domestic labor does not create value or the definition of value which Marx adopted, but does nonetheless contribute to surplus value by keeping down necessary labor, or the value of labor power, to a level that is actually lower than the actual subsistence of the working-class" (188). Therefore, in times of economic crisis domestic labor plays an increasingly important role. Weinbaum and Bridges (1979) focus on the role of domestic labor in market relations through consump-tion. They maintain that it is the houseworker who does the important work of reconciling consumption needs with the production of com-modities, thus contributing to capital's ability to increase its own profit (1961).

Eisenstein (1979) summarizes these arguments when she states:

Domestic labor—the work necessary to the maintenance of the home—involves production, consumption, reproduction, and maintenance of labor power . . . Domestic labor is indispensible to the operation of capitalist patriarchal society as it *now* exists (170).

The Marxist literature brings to the forefront the contribution of housework to societal economy, and, additionally, illustrates the ways in which "its importance and function are concealed by mystification of dominant ideology" (Oakley, 1980: 11).

Another view of the home, the homemaker, and society is con-tained in Toffler's (1980) *The Third Wave*. He predicts a "home-centered society" with computers and robots enabling all levels of economic life to be controlled from the "electronic cottage." This prediction of the "rise of the prosumer" who combines the functional activities of the producer and consumer opens a new view of the rela-tion between the household and society. In Toffler's terms, the second wave of human development converted agricultural societies into industrial ones, moving major spheres of activity out of the home to central factories and offices. Others have observed the same, as already noted several times here. What is exciting about his *The Third Wave* is his view of the decentralization of work thanks to the computer, decreasing the need for the separation of private and public, home and the rest of societal spaces. Home management then becomes even more complex than it is in certain homes at the present time. It would involve the coordination of work, consumerism, education, stock manipulation, political decision-making, and all kinds of activities in still unimagined areas of life. Thus, the "do it yourself" trend so dominant in American home life of recent generations can be expanded to control all types of societal and familial behavior, increasing the influence of home managers and the in-and-out permeability of boundaries. If Toffler (1980) is right, and there is enough evidence to indicate that his view of the future pointed up important changes, then the trends observed by Aries (1965), B. Laslett (1973) or Parsons (1964) and others of the privatization and isolation of the nuclear family household from not only kin but also societal life will have been reversed. On the other hand, much of the interaction of homemakers and workers in the electronic cottage will be with inanimate objects, replacing face-to-face interaction with other human beings.

Power and Decision-Making

Power, like work, is usually unevenly distributed within the household. Ever since Blood and Wolfe's (1960) publication of *Husbands and Wives*, social scientists have been interested in the direction of power in decision-making between two spouses. As McDonald (1980: 843) pointed out in his survey essay on family power, the Blood and Wolfe (1960) study assumed that the major basis for decision-making power in the family was economic. "The more successful the husband, the less the wife can count on the husband's help at home" (Blood and Wolfe, 1960: 61). McDonald (1980: 843) summarized research which shows other power bases in the home including:

> (1) normative resources—i.e., cultural and sub-cultural definitions of who has the authority . . .; (2) affective resources—i.e., the level of involvement or commitment and the degree of dependence of the other person; (3) personal resources—i.e., personality, physical appearance and role competence; and (4) cognitive resources—i.e., the influence, the perception of power has on the individual and others (McDonald, 1980: 843).

The lack of personal income on the part of the housewife has bothered many a writer. *Redbook Magazine* (1977) devoted an article to this subject, entitled "Is his Money Your Money Too?"

> Once the first child is born and the wife stops working for pay the balance of power shifts—often so subtly that neither partner is aware of it until both are brought up short by some conflict over money or by a major change in life-style—often the wife's going back to work (Olds, 1977: 165).

Olds (1977) recommends that each homemaker establish "an individual savings account in her name," which she can use in any way she wishes without having to ask her husband for money (see also Glazer, 1978).

Class Differences in Household Management and the Two-Person Career

An important contribution to the literature dealing with homemaking focuses on class differences in the way the woman manages the home. Smith (1977) and Glazer (1978; Glazer et al., 1979) specify that the working class woman performs mainly privatized labor in the home for the benefit of her husband and children, some relatives, but few people besides this limited circle. The upper middle class woman, on the other hand, contributes to a broader social circle, especially if her husband is in management or the professions (Fowlkes, 1980; Mortimer, Hall and Hill, 1978; Seidenberg, 1973; Vandervelde, 1979; Wittner, n.d.). Papanek (1973) coined the phrase "two-person career" to explain the situation of women who actively contribute to the success of the husband. These are generally full-time homemakers who maintain a relatively public household to which co-workers, clients, and other associates of the husband in his occupational role are invited, assist the husband to entertain and to be entertained outside of the home, and perform a variety of other duties which help the husband with his job. The initial literature dealing with wives of managerial position husbands tended to be rather negative, dating back to Whyte's (1952/1971) discussion of "the wife problem" in connection with his *Organization Man* (1956). The problem was a lack of upward mobility in life-style and sophistication on the part of the wife whose husband was moving up in status. *Newsweek's* (1963) "Convention Wives—Help or Hinderence" similarly looks at the limitations of homemaker wives of successful husbands. A series of books published during the 1950s and 1960s instructed the wives of the

United States armed service officers on proper etiquette applicable to their situation rather than to wives in general (see Lopata, 1971). Kanter (1977) devoted a major part of her *Men and Women of the Corporation* to the wives of managers and the relation between them and the social circle of the husband at work. Margolis (1979) documents the importance of the wife to the mobility of managers in a large organization headquartered near the East Coast of the United States. A frequently mentioned problem of homemakers married to upwardly moving managers and professionals is the need to remain unobtrusive and noncompetitive, denying individuality (Fowlkes, 1980; Seidenberg, 1973; Vandervelde, 1979). Weiss (1973), Vandervelde (1979), and Bucher (1977) discuss another major problem of homemakers married to upwardly mobile husbands, and that is moving. Until very recently companies successfully socialized their upwardly moving managers into loyalty to the organization and familiarity with the whole system by transferring them frequently. Studies of the wives indicate that this experience can be quite traumatic for them and the children since they must start all over again developing social relationships. The man has an automatically engaging system in the company (Bucher, 1977; Vandervelde, 1979; Weiss, 1973). An early study of Air Force officer wives during the Korean War found them able to set up households in a variety of locations, adjusting to various levels of resources, but dependent upon the armed forces for many of these resources, thus tied to the organization rather than to the community (see Lopata, 1971). The children, however, often went to local schools, creating family role stress.

Finch (1983) has recently developed in detail the ways in which women *Married to the Job: Wives' Incorporation in Men's Work* are influenced by that job. All full-time homemakers are dependent in the style of life they develop on the income produced by the husband, but they vary in how much of this income has to be used to manage a household open to view to the members of the husband's social circle on the job. Time is structured by the demands of a man's job, considered more inflexible than the time requirements in the role of homemaker. Men who work from the home tie their wives even more strongly to the job than do men who leave the household during the day, sometimes even for the whole work week. Finch (1983) argues that the wife contributes not only directly to her husband's work through domestic labor, moral support, peripheral activities, back-up services, and often the work itself, but also indirectly to the work of the organization which employs him. Homemakers involved in two-person careers are generally more educated and have greater resources than is true of working class women, who often do not even know what the husband does on the job, and who are never faced with work brought home or telephone inquiries typical of doctor's wives (Bucher, 1977; Helfrich, 1961; Margolis, 1979; *Newsweek*, 1957, 1963).

Working class women have been described as involved in a never ending routine of work, having many children, a frequently unsympathetic husband, and limited resources with which to manage the household (Rubin, 1976). Rainwater, Coleman, and Handel's (1959) classic *Workingman's Wife* portrayed the woman as highly restricted in her roles because of a lack or knowledge or self-confidence, a fearful view of the world outside of her home, and unpredictable behavior of the husband and older children. Komarovsky (1967), Gans (1967), Cohen and Hodges (1961) supported and detailed this image of the homemaker in the working class and the Social Research (1973) analysis did not find much difference from their portrayal as late as the 1970s (see also Lopata, 1973). Communication between husband and wife has been reported as decreasing with a decrease of education. Homemaking tasks also tend to decrease in creativity and variability (Gans, 1962; Lopata, 1971). The work of the lower class homemaker increases as income decreases, as in the case of depressions or the otherwise caused unemployment of the husband (Gardiner, 1979; Milkman, 1979).

There is a middle range of homemakers who use a personally developed life-style for the management of their homes, having neither the limitations of outlook and resources of the working class women, nor the obligations of a two-person career of the upper-middle or upper-class women. Their role thus varies according to the factors discussed in the beginning of the chapter, household complexity being the basic independent variable used in our analysis of the full-time homemakers in our sample (see also Baruch, et al., 1983). We also include a brief discussion of the degree of involvement by the women in a two-person career.*

---

*The occupation of housewife was not given National Opinion Research Center prestige or Duncan socioeconomic status scores. Several sociologists have attempted to assign homemakers an average score and the most accepted one of 51 points was estimated by Bose (1973; also see Nilson, 1978). It at least provides some base for discussion, although there are tremendous variations in the role, depending upon all the factors discussed before. On the other hand, this can be said of the score for any occupational group. We have seen how varied are the jobs that fall into each category. We will use 51 throughout *City Women*.

The Chicago Area Homemakers

There are 798 full-time homemakers in our Chicago area sample, and 646 of them are currently married. Over a hundred are single parents. Only 6 percent have never been employed, the others coming to this social role from a variety of occupations. It must be remembered that our sample consists of women between the ages of 25 and 54, so it is not surprising that almost all are mothers and have an average of three children. In analyzing the data we finally grouped these homemakers, seen as managers of households, by the complexity of their household. We had initially placed the single parent households as the most complex, since the homemaker has full responsibility and no assistance from a husband. However, we soon found that the absence of a husband contributed more to simplicity than to complexity. It appears that husbands are more work than they are help, and that work and all activity must be organized around their schedules. The classification of households, from simpler to more complex, thus goes as follows: mainly adult, single parent, small (husband and one or two children), and large (husband and three or more children). The small and large households were further divided by the presence or absence of a child age six or under.

SUMMARY AND CONCLUSIONS

The role of homemaker has undergone some very interesting shifts, not just in the composition of the social circle and the content of activities, duties, and rights, but also in status. It became differentiated as a private role with the organization of the world of work into jobs outside of the home and the ideological movement which removed women and children from those jobs. Management of a home in modern urban societies decreasingly involved nonfamily members as contributors to and beneficiaries of the role of homemaker. In fact, even family members, i.e., the husband and school-age children, were removed from the home for most of the day, leaving the homemaker alone to gather the resources for its management. As status accrued to jobs in the society, those which were evaluated and paid according to the new value system, the role of homemaker became (or remained, depending on your view) low. It could not be evaluated, was performed for a private set of people, and thus allegedly did not contribute to the gross national product. Some people advocated that it be abolished, its duties and rights redistributed among several individuals and societal agencies.

A new focus on the role of homemaker points to its unpaid work, which makes possible the life of the society as it now functions. A great deal of business activity, especially in the retail or consumer end, depends on someone, traditionally the homemaker, having the time to reach for, or to receive, services and objects. She is seen as providing services without which the husband and the children could not perform their roles outside the home in the manner in which they are expected to carry them out. The unwillingness, or inability, of many women to be in the role of homemaker full time has raised many new questions as to that set of relations. The view of the relatively passive homemaker, dependent upon the income produced by the husband, is beginning to change in the literature, with a possible swing back (or for the first time) toward a positive re-evaluation of the role and of the women in it. In the meantime, the literature still reports studies of the division of labor in the household, consumerism, and power and decision-making within the household, and the part that the homemaker has in these aspects of household management.

REFERENCES

Andre, Rae. 1982. *Homemakers: The Forgotten Workers*. Chicago: University of Chicago Press.

Anderson, Michael. 1971. Family, Household and the Industrial Revolution. In *Sociology of the Family*, edited by Michael Anderson, pp. 78-125. Baltimore, Maryland: Penguin Books.

Aries, Phillipe. 1965. *Centuries of Childhood*. New York: Randon House, Vintage Books.

Baruch, Grace, Rosalind Barnett and Caryl Rivers. 1983. *Lifeprints: New Patterns of Love and Work for Today's Women*. New York: McGraw-Hill.

Benston, Margaret. 1969. The political economy of women's liberation. *Monthly Review* 21 (4, Spring): 13-27.

Berk, Sarah Fenstermaker, (ed.). 1980. *Women and Household Labor*. Beverly Hills, California: Sage.

Berk, Richard A. and Sarah Fenstermaker Berk. 1979. *Labor and Leisure at Home: Content and Organization of the Household Day*. Sage Library of Social Research. Beverly Hills, California: Sage.

Berk, Sarah Fenstermaker, and Anthony Shih. 1980. Contributions to Household Labor: Comparing Wives' and Husbands, Reports. In *Women and Household Labor*, edited by S. F. Berk, pp. 191-227. Yearbooks in Women's Policy Studies, Vol. 5. Beverly Hills, California: Sage.

Bernard, Jessie. 1981. The good provider role: Its rise and fall. *American Psychologist* 36 (January): 191-227.

―――――. 1974. The Housewife: Between Two Worlds. In *Varieties of Work Ex-*

perience, edited by Phyllis L. Stewart and Muriel G. Cantor, pp. 49-66. New York: John Wiley.

Bird, Caroline. 1979. *The Two Paycheck Marriage: How Women at Work are Changing Life in America*. New York: Rawson, Wade.

Blood, Robert O., Jr., and Donald M. Wolfe. 1960. *Husbands and Wives*. New York: The Free Press of Macmillan.

Bose, Christine. 1973. *Jobs and Gender: Sex and Occupational Prestige*. Baltimore, Maryland: Johns Hopkins University Press.

Bryson, Jeff B. and Rebecca Bryson, (eds.). 1979. *Dual-Career Couples*. Special issue of *Psychology of Women Quarterly* 3 (1, Fall). New York: Human Sciences Press.

Bucher, Judy Darby. 1977. Moving. *Redbook Magazine* (July): 60, 146, 148.

Cohen, Albert K., and Harold M. Hodges. 1961. Characteristics of the lower blue-collar class. *Social Problems* 10 (Spring): 303-33.

Dingwall, Eric. 1956. *The American Woman: A Historical Study*. New York: Rinehart.

Dyer, Everett D. 1963. Parenthood as crisis: A re-study. *Marriage and Family Living* 25 (May): 196-201.

Ehrenreich, Barbara, and Deirdre English. 1979. *For Her Own Good: 150 Years of the Experts' Advice to Women*. Garden City, New York: Anchor Press.

Eisenstein, Z. 1979. *Capitalist Patriarchy and the Case for Socialist Feminism*. New York: Monthly Review Press.

Ferree, M. M. 1976. Working class jobs: Housework and paid work as sources of satisfaction. *Social Problems* 23 (April): 431-41.

Finch, Janet. 1983. *Married to the Job: Wives Incorporation in Men's Work*. Boston: George Allen & Unwin.

Fogarty, M. Rhona Rapoport, and Robert N. Rapoport. 1971. *Sex, Career and Family*. Beverly Hills, California: Sage.

Fowlkes, Martha R. 1980. *Behind Every Successful Man*. New York: Columbia University Press.

Friedan, Betty. 1963. *The Feminine Mystique*. New York: Norton.

Galbraith, John Kenneth. 1973. The economics of the American housewife. *Atlantic Monthly* (August): 78-83.

Gans, Herbert. 1967. *Levittowners*. New York: Pantheon.

Gardiner, Jean. 1979. Women's Domestic Labor. In *Capitalist Patriarchy and the Case for Socialist Feminism*, edited by Zilliah R. Eisenstein, pp. 173-89. New York: Monthly Review Press.

Garland T. Neal. 1972. The Better Half? The male in the Dual Profession Family. In *Toward a Sociology of Women*, edited by Constantina Safilios-Rothchild, pp. 199-215. Lexington, Massachusetts: Zerox College Publishing.

Gavron, Hannah. 1966. *The Captive Wife*. London: Routledge and Kegan Paul.

Glazer-Malbin, Nona. 1976. Housework. *Signs* 1 (4, Summer): 905-22.

Glazer, Nona. 1980. Everyone Needs Three Hands: Doing Unpaid and Paid Work. In *Women and Household Labor*, edited by Sarah Fenstermaker Berk, pp. 249-73. Beverly Hills, California: Sage.

_____. 1978. "Toward a theory of women's social class: Housewives and their work." Unpublished paper, December.

Glazer, Nona, Linda Majka, Joan Acker, and Christine Bose. 1979. The Homemaker, the Family and Employment. In *Women in the U.S. Labor Force*, edited by Ann Foote Cahn,

Hartmann, Heidi. 1981. The family on the locus of gender, clan and political struggle: the example of housework. *Signs* 6 (3, Spring): 366-94.

_____. 1976. Capitalism, patriarchy and job segregation by sex. *Signs* 18 (4 special supplement, Spring): 137-69.

Helfrich, Margaret. 1961. The generalized role of the executive's wife. *Marriage and Family Living*. 23-24: 383-87.

Kanter, Rosabeth Moss. 1977. *Men and Women of the Corporation*. New York: Basic Books.

Kessler-Harris, Alice. 1981. *Women Have Always Worked: A Historical Overview*. Old Westbury, New York: The Feminist Press.

Komarovsky, Mirra. 1967. *Blue-Collar Marriage*. New York: Random House.

_____. 1953. *Women in the Modern World: Their Education and their Dilemmas*. Boston: Little, Brown.

Kriesberg, Louis. 1970. *Mothers in Poverty: A Study of Fatherless Families*. Chicago: Aldine.

Laslett, Barbara. 1973. The family as a public and private institution: a historical perspective. *Journal of Marriage and the Family* 35 (August): 480-92.

Laslett, Peter. 1971. *The World We Have Lost: England before the Industrial Age*. 2nd ed. (no city): Charles Scribner's Sons.

Laslett, Peter, and Richard Wall (eds.). 1972. *Household and Family in Past Time*. Cambridge, England: Cambridge University Press.

Laws, Judith Long. 1979. *The Second Sex*. New York: Elsevier.

Le Masters, E. E. 1957. Parenthood as Crisis. *Marriage and Family Living*. 19: 352-55.

Lipman-Blumen, Jean, and Harold J. Leavitt. 1976. Vicarious achievement patterns in adulthood. *Counselling Psychologist* 6 (1): 26-32.

Lopata, Helena Znaniecki. 1980. The Chicago woman: A study of patterns of mobility and transportation. *Signs: Journal of Women in Culture and Society*. Special issue on *Women and the American City* 5 (3, Spring): 161-69.

_____. 1979. *Women as Widows: Support Systems*. New York: Elsevier.

_____. 1973. The effect of schooling on social contacts of urban women. *American Journal of Sociology* 79 (3, November): 604-19.

_____. 1971. *Occupation: Housewife*. New York: Oxford University Press.

_____. 1966. The life cycle of the social role of housewife. *Sociology and Social Research* 51 (1, October).

_____. 1962. "The dysfunctional effects of social science knowledge." Paper given at the meetings of the American Sociological Association, Washington, D.C.

Lopata, Helena Z., Debra Barnewolt, and Kathleen Norr. 1980. Spouses Contributions to Each Other's Roles. In *Dual Career Couples*, edited by Fran Pepitone-Rockwell, pp. 111-41. Beverly Hills, California: Sage.

Mack, Raymond. 1956. Occupational determinateness: A problem and hypothese in role theory. *Social Forces* 35 (October 1).

Mainardi, Pat. 1970. The Politics of Housework. In *Sisterhood is Powerful*, edited by Robin Morgan. Pp. 447-454. New York: Vintage Books.

Malos, Ellen, (ed.). 1980. *The Politics of Housework*. London: Allison and Busby.

Margolis, Diana Rothbard. 1979. *The Managers: Corporate Life in America*. New York: William Morrow.

McDonald, Gerald W. 1980. Family Power: The assessment of a decade of theory and research, 1970-79. *Journal of Marriage and the Family*. 42 (November, 4): 841-54.

Milkman, Ruth. 1979. Women's Work and the Economic Crisis: Some Lessons From the Great Depression. In *A Heritage of her Own: Toward a New Social History of American Women*, edited by Nancy F. Cott and Elizabeth H. Pleck, pp. 507-41. New York: Simon and Schuster: A Touchstone Book.

Mortimer, Jeylan, Richard Hall, and Robert Hill. 1978. Husbands' occupational attitudes as constraints on wives' employment. *Sociology of Work and Occupations* 5 (3, August): 285-313.

Nelson, Linda. 1980. Household Time: A Cross-cultural Example. In *Women and Household Labor*, edited by S. F. Berk, pp. 169-90. Yearbooks in Women's Policy Studies 5. Beverly Hills, California: Sage.

Newsweek. 1963. "Convention wives—help or hindrance." May 13: 82-83.

Newsweek. 1957. "Sizing up executives' wives." May 13: 93-95.

Nilson, Linda Burzotta. 1978. The social standing of a housewife. *Journal of Marriage and the Family* 40 (August): 541-48.

Oakley, Ann. 1974a. *Women's Work: A History of the Housewife*. New York: Pantheon Books.

_____. 1974b. *The Sociology of Housework*. Bath, England: Pitman Press.

O'Kelly, Charlotte G. 1980. *Women and Men in Society*. New York: D. Van Nostrand.

Olds, Sally Wendkos. 1977. "Is His Money Your Money Too?" *Redbook* Magazine 120 (September): 164-69.

Papanek, Hanna. 1979. Family status production: The 'work' and 'non-work' of women. *Signs* 4 (4, Summer): 775-81.

_____. 1973. Men, women and work: Reflections on the two-person career. *American Journal of Sociology* 78 (4): 852-72.

Parsons, Talcott. 1943/1964. The Kinship System in the Contemporary United States. In *Essays in Sociological Theory*, pp. 194-95. New York: The Free Press of Glencoe, rev. paperback ed.

Pepitone-Rockwell, Fran, (ed.). 1980. *Dual Career Couples*. Beverly Hills, California: Sage.

Pleck, Joseph. 1983. Husbands' paid work and family roles: current research issues. In *Research in the Interweave of Social Roles: Jobs and Families*, edited by Helena Z. Lopata and Joseph Pleck, pp. 251-333. Greenwich, Connecticut: JAI Press.

Poloma, M. M. 1972. Role Conflict and the Married Professional Woman. In *Toward a Sociology of Women*, edited by C. Safilios-Rothschild, pp. 187-98. Lexington, Massachusetts: Xerox College Publishing.

Poloma, Margaret and Neil Garland. 1970. "The myth of the egalitarian family: Familial roles and the professionally employed wife." Paper presented at the 65th annual meeting of the ASA (September).

Rainwater, Lee, Richard Coleman, and Gerald Handel. 1959. *Workingman's Wife.* New York: Oceana.

Rapoport, Rhona, and Robert N. Rapoport. 1980. Balancing Work, Family and Leisure: A Triple Helix Model. In *Work, Family and the Career*, edited by C. Brooklyn Derr, pp. 318-28. New York: Praeger.

————. 1976a. *Dual Career Families: New Integrations of Work and Family.* New York: Harper Colophon Books.

————. 1976b. *Dual Career Families Re-examined.* New York: Harper Colophon Books.

Riesman, David, Nathan Glazer, and Reuel Denney. 1950. *The Lonely Crowd.* New Haven: Yale University Press (also in Doubleday Anchor Books in 1956).

Robinson, John P. 1980. Housework Technology and Household Work. In *Women and Household Labor*, edited by Sarah Fenstermaker Berk. pp. 53-68. Beverly Hills, California: Sage.

Rosaldo, Michelle Zimbalist, and Louise Lamphere (eds.). 1974. *Women, Culture and Society.* Stanford, California: Stanford University Press.

Ross, H. L., and I. V. Sawhill. 1975. *Time of Transition: The Growth of Families Headed by Women.* Washington, D.C.: The Urban Institute.

Rossi, Alice. 1968. Transition to parenthood. *Journal of Marriage and the Family.* 30 (Feb.): 26-39.

Rothman, Sheila M. 1978. *Woman's Proper Place: A History of Changing Ideals and Practices.* New York: Basic Books.

Rubin, Lillian Breslow. 1976. *Worlds of Pain: Life in the Working Class Family.* New York: Basic Books.

Ryan, Mary P. 1979. *Womanhood in America: From Colonial Times to the Present.* New York: New Viewpoints, 2nd edition.

Seccombe, Wally. 1973. The housewife and her labour under capitalism. *New Left Review* 83 (Jan.-Feb.).

Seidenberg, Robert. 1973. *Corporate Wives—Corporate Casualties?* New York: American Management Association.

Smith, Dorothy. 1977. Women, The Family and Corporate Capitalism. In *Women in Canada*, edited by Marylee Stephenson, pp. 14-48. Don Mills, Ontario: General Publishing.

Social Research, Inc. 1973. *Working Class Women in a Changing World.* May: Study No. 287/07. Chicago, Illinois.

Sokoloff, Natalie J. 1980. *Between Money and Love: The Dialectics of Women's Home and Market Work.* New York: Praeger.

Strasser, Susan. 1978. The business of housekeeping: The ideology of the household at the turn of the twentieth century. *Insurgent Sociologists*, No. 7 (2 & 3, Fall): 147-63.

Szalai, A. (ed.). 1972. In collaboration with P. E. Converse, P. Feldheim, E. K. Scheuch and P. J. Stone. *The Use of Time: Daily Activities of Urban and Suburban Populations in Twelve Countries.* The Hague: Mouton.

Tilly, Louise A., and Joan W. Scott. 1978. *Working Life of Women in the Seventeenth Century*. New York: Holt, Rinehart and Winston.

Toffler, Alvin. 1981. *The Third Wave*. New York: Bantam Books.

Vandervelde, Maryanne. 1979. *The Changing Life of the Corporate Wife*. New York: Mecox.

Vanek, Joann. 1979. Time Spent in Housework. In *A Heritage of Her Own*, edited by Nancy F. Cott and Elizabeth H. Pleck. pp. 499-506. New York: Simon and Schuster: A Touchstone Book.

_____. 1978. Housewives as Workers. In *Women Working: Theories and Facts in Perspective*, edited by Ann Stromberg and Shirley Harkess, pp. 392-414. Palo Alto, California: Mayfield.

Veblen, Thorstein. 1899/1934. *The Theory of the Leisure Classes*. New York: Modern Library.

Vickery, Clair. 1979. Women's Economic Contribution to the Family. In *The Subtle Revolution: Women at Work*, edited by Ralph E. Smith, pp. 159-200. Washington, D.C.: The Urban Institute.

Walker, Kathryn E. 1969. Time spent in household work by homemakers. *Family Economic Review*, 3: 5-6.

Walker, Kathryn E., and Margaret E. Woods. 1976. *Time Use: A Measure of Household Production of Family Goods and Services*. Washington, D.C.: American Home Economics Association.

Weiss, Robert S. 1973. *Loneliness: The Experience of Emotional and Social Isolation*. Cambridge, Massachusetts: The MIT Press.

Weinbaum, Batya, and Amy Bridges. 1979. The Other Side of the Paycheck: Monopoly Capital and the Structure of Consumption. In *Capitalist Patriarchy and the Case for Socialist Feminism*, edited by Zilliah R. Eisenstein, pp. 190-205. New York: Monthly Review Press.

Welter, Barbara. 1966. The cult of true womanhood: 1820-1869. *American Quarterly* 18 (Summer): 151-60.

Whyte, William H. Jr. 1956. *The Organization Man*. New York: Simon and Schuster.

Whyte, William H. 1952/1971. The Wife Problem. In *The Other Half: Roads to Women's Equality*, edited by Cynthia Fuchs Epstein and William J. Goode. pp. 79-86. Englewood Cliffs, New Jersey: Prentice-Hall.

Wittner, Judith. "Non-market labor segmentalization: children and household work." Unpublished manuscript.

_____. 1983. Private conversation.

Wylie, Philip. 1955. *Generation of Vipers*. New York: Holt, Rinehart and Winston.

8

MANAGERS, PROPRIETORS, AND OFFICIALS

The Dictionary of Occupational Titles (U.S. Department of Labor, 1965) defines "manager" and then lists 257 different kinds of positions identified in this occupational category.

> A term applied to employees who direct supervisory personnel to attain operational goals of an organization or department as established by management. Classifications are made according to type of work performed or department managed as MANAGER, ADVERTISING: MANAGER, PERSONNEL I (profess. and kin.); or according to type of establishment as MANAGER financial institution (banking; finan. inst.) MANAGER, HOTEL (hotel & rest.) (*DOT*, 1965: 443)

In addition, managers manage "the affairs of athletes," or athletic teams, entertainers, public figures, and buildings. In fact, the term is used loosely, often as a means of separating wage workers from salaried employees, contributing to the cultural emphasis on the gulf between blue-collar or white-collar worlds. Management jobs in large organizations, however, differ considerably from those involving the running of a small store or the supervision of workers on a plant floor, and clothing is not always the distinguishing symbol.

MANAGEMENT: THE LITERATURE

Mills (1956), Weber (1946), Kanter (1977), and many other social scientists have been fascinated by the development of "management" as a major division of organizational structure with the increase in size and complexity of economic systems. Mills (1951) analyzed the changes in *White Collar* work from that of the "ma and pa" store or one person entrepreneurship to the creation of large conglomerates and corporations. Kantor (1977: 15) explains that:

> Nearly 20 percent of the total nonagricultural employed labor force works for local, state, or federal government. Another 30 percent are employed by business enterprises with more than 500 people on the payroll . . . Over 12 million Americans work in firms that employ over 10,000 people.

On the other hand, Danco (1975: 11-12) points out that although there are "over a million corporations in the United States, only 50,000 employ more than 100 people and over 95 percent of business units are privately held, usually family owned."

> Despite public opinion to the contrary, the United States is still mostly a nation of first-generation businesses. The founder is generally still alive, still the owner and probably working (Danco, 1975: 14).

Management as an occupational category includes many people who do not manage men and women directly but provide services or resources which make possible the production and distribution of products and the provision of services.

Businesses with complex management staffs also vary considerably. Lyle and Ross (1973: 79) differentiate between "central firms" and "periphery firms" in relation to the primary and secondary or periphery industrial divisions. They also explain that:

> In both large and small firms, however, management may be stratified both vertically and horizontally. When layered vertically within a firm's organizational hierarchy, management personnel fall into line, staff, and senior levels.

Senior level personnel are called "executives." A vast literature has grown concerning paths of ascent, style of leadership, characteristics and life-styles of such persons. Fascination with executives is reflected in *The Executive Life*, written by the editors of *Fortune* magazine, which originally ran as a series of articles in the periodical and was then published in 1956, or in Mitchell's (1965) *The Business Executive in a Changing World*. Frequent studies of the heads of *Fortune's* 500 largest industrial corporations (Mitchell, 1965: 17) are reported in the *Harvard Business Review* or Chicago's *Crain*.

Hall (1975: 139) refers to Barner's outline of the main functions of the executive as:

The first is the maintenance of communications within the organization, which involves the establishment of positions to form a communication system and the filling of these positions . . .

The second major function of the executive is the securing of essential services from individuals which involves bringing people into cooperative relationships . . . and eliciting the required services. . . .

The third executive function is the formulation and definition of the purposes, objectives, or goals of the organization.

Middle management includes people who:

. . . manage managers, supervisors or professional and technical people and are not vice-presidents of functional or staff areas or general managers (that is they have no profit and loss responsibilities), [they are] responsible for the following activities: . . . Interpretation and implementation of organization policies and goals. Middle managers interpret and translate the intentions of the top executives in terms of specific activities within their respective areas. (also includes) Management of subfunctional and staff specialties. Basically they are specialists in their functional areas and manage a portion of the total function. For example, in a manufacturing operation they would be the managers of production, methods, and quality control. They are expected to provide an area of expertise through their own knowledge and performance and through the persons they manage (Kay, 1974: 106-07).

Most books dealing with managers generally focus either on people in the middle rungs or those aspiring for such positions. Starting with Whyte's (1956) *The Organization Man* and running through Margolin's (1974) "What Do Bosses Do?", McGregor's (1967) *The Professional Manager*, or Margolis's (1979) *The Managers: Corporate Life in America*, or Kantor's (1977) *Men and Women of the Corporation*, we can get a pretty good view of the ideal typical structure within which managers operate.

Management is located not only in central headquarters but also in all branches associated with the corporation or smaller business firms. For example, one of our respondents is a regional manager, defined by the *Dictionary of Occupational Titles* (1965: 448) as a person who:

Directs major policies and programs to coordinate marketing, maintenance, personnel and labor relations, legal negotiations and safety programs for regional division of the (in this case) transportation system.

The occupational category under discussion also contains officials and proprietors, classifications that are so broad that the *Dictionary of Occupational Titles* does not even list them. Ritzer (1977: 199) explained that:

While managers operate in profit-making organizations, officials perform essentially the same functions in such nonprofit-making organizations as hospitals, labor unions, and the government.

In all, the broad occupational category of "managers, officials, and proprietors" encompasses an enormous conglomerate of positions and social roles. Complex corporations, family held businesses, retail establishments, offices, divisions of universities or hospitals, and governmental agencies all need a variety of managers. Factors such as function, size, height of the managerial core, volume of interaction, goods and money exchange, the location of the organization, as well as the location of the job within the system all influence the social circle and the total role of the manager.

WOMEN IN MANAGEMENT AND ENTREPRENEURSHIP

There is a rapidly growing literature on women in management, mainly in complex organizations. The explosion started about the time the United States government added sex to its 1965 Title VII of the Civil Rights Act (Bowman et. al., 1965; Schwartz, 1971), and established the Equal Employment Opportunity Commission. The Act was amended in 1972 by the Equal Employment Opportunity Act (Terborg, 1977). The mass media has repeatedly drawn attention to women who have moved up dramatically or to changes in distribution of women in these positions. *Newsweek*'s stories were reflecting contemporary culture even before then, as exemplified by such features as "Spotlight on Business: the Ladies are Getting Ahead" (September 22, 1958: 93), "Still More Room at the Top" (April 29, 1974: 79), and "Women and the Executive Suite" (September 14, 1981: 65). The topics upon which the literature on women in management focus include the numbers and their distribution, barriers, problems on the job, and techniques for success.

Numbers and Distributions

The number of women in management positions, especially those earning a certain level of salary, and their location in industry have been of great interest in recent years:

In 1971, 1,493,000 women 16 years of age and over were employed as nonfarm managers, officials and proprietors; 1,073,000 of these were salaried managers . . . This means that only five percent of all women workers were in managerial positions and less than four percent were salaried managerial workers. Although women accounted for 38 percent of all workers, we find that they were only 17 percent of all managerial workers [men and women] and only 16 percent of salaried managers (U.S. Department of Labor, 1972: 1).

Women now constitute 22 percent of all managers and administrators in the United States, an increase from 14 percent in 1947 . . . In the mid-1960s, only one percent of managerial trainees were female; now 15 percent beginning trainees are . . . Harvard MBA program did not admit women until 1963 (Brown, 1979: 267-69).

The differences in the figures quoted above are due not only to the years involved but also possibly to the inclusion of a broader category of workers by Brown (1979). The figures generally hovered around 22-23 percent for 1978.

The 1979 Employment and Training Report of the President shows that the percentage of women managers and administrators was 15.9 percent in 1970, 18.5 percent in 1974, and 23.1 percent in 1978 (Powell, 1980: 22).

Bowman et al. (1965: 22) summarized the changes in number of women in management in an article in the *Harvard Business Review* as follows:

In essence, then, the absolute number of women executives has increased dramatically but their proportion to male executives in the workforce has not changed dramatically.

In actuality, they are not talking of women executives but women in management in general.

One of the sub-subjects concerning women in management is their location. Since they have only recently moved into such positions and, as noted above, had not even been allowed into the Masters of Business Administration programs such as that at Harvard University until very recently, it is not surprising that they are located at the entry, or lowest level of the structure. According to Harlan and Weiss (1980b), they "comprise 15 percent of entry level managers, only five percent of middle, and one percent of top levels" (see also Crawford, 1977).

The number of women who are corporate officers of the 1,300 largest U.S. companies, judged too tiny to count just five years ago—stands at 477 . . . and the number of women directors of those companies now exceeds 399 . . . Twenty-six percent of all today's M.B.A. hopefuls are female—compared with three and one-half percent ten years ago and the proportion is sometimes higher at the most prestigious schools. But the revolution in the executive suite has hardly begun. Only six percent of all working women qualify as managers of any sort (*News-week*, September 14, 1981: 65).

The level as well as the functional division of business appears to be influenced by the gender identity of the person. Powell (1980: 23) refers to the "velvet ghetto" when writing about women's careers in management:

> . . . velvet ghettos—those areas which women have typically been re-garded as best suited for—namely personnel and public relations and, more recently, consumer affairs and corporate social responsibility . . . (these) tend to be staff functions, peripheral to the more established and powerful line functions of sales, finance and production . . .

In addition, women are found mainly in small businesses and in trade, rather than in the higher paying manufacturing industries. Bowman et al. (1965), reported in a classic article entitled "Are Women Executives People?" that 50 percent of the females in management were located in companies with less than 50 employees (see also Larwood and Wood, 1978).

Barriers to the Movement of Women Into and Up in Management

Three types of barriers are seen as impeding the movement of women into management and into its upper layers, in spite of govern-mental regulations: structural, male attitudinal, and the characteristics of the women themselves. Epstein (1970; 1975), Lipman-Blumen (1976) and many others have pointed out that the division of the world into two spheres accomplished in the last century resulted in conversion of business and professional activities into male bastions. Psychologist Ellman (1973: 122-23) expresses the dominant philos-ophy of the business sphere:

> This author believes that women will never gain full acceptance in the labor market, nor will they qualify completely for equal pay. Mar-ried or single, their primary role of motherhood must always remain more dominant than the requirements of a job.

There is more to the system than just biased attitudes toward women in any positions other than the traditional secretarial ones. The whole system, its entry lines, scheduling demands, social relations, and pro-cedures for getting the job done are based on the male model of working. The fact that the Harvard Masters of Business Administra-tion program did not admit women until 1963 is but one evidence of of the tightness of the system, as are all the racist policies that kept black men out of white establishments until very recently. The business sub-culture is learned early and few women were directed in the past to business schools or even relevant subjects. The gap between clerical and managerial positions has been enormous, office manager or executive secretary being the end of that line. The male world has accepted tokens, but several studies have indicated that these women must adjust to the system, not vice versa (Kantor, 1977; Schwartz, 1971).

Another structural barrier for the involvement of women in management is the scheduling of work and careers. Business has traditionally demanded extensive commitment of time and energy on the part of people in its more rewarding strata. The job and the career have allegedly top priority, not to be interfered with by involvements in other roles. The two-person career, of which we spoke in the prior chapter, grew out of this culturally approved set of expectations of "greedy" business and the professions (Coser, 1974). Several participants in Columbia University's Conference on Women's Challenge to Management in 1971, whose papers have been published in a book, rather cutely named by the editors Ginzberg and Yohalem (1973) *Corporate Lib: Women's Challenge to Management*, were strongly critical of the rigidity of the business community. Some experimentation with flexible hours and work schedules has occurred throughout the United States since then. Unfortunately, the government's "flextime" participation was stopped by the recent administration's policy. It is unlikely that management of large corporations is going to develop tolerance for nontraditional scheduling of work during the day, the week, the year, or the life course. The insistence that people prepare for entrance through formal schooling, enter at low levels, and then commit themselves through long hours of work and a willingness to be moved geographically forces an either-or dilemma on women given the current organization of family life. The demands traditionally met by men can usually be met only by non married women, those who do not enter that relation or motherhood, or those who have decreased family demands because of widowhood, of voluntary separation from the husband, and of offspring reaching independence. This has been the pattern in the past (see Bird, 1976). A few men are now refusing to meet some of business's demands and the pressure brought by women's groups and the mass media may loosen the system in the future.

Male Attitudes

Although much of the rigidity of the business community in trying to preserve its traditional male system is due to clinging to familiar structures which decrease uncertainty (Kantor, 1977; Tausky, 1978), a large part is due to sex bias. Many men simply do not want women in management, competing, and even—perhaps—surpassing them (Bass, et al. 1971). Male attitudes toward the "unsuitability" of women in management are strong and frequently reported (Ferber et al., 1979; Garland and Price, 1977). We shall present only two surveys of managers in the literature.

One of these studies was conducted by Ellman (1973), whom we quoted earlier. A few more quotes help indicate the manner in which his attitudes reflect those of many men in the business community.

> Women are prone to lie about their age (36).
> In this chapter we have learned that although psychological testing is an accepted tool in business, it is a personnel technique which is generally resisted by women. Perhaps this resistance stems from woman's desire to compete on the basis of her femininity rather than any measurable qualities of intellect (56-7).
> Finally, everyone knows that women love parties and social events, particularly if they are given the opportunity to participate in the planning and production of such activities (91).

Ellman (1973: 102) mailed a questionnaire to "over 500 leading personnel executives" asking their opinions of women workers and received 130 answers (26 percent response), 30 from women executives. According to the respondents, what women want most from their jobs includes: pleasant working surroundings (79 percent), recognition for work well done (75 percent), pleasant people to work with (58 percent), fair and equal treatment (68 percent), desirable job location (58 percent), highest wages (47 percent), and chance to advance (35 percent) (Ellman, 1963: 106). One assumes that personnel directors who do not think that women are more interested in pay and a chance to advance than in pleasant working conditions are not likely to hire and promote women to important positions if given a chance.

The respondents were also asked a series of questions reflecting a strong bias against women in management:

Summary: How the Personnel Executives Answered the
Survey Questions

	Percent Responding		
Statement	Yes	No	Undecided
Do you believe there is a need for using different techniques in training women than men?	56	42	2
Are women generally more concerned with details than men?	72	25	2
Do women tend to take corrections more personally than men?	74	25	1
Is there a higher rate of absenteeism among women than among men in your company?	78	21	1
Do women tend to form cliques more than men?	78	20	2
Do men generally object to having a woman supervisor?	81	11	8
Do you feel that many women could advance to more responsible jobs but they do not want the added responsibility?	65	31	4
Do women have more company spirit than men?	18	75	7

Source: Edgar S. Ellman, *Managing Women in Business*. Waterford, Conn.: National Sales Development Institute Complete Management Library, Vol. XIII, 1973: 106-09. Reprinted with permission.

Eleanor Schwartz (1971) also surveyed business executives, sending questionnaires to 300 men in large corporations selected from the *Fortune* directory, 300 in small corporations, and 300 women managers from lists in trade directories and *Who's Who in American Women*. Her questions focused on generalizations about the effectiveness of women in management:

	Percent Answering Yes		
	Firms		
Statement	Large	Small	Women
Women are too emotional in working with people	58	16	40

Percent Answering Yes

Statement	Firms		
	Large	Small	Women
Women have less motivation than men	78	69	36
Women are not as capable in management positions	38	35	21
Women cannot make precise, clear decisions	23	30	12
Women cannot effectively hire subordinates	45	58	20
Women do not provide as much return for investment in educational and training dollars, employment patterns not stable	90	79	32
Women prefer not to work for women, they are competitive and jealous of other women, so prefer men supervisors	65	54	32
Men prefer not to work for women—they use feminine wiles on one hand and are aggressive and emasculating on the other hand	79	74	37
Women are too personal in giving and receiving criticism	82	76	28
Women are not as apt to become as totally committed to management as men	70	68	29
Men have careers, women have only jobs	72	70	36

Source: Eleanor Brantley Schwartz, *The Sex Barrier in Business*. Atlanta, Georgia: The Georgia State University, 1971, pp. 80-82. Reprinted with permission.

These two surveys certainly point to the presence of strong stereotypes about women on the part of the personnel directors and men in management as late as the 1970s. Even some of the women in business surveyed by Schwartz (1971) held some of the same images of members of their gender in management. The literature is full of titles such as "Exploding Some Myths About Women Managers" (Reif, Newstrom and Monczka, 1978), "Women as Managers—Stereotypes and Realities" (Dipboye, 1978), *Racism and Sexism in Corporate Life* (Fernandez, 1981). Even articles which claim to be helping women prepare for management positions perpetuate the idea that women are basically passive and lack self-confidence, leading them to avoid risk-taking. The interesting thing is that even male owners of small businesses, which form over 95 percent of the corporate world, do not even consider, for the most part, preparing their daughters to take over the business, concentrating only on sons or sons-in-law (L. Danco, 1975; K. Danco, 1981).

Women's Characteristics

This leads us to the third category of writings about women and business management, that of blaming the woman herself for her absence from top positions. This literature focuses on alleged personality characteristics or on the unwillingness of women to meet the demands of corporate life. Plenginger and Small, writing in 1981 in *Overcoming Women's Career Obstacles*, state flatly that women refuse to transfer, assume sexual advances in interaction with male managers, and should not travel on the job. Reflecting the male mentality they state that:

> The younger woman is less apt [than the young man] to have a car and may possibly lack a driver's license, but she will usually have more personal belongings, including clothing, personal care items, heirlooms, and trousseaus.

Thus, the young women would have difficulty traveling on the job. Too many heirlooms.

The reported unwillingness of women to take jobs with added responsibility is frequently discussed in the literature. Vwynon and Blackburn (1972: 88) asked workers in a factory why they did not take the opportunity to move into management.

> When respondents were asked to explain why they hadn't applied to be supervisors, about half of the men and over 80% of the women gave answers indicating that they didn't want the job.

The authors found that women and men gave different reasons for their unwillingness to move up the ladder, women not wishing to lose friends or take on additional responsibility.

Hennig and Jardim (1977a) develop in detail the theme that American men and women are socialized so differently concerning their involvement in the world of work outside of the home that they approach management jobs in very diverse ways at a disadvantage to the women. Men are accustomed to teamwork and lateral relations through sports, depersonalizing interaction rather than focusing on the relation itself. They learn early that they will have to support at least themselves and focus on careers as a series of jobs in "a path leading upward":

> Women see a career as personal growth, as self-fulfillment, as satisfaction, as making a contribution to others, as doing what one wants to do . . . Women separate the two [job and career] issues completely: a job is in the here and *now* and a career is an intensely personal goal

which the individual alone can judge whether she has achieved (Hennig and Jardim, 1977a: 14-15).

Harlan and Weiss (1980b: 196) found that women aspired to lower levels of organizational achievement than men, Fretz and Hayman (1973) that they are unwilling to relocate for the job, and both Schein (1977) and Lannon (1977) conclude that the characteristics regarded as typically feminine are out of place in management, which is masculine. Bringing in women would change the system, because they are more concerned with caring while men are competitive, aggressive, firm, rational, vigorous, and so forth (Lannon, 1977; Schein, 1977). Horner's (1972) fear of success thesis, stating that women fear that success would make them unpopular with men and prevent marriage and "fulfillment as a woman," certainly gained popularity within a very short period of time, in a "blaming the victim" style. *Women in Management*, edited by Gerrard and Williams (1976), contains three articles on this subject.

There are books and articles, too numerous to mention, advising women how to manage their careers, including the widely read *Games Mother Never Taught You: Corporate Gamesmanship for Women*, by Harragan (1977). Also relevant is Crouch's (1977) "Going Up: New Rules for Women on the Job" in *Redbook* magazine. Finally, there are many more or less scientific studies of women who "have made it," that is, who are successful (Adams, 1979; Williams, 1976). Harlan and Weiss (1980b: 45) point out that the tendency to downgrade women's achievements is partly due to the fact that "women's experiences have been compared to a 'successful male myth' rather than to men's actual experience." They themselves studied both men and women involved in career advancement in management, showing lines of control which lead to power in the system. Hennig and Jardim (1977b) selected management styles that have led to success, regardless of sex, and Fenn (1978; 1980) has two books on women executives. Donnell and Hall (1980), who studied over 18,000 managers over the years, found no significant difference in their styles of managing once they reached that level of achievement.

Chicago Area Managers

Women in the Chicago area sample who were managers in their last job tended to remain in this position, rather than withdrawing to the role of full-time homemaker. They reached this job, or that of proprietor or official after having been first in a clerical job. This holds true if their work is in construction or manufacturing industries, or in the professional/administrative area. The largest number of our managers work in trade establishments, mainly in retail stores. The industry makes a difference in the management positions of the women. However, few are involved in "management" sectors of large corporations, unless they run the offices. Thus, the literature dealing with the movement of women into that type of management focuses on an elite not likely to be found in the 1978 sample of Chicago area women. That does not mean that they are totally absent, since some hold very nontraditional supervisory positions, especially in manufacturing, construction, and transportation. Managers or entrepreneurs in retail trade tend to have the most discontinuous employment careers, but they are the most educated of the managers, as far as formal schooling rather than job training is concerned. Those in construction and manufacturing see their job as highly complex while those in trade are the most likely to score theirs as low on all dimensions of complexity. Most of the women experienced upward mobility in the jobs they have held and they like the independence of the present position. They use their own judgement of their role performance as a reference much more often than do women in the other occupational categories. Thus, they present an image of new movement toward jobs they enjoy and which are better than prior ones.

SUMMARY AND CONCLUSIONS

The expansion of the groups which operate to produce goods and services in the various industries of a large and complex society requires various levels of managerial staff. These may be concentrated within a central headquarters in a single unit firm, or spread out in various locations. Thus managers vary in what they manage, whether it is a single unit or a group of people and activities. Entrepreneurs who start their own business can continue to also manage it, and similar roles are contained in even voluntary organizations. Managers also differ by the size of the social circle within which they operate. The business world has been very male-dominated, with specific exceptions, both in numbers and in sub-culture. For that reason, it has been very difficult for women to move from their traditional role of clerical worker into that of manager of any but women of that office or that store. However, a recent movement of young women into colleges of business administration, as well as the legislative acts forbidding discrimination, have opened some of the doors of management, if rarely of the executive suite. Most of the literature dealing with women in management points to their traditional absence and gradual movement into, if not up, the ladder. Social scientists and other observers of the business and administrative worlds have studied the few women who have become successful in it. Others provide advice as to the rules of the game, as the business world at least, is visualized. An interesting new but scarcely large movement is the one mentioned above, of women starting or taking over businesses. Traditionally, family-owned establishments have been started by male "founders" and passed on to sons or sons-in-law, wives entering only as widows and daughters taking control as extreme exceptions. As the culture changes, women gaining greater acceptance in most areas outside of the home, we can expect more men to "trust" women into inheritance of management or as "protegees" and even partners.

REFERENCES

Adams, Jane. 1979. *Women on Top: Success Patterns and Personal Growth.* New York: Hawthorn Books.

Bass, Bernard M., Judith Krusell, and Ralph Alexander. 1971. Male Managers' Attitudes Toward Working Women. In *Women in the Professions: What's All the Fuss About*, edited by Linda S. Fidell and John DeLamater, pp. 63-78. Beverly Hills, California: Sage.

Bird, Caroline. 1976. *Enterprising Women.* New York: New American Library. A Mentor Book.

Bowman, Gerda W., N. Bernice Worthy, and Stephen A. Greyser. 1965. Are women executives people? *Harvard Business Review* 43 (July-August): 14-28.

Brown, Linda Keller. 1979. Women and business management. *Signs: Journal of Women in Culture and Society* 5 (2, Winter): 266-88.

Collins, L. G. C. and Timothy B. Blodgett. 1981. Sexual harassment . . . some see it . . . some won't. *Harvard Business Review* 59 (March-April): 76-95.

Coser, Lewis A. 1974. *Greedy Institutions: Patterns of Undivided Commitment.* New York: The Free Press.

Crawford, Jackelyn S. 1977. *Women in Middle Management.* Ridgewood, New Jersey: Forkner.

Crouch, Dorothy R. 1977. "Going up: New rules for women on the job." *Redbook* 102 (August): 192-97.

Danco, Katy. 1981. *From the Other Side of the Bed: A Woman Looks at Life in the Family Business.* Cleveland, Ohio: The Center for Family Business.

Danco, Leon. 1975. *Beyond Survival: A Business Owner's Guide for Success.* Reston, Virginia: Reston.

Dipboye, Robert L. 1978. Women as Managers—Stereotypes and Realities. In *Women in Management*, edited by Bette Ann Stead, pp. 2-18. Englewood Cliffs, New Jersey: Prentice Hall.

Donnell, Susan M., and Jay Hall. 1980. Men and women as managers: A significant case of no significant difference. *Organizational Dynamics* (Spring):
60-76.

Ellman, Edgar S. 1973. *Managing Women in Business.* Waterford, Connecticut:
Prentice Hall.

Epstein, Cynthia Fuchs. 1975. Institutional Barriers: What Keeps Women Out of
the Executive Suite. In *Bringing Women into Management,* edited by Francine E. Gordon and Myra H. Strober, pp. 2-21. New York: McGraw-Hill.

————. 1970. *Woman's Place: Options and Limits in Professional Careers.*
Berkeley, California, University of California Press.

Fenn, Margaret. 1980. *In the Spotlight: Women Executives in a Changing Environment.* Englewood Cliffs, New Jersey: Prentice Hall.

Ferber, Marianne, Joan Huber, and Glenna Spitze. 1979. Preference for men as
bosses and professionals. *Social Forces* (December): 466-76.

Fernandez, John P. 1981. *Racism and Sexism in Corporate Life.* Lexington,
Massachusetts: Lexington Books.

Fortune. 1956. *The Executive Life.* New York: Fortune.

Fretz, C. F., and Joanne Hayman. 1973. Progress for women—men are still more
equal. *Harvard Business Review* 51 (Sept.-Oct.): 133-42.

Garland, Howard, and Kenneth H. Price. 1977. Attitudes toward women in management and attributions for their success and failure in a managerial position. *Journal of Applied Psychology* 62, No. 1: 29-33.

Gerrard, Meg, June Oliver, and Martha Williams (eds.). 1976. *Women in Management. Proceedings of the Conference Women and Men—Colleagues in Management.* Austin, Texas: The University of Texas at Austin.

Ginzberg, Eli, and Alice M. Yohalem. 1973. The New Reality. In *Corporate Lib:
Women's Challenge to Management,* edited by Eli Ginzberg and Alice M.
Yohalem, pp. 1-8. Baltimore, Maryland: Johns Hopkins Press.

Goode, William. 1973. Family Life of the Successful Woman. In *Corporate Lib:
Women's Challenge to Management,* edited by Eli Ginzberg and Alice M.
Yohalem, pp. 97-117. Baltimore: John's Hopkins Press.

Hall, Richard. 1975. *Occupations and Social Structure.* Englewood Cliffs, New
Jersey: Prentice-Hall.

Harlan, Anne, and Carol L. Weiss. 1980a. Career Opportunities for Women Managers. In *Work, Family and the Career: New Frontiers in Theory and Research,* edited by C. Brooklyn Derr, pp. 188-99. New York: Praeger.

————. 1980b. "Sex differences in factors affecting managerial career advancement." Wellesley College: Working Paper No. 56.

Harragan, Betty Lehan. 1977. *Games Mother Never Taught You: Corporate
Gamesmanship for Women.* New York: Warner Books.

Hennig, Margaret, and Anne Jardim. 1977a. *The Managerial Woman.* Garden City,
New York: Anchor Press/Doubleday.

————. 1977b. *Women and Management.* New York: Doubleday.

Horner, Matina S. 1972. Toward an understanding of achievement-related conflicts in women. *Journal of Social Issues* 28, No. 2. 157-79.

Jewell, Donald O. (ed.). 1977. *Women and Management: An Expanding Role*. Atlanta: Georgia State University.

Kanter, Rosabeth Moss. 1977. *Men and Women of the Corporation*. New York: Basic Books.

Kay, Emanuel. 1974. Middle Management. In *Work and the Quality of Life: Resource Papers for Work in America*, edited by James O'Toole, pp. 106-29. Cambridge, Massachusetts: The MIT Press.

Lannon, Judith M. 1977. Male vs. female values in management. *Management International Journal* 17: 9-12.

Larwood, Laurie, and Marion Wood. 1978. *Women in Management*. Lexington, Massachusetts: Lexington Books.

Lipman-Blumen, Jean. 1976. Toward a Homosocial Theory of Sex Roles: An Explanation of the Sex-segregation of Social Institutions. In *Women and the Workplace: The Implications of Occupational Segregation*, edited by Martha Blaxall and Barbara Reagan, pp. 15-31. Chicago: University of Chicago Press.

Lyle, Jerolyn R., and Jane L. Ross. 1973. *Women in Industry: Employment Patterns of Women in Corporate America*. Lexington, Massachusetts: Lexington Books.

Marglin, Stephen. 1974. What do bosses do? The origins of hierarchy in capitalist production. *Review of Radical Political Economies* 4: 60-112.

Margolis, Diane Rothbard. 1979. *The Managers: Corporate Life in America*. New York: William Morrow.

McGregor, Douglas. 1967. *The Professional Manager*, edited by Caroline McGregor and Warren G. Bennis. New York: McGraw-Hill.

Mills, C. Wright. 1956. *White Collar*. New York: Oxford University Press.

Mitchell, William N. 1965. *The Business Executive in a Changing World*. New York: American Management Association.

Newsweek. 1981. "Women and the Executive Suite." 98 (Sept. 24): 65-68.

Newsweek. 1974. "Still More Room at the Top." 83 (April 29): 74, 79-80.

Newsweek. 1958. "Spotlight on Business: The Ladies are Getting Ahead." 52 (Sept. 22): 93-96.

Olson, Jon and Jon Miller. 1983. Gender and Interaction in the Workplace. In *Research in the Interweave of Social Roles: Jobs and Families*, edited by Helena Z. Lopata and Joseph Pleck, pp. 35-58. Greenwich, Connecticut: JAI Press.

Pleninger, Andrew, and Elaine Small. 1981. *Overcoming Women's Career Obstacles*. New York: Vantage Press.

Powell, Gary N. 1980. *Career Development and the Woman Manager—a Social Power Perspective*. AMACOM (a division of American Management Association).

Reif, William E., John W. Newstrom, and Robert M. Monczka. 1978. Exploding Some Myths about Women Managers. In *Women in Management*, edited by Bette Ann Stead, pp. 11-24. Englewood Cliffs, New Jersey: Prentice Hall.

Ritzer, George. 1977. *Working: Conflict and Change*. Englewood Cliffs, New Jersey: Prentice Hall, 2nd ed.

Rosen, Benson, and Thomas H. Jerdee. 1974. Sex stereotyping in the executive suite. *Harvard Business Review* (March/April): 45-58.

Schein, Virginia. 1977. Think Manager–Think Male. In *Women and Management: An expanding Role*, edited by Donald O. Jewell, pp. 219-27. Atlanta: Georgia State University.

Schwartz, Eleanor Brantley. 1971. *The Sex Barrier in Business*. Atlanta: Georgia State University Press.

Tausky, Curt. 1978. *Work Organizations, Major Theoretical Perspectives*. Itasca, Illinois: F. E. Peacock, 2nd ed.

Terborg, James R. 1977. Women in management: A research review. *Journal of Applied Psychology* 62, No. 6: 647-64.

Terborg, James R., Lawrence H. Peters, Daniel R. Ilgen, and Frank Smith. 1977. Organizational and personal correlates of attitudes toward women as managers. *Academy of Management Journal* 20, No. 1: 89-100.

U.S. Department of Labor. 1972. *Women Managers*. Washington, D.C.: U.S. Government Printing Office (February).

U.S. Department of Labor. 1965. *Dictionary of Occupational Titles* Vol. II. *Occupational Classification*. Washington, D.C.: U.S. Government Printing Office, 3rd ed.

Vwynon, H. and R. M. Blackburn. 1972. *Perceptions of Work Variations within a Factory*. Cambridge, England: Cambridge University Press.

Weber, Max. 1946. *From Max Weber: Essays in Sociology*. (Translated by H. H. Gerth and C. S. Mills.) New York: Oxford University Press.

Whyte, William H., Jr. 1956. *The Organization Man*. New York: Simon and Schuster.

————. 1953. "The transients." *Fortune* (5 part series).

Williams, Martha. 1976. Women and Success in Organizations. In *Women in Management. Proceedings of the Conference Women and Men—Colleagues in Management*, edited by M. Gerrard, June Oliver and Martha Williams, pp. 52-59. Austin, Texas.

9

PROFESSIONALS, TECHNICIANS, AND RELATED WORKERS

Looking at the extremely complex structure of American occupations, one can but wonder about the history through which each passed before becoming the social role, or set of roles, which characterize it today. How did a set of functions get pulled together? How might the characteristics of the social person (who is to be the focus of the role) and of the segments of the social circle without which the job could not be performed be determined? Unfortunately, we do not know much of the history of the occupations existing in modern capitalistic societies. Even when we reach the professions that have been studied extensively—at least, those which are considered to be the top of the structure have been studied extensively—we still fail to understand the processes by which they developed. Why did some duties become the province of doctors, others of nurses? Health care, health maintenance, care during illness, and control of plagues and other contagious diseases are necessary and found as part of many social roles in societies. However, this care has been pulled into many different social roles and, as we saw when examining service jobs, old ones are being modified and new ones introduced. These are fitted, albeit with great difficulty, into the existing hierarchy of the medical field, recently, however, leaving the role of doctor on top (Starr, 1982). The process by which the role of doctor became forged out of other roles and a whole system of relations and ideologies built in and around it is fascinating, and we will deal with it to some degree in this chapter.

We are able to see some of the processes by which new occupations are created and fitted into the existing structure in the case of the astronaut. There is a growing literature documenting the stages by which the planners determined what the role should be and who would best fit its new requirements. An image of the "perfect" astronaut was created, the society was combed for people matching it most closely, and training as well as role playing were used to round out the persons selected. The astronauts, as well as the members of the circle, were carefully selected from other roles in conformity to the assumed needs of the system (see James Michener's *Space*, 1982 and Tom Wolfe's *The Right Stuff*, 1979, book and film). Women and minorities were not part of the initial sweep which drew future astronauts, mainly because the specialties that were sought had not included anyone but white males (Dolan, 1983). The role has changed over time so that knowledge specialties other than piloting aircraft have been brought in. It is interesting to note the response of American society to the announcement, and successful trip, of the first woman astronaut.

It is not in the province of this study to trace the histories of all the different jobs which fall into the professional, technical, and related spheres of the American occupational structure, even if we had such knowledge. We are studying jobs as currently defined by the U.S. Census and the U.S. Department of Labor, which are included in the categories so labeled. First, we will look at the literature dealing with the occupations labeled as technical and professional, then we will focus on those studies devoted to the presence, problems, and successes of women in those occupations. Throughout, much of this literature deals with changes in the situation, shifting from an attempt to explain sexual segregation in the professional and technical occupations to recommended entry points and appropriate behavior of "pioneers" or "tokens," and to the dramatic influx of women into training and actual involvement in such jobs.

PROFESSIONALIZATION

Sociologists have been fascinated by the professions. Hughes (1971b) explained in one of his delightful excursions on the world of work that he had to change the title of one of his courses, first introduced in 1939, to "Sociology of Work":

> In 1939, I began to teach a course on professions. People from various departments of the university and from many occupations came into

the course; many of them wanted to write about the efforts of their own occupation to have itself recognized as a profession. . .I soon changed the name of the course to the "Sociology of Work," both to overcome to some extent the constant preoccupation with upward mobility of occupations and also to include studies of a greater variety of occupations and problems (Hughes, 1971b: 418).

The fascination with the traditional professions—law, medicine, the clergy, science, and academia—and with occupations currently attempting to upgrade their stature and reach that of the professions, is without doubt partly due to their prestige. However, they are also easy to study because the very process of professionalization forced these occupations to specify the roles and the relations within them, as well as their relationships with other occupations, and to develop an ideology that would justify them. Few occupations of lesser societal license and mandate have been so self-conscious in their explanation of themselves. Habenstein (1970: 104) provides the most informal definition of the professional ideal type as well as the decreasing availability of such persons in modern society:

> Traditionally, the notion of independent skilled practitioners giving esoteric advice to the trusting client in the context of face-to-face relations probably came close to filling the bill. But the face-to-face relationship with the independent practitioner comprises increasingly less of the professing done these days, while the growth of the professions, as revealed by census and manpower reports, increases rapidly.

There are two ways in which sociologists tend to study the professions and related occupations: by taking the ideal typical image of the medical doctor or lawyer and showing the characteristics which distinguish these people from those in other occupations, or by tracing the process by which they got where they are now. Bledstein (1978), Larson (1977), Ritzer (1977), Vollmer and Mills (1966), among others, favor the latter approach. They have studied the process by which occupations gain varying degrees of the following set of characteristics:

1. A body of esoteric knowledge developed and transmitted by members of the profession to prospective members through a lengthy educational process
2. Licencing of new members by the state after they pass examinations, also controlled by the profession
3. A mandate to help solve important, even life and death problems of relatively helpless and ignorant patients or clients

4. Self control by members following a code of ethics and by peers in cases of alleged deviant behavior (Goode, 1956; Haberstein, 1970; Hall, 1975; Larson, 1977; Vollmer and Mills, 1966; Wilensky, 1964)

Members of a profession belong to a community, according to Goode (1956), not only because they are co-members of professional organizations in their field, but also because they share a culture and a sense of identity. Bucher and Strauss (1961), however, point out that a profession is segmented by specialty and social role. Davis and Moore (1945) attempted to explain the position of occupations in the hierarchical system which obviously exists in America, and elsewhere, by claiming it is part of the reward structure accrued because of the functional importance of that job to the society. However, recent analyses of the process of professionalization have stressed the importance of organization and power.

> I see professionalization as the process by which producers of special services sought to constitute and *control* a market for their expertise. . . . Professionalization is thus an attempt to translate one order of scarce resources—special knowledge and skills—into another—social and economic rewards (Larson, 1977: xvi-xvii).

All students of professionalization and the professions stress the importance of the development of specialized knowledge. The guilds obtained their control over markets through control over skill and entrance of newcomers, thus cutting out competition. The professions focused on education obtained in universities, appropriate to a "gentleman." Bledstein (1978) considers America of the nineteenth century to have been a breeding ground for the formation of professions because of the presence of an expanding middle class and the absence of a dampening traditional gentry, as in England and other Western European countries.

> And the professions as we know them today were the original achievement of Mid-Victorians who sought the highest form in which the middle class could pursue its primary goals of earning a good living, elevating both the moral and intellectual tone of society, and emulating the status of those above one on the social ladder. Americans after 1870, but beginning after 1840, committed themselves to a culture of professionalism which over the years has established the thoughts, habits and responses most modern Americans have taken for granted, a culture which has admirably serviced individuals who aspire to think very well of themselves (Bledstein, 1978: 80-1).

Although higher education, with the help of professional associations, was instrumental in enabling such fields as theology, law, medicine, dentistry, pharmacy, and veterinary medicine to strive for higher status in the society, the creation of a market required extensive effort. The associations started in America in 1864, with the formation of the American Ophthalmological Society; the years between 1870 and 1890 saw the establishment of an additional 200 or so societies (Bledstein, 1978: 86). According to Bledstein (1978: 102), one way the professions established a market and were able to demand and receive a liberal mandate to control their own roles was through the exploitation of "the weaknesses of Americans. . . fears of violent, sudden, catastrophic and meaningless forces."

Larson (1977: 14) attributes the creation of professional markets to shifts in the value systems in Europe and America to a market-oriented system, the tightening of membership, the establishment of a distinctive "commodity" of service by "producers" highly trained in their areas, and the standardization of the activity and the elimination of competing "products."

> Because of the pre-existing competition, this task demanded strong and quasimonopolistic protective devices. . .The proved institutional mechanisms for this negotiation [of cognitive exclusiveness] were the license, the qualifying examination, the diploma, and formal training in a common curriculum (Larson, 1977: 15).

Starr (1982) adds to the analysis of the process by which medicine acquired status to its acquisition of "cultural authority" or lay deference and dependence.

The professions, particularly law and medicine, did gain a strong mandate and license to practice, particularly in American society, as Hughes (1971a, 1971b, 1971c) repeatedly reminded his students and readers. However, recent changes have begun to undermine the power of the major professions. Knowledge monopolization is becoming increasingly difficult in modern society due to mass communication and the increased educational achievement by clients who demand greater explanation of services (Lopata, 1976). The revolt of the client has been documented in a variety of situations (Freidson, 1960; Haug and Sussman, 1968; Lopata, 1976). Burnham (1982) claims in his "American Medicine's Golden Age: What Happened to It?" that the public image of scientific medicine improved in the twentieth century until it reached a peak several years ago and has recently gone down in prestige and power. The *Wall Street Journal* (Wermiel, 1983) headlined the following story on the front page, "Negative Verdict: Lawyers' Public Image is Dreadful, Spurring Concern by Attorneys: Devious Tactics, High Fees, Big Damage Suits Hurt; But They Defend System." The alleged drop in the prestige and the routinization of many professional jobs lead Carter and Carter (1981) to title their examination of women in these jobs, "Women's Recent Progress in the Professions, or Women Get a Ticket to Ride after the Gravy Train has Left the Station." According to Starr (1982) the medical profession's success is actually undermining its influence in American society.

While the attention of the public and sociologists is being drawn to the failure of the traditional professions to maintain their status and code of ethics, other social scientists have focused on several aspects of professional life. This literature includes studies of relations with "semi-professions" and "marginal professions" in their attempt at "full" professional status (Etzioni, 1969; Ritzer, 1977); barriers to such movement (Wilensky, 1964); choice of professions and training (Bucher and Stelling, 1977; Helfich, 1975); and the effects of the process upon status attainment (Tinto, 1980); professional identity and work satisfaction (Haas and Shaffir, 1982; Walsh, 1982); control over one's role in view of technological change (Morrisey and Gillespie, 1975); competing encroachment (Child and Fulk, 1982); and client "atrocity stories" (Dingwall, 1977).

Wilensky (1964) outlines some of the barriers to "the professionalization of everyone," including organized competition when established professions become threatened in their autonomy, lack of a solid knowledge foundation, practical limits to role creation, the inability of most striving professions to gain control over their relations and even training, and the difficulties of establishing credibility in the eyes of the public. That public must be convinced that it needs the services of the aspiring profession rather desperately, and that the practitioners of that profession are the only ones able and willing to offer this service for a just fee. The profession strives to keep out charlatans, unqualified and unscrupulous pretenders to the knowledge. Few occupations can succeed in this fight, especially now that the occupational structure has become so highly controlled by the established professions. Still, there is movement and the process of professionalization is a constant one in many occupations.

Some of the "marginal" professions include pharmacists, chiropractors, and funeral directors. These are allegedly independent entrepreneurs who offer services needed by the public (Ritzer, 1977).

However, according to Kronus (1975), several characteristics of the job of pharmacist prevent it from being a profession. This includes a lack of control over the product and service, since it is the doctor who determines what a patient needs, as well as conflict between the business and the professional aspects of the enterprise. Pharmacists continue to advertise, have failed to develop a strong organization to control members, and are often simply salaried employees of chain stores or "mini-department stores in which virtually everything including hardware, food, toys, and electrical appliances are sold" (Ritzer, 1977: 192; see also Kronus, 1975).

WOMEN IN PROFESSIONAL AND TECHNICAL OCCUPATIONS

A few, albeit rather a very few, subjects emerge when social scientists and the mass media turn their attention to the presence of women in the professions and related technical fields. These subjects can best be examined chronologically, as they arose and expanded since the 1960s, although old ones do not necessarily fade away as new ones come along. The first major area of concern, expressed as such, was the discovery that many wives, even mothers, were returning to school in preparation for professional involvement, taking such jobs even after having entered family roles and that the younger ones were continuing employment in spite of such involvement. The Women's Bureau of the United States Department of Labor has been documenting the facts about women's employment in its *Handbook on Women Workers* (1966, 1969, 1975b), and Oppenheimer (1970, 1973) pulled all the data together and showed the consequences of social structure upon the presence and location of women in the labor force and vice-versa.

Observers then turned their attention to an examination of the characteristics of female workers. The third general topic became the alleged consequences of working wives and mothers upon children, marriage, and, finally, the women themselves. This shifted to an interest in the two-paycheck marriage, and two-career families. A fifth subject has been the location of women in the labor force, by occupation and industry, with special emphasis on what has been called the "semi-professions" and on "pioneers" or women entering the male-dominated professions. The final topic to be discussed here has been the study of women in their jobs as professionals and technical workers and in their careers.

The original interest in the employment of women outside the home focused only on that fact, not on the occupational distributions or on the differences in demands made upon these women by the types of jobs they entered. Thus, the traditional question, "Who are the working wives and mothers?" is underlined by the assumption that wives and mothers belong at home. Explanations of reasons for leaving the home in terms of economic need are readily available and easily accepted in modern American society. Numerous studies concluded that the women who combine employment with home roles are not being financially supported, or are inadequately supported, by a male head of household. In recent years, inflation has supplied an additional weight to this explanation. Traditionally, women whose husbands were earning "adequate" or "superior" salaries were not in the labor force. Gradually, however, it became apparent that this was no longer, if ever, necessarily true. Besides the women who obviously have to work to support themselves and their families, the most apt to be employed are the women with the highest educational attainment and professional jobs. In fact, a higher proportion of professional than of lower status or poor women hold jobs, even when there are children in the home (U.S. Department of Labor, Women's Bureau, 1975b: 187-91). These women were hard to understand, given traditional explanations: They obtained an education beyond that which was fashionable and entered demanding jobs that were likely to lead to role conflict. Thus, the literature gradually became polarized, one segment devoted to the description of the problems of blue-collar women on the job and in trying to maintain a family with few financial or service resources (Garson, 1975; Walshok, 1981). The second segment became focused on the professional and managerial woman and the means by which she entered jobs organized around the male dominant two-person career, or at least the male occupational commitment model.

When faced with the "career woman" in such jobs, early commentators were very unsupportive. The most damning of such women were Helene Deutsch (1944) in *The Psychology of Women*, and Ferdinand Lundberg with Marynia Farnham (1947) in *Modern Woman: The Lost Sex*. The very popular movie "Lady in the Dark" dramatized the psychoanalytic view of the career woman, with the then inevitable result of her "cure" through withdrawal from aspirations which compete with "feminine" roles (see also Coser, 1975; Coser and Rokoff, 1971). Prather (1971) saw this conflict as inevitable in a society which views women only as sex objects and servants.

That intensity of hostility against the "career woman" was most often expressed in the decades of the feminine mystique (Friedan,

1963). However, the instant popularity of Horner's (1972: 65) thesis that young women fear success in the professions because "femininity and individual achievement continue to be viewed as two desirable but mutually exclusive ends" certainly documents the continuation of this view well into recent years. Yogev (1983) finds the theme of psychological role conflict for women in the professions a prevalent one of the 1960s, but increasing since:

> Modern theory and research display two patterns: the early pattern of the 1960s, which viewed professional women as violating sex stereotypes, lacking femininity, and having personality disturbances; and the contemporary view, which emerged during the 1970s and suggests the possibility of combining career with family without psychological conflicts and personality disturbances. A critical appraisal of the literature in four areas [psychological role conflict, fear of success, comparison between housewives and career women, and comparisons between women in traditional and pioneer occupations] concludes that little evidence supports the view that professional women have personality disturbances because of their career (Yogev, 1983: 219).

Interest in women who obtained higher education, especially those who went to prestigious schools and specialized in professional training after they finished this schooling, has drawn several researchers. Komarovsky (1953) was one of the first to examine the life of American educated women who chose one of three life patterns: those who became full-time homemakers, those who combined family and professional roles, and those who focused on a career. Much of her book is devoted to the problems of the second life pattern and the frustrations of homemakers who had hoped to continue their career, but found the role conflict too difficult. She also described the ways in which the professional women handled home problems and that role conflict, when it occurred. Ginzberg and his associates (Ginzberg and Yohalem, 1966; Ginzberg et al., 1966) studied the top students graduating from the Columbia graduate school in the 1940s and found many of the employed women not married or without children, and only 36 percent with continuous work histories. The most apt to be working had obtained their degrees in medicine and law, the least likely were graduates of business or journalism (Ginzberg et al., 1966: 78). The team found four major life patterns, translated into types of women:

1. The planners—know what they want fairly early and arrange lives in order to realize plans

2. Recasters—know what they want, set out, but meet opportunities which permit them to consider more attractive goals, or meet obstacles and change
3. Adapters—recognize early the inherent fluidity of a woman's life and avoid commiting themselves irrevocably to any particular goal
4. The unsettled—still groping (Ginzberg et al., 1966: 78).

The professional woman probably has fewer mechanisms than the man for coping with the expectations of the over-demanding role networks revolving around her sex-linked and occupational statuses (Epstein, 1970: 93).

While early studies of employed women, especially of those in demanding occupations, focused especially on the consequences of their absence from the home on the children, the emphasis appears to have shifted to the dynamics of family relations, and to societal responses to the dual-career family (Holmstrom, 1973). The first book published by Nye and Hoffman in 1963 was devoted mainly to proving that the children were not negatively affected by the employment of their mothers outside the home. The concern became transformed in recent years to a critique of American society for its failure to provide childcare resources to families without a full-time homemaker (Kahn and Kamerman, 1975; Roby, 1973). Interestingly enough, the professional woman is expected to be able to afford childcare at home, so the concern here is more with women in less economically rewarding jobs. This new theme of concern for all family members appears in the 1974 Hoffman and Nye *Working Mothers: An Evaluative Review of the Consequences for Wife, Husband and Child*. But the assumption is still being made that the woman had been a homemaker and that the adjustment is made to her new "career" outside the home. In fact, the interest of most social scientists has focused on the "two-career" rather than the "two-earner" families. The latter was, however, dramatized by the movie "9 to 5".

Poloma (1972) and Poloma and Garland (1970, 1971) warned in the 1970s that the problems faced by professional women in combining that role with those at home are generally met by her alone—all is not equal in such homes. It is the wife who carries the major share of homemaking and adjustment to the mate's job demands. They were harshly criticized for their conclusions at the time of enthusiasm over women's "liberation," but every study since has corraborated their findings. Bird's (1979) *Two-Paycheck Marriage* describes very interestingly the sources of strain and conflict between the wife and the husband if she has a demanding job. Blumstein and Schwartz's 1983 book on *American Couples* documents that the strain can be experienced by couples living together even when there is no marriage and even in homosexual unions.

The Rapoports (see Fogarty et al., 1971; Rapoport, Rhona and Rapoport, Robert, 1972; Rapoport, Rhona and Robert, 1976; Rapoport, Robert and Rhona, with Bumstead, 1978) were pioneers in research analyzing the ways in which two-career marriages actually work, and others have followed (see Pepitone-Rockwell, 1980). Holmstrom (1973) found that the wife in *The Two-Career Family* eventually succeeded professionally, despite frequent part-time work when the children were young. Hall and Gordon (1973) concluded that, although there is a strong preference for part-time work among women professionals, those who obtained such an employment schedule displayed less job satisfaction than full-time workers, despite the self-perceived conflict among the full-timers. Fava and Genovese (1983) state that individual and professional development of the husband and the wife require flexibility in their interaction. Bielby (1978) studied college educated women in sexually atypical careers and found that they credited a supportive male as extremely important in their being able to maintain involvement and commitment to careers. She suggests that a recent redefinition of major social roles of women, which she had spotted in the years between 1961 and 1968, will make it easier for them to integrate the role cluster, "capitalize upon their educational investments," and become more involved in professional careers (Bielby, 1978: 22; see also Hunt and Hunt, 1977). The redefinition is not only cultural, or within the construction of reality by the women; it must also evolve within the couple's interrelation in order to reduce the "marriage versus career" role dichotomy.

Our team (Lopata et al., 1980) studied the contributions each spouse makes to the other's roles both inside and outside of the home. This study finds that both the husband and the wife are perceived by the wife as helping the other reduce role conflicts. However, the wife sees herself as making more concrete contributions to the husband's job than he makes to hers. Of course, the jobs may require different amounts of out-of-the-workplace activity. Pleck (1983) deals with the dual role of each marriage partner from the perspective of the husband.

Farmer and Bohn (1970) also speak of home-career conflict reduction, while Kahne (1976) looks outside of the marital unit in asking for more flexible work schedules, the same argument made by

Lopata (1978). Helson (1972) claims that the changing image of "career woman" will make the reduction of role conflict easier:

> Recently, new pressures have developed to enlarge and enhance the participation of women in the labor force. Among these pressures are the trend to population control with the consequent need to de-emphasize women's reproductive role and the contraceptive revolution making it possible to do so, the increased number of divorced and widowed women who expect to support themselves and their children at more than a subsistence level; and the strength of anti-establishment ideology, particularly a new sophistication in exposing discrimination, which has been seen by women to be useful in furthering their own cause (Helson, 1972: 40).

Helson (1972: 37) also claims that the "case against the career woman was never as strong as it was made out to be." The mass media have now begun to treat two-career couples as a natural part of the ever-changing scene. The *Wall Street Journal* started doing so as early as 1976 (Otten, 1976: 1):

> In most families where both husband and wife work, they labor at more or less routine jobs and chiefly to enlarge family income. In two career marriages, however, money is rarely the major motivation; each partner, usually well educated, aims to advance steadily in the chosen business or profession, seeking psychological as well as financial rewards.

In 1983, the *Chicago Tribune* ran an Associated Press story, "More Wives Deciding Where Couples Live: For Some Spouses, Egos and Economics can Balance Out." *Working Woman* recently ran a whole series of articles on women who must travel, with pointers as to hotels and restaurants for those unaccustomed to going to such places alone.

Most of the literature on women in the workplace deals with specific occupations. Some, however, cover more than one occupation or location. For example, Stolte-Heiskanen (1983) examines the roles and positions of women in a variety of scientific research groups in several countries, finding that their contribution is often peripheral, because of their assignments and time limitations. Interestingly enough, the male and female scientists were not asked about their family roles, which she thinks may be the major cause of these limitations. Olson and Miller (1983) also find women in large organizations lacking contacts and information channels necessary for effective role performance. Macke (1981) found great similarities in self-esteem among professional men and women who answered a *Psychology Today* questionnaire, but significant differences between them and semi-professional women. Of course, that is a highly self-selected sample, but it is interesting that she supports Kanter's (1977) thesis in that she found "low levels of commitment—a characteristic often thought to be true of women—among men in occupations with structural impediments similar to many female-type occupations—i.e., little chance for advancement" (Macke, 1981: 34).

WOMEN AND THE SEMI-PROFESSIONS AND WOMEN IN MALE-DOMINATED PROFESSIONS

This brings us to a subject which is impossible to avoid when discussing women in the professional and technical occupations—the "semi-professions." The concept predates (Etzioni's (1969) book devoted to this subject, but that effort contributed to establishment of the idea in American occupational sociology:

> The 1949 edition [of the *Dictionary of Occupational Titles*] describes in brief detail over 20,000 more or less distinct occupations . . . [it included] an abortive attempt to create a "semi-professional" major work category and a list of over 400 "semi-professional occupations" (Habenstein, 1970: 103). . . . its purpose was to separate out of the 20,000 or so jobs listed in addition to professions those:
>
>> occupations concerned with the theoretical or practical aspects of the fields of endeavor that require rather extensive educational or practical experience, or a combination of such education and experience for the proper performance of the work . . . [but] are less demanding with respect to background or the need for initiative or judgement in dealing with complicated work situations than those fields which are considered as 'professional'. These occupations are typically confined to relatively restricted fields of activity, many of them being concerned with the technical or mechanical details of the broader and possibly more theoretical fields of endeavor (U.S. Department of Labor, 1949, quoted by Habenstein, 1969: 6).

Although the passage quoted by Habenstein (1970) referred mainly to technical or mechanical jobs, the concept was shifted to a set of three female intensive occupations: teachers, nurses, and social workers by the publication of Etzioni's (1969) edited *The Semi-Professions and their Organization* and have remained in that location ever since. In their generalizing chapter on women and bureaucracy in the semi-professions, Simpson and Simpson (1969) explain the connection mainly in terms of women's failure rather than that of the social system. The structural constraints on those who work in the semi-professions include a lack of autonomy, accountability for performance to superiors, location in strictly hierarchical structure and lack of a mandate for independent care of patients or clients (see also Grimm, 1978). The set of characteristics of women which account for these differences between the semi- and the true professions includes a lack of "reference group orientations to colleagues," strong "competing attachment to their family roles and to their clients," and agreement with "the general cultural norm that women should defer to men" (Simpson and Simpson, 1969: 198-99). They tend to have decided on an occupation late in life and are not motivated toward the scholarly aspects of their work. They feel inadequate "to succeed in other fields" and are attracted to the emotional, service feature of the job for life satisfaction. Their careers tend to be discontinuous, with frequent part-time employment and high job turnover rates. They desire sociability and lack ambition, are compliant and deferential. On the other hand, Simpson and Simpson (1969: 198) do mention the fact that the American public is "less willing to grant autonomy to women than to men" and admit the presence of discrimination:

> The low motivation and discontinuous work histories of women raise questions about the prevailing assumption that women are discriminated against in occupations where they compete with men. . . . But a case can be made that women's lack of occupational success is not always due to discrimination, and that when discrimination does occur, there may be valid grounds for it from the organization's standpoint (Simpson and Simpson, 1969: 221-22).

One can but speculate as to the reason male dominated occupations within bureaucratic organizations are not also labeled semi-professions. This could include artists in commercial establishments, writers in advertising, employment counselors, and "head hunters," MBAs (Masters of Business Administration) with specialties on staffs rather than in management positions, and so forth. The differences in the jobs of nurse, teacher, and case worker are also tremendous, with varying degrees of autonomy of action.

When social scientists and related observers of the American scene are not focusing on the semi-professions and their domination by women, they tend to turn their attention to the professions in which women are relatively absent (Patterson and Engleberg, 1978):

> An increasing demand for skilled and highly trained workers has accompanied the rapid growth and changing technology of our economy. Women have shared in the rising number of professional and technical workers. Prior to World War II women employed in professional and

technical positions numbered about 1.6 million. In October, 1966 they numbered 3.6 million. However, men have moved into these jobs at an even faster pace. As a result, women held only 38 percent of all professional and technical positions in October, 1966 as compared with 45 percent in 1940 (U.S. Department of Labor, 1966: 1).

The U.S. Department of Labor's (1966) "Fact Sheet on Women in Professional and Technical Positions" makes an important point often overlooked when people speak of the decrease in the percent of professional and technical jobs that are taken by women. It is the rate of men's involvement, not the withdrawal of women from these fields, that has changed the proportions. On the other hand, it must be remembered that most of the women in this broad occupational category are still nurses and teachers. The occupational distribution in some of the occupations which fall into the category are contained in Table 9.1.

Table 9.1 documents some interesting changes and continuities in the percent of women employed in the different occupations which are classified under the heading of professional, technical, and kindred in the ten-year period between 1972 and 1981. There has been a dramatic increase of women accountants, computer specialists, lawyers, life and physical scientists, including chemists, operations and system analysts, personnel and labor relations workers, health therapists, social scientists, engineering and science technicians, and other technicians, designers, public relations specialists and publicity writers, and research workers (not specified). On the other hand, there are still very few women architects, engineers, dentists, or clergy. Women also form either a minority or the dominant majority of many traditional occupations. Thus, Gross's (1971) conclusion that things have not changed much as far as occupational segregation is concerned is only partially true as of the 1980s. Certainly men are not moving into the female-dominated professions to any extent. The figures are, of course, estimations based on limited samples and fluctuations by year can be expected, but the patterns are clear. The increase in numbers and percentages of women in previously (and still) male-dominated professions is anticipated to continue for an indefinite future, in spite of some backlash and the shrinkage of some of these occupations. Predictions as to this trend come partly from the educational figures of recent years. Table 9.2 contains the figures that give rise to optimism on the part of people positively evaluating the decrease of women's confinement to the few traditionally female professions.

Table 9.1 Percentages of Women in Selected Professional, Technical and Kindred Occupations, 1972-1981

Occupation	1972	1973	1974	1975	1976	1977	1978	1979	1980	1981
Professional and technical	48.4	48.7	49.3	53.2	42.0	42.6	42.7	43.3	44.3	44.6
Accountants	26.7	21.6	23.7	24.8	26.9	27.5	30.1	32.9	36.2	38.5
Architects	3.0	2.7	2.8	4.3	3.2	3.4	5.8	6.0	6.7	4.3
Computer specialists	16.8	19.5	19.0	21.2	19.1	23.2	23.1	26.0	25.7	27.1
Engineers	0.8	1.3	1.3	1.1	1.8	2.7	2.8	2.9	4.0	4.4
Lawyers	4.0	5.8	7.0	7.2	9.3	9.3	9.4	12.8	13.0	14.2
Librarians, archivists	81.6	82.1	81.7	78.4	80.7	79.8	80.7	78.1	81.4	82.8
Life and physical science	10.0	11.5	15.9	14.4	12.1	15.6	17.9	18.9	20.3	21.9
Chemists	10.1	11.2	14.0	14.5	11.4	13.7	14.4	15.2	20.3	21.7
Operations and system analysts	10.8	13.7	11.5	15.3	14.6	20.5	21.7	21.2	23.5	26.1
Personnel and labor relations	31.0	33.7	34.9	36.5	39.7	43.5	43.7	45.5	46.9	49.9
Dentists	1.9	1.9	1.0	1.8	1.9	2.9	1.7	4.6	4.3	4.6
Physicians	10.1	12.2	9.5	13.0	12.8	11.2	11.3	10.7	13.4	13.7
Nurses RN	97.6	97.8	98.0	97.0	96.6	96.7	96.7	95.8	95.5	96.8
Therapists	59.1	64.2	58.3	80.5	67.3	68.5	70.4	72.9	73.7	70.5
Health technologists	69.5	71.5	70.6	73.2	72.9	71.4	70.9	69.5	70.8	72.3
Religious workers	11.0	10.7	10.1	11.8	13.1	13.0	14.8	13.3	11.4	11.9
Clergy	1.6	2.4	3.0	2.8	1.5	3.5	3.8	4.6	4.2	5.0

Social scientists	21.3	22.6	23.5	24.3	24.4	26.6	33.7	34.5	36.0	33.8
Social, recreational workers	55.1	56.9	57.7	58.5	60.4	60.8	61.0	61.0	63.3	62.4
Teachers, university	28.0	27.1	30.9	31.1	31.3	31.7	33.8	31.6	33.9	35.2
Adult education	37.7	40.0	45.0	46.4	41.1	46.1	49.4	51.3	47.2	42.1
Elementary	85.1	80.7	84.3	85.4	84.8	84.2	84.0	84.3	83.7	83.6
Secondary	49.6	49.5	48.3	49.2	50.5	51.2	51.6	50.7	52.1	51.3
Other	74.1	74.8	75.8	76.1	73.1	75.2	75.9	75.9	72.7	73.8
Technicians, technicals, science	9.1	10.2	11.4	11.8	13.6	14.9	13.4	15.9	17.8	18.8
Technicians *not* health, science	11.2	13.0	11.3	11.7	13.7	19.9	13.4	15.9	19.3	22.4
Vocational and educational counselors	50.0	48.3	48.4	48.8			52.6	53.3	55.8	53.7
Writers, artists	30.8	36.8	33.6	34.4			35.5	37.8	39.3	39.8
Designers	18.2	21.1	24.0	25.8			27.3	28.5	29.5	29.4
Editors, reporters	41.1	40.4	43.6	44.8			42.4	42.3	50.0	50.2
Musicians	31.4	31.7	30.7	31.7			30.9	35.9	29.4	24.8
Painters, sculptors	43.4	42.6	41.6	48.8			44.6	46.6	49.7	50.7
Publications	29.9	28.1	28.8	32.2			40.5	43.8	46.8	45.5
Research	27.9	25.0	27.8	32.5			32.0	37.1	36.6	38.9
Other	35.8	39.7	41.8	36.0			37.0	39.1	40.0	38.2

Source: U.S. Department of Labor. Labor force statistics derived from the Current Population Survey: A Databook, Vol. I. Washington, D.C., U.S. Government Printing Office. Table B-20, pp. 651-67.

Table 9.2 Percentage of Women among Degree Recipients by Discipline 1975-76 and Percent Change Between 1975-76 and 1979-80

Discipline Division	Bachelors		Masters		Ph.D.s	
	1975-76	% Change to 79-80	1975-76	% Change	1975-77	% Change
Agriculture and natural resources	18.3	90.1	14.3	37.0	6.6	83.6
Architecture and environmental design	19.2	45.0	20.8	34.3	15.9	—
Area studies	55.5	-12.7	45.3	-13.8	31.9	-13.8
Biological sciences	34.8	4.5	31.8	15.3	21.5	29.5
Business and management	19.8	121.9	11.6	148.4	5.4	121.2
Communications	41.5	69.8	41.8	19.0	24.5	44.0
Computer and information sciences	19.8	202.4	14.5	102.7	9.4	17.4
Education	72.8	-21.8	64.3	-11.9	33.4	35.8
Engineering	3.2	334.4	3.6	96.2	2.3	43.9
Fine and applied arts	60.9	.3	48.9	7.6	27.9	39.9
Foreign languages	76.4	-28.0	66.7	-32.9	47.9	-23.9

Health professions	78.8	24.1	66.5	35.4	28.8	111.4
Home economics	95.9	5.5	91.5	22.7	71.3	15.0
Law	18.8	211.0	12.8	65.3	3.4	33.4
Letters	56.9	-18.2	58.3	-21.6	36.5	-14.1
Library science	93.1	51.8	78.3	-30.6	45.1	18.8
Mathematics	40.7	-26.0	34.0	-21.1	11.0	6.4
Military science	0.2	400.0	—	—	—	—
Physical sciences	19.2	36.5	15.0	18.2	8.7	28.7
Psychology	54.4	-17.0	46.7	21.6	31.7	43.0
Public affairs and services	43.7	43.6	45.3	34.9	32.0	35.3
Social sciences	37.9	-5.5	31.6	-11.9	21.6	-2.9
Theology	27.3	15.7	32.1	15.0	4.1	83.3
Interdisciplinary studies	45.0	18.8	46.5	18.7	32.2	34.1
All discipline divisions	45.6	8.6	46.5	1.8	22.9	24.1
	934,443		313,001		34,076	

Source: George H. Brown NCES—336.A, 336.B, 336.C. U.S. Department of Commerce, National Center for Educational Statistics *Earned Degrees Conferred 1979-1980*. Washington, D.C.: U.S. Government Printing Office, 1981.

The only areas of study in which there have been a drop in the percent of women earning bachelor's degrees have been in education, home economics, letters, and public affairs and services. The drop is not large, but it is significant in view of the increases in the more technical fields (see also Astin, 1969; Baker, 1981). There has also been an increase in the percent of women earning masters and doctorate degrees. This increase is across the board as far as the latter is concerned. Brown (1978A: 2) pointed to the fact that women in 1976 still tended to choose feminine fields in terms of numbers of Ph.Ds and related degrees. Nevertheless, the increases in nontraditional fields are definite and they have expanded dramatically. We will return to this subject when discussing women in acedemia.

One interesting and very important fact about the entrance of women into schooling and job training, as well as into the jobs themselves, in male dominated professions has been their age distribution. Due to the failure of guidance toward, and models within, such fields early in their education and the traditional tendency of women to "choose a life-style not an occupation," many future professionals and scientists did not follow the typical ideal male path of consistent preparation for such a career (Ahrons, 1976; Almquist, 1974; Angrist and Almquist, 1975; Hansen and Rapoza, 1978). Wilensky (1961) found many blue-collar workers having "disorderly careers" in terms of job changes. Even on the professional level all people, men included, do not necessarily progress straight through educational and occupational systems. Gross (1958) comments on the fact that many sociologists are former preachers, school teachers, and newspapermen (sic). Students entering medical and dental school fall into four types, depending on the paths they followed into professional schools: decision made during high school and carried straight through; work following graduation from high school with later return; decision made during college; and entrance into the professional school after finishing college and working for a period (Helfrich, 1975). Davis and Bumpass (1976) found that:

> Over one-fifth of all women have attended high school or college since marriage; over one-third either have returned to school or anticipate returning to an academic institution sometime in the future . . . Examination of differentials reveals for both blacks and whites that post-nuptual education is higher among women who: (1) attended college before marriage, (2) married early, (3) are currently separated or divorced, (4) support egalitarian sex-role attitudes, or (5) whose most recent occupation is in the professional, managerial or administrative category (Davis and Bumpass, 1976: 161).

As we shall see in Volume II, a high proportion of the Chicago area professionals have returned to school after leaving it for the first time and a total of 43 percent of the women have done so. The Davis and Bumpass (1976: 171) sample of 1970 showed 40 percent of women in the top occupations as having returned, even when the figures are adjusted for the effects of the other variables they tested. Perusal of our interviews and biographical sketches in mass media publications indicates the possibility that returning students are more likely to choose better paying and less traditional professions than is true of women who went straight through. Working outside the home may increase their awareness of occupational opportunities. Recent years witness a greater tendency for women to prepare earlier in life for the less traditional professions, thanks probably to the women's movement and to the publicity surrounding women who have gone in this direction (see also Almquist, 1974 for early pioneers).

In much of the literature, the documentation of the dearth of women in professions other than those dominated by women is followed by explanations of this phenomenon. In the 1950s Ruth Cavan (1957) explained it in terms of women's choices. She stated that they prefer fields with less training, those which are extensions of traditional women's work and require less competitiveness while allowing control to remain in the hands of men. The consequences of the failure of women to enter the fields which men dominate are both negative and positive according to Cavan. They are negative in that there is a "public loss due to the incomplete training and use of women's minds" and positive in that they are able to carve out an area of specialization which permits them "to turn their attention to the rearing of children without qualms of conscience over the expensive professional education that is not used, or a top level position in which responsibilities are not readily set aside" (8-9).

Alice Rossi (1965a), in speaking to a symposium at the Massachusetts Institute of Technology, outlined the "Barriers to the Career Choice of Engineering, Medicine or Science among American Women." She focused on the inability of women to devote the same number of hours to professional work as men do, unless they are willing to forego marriage and motherhood. Even with the necessary training, a woman would have to postpone marriage, thereby decreasing the possibility of finding a husband not threatened by her achievement. At that time Rossi (1965a) was in the process of completing a study of college graduates of 1961, who were followed until 1964. These were divided into (1) homemakers, who had no career goals other than that role; (2) traditionals, women who planned on being in female intensive professions; and (3) pioneers, "whose long-range career goals were in predominantly masculine fields" (Rossi, 1965a: 79-80). Very few were defined as pioneers and Rossi develops in great detail the occupational stereotypes of many professions that discourage women from wanting to enter and to achieve in them. These include the tremendously demanding nature of the careers and the lack of part-time work available during child-rearing years. The obstacles women see to their involvement in such jobs are also perceived by people around them, even by potential husbands. At the same conference, Erikson (1965: 242) explained the lack of women in the sciences and engineering in terms of their "inner space" of the womb which makes "scientific training more or less peripheral to the intimate tasks of womanhood and motherhood." Rossi (1965b: 615) published an article in *Science* in which she further documented that women who had trained for selected professions withdrew from labor force participation in 1960 at ages (25 to 44) when greatest commitment is expected in such fields. This included 51 percent of the natural scientists, 31 percent of the engineers, 34 percent of secondary school teachers. Only 19 percent of physicians-surgeons were not working full-time when studied. The feminine mystique appears to have been working well in those years for all women, despite their educational attainment or career aspirations.

The difficulties facing women who move into predominantly male occupations can be analyzed in a broader framework, as Lipman-Blumen (1976), Epstein (1970), Lorber (1979), and Kanter (1977) have done. Lipman-Blumen (1976: 15) discusses what she calls a "homosocial theory of sex roles":

> In conclusion, we have tried to demonstrate that the absence of women from certain segments of the occupational world is part of a much larger pattern of a male homosocial world. Women are excluded from this world because their lack of resources makes them less useful and interesting both to men and to other women. Men, recognizing the power their male peers have, find one another stimulating, exciting, productive, attractive, and important, since they can contribute to virtually all aspects of one another's lives (31).

The lack of resources on the part of women refers to their lack of influence in the public sphere, which increased in importance dramatically in industrializing and urbanizing societies and was defined as the province of men, as noted before. It was during the nineteenth century, according to Bledstein (1978), that the professions emerged as powerful occupations and consolidated their control over their own area of expertise. Controlling the educational system, males prevented the entrance of women into educational roles that would prepare them to enter the professions (see also Starr, 1982). Peripheral occupations, such as midwifery, so defined in constrast to the powerful ones, lost their competitive strength. Each profession, and those aspiring to such status which became male-dominated, developed its own sub-culture and "community" as described by Goode (1956).

In view of the fact that women were assigned to the domestic sphere and that the professions, as well as the business community, developed outside of it and was male-dominated, it is not surprising that women have had trouble integrating into such occupations (see also Bird, 1972). Kanter (1977) found that men of the corporation turned to those people who were a known entity, whom they could trust in an uncertain world. Few of these trusted confidants are women. Lorber (1979) argues that the need to trust colleagues, seen as a brotherhood, prevents men from investing in people with a different background—this includes women. The situation is complicated by the fact that men have been taught to relate to women mainly as sexual objects; this results in difficulties in converting them into colleagues. Furthermore, male clubs, washrooms, and other places of informal contact are imbued with male culture and closed off from women. The historical tendency has been for professional women to withdraw from the field or from intensive work when family problems arose, since no one in their family unit or in society shared that responsibility. According to the male culture, this has increased their "untrustworthiness" as members of the team. Men are also afraid to sponsor women, or become their mentors because of an expectation that they will face jealousy from their wives (Epstein, 1970, 1983; Kanter, 1977; Lorber, 1979). As in the case of the *American Dilemma* (Myrdal, 1944), the need to continue discriminating against women and other minorities in the world of work, in spite of the ideal of equal treatment built into democracy, has resulted in a complex subcultural set of beliefs as to the nature of women. This set of beliefs precludes women from having characteristics required of professionals.

> Thus, American society holds that women cannot be good engineers or lawyers because these professions call for qualities which are not feminine (Epstein, 1970: 155).

All in all, the current situation is that women, who are now legally allowed to enter the educational and apprenticeship channels for professional and skilled work and to be hired for previously male only jobs, still feel uncomfortable, are cut off from informal channels of communication, have difficulties finding sponsors, and are often forced to self-exclusion and low profile visibility or, conversely, to open competition on male terms (Epstein, 1970). An excellent set of studies documenting these problems was conducted by Epstein (1971, 1979, 1983) on women encountering the Wall Street establishment of male lawyers. One way women dealt with these problems was by forming professional associations composed exclusively of members of their own gender (Epstein, 1970; Schwartz, 1973) and "networking" or developing loosely organized networks of women in similar occupations but with different employers (Kleiman, 1980).

Of course, the structure of the occupations and the sub-culture by which their composition and relations are justified, vary by society. For example, there is an abundance, if not a preponderance, of women physicians, dentists, lawyers, and engineers in Poland, the USSR, and other Communist countries (Sokolowska, 1965). This is partly a consequence of the loss of men in such occupations during World War II and partly an attempt to follow the Communist ideology. However, two important facts must be kept in mind when comparing American to Polish figures: One is that occupations such as that of physician have never had the status and power in those countries as they have here, so that there is no strong professional organization determined to keep women out. Since those societies have a strong patriarchal history, the status was lowered even further by the high proportion of women in those occupations. Secondly, the profession itself became redefined in those countries upon the influx of women. Physicians should be persons with empathetic, kind, "motherly" personalities, not hard scientists. It is "natural" that women are better than men in certain forms of engineering, civil rather than electrical, and so forth.

Even in America, the ease of finding a job on the part of a woman is related to the strength of the professional male establishment:

> Thus, where professionals themselves do the hiring, few women are employed. As control of the occupation moves out of the hands of professionals, women are employed in much larger numbers, but in relatively less desirable sectors of the profession (Carter and Carter, 1981: 479).

FOUR CATEGORIES OF WOMEN PROFESSIONALS AND TECHNICIANS

In analyzing the women whose occupations fell into the category of professionals, technicians, and related workers in the Chicago

sample, we found a natural split which encompassed more characteristics of the job than the traditional division into male- and female-
intensive fields. The *object-focused* occupations include scientists,
draftswomen, laboratory technicians and technologists, engineers
and related technicians, radio operators, designers, artists and writers,
and unclassified researchers and technicians. The second sub-category
includes all the *teachers*, whether they work in the public school system or in universities or give private lessons. The *health and welfare*
sub-category contains social workers, physicians and surgeons, dieti-
cians, registered nurses, therapists, and health technologists. *People-
focused* occupations cover librarians, public, personnel and labor
relations workers, clergy and related religious workers, educational
and vocational counselors, lawyers, and editors and reporters. I have
organized the literature review according to these four fields. The
reader can find detailed descriptions of the histories, job characteristics and self-constructed reality and role complexes of the Chicago
area women in such occupations in Volume II.

Women in Object-Focused Occupations

Object-focused occupations are those whose main function is
working with objects—as the label indicates—whether they are "things"
such as sculpturing material or laboratory equipment or data, as
handled by accountants, draftswomen, or economists. We contrast
this type of work to people-focused occupations in which the primary
set of duties is the provision of services, other than health or teaching
ones, or interaction with other human beings. The object-focused
occupations cover a wide spectrum of jobs ranging from the scientific
professions to artistic and technical. One of the variables differentiating
the people in these occupations is education, college degrees usually
being the minimum requirement, except among some technicians:

> In some fields the title *technologist* is used for a person with baccelaure-
> ate level training, and the title *technician* refers to someone with one or
> two years preparation. There are exceptions to this usage, and there is
> a lack of general agreement about the educational qualifications that
> differentiate technologists from technicians (Sorkin, 1977: 44).

Koch (1974: 177) describes some of the characteristics that technicians
share, in spite of the diversity of locales in which they work:

> At most they have the following characteristics in common: (1) their
> tasks entail the application of scientific or technical knowledge to work-
> able and practical reality; (2) their educational preparation generally
> includes some specialized training beyond high school in proprietary

vocational schools, colleges, or 'in house' organizational training programs; and (3) their work is generally supportive of the work of professionals, whether they be doctors, scientists, engineers, or managers.
Aside from these few unifying threads, technicians form an incredibly
mixed population, ranking among the most heterogeneous of all occupational groups (Koch, 1974: 177).

Women are beginning to enter all technical occupations. They can be
found as technicians in electronics and chemical science; and radio
operators (Malveaux, 1980). In fact, the technician's is often the entry
level job which leads some of them into greater specialized education
and scientific occupations (Bernard, 1965). So few professors in science and engineering are women that few students look to these fields
on a doctoral level when they originally think of a career. The increasing demand for doctoral degrees in engineering discourages many
young women from considering them. However, since they are obtaining high degrees in other areas in increasing numbers, it must be
the combination of degree and field which has limited the number of
women in engineering. Since the M.I.T. conference in 1964 on women
in science and engineering, social scientists and psychologists have
worried about, and tried to explain, the relative absence of women
from such occupations. The conference involved people other than
Rossi (1965a) and Erikson (1965), whose explanations we already discussed. Bernard (1965) pointed to the gap between the need for scientists and engineers and the employment of women already trained
in engineering. Bolt (1965) presented data showing that women with
this training tended to choose jobs in research in academic or industrial
firms but did not enter development pioneering. However, he found
that there had been an increase of women in mathematics and statistics,
the traditional source of "anxiety" of female students. Hill (1965)
stated that General Electric, with which he was familiar, had only
two women engineers in 1924, but at the time he was writing his
contribution to the symposium there was a total of 360, "which repre-
sents something more than 1 percent of our total number of techni-
cally trained college graduates" (196). All in all, the figures were
small and each participant found several reasons for this fact. By 1978,
Florman (1978) published an article in *Harper's* magazine, "Engineering and the Female Mind," which introduced two new themes. One
reason that only 1 percent of professional engineers in American society were women at that time may have been because of the blue-
collar, craft background of those specialities now combined into this
occupation. Women entering higher education may shy away from

this identification, as well as from the "male image" (see also Robin, 1971). However, he felt that the male image explanation was no longer adequate for "female aversion to the profession," since so much of modern advertising shows women in similarly dominated occupations (Florman, 1978: 58). His second explanation was that modern women, influenced by the feminist movement, avoid engineering because they want power, and the field is seen as powerless. He tries to convert women into seeking participation in the societal occupational structure at all levels and areas and states that change is occurring. He points to the existence of the Society of Women Engineers:

> The society, founded in 1950 by fifty women engineers, has grown in the past five years from just a few hundred to its present membership of 7,000, half of whom are college students (Florman, 1978: 60).

In addition, the headquarters of the society was being flooded by correspondence from interested young women.

As mentioned in connection with the discussion of women engineers in Communist countries, even this occupation, which has been restricted mainly to men in America, has within it specialties that are more open to women than are others. In 1979 women formed 2.9 percent of all engineers, but only 1.3 percent of mechanical, 1.6 percent of aeronautical and astronautical, 2.2 percent of electronic and electrical, 2.5 percent of civil, and 7.3 percent of industrial engineers (Malveaux, 1980: 107).

An interesting development as far as gender distribution is concerned has occurred in the computer related fields. According to Kraft (1977) women were the original workers with computers, since the required skills were considered to be basically clerical in nature. However, as programming increased in complexity and the consumers inability to translate their wants into computer language became more apparent, men entered the field with top pay and high levels of autonomy. Gradually, when software became more standardized, the less expensive female labor force returned, at the lower levels.

> As older, white male [and relatively expensive] specialists are phased out of programming, they are being replaced with programmers who are more female and nonwhite as well as less well trained and with fewer formal credentials. They are also paid considerably less on an average. It should be stressed, to avoid confusing cause and consequence, that the de-skilling of the 'average programmer' has not come about because of the influx of the less skilled women, black and/or brown employees.

> On the contrary, management-designated routinization has made it possible to use less well trained and less skilled workers to begin with (Kraft, 1977: 106).

As of 1979, women formed 26 percent of computer specialists, and of these, 29 percent of the programmers and 24.3 percent of the more complex system analysts according to Malveaux (1980). Table 9.1 shows the percent as 27 in 1981. There are many levels of workers now in the area, some, such as coders, having little prestige. The higher levels are still connected with the mystique of the technology itself.

> Computer workers are important because they occupy a place near the top of the white collar class pyramid in terms of income, status, power, skill and centrality of function (Loseke and Sonquist, 1979: 157). Although they are generally highly educated, they are in the position of performing labor which some writers see as becoming increasingly routinized (158) . . . Frequent job change is a common practice among workers in the computer industry, renowned for its high rate of labor turnover (163) . . . Some women interviewees reported feeling underutilized because of stereotyping into 'female' tasks [routine work, keypunching, and the like] (173-74).

Thus, another field, newly introduced into a society, has peaked, then gone through the devaluation of status process, decreasing autonomy, and the demand for creativity, as it becomes better established. One wonders if the occupation of astronaut will be lowered in status or divided into that of pilot and that of scientist in a bureaucratic organization, with decreasing uncertainty and increasing experience. Twenty-six percent of computer programmers are women and, unlike accountants, have a median years of schooling above that of the males (15.84 to 14.83); the programmers tend to have had vocational training in addition to formal schooling. Most work full-time, 50 to 52 weeks a year. They are subjected to less close supervision than a person with an average job and face above average responsibility (Otto et al., 1980: 13-14).

Painters and sculptors tend to be women much more often than is true of any of the other object-focused occupations. A total of 42 percent of the people in this work are women, and 97 percent of the total are white (Otto, et al., 1980: 113-14). Both males and females have virtually the same median amount of education, below college graduation (13.75). Although vocational training has been undertaken by 40 percent of the workers, many are not employed full-time. Not closely supervised, their work itself is less repetitive than that of other occupations. Women in this field tend to be part-time workers more often than men and earn less than $4,400 a year at the height of their careers between ages 53 and 57. Obviously, those in their thirties who do not earn even $2,000 can not support themselves from this occupation alone. The men reach their height of income of $12,000 at ages 33 to 37. It is impossible to estimate why women earn so much less and do not reach a peak of even this minimal income until so late in life, unless it is because women enter the field at a later age. Rosenberg and Fliegel (1971) claim that there is strong "prejudice against female artists" on the part of gallery owners, art dealers, collectors, and even peers (see also Chicago, 1977).

Although the work of artists, sculptors, painters, writers, and to some extent, dancers and choreographers can be organized into a variety of social roles and performed part-time, it can be very demanding in terms of the time, energy, and concentration required of those who enter it. Agnes de Mille (1958) points to the fact that, although dancing "ranks with women's oldest professional careers," it is often considered so demanding as to exclude any kind of commitment to family roles. Greer (1979: 327), who entitled her book on women painters *The Obstacle Race*, concludes her discussion of the scarcity of such artists with a Freudian explanation:

> You cannot make great artists out of egos that have been damaged, with wills that are defective, with libidos that have been driven out of reach and energy diverted into neurotic channels.

As is true of recent analyses of women in other professions, literature dealing with this field is now less concerned with the scarcity of women in object-focused occupations, and more with changes in their employment and power. Thus, Blau (1979) has studied expertise and power of architects, including women, by their area of specialization and size of firm. As we saw in Table 9.1 women comprised 4.3 percent of architects in 1981. The relation between education and employment is of special interest to Hornig (1982), and Vetter (1980 and 1981) has contributed to our knowledge of women scientists and engineers in two articles in *Science*. In these she documents the number of science and engineering doctoral degrees awarded between 1956 and 1980 and shows an increase in all fields from 744 to 4,099. This increase includes a jump from 297 to 2,165 in the social sciences and psychology. Women doctorates went up from 263 to 1,342 in life sciences but grew only from 127 to 386 in physical sciences, from 50 to 116 in mathematical sciences, and from 7 to 90 in engineering

(Vetter, 1981: 1314). Women, much more than men, are employed in educational institutions, especially if they are in physical, life, or social sciences. Fifty-six percent of women with doctorates in the physical sciences are employed in educational institutions, only 26 percent (compared to the men's 43 percent) are in business and industry, 8 percent are in the government. Only in computer sciences and in engineering are women more apt to be in business and industry than in educational institutions. The general demands of these occupations, more than differences in the orientation of women who work in these fields, accounts for this fact. All in all, 14 percent of the Ph.D.s are in business, 66 percent in educational establishments, and 9 percent in the government (Vetter, 1981: 1377). The academic positions women hold are still concentrated at the assistant professor level in 44 percent of the cases, and 7 percent are on research staffs. The few women in engineering, mathematics, computer sciences, physics, astronomy, chemistry, and environmental sciences are disproportionately involved in research (Vetter, 1981: 1377). There is very little data on their social roles within such occupations.

Object-focused occupations in the professional and technical category include accounting:

> In the past, the accounting profession was not a good place for women, and although the field is opening up, women are still underrepresented. Currently there are only 52 women among the more than 6,000 partners of the international Big Eight accounting firms ... that dominate the accounting marketplace. That low number reflects both sexist hiring practices in past decades and limited mobility for women who did join these firms (Bekey, 1982: 46).

Although the more established firms are beginning to demand people with an MBA (Masters of Business Administration), doctors of law or masters degree in business taxation, women entering accounting average 12.31 years of schooling to the male median of 15.50 (Otto, et al., 1980). According to Otto and associates (1980), women compose 17 percent of all accountants in America and can go into public, private, or solo practice. Table 9.1 finds 38.5 percent of accountants to be women, so the classification schemes are apparently different. Accountants work an average of 47.44 hours per week and are classified as having an above average competency in the manipulation of data. Although their jobs are classified as providing little variety, they are considered as having above average responsibility. The tasks may be repetitive, but their roles are highly varied because social circles and problems are divergent. They leave their place of work and enter the establishments of clients in order to go over their accounts, or else the client, if small in budget, brings the documentation to the accountant's office. Women earn a much smaller salary than men in this occupation, as in other professions.

Teachers

It is hard to imagine any social role that would not involve the transmission of knowledge, that is, learning or teaching (Znaniecki, 1940). The basic questions, whose answers differentiate types of teaching roles, are: Who are the teachers? Whom do they teach? What do they teach? How do they teach? and How does the learner learn? (Williams, 1970). In order to differentiate among systems of knowledge transmission, segments of American society that are not directly involved in educational institutions but who are devoted to the teaching of practical knowledge such as business designate people and programs by the term "training and development." External consultants prepare the programs or conduct seminars for employees or potential employees of business establishments, and large organizations have their own personnel to meet this need.

This leaves us with the social role identified in American society as that of "teacher." However, we are still faced with a great variety of social persons, social circles, and relations among them. Specifically, in our sample, there are teachers in public or private school systems, from kindergarten through primary and secondary grades and the higher education complex, as well as specialized teachers who offer private lessons or who are hired by a variety of organizations to offer academic "courses." The pupils or students are part of an educational institution which prepares potential members of a functioning society and provides generalized knowledge or training into specialties. Each area of knowledge is taught somewhat differently, but the system as a whole has a surprisingly national scope—surprising in view of the complexity of the society and of the teaching and learning roles (Lortie, 1975). Like the hospital or the corporation, each school fits into the larger institution and adds knowledge, it is hoped, to the people who pass through its various levels. The sociology of education studies the social conditions which influence the structure and content of the system in each society and the consequences of these conditions on the system and on those involved in it (Corwin, 1961: 63). This book, *City Women*, focuses on the role of teacher as pre-

sented in part of the literature, with special emphasis on the characteristics and careers of female teachers.

As teaching gradually evolved into an occupational role, with
specified social person qualifications and a specific composition of
social circles, it developed its own ideology regarding who should
teach whom, what, and how. In American society the schoolteacher
who taught in a school with children as pupils emerged as a male who
was usually young and on his way toward a more prestigious or better paying job (Lortie, 1975). Within the last decades of the nineteenth century, this role shifted from being male in stereotype and
dominance to being female on the primary grade level. There are many
explanations for this shift, mainly showing the juxtaposition of social
structure and the availability of the specified kind of social person.
Morain (1980) studied the change in nineteenth-century Iowa:

> In general, studies have tended to stress a combination of factors [for
> the departure of men from teaching] to explain the phenomenon: the
> formation of a leisured class, the opening of post-elementary education
> to women, the appearance and expansion of tax-supported public edu-
> cation, rapid population increases, a Victorian gender formation which
> maintained that the female is innately superior in the care and education
> of young children, and the willingness of women to teach for substan-
> tially lower salaries than men (Morain, 1980: 161) . . . When higher
> standards began to require an investment of time and money in prep-
> aration for positions which paid little more than subsistence wages,
> they strongly tended to discourage those who had other occupational
> options. In the late nineteenth-century Iowa, men had choices; women
> did not (170).

Most other observers of the development of education in America
point to similar factors in the takeover of public teaching by women.
These comments refer mainly to primary school teaching (Richardson
and Hatcher, 1983). Current arguments as to this domination are not
very different from the Victorian ones. Women allegedly have a
"natural" interest in educating children and maintaining contact with
young people. They are attracted by the time compatibility and work
schedule of the school system, especially if they themselves have offspring with a similar schedule. They are more apt than are men to
remember school as a pleasant place in which they proved to themselves and their teachers that they were competent. Labeling by significant others and the self in terms of school success is augmented
by the presence of female role models. Thus, it is easier for girls than
for boys to identify with the role of teacher of young children. Coming

from higher status homes than men in the occupation, they see it as a more secure occupation and one more acceptable to their families than other occupations for which entry is blocked by many factors (Lortie, 1975, ch. 2).

Despite its white collar and "professional" status and self-imagery, teaching of elementary school pupils is not a high status or high paying occupation. Those men who do enter it often come from blue-collar backgrounds and use teaching as a stepping stone to more lucrative careers. There are many explanations of the low status of this set of jobs:

> Although teachers deal with people rather than with things [an ancient distinction], the people they deal with are minors. They miss the rewards, psychological and political, of serving people with high status and power. Their daily work is often programmed by state departments of education, non-teachers supervise and direct them in ways which make the autonomy prized by traditional professionals and entrepreneurs impossible. Under such conditions, we should not be surprised that the recruitment of committed [teaching] professionals is difficult (Geer, 1968: 564).

Actually, it is mainly the professional cadre of the society which would consider the characteristics of teaching as lacking autonomy. Teachers themselves and the public at large visualize the classroom situation as relatively autonomous, or cellular with self-contained units (Lortie, 1975: 14). However, despite the psychic rewards, the whole situation of the teacher, especially in public elementary schools, is a source of numerous role strains. We can examine some of these strains at this point.

Public school teachers are trained and hired as professionals, but must also conform to the demands of the bureaucratic system which is their employer (Lortie, 1969; 1975). Although they come into the school with special knowledge, which is used within their role, they do not function as autonomous workers and they have not produced this knowledge. Their job is to communicate it to students who are assigned to them without choice on the part of the teacher. This job must be carried out within the constraints demanded by the local community school board, the superintendent, and the principal (Etzioni, 1969; Lortie, 1969, 1975). The administration regards teachers as employees and not always as professional ones. This is mainly because it can hire and fire teachers easily until they receive tenure and can pretty much dictate what is taught and how it is to be communicated. Hall (1975) describes teachers as working in heteronomous organizations where mastery of knowledge is only one condition of being an employee. In heteronomous organizations autonomy is minimal, because the teaching staff and other segments of the circles are subordinated and confined by an administrative work structure. Within this framework there exists a system of rules for supervision which controls nearly all tasks, including the communication of knowledge. Heteronomous organizations are typically service oriented public agencies, with the public being invested in the operation of the system and the performance of the professional employees. Thus, as Hall (1975) points out, the professional employee in an heteronomous organization, i.e., the teacher in a school, cannot exercise her own judgment and is accountable to both administrative controls and external norms of performance. The juggling of both sets of values, the local and the cosmopolitan, creates strain (Goode, 1960; Gouldner, 1957; Merton, 1968).

More personalized sources of strain can come from relations with members of the teacher's social circle. Superintendents and principals are often trained in occupations other than teaching and "do not understand" the teacher's needs. Assignments to schools and classes are made in order to satisfy the system, rather than the teacher or the student. Students are also assigned without choice; they are incompletely socialized at entrance to function as students in a group situation where the unit's goals rather than their own must be met (Lortie, 1975). The teacher must combine instrumental and expressive leadership qualities, teach many students, maintain order, gain attention, and carry forth all the other duties of the system, such as clerical work and participation in its activities. Teachers frequently complain of interruptions making their major duties difficult to carry forth. Students can be sources of trouble if they are uncooperative and make teaching of others less than effective (Lortie, 1975). Parents are often hostile, being interested mainly in the attention given to their own child, while the teacher must look after the welfare of the whole class. At the same time, the teacher is dependent upon the parent to prepare the child psychologically to learn and to cooperate with the teacher, to send the child to school in proper health and general physical condition, to insure an environment enabling learning at home. Becker (1972) claims that "A school is a lousy place to learn anything in," quoting Herndon's

> ... hypothesis that nobody learns anything in school, but middle-class children learn enough elsewhere to make it appear that schooling is effective; since lower-class children don't learn the material elsewhere, the schools' failure to teach them is apparent (Becker, 1972: 90).

Often, the teacher wants to "motivate" children for achievement in American society, while the parents' whole value system is being undermined by this very process. The conflict between what the teacher wants for the child and what the parent wants is especially apparent in cases of immigrant families (Denzin, 1973). The need to control the classroom, preventing disruptions by disorderly children without help from the school system or the parents (who are often unable to control their own children), has led in some cases to medicalization of social control through psychoactive drugs, with the help of the label "hyperkinesis" (Conrad, 1975). The alleged failure of teachers to teach American children led to extensive coverage in popular American magazines during the summer of 1983. The status of teachers was not helped by the statement that all too often they (the teachers) are the ones who couldn't become engineers, lawyers, or M.B.A.s. Lortie (1975: 33-34) found that three-quarters of the teachers he studied "considered another occupation before teaching." The assumption here is that other people in other occupations do not contemplate alternatives before setting out on one path.

Other sources of strain within the role of teacher, besides working in heteronomous organizations, the actions of superintendents, principals, and local school boards, students, and their parents, can come from the colleague group of other teachers. In actuality, because of the cellular nature of the self-contained classroom, contact with other teachers tends to be minimal, or on the peer level only. Lortie's (1975) sample and the teachers in our report (see Volume II) used other teachers for companionship, as sounding boards for sharing frustrations, and as a reference group. The main source of strain reported by Lortie (1975) and others arises from the difficulty of meeting the goals teachers assign themselves, that of making a significant contribution to their students' learning. One problem is the "gap between social expectations and the technical capacity" of the teacher, due partly to rigidity and unwillingness on the part of the system and the teachers themselves to introduce new teaching methods. Standards of achievement are indefinite, ambiguous, intangible, and anxiety producing. Self-assessment is hard and there is an absence of authoritative reassurance. Teachers are deeply involved in the classroom scene and its events, yet are faced with what Lortie (1975: ch. 6) calls "endemic uncertainties."

The high-school teaching scene is somewhat different, in that the teacher enters with a specialty of one field of knowledge, or at the most a set of allegedly related fields. Different students enter into more restricted relations with the teacher, and parents are often not as important to the in-classroom interaction. At the same time, the students are older and often much harder to control than is true of elementary school pupils. High schools have fewer women teachers, and men are paid more. The amount of knowledge, rather than teaching technique, allegedly is a source of judgment, thus providing a better environment for the ideology of "professionalization." Psychoanalytic interpretations of the motivating forces and "career dreams" of teachers state that those who enter grade schools were especially attached to and formed romantic images around their fathers, while high school teachers focus on school role models, leaving the family behind (Wright and Tuska, 1971). Ziegler (1971) finds "differing perceptions of the teaching experience" on the part of male and female high school teachers, due to what he claims is a female domination of the educational establishment, which reaches even to the higher level schools. Men have trouble establishing their authority and masculinity in such an environment and tend to act out male role models. This may in fact be the reason they were induced to enter the high school system anyway—because of the community concern over a lack of such models for boys in school. Grandjean and Bernal (1979: 97) found little difference between male and female teachers in Catholic secondary schools in Texas, except for "lower job stability, stronger service orientation, and greater concern for interpersonal relationships" on the part of the women. Men are reported in most studies to leave for higher status jobs, women for family roles, but those who leave or those who stay do not necessarily express dissatisfaction with the job (Chapman and Lowther, 1982). Other studies, including Lopata-Hayes' (1983) review of the literature, report frequent teacher "burnout," resulting in purposeful withdrawal from this occupation. Some of the sources of strain, especially the lack of control over their lives on the job, are being addressed by the recent trend toward unionization, including as established in 1983 in several cities, the willingness to strike to establish demands (Wildman, 1971).

Higher education presents its own set of problems and challenges to women faculty. It is here that we find some very interesting current changes. In order to be allowed to teach in a college or university, a person must have obtained a Ph.D., sometimes only an M.A. or its equivalent, depending upon the field and the school. Teaching in academia is very field limited, as evidenced by a structure which is along discipline lines. A student decides upon a major, or a combination of two, and minors sometime during undergraduate years. A master's degree already involves further specialization, and each Ph.D. has to be earned with expertise in one area. Changes in the distribution of women in academia are evident in the degree receiving level more than in professorial ranks. This is partly due to the newness of women's branching into various disciplines—encouraged by federal pressure against outward discrimination and by the women's movement—and partly due to a difficult to measure combination of latent discrimination and problems in role conflict. Looking again at Table 9.2 we can easily note the areas within which women decreased and those in which they increased their involvement on the bachelors, masters, and doctoral degree levels. With the exception of mathematics, education, and psychology, the increase has been across the board. One of the surprising findings is that 41 percent of the B.A. degrees awarded in mathematics in 1975-76 went to women. This proportion dropped considerably by the 1979-80 degree years, and also holds for masters degrees. On the other hand, there is a slight rise in women obtaining Ph.D.s in mathematics. Women withdrew somewhat from the traditional field of education in the B.A. and M.A. levels, but increased their share of Ph.D.s. This could be considered an interesting indication of greater professionalization. One reason that the percentage of change in woman's share of Ph.D.s is so dramatic in certain fields, of course, is that so few were there in 1975-76. This is true of business and management, health professions, engineering, theology and, to a lesser extent, physical sciences. Women still form a very small minority of persons receiving doctorates in 1979-80 in architecture, mathematics, and they appear to be withdrawing from the social sciences.

Bernard (1964) documented the scarcity of women in academia, their lower level of productivity than that of men, and the tendency of those who became professionally committed to never marry, to be divorced and, at any rate, to have children less often than was true of women in the general population. Her data go back to the 1950-1960 period and are corroborated by other studies of that time period. Centra (1975: 1) conducted a survey of 3,658 recipients of Ph.D. or Ed.D. degrees in 1950, 1960, and 1968 under the auspices of the Graduate Record Examinations Board. More of the 1968 graduates than of the prior group were married, and one-third of the Ph.D.s were not employed at the time of the survey:

> Over half of this group gave reasons for not working that were related to marital and family responsibilities. The most common reasons, in order of frequency, were pregnancy, the lack of suitable jobs in their

husbands' locales, the anti-nepotism policies of their husbands' employers, the absence of domestic help or day-care facilities, and their husbands' resistance to their working (Centra, 1975: 1).

The last named reason appears surprising, since many of the respondent women had started their degree work after marriage and since the men who married already degreed women certainly knew the heavy socialization toward professional activity experienced in graduate school. Those academics who are employed often delay total committment to the profession. According to Centra (1975: 2), "Men clearly outdistance women—an average of 15 publications for men to 9 for women." The only factor which made women comparable to men in their publication record was single marital status; years of experience, kinds of employment, and discipline did not make any significant difference.

The conclusion about productivity differences between women and men academics does not hold up when faculties at specific four-year universities are studied. Glenwick et al., (1978) examined, among other things, productivity by gender in 1970 at Cornell University and 1975 at the University of Rochester. Their conclusions contradict those of Centra (1975), and they support other studies with parallel results:

> This similarity [between male and female assistant professors] in job role—measured by such variables as degrees, number of publications, membership in professional organizations—has been documented in other recent surveys and is at variance with the popular stereotypes of women as less competent and less involved in their careers than men (Glenwick, et al., 1978: 520).

Widom and Burke (1978) used a mailed questionnaire to the full-time faculty of two universities with relatively elite status in the Northeast and found some very interesting things from their, unfortunately, small return sample. The job performance was similar for women and men; in fact, the former tended to be more conscientious in meeting their obligations. However, the women junior faculty tended to edit more articles and books, while the men more frequently wrote them. The main point they make is that the women underrated themselves in comparison to others, as far as their reputation as a teacher or a well published scholar with a professional reputation was concerned, even when they were the same in status as the men. The conclusion is that the men were "fairly accurate" in their appraisal of their standing while women were not.

We are suggesting that females have been socialized to believe that *all* these activities [the duties and obligations] are important for success and, hence, are somewhat misguided. Misguided and misdirected ability, no matter how outstanding, will not lead to productivity and success (Widom and Burke, 1978: 561).

The lack of self-confidence in one's status, combined with naivete as to the professional activities which are rewarded by academia, such as writing, rather than editing books, is undoubtedly a consequence of the newness of the academic role to so many women without female models in their families or graduate training.

Since the role of academician is probably one of the least gender imbued in the professional world, researchers have been interested in the mobility of women and men after they enter it (Bayer and Astin, 1975; Cole, 1979; Ferber & Loeb, 1973; Rossi and Calderwood, 1973; Simon et al., 1967). Consistent among the findings is the earnings gap between men and women in each of the academic ranks. This is documented for each field, as in sociology (Lewis et al., 1979; Patterson, 1971), or political science (Burton, 1979; Converse and Converse, 1971; Finifter, 1973). It is not the purpose of this book to document all the findings of the surveys and biographical sketches, but the overall picture is of women increasingly oriented toward academic work, still in lower rungs of the ladder, consistently underpaid, but facing fewer direct forms of discrimination. The change is attributed to the fear of universities in having affirmative action cases brought against them, especially in the years when the federal government took the anti-discrimination laws and policies seriously, and since most universities are heavily dependent upon federal money. Studies of sexual harrassment at graduate school level abound, and many academicians report prejudice or discrimination of less overt form. The Modern Language Association of America brought together a number of personal accounts of problems in academia, in part-time careers, dual careers, and shared appointments (Hoffman and DeSole, 1976). Many of these problems arise because women who marry academics either before or after furthering their own education, find themselves unable to get full-time positions. Others frequently give up jobs to move with the husband.

As in most other professions, women have been making gains in academic employment ... Affirmative Action has been a force in virtually every academic discipline and college and university in the country. Nevertheless, the discrepancy between males and females remains. Females continue to be more highly represented in the lower-status colleges and universities. They continue to be overrepresented at the bottom of the academic hierarchy [instructors and assistant professors] and underrepresented among associate and full professors (Ritzer, 1977: 340).

In spite of the increasing flexibility of academia in reference to admission and scheduling of adult students, the structuring of faculty careers remains rigid. The newly entering faculty member must establish her- or himself rapidly, with no variation in stages, through the main channel of research and publication. In the meantime, it is the young faculty member who must also carry the burden of committee work and such tasks as help with registration, all of which cut into either class preparation or the more promotion rewarding work. The combination of a heavy teaching schedule in most schools, especially at the lower ranks, and the committee work in addition to the need to establish oneself in the scientific field or discipline, makes it almost impossible for women to add family roles at the very age when they are biologically and socially most encouraged to do so. Thus the figures that Bernard (1964), Yogev and Vierra (1983), and others present as to the high rate of childlessness among academic women may not be a consequence of a desire to be "child free" but of the inability to establish both the academic career and motherhood during the same time period.

The literature is replete with discussions of the problems, or lack of them, of academic women combining this role with that of wife and/or mother (Bernard, 1964; Glenwick et al., 1978; Simon et al., 1967; Yogev and Vierra, 1983). Yogev (1981) asks the question: "Do professional women have egalitarian marital relationships?" and comes to the surprising conclusion that they do not, and that many do not want to be freed from their home duties:

> Having an egalitarian marital relationship which also involved egalitarian sharing of housework and child care seems, therefore, to be beyond the identity tension line for today's professional woman. These women as a group thus seem to be currently undergoing a role expansion process which allows them to expand their horizons in an internal and psychological manner, without abandoning traditional functions and obligations (Yogev, 1981: 870).

This is a very interesting finding concerning women faculty at Northwestern University and fits with some other comments frequently heard, that women really do not want to give up or fully share those roles with which their identity has been tied in the past and in their own socialization. More research is needed here. It supports some of the other findings as to the influence of new occupations upon identities and role clusters discussed in this volume.

Sources of strain for women academics within the role are somewhat different than those for women at lower levels of the educational institution. Entering a male dominated academe, they face the same colleague and administration discrimination and problems of mobility experienced by other women in male intensive and culture infused professions (Davis, 1971b). They are a minority. In addition, although they need not deal with parents and have relative autonomy in the selection of course materials and techniques, they and their students are apt to have different goals. Students often see women university faculty as simply extensions of grade and high school teachers and refuse to admit their professional or scientific orientation. Students can also slip into the role of child vis-à-vis the mother, demanding personal time not requested of male professors (Lopata-Hayes, 1983). On the other hand, university faculty spend fewer hours in the classroom and have more energy and time for their creative work. The ideology of academic equality is more apt to exist in universities than in business or other professional worlds, so that hostility may be less overt. In sum, however, most reports on the situation of women in academia show evidence of role strain and role conflict and the unwillingness of the system to adjust to time schedules and career lines different from those established for males when they functioned in a two-person career situation with back up wives. The old system provided "fringe benefits" to universities derived from highly educated wives who were not directly involved in the university structure (Bernard, 1964; H. Hughes, 1977).

Health and Welfare Professionals and Technologists

The tight control American medical practitioners have over entrance into training and licensing for the professions of physician and dentist has resulted in a shortage of people in these occupations. This shortage is not so much nationwide, but is pronounced in the locations in which the survivors of the filtering system do not want to practice. The shortage almost guarantees lucrative practices in more prestigious communities, but denies entrance into these professions to people who would be willing to provide health services in less traditional ways and to less "desirable" segments of society. The work load facing prestigious physicians and dentists is such as to lead to the creation of numerous occupations in allied fields. The allied health occupations include:

> all those professional, technical and supportive workers in the field of patient care, community health, public health and public related research who engage in activity that supports, complements, or supplements the professional function of administrators, physicians and dentists (Carter and Carter, 1981: 489) . . . In 1977, when only 13 percent of all full-time health practitioners were women, women accounted for 83.4 percent of all full-time allied health professionals (490).

As we saw in Table 9.1, very few women are dentists, and relatively few as yet are practicing physicians although many are attending medical school. On the other hand, the traditional occupations of nurse, dietician, health technologist, and health service worker are still dominated by the female worker in American society. A list of full-time federal white-collar employees includes those in: nuclear medicine, pathology, medical radiology, medical technical assistance, restoration, dental hygiene, public health dental hygiene, and occupations such as orthodontist, prosthetist, medical record librarian, prosthetic representative, medical record technician, environmental health technician, and so forth. These technical occupations vary not only by task and location in the health system, but also by gender dominance (Pennell and Showell, 1975: 22). For example, although 100 percent of public health hygiene is carried out by women, only men are prosthetic representatives, and most of the restorative work on body parts is done by them.

We will proceed in our discussion of the health professionals and technologists from the "semi-profession" of nursing to some of the newer allied occupations and then to the woman physician and dentist. Social workers, who may or may not work in a medical setting, will close this section.

> Nursing, an ancient activity, was long performed mainly within the family, or by religious sisters. It has become so professional that women may nurse strange men. Nurses exert great authority and perform services requiring higher education. But nursing is not part of an apprenticeship to the medical profession (Hughes et al., 1958: 6-7).

> Healing was female when it was a neighborly service, based on stable communities where skills could be passed on for generations and where the healer knew her patients and their families. When the attempt to heal is detached from personal relationships to become a commodity

and a source of wealth itself—then does the business of healing become a male enterprise (Ehrenreich and English, 1979: 41).

Much of the literature dealing with nurses focuses on their "semi-professional" status, attempting to explain the occupation's origin and to predict the success of attempts to change it. The profession (we will call it that, since it is so listed in all discussions of occupational structure) grew separately from that of medicine as practiced by doctors. Florence Nightingale is credited with organizing the care of nonfamily members of the society into the modern occupational role of nurse. She insisted that the nurse be trained and coordinated clinical and academic programs of schooling and refresher courses to keep nurses up to date with medical advances throughout their careers. She envisioned the role as collaborative with that of the doctor, rather than as subordinate (Cope, 1958; Dolan, 1973). Modern authors contend that her Victorian emphasis on chastity and "womanly" behavior further established the nurse as the doctor's handmaiden, rather than as his partner (Bullough, 1978; Cope, 1958; see also Bullough and Bullough, 1978).

One of the important characteristics of nursing is that most of the jobs are within hospitals, hierarchically organized, bureaucratically managed complex systems, with control of medical care in the hands of physicians (Hall, 1975). The simultaneous growth of hospitals and the increase in authority over medical care that is in the hands of physicians brought women into the system as nurses and, in recent years, as various service workers who are generally under nurses in status and control. The duty and right of physicians in hospitals is to diagnose patients and prescribe methods of treatment, but not to care for them on a day-to-day basis. Such care became the job of the nurse (Ehrenreich and English, 1973, 1979). In early years, nurses were recruited primarily from the servant classes in Europe and America, except during wars when upper-class women often volunteered to care for wounded service men. The job of a hospital nurse was hard, dangerous before medical knowledge decreased contagious diseases, and often embarrassing. It was considered inappropriate for a young lady of "breeding." It has been suggested by observers of the situation of modern nurses that this conception of the occupation has continued to limit the status and function of nurses even to the present day (Devereux and Weiner, 1962; Montagna, 1977).

The literature on nursing has also focused on the alleged "feminine" traits of nurses, who are seen as dependent, passive, conformist, and deferential (Davis, 1971a; Goffman, 1956; Hudson-Rosen, et al., 1974; Hughes, 1971d; Wilson, 1971). The subordinate position of nurses is reinforced by the sex stratification in the society in general and the medical professions in particular. Nurses are predominately women, while doctors have been mainly men. This immediately establishes a power differential, as with the dental hygienist, except that the latter is likely to be working in a small office. Nurses have been trained in the past to follow doctors' orders, further legitimating their authority within the hospital. Nurses may administer many medications, following doctors' orders, but they may not prescribe medications themselves, even in emergency situations. They are often limited in the amount and kind of information they may pass on to the patient concerning her or his condition. And, in most states, the role of nurse is specifically outlined and limited through the administration of state nurse practice acts. Such laws are currently under debate, but nonetheless they have profoundly influenced the development of nursing as a profession dependent on that of physicians.

After establishing the semi-professional nature of nursing, the literature often turns to discussions of ways through which women in this occupation manage to manipulate the physicians. They do this indirectly, through subtle "games" which do not threaten the authority system:

> They do this by means of hints, flattery, and feminine wiles, rather than by making open statements. Such an approach is not unusual among groups of people who have little formal power; they learn to negotiate power by devious means (Bullough, 1978: 52).

Nurses vary considerably by their training and the locales within which they practice. There has been a great deal of change undermining some of the traditional aspects of these roles, while the desire to change others meets with stiff resistance from the established professionals.

One of the main problems of the nursing profession has been a lack of agreement, in fact, a conflict internally over the best ways of establishing itself and educating new generations. Hall (1983) points to the weakness of the main organization, the American Nurses' Association, to which only 30 percent of all nurses are members, and which is not functioning effectively. Multiple and conflicting goals interfere with its being able to coordinate efforts and the split over education is dramatic.

The dependence of nurses upon doctors grew in large part due to their early training within hospitals, with limited medical knowledge and a system most resembling apprenticeship. The movement to professionalize nursing included the development of its own body of knowledge, transmitted in an academic setting. In recent years, this setting has increasingly been a university, with practice in several different hospitals, rather than only in the one affiliated with the educational establishment. As of 1980, there were 1,403 nurse training programs in the United States, as well as 127 master's programs, and several universities offered a Ph.D. in nursing (U.S. Department of Labor, 1982). Heyrman (1982) found two distinct subgroups represented in nursing education: educators with a university affiliation and clinicians who are primarily associated with a hospital (Rowland, 1978). Alutto, et al., (1971) claim there is little difference in professional organizations or clinical commitment among nurses trained in different programs, but Heyrman (1982), Corwin (1961), and Orzack (1971) disagree. Kramer (1976) reports that clinicians see bachelors programs as counterproductive because they are not adjusted to the reality of hospital life and fail to provide sufficient professional socialization (Becker, et al., 1968; Psathas, 1968). The professional identification of nursing students has been a source of concern. The seventies have seen the pendulum swing back to a "collaborative model of practice and education" (Grace, 1981; Heyrman, 1982; MacPhail, 1975; Purik, 1973; Simpson, 1967).

In 1980 there were approximately 1,105,000 registered nurses employed, with about one-third of them working part-time (U.S. Department of Labor, 1982). Almost all of the registered nurses are women (98 percent). The demand for nurses has risen greatly in response to population growth, the increased availability of public and private health insurance, and increased interest in preventive and rehabilitative care. According to Davis, Olesen and Whittaker (1966), however, only 54 percent of nursing students chose this occupation as their first or second role upon graduation. Approximately 25 percent of all RNs left the field completely in 1980, and it was estimated that only 60 percent of all licensed RNs are working at any one time (Saleh et al., 1965; Sloan and Richupan, 1975). The shortage of nurses in the 1970s and 1980s has not been met by an increase in salaries, the nurses being very conscious of the gap between their earnings and those of physicians.

Each locale within which nurses practice has its own sources of role strain. We mentioned some of these above. Looking at the whole bureaucratic structure, we find pressure from the medical profession to follow its model of the perfect nurse as obedient to the doctor, while the nurse would like to organize and control the care of the patient from her perspective (Katz, 1969; Montagna, 1977; Rushing, 1971). The expansion of allied medical workers on the hospital scene has added a new source of role strain for the nurses.

> The central conflict in the hospital is the classic one between management [and doctors] on the one side and labor on the other—the governors and the governed. The contest is also a de facto sexist conflict with the governors as largely male and the governed female.
> A secondary struggle also occurs in the hospital because a buffer class—the RNs—stands between the main contestants. While RNs have had notorious difficulties with those above them, their main conflict is with ancillary staff. . . .this secondary conflict tends to obscure the main one (Sexton, 1982: 47).
> . . . The relationship between registered nurses and practical/vocational nurses is a smoldering issue that threatens to erupt now after growing in intensity for many years (Goldstein, 1983: 14).

Besides direct patient care, which involves "observing, assessing, and recording the patient's reactions, symptoms, and progress, most hospital RNs are supervisors in charge of a work group, which is the source of problems mentioned above (U.S. Department of Labor, 1975a, 1982). Time spent on supervision and administration leaves much of the day-to-day care of the ill to *The New Nightingales* (Sexton, 1982), or the lesser trained personnel (Habenstein and Christ, 1955; Montagna, 1977).

The second largest group of nurses (86,000 in 1980) work in long-term care facilities dealing with chronically ill or slowly recuperating patients, their duties being less dramatic and perhaps more mundane than those of the hospital nurses (U.S. Department of Labor, 1982: 170). In addition, 70,000 nurses worked that year in doctors' or dentists' offices, where they are directly answerable to one or a limited number of physicians. They prepare patients for examinations and assist the doctor in routine and emergency medical tasks. They are often called upon to do other tasks, relegated to different personnel in larger offices. Community health nurses are also a significant segment of this occupational group (63,000 in 1980). They care for patients in community and home settings and are likely to be heavily involved in educating the public regarding health issues. School nurses accounted for 40,000 members of the profession and 25,000 RNs were located in industrial settings in 1980. They usually administer first aid, plan and carry out general health programs, maintain health records, and educate the client. The basic difference in their jobs lies in the site of the activities and the age of the clients (U.S. Department

of Labor, 1975a, 1975b, 1982). Private duty nurses may be entrepreneurs controlling their time and type of case, or they may work
through an agency that places nurses in temporary or even relatively
extended positions. They provide bedside care for one patient at a
time. Sometimes this takes place within a hospital, but more often
private-duty nurses work within the homes of the patients themselves.
Such jobs offer more autonomy and greater opportunities for intense
and personalized patient interaction than is true of the hospital setting.

Literature dealing with the commitment of nurses to their profession is mixed. The high rate of drop-out in school and emphasis on
family roles are used as evidence of the problem of developing strong
occupational commitment on the part of young women in America
(Davis, 1966; Davis, Olesen and Whittaker, 1966; Katz, 1979; Simpson, 1967; Simpson and Simpson, 1969). A great deal of the relevant
literature concentrates on the initial socialization of the student
nurse. Psathas (1968) claims that upon entering nursing school the
idealistically inclined students soon lose that idealism and Krueger,
(1971) that the most obedient nursing students do not necessarily
make the best nurses in a hospital. Both Davis (1971a) and Olesen and
Whittaker (1969) focus on the importance of changes in the self-
concept of the young woman as she becomes a nurse. The students
must accept the profession's definition of the role and their own definition of themselves as in it and as "a nurse." Olesen and Whittaker
(1969: 291) call the socializing process *The Silent Dialogue* which
also involved an identity shift:

> This interior landscape quickly became populated with self-installed
> signposts and way stations as the student began to regulate her own
> socialization through self-testing, self-pacing, and, most importantly,
> self-legitimation—in short, according herself the role of nurse.

According to these authors, the women who survive the training retain the identity of nurse, even if they leave the field, especially if
they stop nursing for homemaking rather than for other occupational
roles. Orzack (1971) found four out of five nurses committed to work-
centered goals and Montagna (1977) reports that they received personal satisfaction and meaningful informal group relations at work.
These satisfactions vary according to whether the woman is a "tradi-
tionalizing nurse" who is highly dedicated and uncritical of the hospital and her status, the "utilizing" nurse who has a "strong commitment neither to professional knowledge nor to traditions of the
hospital or medicine" and who just wants to do her job, or a "profes-

sionalizer" who takes seriously the scientific aspect of her role (Habenstein and Christ, 1955). A major problem for employers is the high rate of turnover (Brief and Aldag, 1980). Several observers suggest that the older nurse, without children or returning after her children have partly grown, tends to be more committed than the young woman awaiting involvement in family roles. This finding, however, ignores the newly socialized nurse who sees herself as a professional and part of a medical team. All in all, the nursing profession contains a wide range of practitioners, who vary in the amount and kind of training they receive, the work they do, the settings within which it is done, and the attitudes they hold toward being a nurse and the self as a nurse.

The training most nurses obtain prepares them mainly for hospital in-patient, crisis care even if they end up working in nursing homes in which these skills are rarely required.

A new category of nurse practitioner has recently been added. These are registered nurses with additional training "to qualify as a primary care provider" (Gibbons and Grosgebauer, 1976: 10).

> Approximately 300 schools of nursing across the country offer training programs of from one to two years that prepare participants for certification by the American Nurses' Association. . . . Nurse practitioner programs prepare the nurse to conduct physical examinations, administer diagnostic tests, compile histories, and to treat the myriad of minor colds, bumps, cuts and infections that account for the majority of doctor's office visits (Gibbons and Grosgebauer, 1976: 10).

These health workers can set up private nursing practices, but most work in close association with physicians, "in hospitals, outpatient clinics, health maintenance organizations, and in the offices of private physicians" (Gibbons and Grosgebauer, 1976: 11).

Nurse-midwifes have finally established themselves as a legitimate occupation, having been pushed out of the care of pregnant women and the delivery of children with the tightening of competition controls by the obstetricians, who are mainly men. Modern women have been organizing a revolt against the depersonalized delivery practices of hospitals in which the mother is made passive, usually with the help of anesthetics. The American College of Nurse-Midwives was established in 1955, and the 1970s saw a hesitant, but definite reception of their practice. As of 1976, however, there were only about 1800 certified nurse-midwives practicing in the United States (Gibbons and Grosgebauer, 1976: 12). Certification can be followed by licensing "by the legal jurisdiction in which she is employed" (Gibbons and Grosgebauer, 1976: 12), which is often difficult, even impossible to obtain. The women are trained to give more complete care to the women before, during, and after delivery than busy obstetricians are allegedly able to offer. One of the processes by which the allied medical occupations have worked to acquire near professional status has been through a credentials process that attempts to standardize the competency of all those who use the occupational label. The associations responsible for credentialing are supposed to control not only entrance, but also the action of the professionals, guaranteeing disciplinary action in abuse cases. National credentialing enables geographical mobility currently unavailable to physicians who must pass the examination of each state in which they practice (Wilson, 1976).

Women in the new role of physicians' assistant often practice in rural or small town areas where they are allowed to diagnose, prescribe, and treat, but under general supervision of a physician in difficult cases (Clark, 1980). Many doctors will not use them, while others become quite dependent upon such relatively independent co-workers.

> A physician's assistant is a person who is specially trained to provide a variety of medical services to patients under the supervision of a licensed physician. The American Medical Association recognizes three basic types of assistants:
>
> Type 'C' represents the lowest level of training and skills. Tasks performed by these individuals require no judgmental decisions and are performed under the direct supervision of a physician.
>
> Type 'B' assistants usually possess specialized training in a specific area, like surgery, but lack a broad range of general medical skills.
>
> Type 'A' assistants have passed a certifying examination prepared by the National Board of Medical Examiners. Certificate holders possess a broad range of medical skills, are capable of making medical judgments, and are able to function away from the direct surveillance of a physician (Gibbons and Grosgebauer, 1976: 8).

Medical assistants are trained to work in a physician's office, to take X-rays, perform EKG (electro-cardiographs), carry out laboratory work, and also conduct office procedures.

Another major and relatively new occupation that is striving for professional status is that of dental hygienist. "The traditional role of a hygienist has been one of working for a dentist to increase the dentist's productivity" (Green and Jong, 1980: 377). The attempt to professionalize, modeled after that of the nursing occupation, has involved two actions: removal of control by the dentist and the formation of a unique body of knowledge in a university setting by a "community of scholars" (Brine and Rossman, 1979: 219).

> With an expanding knowledge base, dental hygiene would become accountable among health professionals for decision-making and would function in a significantly different manner from the present boundaries of dental hygiene practice (Brine and Rossman, 1979: 219).

One of the major problems of dental hygiene as an occupation has been the traditional emphasis of the training programs on the technical, rather than the knowledge base of the practice. Another is the fact that people, mostly women, can enter practice from any of four different training centers. This includes the two-year program, after which the woman can practice with as much authority (or lack of it) as does a four-year baccalaureate graduate. This "stifles" the "incentive to pursue advanced study" (Brine and Rossman, 1979: 220). The movement to develop a knowledge base and training for Ph.D. degrees is ambitious and, as Brine and Rossman (1979) state, risk-taking because even the teachers of dental hygiene do not possess more than a master's degree. In the meantime, the American Dental Hygienists' Association has been pushing the Federal Trade Commission to "seek nullification of state restrictions that require dental hygienists to work under dentist supervision" (Green and Jong, 1980: 380).

One of the facts that drew our attention when looking at the Chicago area respondents in our study was that ten women reported dental hygiene occupations in their last job, but none of them are currently working in it. One reason for this is that the occupation is relatively new and most of its practitioners are young and without children (Green and Jong, 1980: 378). They are the most apt to withdraw from the labor force in the next few years. On the other hand, the literature directed to and about dental hygienists reports a definite alienation from the occupation, rather typical of the semi-professions of recent years, or practitioner cohorts. McAdams (1976) lists four problems of the occupation and basic "Reasons Dental Hygienists Dislike their Practice."

> Four problem areas facing dental hygiene today: the increased demand for dental care; the expected dental manpower shortages; the disparity between dental hygiene education and the professional practice; and the high attrition rate of recent graduates from the practice of dental hygiene . . .(McAdams, 1976: 563).

She studied members of the Northern California Dental Hygienists' Association in 1974 and found that what was most unacceptable to the women were the limitations on their practice "imposed by law: and the lack of influence on how the dental practice was carried forth." Dentists are accustomed to operating independently and do not consider it necessary to hold staff meetings and ask for opinions from young women. Hygienists are trained as "professionals" and complain that they infrequently can refer patients to a periodontist. They are often treated as simply dental assistants, there to ease the work load of the dentist instead of as experts in their own right. The gap between the authority they are educated to expect and the rights they are given, or not given, in the dentist's office is the major problem here, as in many situations in which the person whose territory and practice are established attempts to work new components into his (or her) social circle. This is particularly true if the established practitioner, medical, legal, or other independent specialist is a male, older than the newcomer who is a young female. Strain abounds from each direction (Cole and Cohen, 1971).

The final health-related professions we will discuss in this section on health and welfare form the top of the structure of this industry: physicians, psychiatrists, and dentists. These are traditionally labeled as male occupations in American society. Gross (1971) found these occupations to be the least changed in terms of the presence of women in the last few decades. An expanding literature has focused around this topic—on the shortage of female practitioners, the characteristics of women who have entered these fields and areas of specialization, as well as role strain and role conflict. As far as physicians are concerned, the topic has also been the rapid recent increase of women in medical schools and their attempts to establish different kinds of practice. As far as dentists are concerned, the topic is still the dearth of women. The fact that so much literature focuses on the women in the medical professions is of itself interesting, since as Lorber (1975) has pointed out, they have been invisible in medical sociology in the past (see also Marieskind, 1980).

We mentioned before that the medical profession squeezed women out of any but informal or highly controlled health care occupations (Starr, 1982). One reason women themselves have been traditionally hesitant to enter the medical field was the length and expense of education. Families and schools were less willing to invest in such schooling for women than for men, and most women were reluctant to give up the early childbearing years and possibly forego parenthood entirely. It took the women's movement and the action of the federal government to open up the doors of medical schools to women, albeit this was not done very gracefully. Traditionally, the medical profession once established has favored white males of the higher social classes. Observers admit, however, that it is changing. Although it is still hierarchical in its specialties, with women entering the least prestigious fields (pediatrics or obstetrics; almost never surgery), the profession has moved toward increased involvement in community and family health (Kosa and Coker, 1971). Women are more apt to take on such positions or to enter government medical jobs. Some are able to combine private practice with family responsibility (Lorber, 1982).

Social scientists have tried to determine how women who enter occupations dominated by men, in which they are apt to be tokens or at least in the minority, choose such an unusual path. We mentioned this interest in discussing women in nontraditional blue-collar jobs; it is repeated in reference to professional and technical roles. Why do some women become physicians and dentists instead of nurses and medical rehabilitators? (Smock et al., 1980; Trigg and Perlman, 1976). According to Smoth and associates (1980), the professionals in newly opening occupations had mothers who worked and who had been relatively well-educated themselves. Mothers of male physicians were less likely to have been employed. Fathers of the female physicians were encouraging and the daughters obtained their socioeconomic status through their own occupation, rather than through their husband's (Smock et al., 1980). Trigg and Perlman (1976) found the father's education also to have influenced the daughter's professional choice:

> Crucial factors encouraging women to pursue a nontraditional health science career include: low need affiliation, high need achievement, perceiving support in the attitudes of others [particularly mothers], a low need to have children, and perceiving the need to have a family as being compatible with a nontraditional career (Trigg and Perlman, 1976: 149).

According to Cartwright (1977, 1978), who studied graduates of the University of California, San Francisco medical school after 8-11 years of practice, once women enter practice as physicians, they tend to become more traditional as to role demands. Their push for success decreased as did their need to impress others, and they became more conservative and settled. Although they saw less conflict in their role complex than they expected, these women drifted into the more traditional specialties, and those with many children expressed problems. Being out of a school environment enabled them to relax professional norms.

One of the arguments against women's entrance into demanding professions, such as medicine, is the possibility that they may interrupt their careers to have children. Quadagno (1978) found that men in the cohorts she studied around retirement age had also interrupted their careers, but for different reasons. As Holmstrom (1973: 54) pointed out:

> In a curious paradox of human values men have been criticized only slightly for career interruptions in which their task was to kill off other members of the human race; but women have been severely criticized for taking time away from their profession in order to raise the next generation.

Quadagno (1978) did not find any difference in the commitment to the medical career between those physicians who did and those who did not interrupt their careers. Lorber (1982) studied the influence of the spouses on each other's careers, using physicians and numerous other studies dealing with role conflict. Strain within occupational role was reported to be a result of working with terminal patients (Vachon et al., 1976, 1978), as often as it arose from the presence of gender differences. The process of professional incorporation is a long one, and women often lack sponsorship to a prestigious hospital or referrals from other physicians that are so necessary to a career. Still, it does occur (Hall, 1948; Ortiz, 1975). Yet, and in spite of all the difficulties, most women physicians do persist in their career, especially in cases in which the interest in becoming a physician began early and identification through association with physicians enabled easy role taking (Mandelbaum, 1976).

Women psychiatrists face similar problems to those of other physicians, with a few additional complications. Especially when influenced by Freudian theories, the profession was not favorable toward women as participants of this or of any other demanding and "masculine" occupation. In addition, many women psychiatrists work alone and feel isolated from female contact (Kirkpatrick, 1975). In forming consciousness-raising groups in several parts of the country, but especially in Southern California, women in this field were able to compare their problems, especially in situations in which they "felt ourselves to be seen as openly competing with men—for position, for money, for the right to speak, for 'room at the top'" (Kirkpatrick, 1975: 207).

Women dentists are few and far between. In 1970 only 49 percent worked full time, 19 percent specialized in periodontics or orthodontics, and 55 percent in general dentistry (Boquist and Haase, 1972).

Linn (1971) states in "Women Dental Students: Women in a Man's World," that "the number of women dentists in the United States is uncertain" and women students in dental schools formed only a little over 1 percent. This situation is very different from that in the USSR, Greece, and even Denmark. Many of the women dentists practicing in the United States were trained elsewhere (see also Lemkau, 1979).

Social workers, who can be located between the health and welfare workers and the people-focused occupations, work in a variety of settings and have widely diversified social circles.

> Matching the variety of training undergone and tasks performed by [social] workers is the diversity of settings in which they operate, some few functioning as solo practitioners, most typically as family counselors, others working for specialized private agencies and the majority serving as employees in a variety of public settings—schools, hospitals, correction facilities and public assistance agencies (Scott, 1969: 83).

Fink (1974a) traces some of the ideology surrounding social work to England and the Elizabethan Poor Laws. As we mentioned before, concern with members of the society who had problems maintaining themselves economically and psychologically, including women and children, was tinged in America with a moralistic judgment. Care of such people began in this country as a purely voluntary social service. The Charity Organization Societies, originated in London, spread to this continent's cities and its volunteer "friendly visitors" took upon themselves the obligation to investigate every applicant for relief:

> An attitude that regarded the needy as victims of their own vices and failings tended to absolve the social order of any responsibility for the conditions that reduced individuals to destitution . . . [making] relief as unattractive as possible (Fink, 1974b: 39).

Only gradually did local communities, then states, and finally the federal government decide that the society is at least partially responsible for many of its members' problems (Fink, 1974b). Aid to blind needy, widows and children, older people, the unemployed, and other groups at risk gradually became incorporated into the system. Social Security was introduced in 1935, modified to include dependent wives, widows, and minor children in 1939. Two separate systems emerged, an income maintenance program, (social welfare) and a social service program which helps people utilize community resources. These required an army of social workers, or paid public or private employees (Wiltse, 1974). The history of upper- and middle-class volunteerism shows it assisted the newly developing social work occupation in its attempt to establish professional status. The first professional journal was founded in 1891, a rather limited summer school was established in 1898, and several professional associations were organized (Fink, 1974b). However, the occupation remains identified as a semi-profession in spite of all these attempts. Gurin and Williams (1973) quote Flexner, who studied the major professions in and around 1915 and concluded that social work had not achieved such a status because it lacked an area of intellectual knowledge distinctly its own, and was not based on "standards of *individual* responsibility" on the part of the practitioner. The occupation does not control the employer, and it is that establishment, not the organization of social workers, which judges performance and determines caseloads and the form of assistance. Although social workers can obtain master's degrees for certain specialties and even Ph.D.s, few go as far as the higher degree, and the more educated turn to research or teaching in universities, rather than to practice. In fact, entrance into the occupation is quite open, with many practitioners having in essence no relevant training (Gurin and Williams, 1973). Toren (1969, 1972), in both her chapter for the Etzioni (1969) book on the *Semi-Professions* and in her own book published later, makes a strong point concerning the lack of "pure" professional status on the part of social work. The original placement of the field into that classification was probably Carr-Saunders in 1955 (see Toren, 1969: 145), and he stressed the lack of practitioner autonomy. The main argument, similar to the one used to describe teachers as semi-professionals, is the dependence of the role on the public or private bureaucratic organization, within which most social workers are located (see also Scott, 1969). It is this location that is reportedly a major source of strain in the occupation. Social workers tend to enter the profession with idealistic goals of helping people, but the organization which employs them is usually tax supported and must operate within tight constraints. Since Americans are very individualistic and moralistic toward people with problems and are concerned over "welfare," which is surrounded by many myths of cheating, social workers are highly regulated as to the help they can actually offer (Toren, 1972; Tropman, 1971). A fairly recent (1968) law no longer requires that workers in family income maintenance programs (AFDC) have to look in the household for signs of a male who could be a breadwinner, but strain is inevitable for social workers in relations with clients (Handel,

1982; see also Lopata, 1984). For example, much of social service work is connected with problems of children. It is the social worker who must often decide whether or not there is child neglect or abuse in a family and whether to remove the youngster for placement in a foster home (Fink et al., 1974; Kennedy, 1974; Lopata, 1984; Taber, 1974; Tropman, 1971; Wittner, 1978). Social workers who are located in schools deal not only with the children, but also with parents, teachers, school administrators, outside agencies, and so forth (Kennedy, 1974). Those located in hospitals or clinics have medical personnel as part of their social circle. The role in general is a mediating one between the person needing help and the agencies involved. Often the agencies in the community have different ideologies and views of the situation than does the social worker. This is usually the case of probation officers dealing with the police, judges, and lawyers (Albrecht, 1979). Some of the neighborhoods into which social workers venture can be dangerous and the person-role strain immense. Mayer and Rosenblatt (1975) studied the means by which social workers cope with danger both psychologically and in attempts to protect themselves from assault.

Social work is dominated by women, especially at the lower levels, and these women traditionally come from fairly middle-class families (Gurin and Williams, 1973). However, as Toren (1969) points out, they are increasingly drawn from "lower social strata" and, according to Gurin and Williams (1973), from minorities. One reason for the need to constantly recruit new practitioners is the high attrition rate, usually explained not just by the presence of childbearing women, but also by burnout. The combination of strain in relations with clients and in relations with supervisors is a strong one. The history of social work is grounded in reform impulses and in the simultaneous need to help people adjust to what can be seen as unfair and discriminatory social systems. This creates a double-bind situation aggravated by the helplessness of achieving the reform of the person or the system (Toren, 1969; 1973; Tropman, 1971). In addition, the rewards, in terms of prestige, money, or positive feedback are not great (Bucklew and Parenton, 1971). Some of the strain has been decreased by the movement of the field of social work away from Freudian psychoanalytic theory and practice to community work and sociological theory (Toren, 1969). Individual casework is noted for its burnout effect, while community and group work is apparently more rewarding. An important impetus to this movement came from the Chicago Settlement home development.

Women in People-Focused Occupations

As with all the categories of occupations falling under the professional and technical umbrella, the "people-focused" category encompasses a wide variety of jobs, most of which can be called semi-professional if gender domination is not the primary criterion for the label. This includes librarians, vocational and educational counselors, personnel and labor relations specialists, public relations consultants, management consultants, editors, reporters, and other media news specialists, and lawyers. Included are also religious workers such as clergy and lesser status professionals.

> Library work is divided into two basic functions: User services and technical services. Librarians in user services—for example, reference and children's librarians—work directly with users to help them find the information they need. Librarians in technical services—such as acquisitions librarians and catalogers—are primarily concerned with acquiring and preparing materials for use and deal less frequently with the information user (U.S. Department of Labor, 1982: 138).

Librarians, archivists, and curators are predominately female and white (Otto, et al., 1980). The median level of education reached by the women in such jobs is 15.13 years, that of the men in the occupation a full year higher. This means that the occupation contains many people with graduate education, a requirement that has recently come to be demanded by the larger public and more prestigious educational institutions. Only 16 percent of the workers obtained additional vocational training. People in these occupations tend to work part-time (24 percent) more often than many other professionals; 19 percent were employed only 40 to 47 weeks per year. The schedule is due mainly to involvement in school systems which lack summer programs that include library hours (Otto, et al., 1980). Library jobs are identified as above average in complexity in dealing with data and people, in variety of work, responsibility, and overall complexity (Otto et al., 1980). Women are often substantially underpaid in librarianship, with average earnings which never reach those of men, regardless of age category.

Of primary interest to us here are librarians who work with people in public or school organizations. School and academic libraries together accounted for roughly seven out of ten librarians (U.S. Department of Labor, 1982: 139). Librarianship is frequently identified as being one of the female-dominated (83 percent in 1981, see Table 9.1) semi-professions, and men tend to identify themselves in terms of administrative career paths. The occupation is lumped together with social workers, teachers, and nurses, although each is very different from the others (Ritzer, 1977: 178). Role strain arises often, since librarians are limited in the services they can provide, the resources they can muster, and their relations with others by the structure of the larger organization within which the library is located, the administrators, their "clientele," the community and financial constraints. School librarians must acquire books recommended by teachers, sometimes with the guidance of school boards and are discouraged from leading students toward knowledge areas not favored by others in the system. Their desire to encourage students at all levels to expand their knowledge may thus be thwarted by those teachers and administrators who wish to focus learning to limited subjects. Even parents may impinge on role performance. They face the same sources of strain as other marginal professions (Ritzer, 1977). Librarians in elementary schools have less status and fewer benefits than do those servicing a more prestigious set of users, such as scholars or societal leaders, as is true of those in the United States Library of Congress.

Blankenship (1971), in studying college librarians, found that:

> There are opportunities for administration minded people of either sex in librarianship, [but] men are more likely to be head librarians of publicly supported colleges; of larger colleges; women head librarians tend to change positions less often than men; [and] men become head librarians at an earlier age than women (Blankenship, 1971: 101-2).

Vocational and educational counselors also tend to be primarily white (89 percent), but they are more evenly distributed by sex than are the librarians. In this case, the women have more schooling than the men, with a median of 18.0 to 17.83 years, though the differences are not large. The counselors work an average of the full 40 hour week, but a third are employed less than 50 weeks a year, probably because so many are associated with schools. The job is defined as above average in all job characteristics except complexity of working with things and closeness of supervision (Otto et al., 1980: 103). Most of it involves counseling of youths in schools and colleges on a one-to-one basis, although other persons may be brought in if the counselor determines a need. A survey of guidance and counseling divisions of state departments of education (Pressley, 1974), given impetus by a recent formation of a Commission for Women by the American Personnel and Guidance Association, reported that 65 percent of the elementary counselors, but only 43 percent of the secondary school counselors are women. Concern with the influence of counselors upon the occupational choices of girls led the association in 1973 to finally sponsor programs for counseling of all age women in a number of universities. However, 70 percent of the counselors who returned the survey (an 88 percent return rate) were not aware of any pre- or in-service programs aimed at decreasing the admitted bias (see also resolutions of March 26-29, 1972). Ahrons (1976) studied the counselors' perceptions of career images of women in view of the fact that:

> Studies on the effect of traditional or marriage socialization on women indicate that it has a significant effect on their vocational decisions by restricting their range of vocational choices (Ahrons, 1976: 197).

The Wisconsin state school counselors she studied perceived the concept of career woman as being in conflict with other female "appropriate" concepts, with the exception of traditionally female occupations, such as nursing. "The findings of this study suggest that counselors expect women to experience conflict in vocational choices that men do not experience" (Ahrons, 1976: 205).

The creation of large-scale bureaucracies in modern, industrialized, and urbanized societies has necessitated many layers of workers between management and employees. One of the staff functions of organizations has been the personnel or, as recently redefined, the human resource department. Two major sets of activities requiring professional, or semi-professional, staffs are personnel and labor relations.

> ...many enterprises have become too large to permit close contact between management and employees. Instead, personnel and labor relations specialists provide this link—assisting management to make effective use of employees' skills, and helping employees to find satisfaction in their jobs and working conditions (U.S. Department of Labor, 1982: 43).

Personnel departments often include recruiters who search out applicants, interview, and recommend and/or hire workers. Sometimes they are saddled with the job of firing them. Affirmative action coordinators protect the firm from trouble with the Equal Employment Opportunity Commission. Duties may also involve the training, "motivating," and counseling of workers and managers, as well as providing programs for the maintenance of morale in general. Cawsey (1980) claims that much role strain in personnel work comes from the absence of clear cut definitions, and lack of an hierarchical classification of functions. His solution is to place "motivators" or activities which increase worker satisfaction and production above the administrative/mechanistic or hygienic activities. Other sources of strain arise from the staff responsibility of the department which relies on persuasion rather than authority relations.

Cawsey (1980) found that personnel managers resort to stereotyped stances in an effort to cope with this gap between function and resources, such as "the clerk," "the bureaucrat," "the entertainer," and "the scapegoat," blamed for almost everything that goes wrong in the organization. Women have additional problems in this occupation when dealing with men. The occupation has social work backgrounds and is seen by management as a means for keeping workers "happy," so that it is not granted authority, but is encouraged to act as "sounding boards." This is especially true of women workers. The organizations themselves may be facing many problems in relations to workers, with absenteeism and sabotage, plus inefficient work due to alienation, alcoholism, and drug addiction, but the personnel semi-professional is generally powerless in dealing with these in the absence of authority to restructure the system or the work roles. Labor relations specialists serve as a link between management and the union. The mediator role is a very difficult one. Women are used here mainly when the workers are also women, but men have greater influence on management, at least in the minds of union members.

Associated professions that are either part of a large bureaucracy or that developed independent organizations include those of public relations (Kleiman, 1983). According to the Public Relations Society of America, about 60,000 people are in the field, which has become an important marketing hook for business and private organizations. Public relations jobs require a high "sense of commitment and survival" and are so organized that the rhythm of work is uneven and difficult for women involved in family roles.

One of the professional fields in which women have become increasingly involved is that of mass communication, working as editors and reporters of the press and television or radio news. They have been in motion pictures and television as actresses for years, but Chicago is not a center for such activity. Therefore, none of our sample fell into the actress category. On the other hand, we do have editors and reporters, and one newscaster. The occupational group combining editor and reporter is almost evenly split between men and women but members are most apt to be white (Otto et al., 1980: 109). The median number of years of schooling achieved by women in this field is 15.90 years, by men 15.65 years. The greatest percentage,

73 percent, work between 50 and 52 weeks a year, which is high in comparison to other professionals whom we have been discussing. The latter are often connected with the educational system and its nine-month schedule, while the media operates the year round. The older women in the field earn very little, compared to the youngest who have entered it recently and those aged 38 to 53. They earn less than a third of what men their age (53-57) do. Interestingly enough, these jobs are evaluated as being only average in the variety of work entailed. On the other hand, they are scored as below average in repetitiveness and closeness of supervision. Although assignments are often involuntary for reporters, they allow a great deal of latitude in gathering data and interpreting them. Role strain occurs at all levels, since the reporters and newscasters must get the information even when subjects are unwilling to disclose it. There is often hostility between the media and organizational representatives, the public, officials of government afraid of "exposés," and so forth. There is reportedly a great deal of turnover from employer to employer and, especially on the part of younger workers, out of the occupations (Becker, et al., 1979). Ginzberg and his associates (1966) found the women who obtained higher degrees at Columbia University in journalism to have a lower employment rate a few years later than did the scientists. Becker et al., (1979) found no difference between women and men in terms of professional and organizational commitment, but marital status and the presence of children were significantly related to such commitment. They did not separate the genders on these variables, but it is not hard to guess, in view of all the evidence thus far presented, that it is the women for whom marriage and parenthood make a difference in the degree to which they are committed to their profession of reporter and to their employer.

The dramatic increase of women in television network news in recent years is visibly apparent. Few women were active in this area prior to the 1970s.

> This began to change in the 1970s when, aided by federal affirmative action policies and citizen group agreements, more female reporters began to appear on local and network news programs (Singleton and Cook, 1982: 487).

However, Singleton and Cook (1982: 488), decided to test the hypothesis that "female reporters in print and electronic media were being assigned less newsworthy beats than males." They concluded that "the scope and importance of women's reporting assignments have improved in recent years." In spite of this:

> Females are assigned more U.S. government stories and less foreign affairs, more social problems and fewer disasters, more 'women's issues' and fewer stereotypically male-associated topics such as business and sports (Singleton and Cook, 1982: 489).

One of the problems facing women in the mass communication media, to which Tuckman (1978) drew attention, is associated with the feminist movement and the dual obligation many felt to their professional field and to the goals of the movement. Journalism has traditionally operated from a male perspective and "construction of reality" except for the special sections of newspapers, periodicals, or programs devoted to "women's issues." As noted above, Singleton and Cook (1982) researched the influence sex-stereotyping of television reporters had upon their assignments. The other problem being discussed here is the reporter's way of handling herself both in the gathering and in the presentation of news. The women's movement has tried to change the male dominated view of the world, and it initially (still?) was met with hostility by many segments of the society and certainly by the media. This made the role of the feminist reporter, or any woman reporter who had to deal with the ostracism and ridicule of the movement, very difficult (Tuckman, 1978: chapter 7). One way the media handled the situation was to place any news associated with the women's movement and feminism in the women's section of their media, as though it were of no concern to the society at large, as Epstein (1978) and Tuckman (1978) observed. The role strain problems, including that between person and role, have not been resolved for many women in the media, or in any of the other professions.

Another field in which women have dramatically increased their presence in very recent years is law. There were very few women in law since the profession became organized and male domination prevailed. The author's mother graduated from the University of Chicago Law School in 1914, but she was one of only two women in her class—and the only job she could get was with Legal Aid. Students now entering law school, as well as the pioneers, come from families with a high educational background, often having fathers who were in law. However, Epstein (1983) reports that many were strongly influenced by the mother, with somewhat passive support of the father. The mothers were working women, "doers" as Epstein calls them, active in the community if not working for pay and considered successful. The mothers guided them into law (Epstein, 1983: 30).

Even after law schools stopped their practice of barring women, or admitting a very low quota, the female students reported hostility from professors and antagonism from peers. The proportions of women in such training have changed, partly due to wars emptying classrooms of men but mainly due to the Civil Rights Act of 1964 and the 1967 Executive Order 11375 which forbade sex discrimination in organizations with federal contracts of more than $10,000 (Epstein, 1983: 94; Fossum, 1983). Spangler, Gordon, and Pipkin (1978) tested Kanter's (1977) "hypothesis that minority achievements are diminished by the underrepresentation of minority persons in majority-dominated work groups." They studied women in two law schools, one with a skewed ratio of women to men of 15.85, the other with a "tilted" ratio of 35 women to 65 men. They concluded that being a token in a highly male-dominated school was detrimental to the women's performance, and adding to the likelihood of social isolation and role entrapment in female stereotyped areas of law (Spangler, et al., 1978: 169).

Epstein (1983) finds the whole profession of law greatly changed as a result not only of the presence of women, but also of the societal upheaval of the 1960s and 1970s. This does not necessarily mean that prejudice against minority lawyers has vanished:

> The entry of women into the legal profession is as much a part of the changing context of the legal profession as any of the other factors that have contributed to its changing size, shape, and focus. From a negligible 6 percent of law school enrollments in 1968, women today constitute 31 percent of the total, and at some schools the figure is 50 percent or more. Their dramatic increase in numbers is part of the new fabric of the legal profession. Women lawyers experienced severe discrimination in the past; today their presence is met with responses ranging from receptivity to rejection, with a high component of ambiguity (Epstein, 1983: 21-22).

The figures concerning women in law appear repeatedly in the literature. The American Bar Association's survey found that:

> While the size of the nation's legal profession has doubled in the past decade, the number of lawyers who are women has increased more than seven-fold (94,000 of 606,000; Fossum, 1983: 1389).

Although more women are now "encountering the male establishment" than when Epstein (1971, 1979) first studied them in the late 1960s, and these women have been found competent, problems remain:

A 1958 U.S. government publication advised women lawyers to concentrate on 'real estate and domestic relations work, women's and juvenile legal problems, probate work and patent law,' reflecting the wisdom of insiders about areas in which women were apt to find work (Epstein, 1983: 81).

Women still tend to be stuck in fields which senior law partners consider "appropriate," in trusts and estates, divorce, and other family law. The demands placed on young lawyers, and many are young, make it difficult to combine practice with family roles. Long hours are required and women who leave the office early to attend to family duties are viewed with suspicion (Epstein, 1979; Fossum, 1983). Thus, a much higher proportion of women than of men lawyers have never married (32 to 8 percent), or have divorced (10 to 2 percent) (Epstein, 1983: 330). In fact, 87 percent of male but only 46 percent of female lawyers were married in 1960; the divorce rate of women has doubled between 1963 and 1975 (Epstein, 1983: 330). In 1983, 46 percent of the women lawyers studied by the research organization commissioned by the American Bar Association were not married and 59 percent had no children. Of course, the women lawyers were young, 60 percent being under the age of 35 (Winter, 1983: 1385 and 1388).

The older female lawyers tended to have entered law school at a later age than male counterparts. However, the younger women are following the pattern of men by going straight into law school after college (Winter, 1983: 1385). Women earned a median of $33,000 in 1983 to the men's median of $53,000 a year. Much of the difference, but not all, comes from their newness in the field and relative youth. Fewer women are partners in law firms (20 percent to the male 44 percent) and only 20 percent, (to men's 33 percent) are in solo practice, as individual entrepreneurs (Winter, 1983: 1386). Ten percent hold government jobs, which is relatively high. Many women have gone into poverty law and public interest cases, which do not rank high because of association with "clients whom society looks down upon" and pay poorly (Epstein, 1983: 124). Some women have started feminist firms, which frequently could not withstand the problems created by the newness of the role for them and for their women clients, as well as by value dilemmas:

The need to make money and desire to avoid money considerations in the choice of cases
The wish to serve the special needs of women clients though women often brought matrimonial and other problems the firm did not wish to handle

The wish to conduct business in a non-authoritarian manner though this
produced objectionable reactions in clients
The wish to make their partnership entirely equal although they found
it difficult to reconcile their sense of justice with inequities of participation (Epstein, 1983: 145).

Feminist lawyers have numerous problems with their demeanor. Those
who "have been troubled by men's use of barriers" in relations with
clients find it difficult to fight prejudice against women lawyers without the protection of these defenses (Epstein, 1983: 154). They even
find problems with the staff, which does not expect to have to work
as hard for women as for men. At the same time, Epstein (1983) feels
that they have contributed to the legal profession and to women in it
by being visible, performing exceptionally well, and trying to avoid
discrimination within a more enlightened environment than typical
of legal offices (Epstein, 1983: 159).

Women lawyers in male-dominated firms also face role strains.
One situation which both genders define as problematic for women
is obtaining new business, due to the anti-feminine prejudice of busi-
nessmen accustomed to men lawyers (Epstein, 1971, 1979, 1983;
Fossum, 1983). This is one reason they are pushed into noncorporate
law, especially that dealing with family issues and inheritance. Sorenson (1983) advises women lawyers to develop special skills, expertise
that will be respected in the firm and by potential clients. Finding a
flexible firm is important, according to him, because of the need for
flexible hours and assignments if practice is combined with parenting.
Quade (1983) presented "Twelve Success Stories" as part of the *American Bar Association Journal* cover story on women lawyers, explaining how some of them solved the problems of conflict between law
and home roles. On the other hand, *The American Lawyer* ran an extensive story about a case in which a woman is suing a major Atlanta
law firm for sex discrimination in not promoting her to partnership.
The case is being followed by most lawyers with great interest. The
description of the Atlanta legal world is very interesting:

The legal community in Atlanta is like a small town within a major city.
Most large firms are in walking distance of each other; the lawyers in
those firms meet often for lunch at the Commerce Club or the Capital
City Club; most have friends or relatives in neighboring firms. Lawyers
still practice law in what seems to an outsider an old-fashioned way: A
great deal is done through accommodation, and many agreements are
oral. In such an inbred, highly civilized world, where the norm is cooperation and living by the rules, Hishon's action [suing the firm] —even

if she had a strong case on the merits—could be taken as a terrible breach of conduct (Bruck, 1983: 101-2).

The community is reportedly taking out their frustration over her "ungentlemanly" action on her husband's law firm.

The woman's law firm turned to the U.S. Supreme Court claiming that she could not bring suit under the Fair Employment Act because partners are not employees. The court decided in 1984 that she was hired with the understanding that, if she progressed normally she would become a partner, so that the situation is one of employment. The case now goes back to trial court.

And yet, as Epstein (1983) found, there are benchmarks of success—women law professors, in the judiciary, in higher income brackets and partnerships in male-dominated firms. Sandra Day O'Connor is a frequent reference point (Bodine, 1983). Black women lawyers, of whom there are still very few, face additional problems (Burlew, 1982).

A subject of great current interest in American society, as well as in Europe, has been the attempt to change the roles of women in religious organizations. Two areas of discussion have appeared in the literature: ordination and changes in the roles and whole life patterns of Catholic nuns. Each hierarchically structured religious group shares a foundation of ideology which explains and justifies the location of members in the system. Almost all major European and American religions and denominations have until recently ordained only men and provided women with specialized roles of lesser importance and status. This is clearly evident in Judaism, Catholicism, and most Protestant denominations, with the exception of some black churches. Thus, in order for women to enter the male hierarchy of these religious organizations, the ideology defining male and female roles must undergo reality reconstruction. Some branches of Judaism have recently ordained women rabbis and some Protestant denominations have allowed women to become pastors.

When the history of American Protestantism during the 1970s is written, surely one of the important developments to be chronicled will be the entry of large numbers of women into the ranks of the ordained clergy, with attendant conflicts and changes surrounding their entry. For some denominations, this dramatic increase in women clergy built on a previous history of ordaining women to the ministry (we use the terms clergy, organized ministry, and pastor interchangeably). For others, notably the Episcopal Church, the decision to ordain women came only in 1977, and was preceded and followed by bitter controversy (Caroll et al., 1981: 1-2).

Caroll et al., (1981: 4) document the increase of women ministers in America from 3,276 in 1930 to 11,130 in 1980. Table 9.1 in this chapter shows the increase of women clergy to be very slow. The category of religious worker must have changed after 1960 since the Bureau of Labor Statistics records 61.4 percent of such workers to be women that year but only 11.0 percent in 1972.

The newness of women's entry into clergy positions, the pioneers opening the doors only in the late 1960s, results in a two-layered age composition. Many of the clergywomen are in their "second career," having previously been homemakers or in other occupations, because of the unwillingness of the churches to accept their "calling." Others have entered directly into the seminaries as young women. Bock, studying such professionals in 1971, found the women to be older and with less education than their male counterparts, partly because proportionately many were affiliated with "negro churches," and partly because of the second career entrants. Caroll and his associates (1981) found seminarians in their study of women clergy in nine Protestant denominations split by age. The younger pastors were also frequently lonely unless they were married. The women clergy tended to be located in smaller parishes, with older parishioners more often than was the case for men. On the other hand, the lay leaders in their parishes are very likely to be more liberal than those choosing male pastors. Caroll and associates (1981) concluded that women experience "dilemmas and contradictions of status" beyond the strain felt by the men, often because the ministry has traditionally been seen as the province of men. Many religious leaders point to Jesus and his disciples as models of maleness, and as by implication rejecting women in leadership roles. This masculinity is somewhat incongruous, in view of the feminization of religion in America during and after the Victorian nineteenth century (Douglas, 1977). The contradictions between the self and the male image of pastor are handled by the women in a variety of ways, similar to those of women entering other male-dominated and male-imaged professions. Some attempt to relate to people in their social circle according to the male model. Others try to modify the model to include behavior into which they have been socialized as women, running a parallel track to that of men. Finally, there have been attempts to modify the role of minister along androgynous lines (Bock, 1971; Jones and Taylor, 1971). Caroll and associates (1981: 40) reiterate the statement that the past century divided

> social life into two increasingly separate spheres, the public and the private. It may be, in fact, that the division is becoming tripartite, with

much of the educational institution in its own separate sphere. But what is most relevant here is the separation of church and family, as institutions of private life, from the economy and government as public institutions (Caroll et al., 1981: 40).

The situation facing women in the Catholic church is quite different. Pope Pius XII and Vatican Council II introduced many changes in the lives of religious women since 1952. These changes were not directed toward ordination, and the present pope has steadfastly resisted pressure toward the redefinition of women as potential priests. Nevertheless, many nuns and lay Catholic women continue to push for ordination. The Detroit Ordination Conference of 1976 is an example of the organized attempt to redefine the position of women in the church, especially vis-à-vis male domination. However, the movement is not homogeneous and has met with little success. The proceedings of the 1976 Detroit Conference demonstrate the great variation of opinion as to women's roles in the church (Gardiner, 1976). Swindler (1976) recommended that women perform roles directed toward other women as the beneficiaries. He presented a model of sisterhood very different from that of priesthood:

I urge that you not identify with the male clergy as over against the laity. The last thing the Church [and the world it ministers to] needs is an expanded clericalism! It will only be when our sisters, your *lay* sisters have reached their maturity, have taken their full roles, as leaders as well as followers, in the Church and the world, that your priestly ministry will have begun to be fulfilled. Then it will be true to say, in every sense, 'sisterhood is powerful!' (Swindler, 1976: 134).

At the same conference, women like Rosemary Radford Reuther (1976) of the Theology Department of Harvard University were arguing for ordination and extensive changes in the "consciousness" of the church. She recognized, however, that

The struggle for ordination of women in the Roman Catholic Church will be a long and frustrating one, with no immediate success forseeable (Reuther, 1976: 34).

Although the attempts to create a role of woman priest have not been successful as yet, there have been dramatic changes in the role of nun in Catholicism. We are considering nuns in this chapter on professions in spite of the fact that this is more of an all-encompassing identity than an occupation and women can be assigned to teaching, nursing, or other work for the church once they enter an order. The change in the role cluster of nuns, and in their whole style of living, has taken place very recently under the mutual influence of pioneer nuns and the Catholic hierarchy itself. Before about 1960, nuns led very cloistered lives, distanced from the rest of society also by their distinctive clothing and with routinized schedules, strict obedience to superiors, and minimal choice over their occupation. One of the really distinctive features of the lifestyle is celibacy. The church has traditionally refused to allow its priests and nuns to marry and have children, thus avoiding role conflict typical of other professionals. It is interesting to note, however, that priests swear to individual celibacy, while nuns are "married to Christ" and even wear wedding rings.

The whole style of life of the 170,000 nuns present in American orders prior to the changes also discouraged higher education in many cases. Michael Novak (1968) provides some of the history and significance of the changes in his contribution to *The New Nuns* (Burromeo, 1968). He traces the reform movement within the orders to a few pioneers as early as 1949 and to the organization of "Sister Formation Centers" around the United States. Ebaugh (1977) concluded from her study of nuns and the orders that changes introduced by them and encouraged by the Catholic church hierarchy had many unforeseen consequences. The by-play of change includes Pope Pius II's insistence in 1952 that nuns be better educated, even, if necessary, in secular universities. Vatican II then promulgated a document entitled 'Decree on the Appropriate Renewal of Religious Life' in 1964 and, by 1966, Pope Paul VI directed all religious orders to change their way of life and become more involved in the problems of the society (Ebaugh, 1977: 7). Ebaugh (1977) uses Lifton's *Thought Reform and the Psychology of Totalism* to sharpen the contrast between the Pre-Vatican II life in orders seen as total institutions and the Post-Vatican II life in the open society. The shift has had many ramifications, described in writing by leaders and many of those who have experienced it. Not surprisingly, a number of nuns, when offered these suddenly expanded choices and deprived of the security of the total institution, opted to leave the orders and enter the role cluster of wife-mother-worker, considered more "normal" for American women (see SanGiovanni's 1978 *Ex-Nuns: A Study of Emergent Role Passage*, and Ebaugh's 1977 *Out of the Cloister: A Study of Organizational Dilemmas*).

The literature focusing on nuns is interesting for occupational sociologists, because the professional commitment was based on a religious motivation rather than on an occupational one. The rapidity of change has led to great heterogeneity and dissension but also to an attempt to better understand roles, role complexes, and life-styles of women in both the private and the public domains.

Chicago Area Women in Professional and Technical Jobs

The professionals and women in technical jobs who are in the Chicago area sample fall fairly evenly into the four subcategories we have created: object-focused, teacher, health and welfare, and people-focused occupations, except that the first category is over-represented. The various types of technicians are located here, but so are accountants, artists such as sculptors and painters, writers, and research workers. The teachers are mainly in elementary schools, but we also have a relatively large number of women who transmit specialized knowledge and skills to private students or unusual groups. The health and welfare workers are mainly nurses, but we also have two surgeons and several social workers. The women in people-focused occupations include public relations writers, newspaper editors and reporters, librarians, personnel and labor relations workers, and consultants or guidance counselors. We have four religious workers, three of whom are nuns.

Women working in these fields, which form the highest rung on the occupational ladder, tend to be more educated, earning more money than are the others. Many are not married, having never entered that role or exited it through divorce. Many of the object- and people-focused workers are in their second career, having started employment in other types of jobs, often as clericals. Nurses and teachers are most apt to have gone straight through with occupational preparation and involvement in these areas. Many former teachers, all the dental hygienists, farm management advisers, and half of the social workers whose last job was in these specific occupations have withdrawn from the labor force into full-time homemaking. Many factors account for this attrition rate, and they vary by occupation and the age of the worker.

SUMMARY AND CONCLUSIONS

It is apparent from the length of this chapter, compared to that of the other chapters in this volume, that there is a great deal of literature focusing on women in professional and technical occupations. This analysis of the literature, organized with the help of sociological concepts, illustrates the importance of knowing at least some of the history and location in the broader structure of the world of work of each occupation, as well as the changes in their social role characteristics. The complexity of knowledge needed to understand these professions become even more evident when we combine what we have learned from various sources describing and analyzing the professional roles of American women with what the women themselves have experienced. Volume II of *City Women: Work, Jobs, Occupations, Careers* provides a benchmark of knowledge of "things as they were" and the construction of reality of women aged 25 to 54 in one of the major metropolitan areas of American society in 1978. I dove into Volume I with the confidence that someone, somewhere, has studied, or at least described with even less claim to scientific objectivity, each of the major occupations in which the Chicago women are involved. When it comes to the professions, there is a lack of uniformity of background literature, depending on the interest of particular researchers or writers. There is a wide range of material available to sociologists about the role of nurse, very little about some of the technical professions. A blooming literature on women in law is emerging, although none of the women in our sample are practicing in this field. The explanation for this gap is simple: the movement of women into law school and jobs which is described by Epstein, 1983 and the *American Bar Association Journal* (1983) is so recent that it postdates numerical prominence in the Chicago of 1978.

There are several themes which recur in the literature describing women in professional and technical occupations. One of these is the importance of gender authority and numerical domination. This theme appeared before, but it is prominent in discussions of high status occupations. The model combining these two variables appears in Figure 9-1.

Thus far, we find few professional and technical fields dominated in terms of both authority and numbers by women, since the world of occupations in America has been traditionally (if we limit tradition to the last 100 or so years), the province of men who gained control as occupations expanded and as women voluntarily or otherwise retreated to a privatized world of the home. We are unable to find professions in which the authority structure is dominated by women but the numerical domination is male. As late as 1965 the vocabulary of gender domination was incorporated in the *Dictionary of Occupational Titles*, not only in the labels, but also in the very descriptions of jobs (see also Spender, 1980).

Figure 9.1 Male/Female Domination of Professional/Technical Fields

Authority Domination	Numerical Domination	
	Male	Female
Male	A	B
Female	D	C

Professional/Technical Fields by Gender Domination. In American society at the present time:

A is represented by the still male-dominated roles of doctor, lawyer, minister, etc.

B is represented by the roles of nurse, social worker, elementary school teacher, etc.

C is represented by cloistered sisterhood and schools run for, and by, women, etc.

D is represented by ———.

Two sub-themes concerning numerical domination by either gender occur frequently: one focuses on the reasons for gender segregation, the other on changes in distributions within specific professions. The most frequent early explanation of gender domination is tied to the alleged "naturalness" of fit. Males are ———, the profession calls for ——— so men dominate that profession. The whole image of medicine, engineering, law, and dentistry is different in Poland or the Soviet Union than in America and can accommodate the divergence of gender domination (Sokolowska, 1965). An interesting example of gender labeling of occupations considered along the professionalization spectrum concerns the so-called "semi-professions." Although this concept was being considered for inclusion in the 1949 edition of the *Dictionary of Occupational Titles* to cover some 20,000 jobs which require extensive education, but of a more practical and restricted nature than that developed by the more theoretical established professions, its use became restricted to a few female intensive occupations (Habenstein, 1970). Etzioni's 1969 *The Semi-Professions* solidified the limitation of this label to such occupations as social worker, nurse, and teacher, in spite of the fact that many male-dominated professions in large bureaucratic organizations display similar characteristics of specialized knowledge and limited self or other control. The semi-professions acquired a feminine cast, their limitations are often explained in terms of the alleged attributes of this gender.

A related topic is the explanation of the absence of one gender in the professions dominated by the other. Although sometimes the reasons are still couched in terms of gender-linked personality attributes, greater emphasis is recently placed upon socialization and role models, the function of schools and counselors in guiding students to the gender-appropriate professions, the barriers set up which prevent entrance or success in the "inappropriately" chosen ones. Interestingly enough, though not surprisingly, most of this literature deals with the problems of women's entry into male-dominated professions, not vice versa. We can expect increasing studies of the male nurse, as members of the more prestigious gender start moving into a semi-profession dominated by those of lesser status. Market analyses are now appearing in gender-domination literature.

Sociology is becoming interested in consequences of changes in the gender distributions and in the actual role involvements in the professions. Studies have been made of the experience of "pioneers" or "token" women in male-dominated professions, much as they have been of women in similar blue-collar jobs. As higher education, employers, and professional groups respond to federal laws and policies barring discrimination and the numbers of women in nontraditional professions increase, focus has shifted to the subtle ways in which total cooperation is withheld from newcomers in sex-biased groups. The withdrawal of some of the rights from the social person can make role performance very difficult, as several studies document. Much of the knowledge required for the successful practice of law or medicine is transmitted informally in locations and interactions closed to women. The importance of mentors and sponsors is similar to that in management, and often difficult to obtain, especially in the absence of same-gender models. No roles are so clear-cut and no academic or job training so complete as to prepare a newcomer for the way in which a specific social circle functions. A sculptor or painter needs the cooperation of gallery owners, dealers, and peers. Teachers are dependent upon the school system, students, co-workers, parents, and the community at large and their cooperation is often influenced by the acceptance of the social person with all attributes, including gender. On the other hand, it is possible that the importance of gender in the professions is decreasing and a new contribution to the literature on women in these occupations will be entitled *The Declining Significance of Gender: Women and the Changing American Institutions* in a similar vein to Wilson's (1978) *The Declining Significance of Race: Blacks and the Changing American Institutions.*

Much of the literature on the professions and the processes of professionalization, in fact, does not focus on the subject of male or female involvement. New social movements, professional proliferation and educational shifts have pushed, or been led by, intense self-examination by many groups. They wish to introduce change, prevent it, or move it in certain directions to deal with encroaching occupations and to maintain a semblance of homogeneity and control. Much of this internal ferment is not directly influenced either by the presence or the expansion in numbers of women although much of it is relevant. The role of doctor has been dramatically changed by technology and the development of allied health professionals, with whom relations are often strained. Law is having problems absorbing all newcomers, not just those of female identity and lack of familiarity with LaSalle Street, Chicago, let alone Wall Street, New York. Scientists in object-focused or people-focused occupations but in profit-making organizations, teachers in unions, pharmacists attempting to move from a marginal status as professionals in spite of their business connections, and so on, all face strain.

One topic that is frequently mentioned in the literature dealing with women in the professional and technical occupations is role conflict. Unlike the early concern with all women who leave their families and home to work for pay in jobs, the focus is now on those women who hold very demanding jobs. In the past, the effects on them, their children, their husbands, and the community have been examined through the prism of individual choice and solution. Attention is now moving to the questioning of the traditional model of professional work and career scheduling. This traditional model assumes that the professional (male) has a back-up person (female) at home to facilitate effective functioning, providing services and preventing or easing role conflict, in a "two-person career" fashion. The professions, more than any other occupations except those in business management, are "greedy institutions" and have changed little to accommodate newcomers who do not have such resources or who do not want to make such strong commitments during their role complex building years (see Coser, 1974). A new problem in the professions and related fields has been the increased pressure by women, and even by some men, to build more flexible work scheduling and career lines to accommodate a more "humanistic" life with multiple commitments. Until the professions and the organizations which hire most of their members are willing and able to introduce such changes, the major focus of studies of professional women, in addition to the way they carry out their professional roles, will be on their individualistic solutions to role conflict.

REFERENCES

Ahrons, Constance R. 1976. Counselors' perceptions of career images of women. *Journal of Vocational Behavior* 8: 197-207.

Albrecht, Gary L. 1979. Defusing technological change in juvenile courts: The probation officer's struggle for professional autonomy. *Sociology of Work and Occupations* 6 (3, August): 259-82.

Almquist, Elizabeth. 1974. Sex stereotypes in occupational choice: The case for college women. *Journal of Vocational Behavior* 5: 13-21.

Alutto, Joseph A., Laurence J. Hubeniak, and Ramon C. Alonzo. 1971. A study of differential socialization for members of one professional occupation. *Journal of Health and Social Behavior* 12: 140-47.

Angrist, Shirley S., and Elizabeth M. Almquist. 1975. *Careers and Contingencies.* New York: Dunellen University Press of Cambridge, Massachusetts.

Astin, H. S. 1969. *The Woman Doctorate in America.* New York: Russell Sage Foundation.

Baker, Curtis O. 1981. *Earned Degrees Conferred, 1979-80.* U.S. Department of Commerce, National Center for Educational Statistics. Washington, D.C.: U.S. Government Printing Office.

Bayer, Alan, and Helen Astin. 1975. Sex differentials in the academic reward system. *Science* 188 (May 23): 796-802.

Becker, Howard S. 1972. A School is a Lousy Place to Learn Anything in. In *Learning to Work,* edited by Blanche Geer, pp. 89-109. Beverly Hills, California: Sage.

Becker, Howard S., Blanche Geer, and Everett Hughes. 1968. *The Academic Side of College Life.* New York: Wiley.

Becker, Lee B., Idowu A. Sobowale, and Robin E. Cobbey. 1979. Reporters and their professional and organizational commitment. *Journalism Quarterly,* 753-63, 770.

Bekey, Michelle. 1982. Careers: CPAs. *Working Woman* (June): 46-48.

Bernard, Jessie. 1965. The Present Situation in the Academic World of Women Trained in Engineering. In *Women and the Scientific Professions,* edited by Jacquelyn A. Mattfeld and Carol G. Van Aken, pp. 163-82. Cambridge, Massachusetts: The M.I.T. Press.

———. 1964. *Academic Women.* University Park: Penn State University Press.

Bielby, Denise D. 1978. Career and career involvement of college educated women: Baseline evidence from the 1960's. *Sociology of Education* 51 (January): 7-28.

Bird, Caroline. 1979. *The Two-Paycheck Marriage: How Women at Work Are Changing Life in America.* New York: Rawson, Wade.

———. 1972. Demasculinizing the Professions. In *The New Professionals,* edited by Ronald Gross and Paul Osterman, pp. 291-316. New York: Simon and Schuster.

Blankenship, W. C. 1971. Head Librarians: How Many Men? How Many Women? In *The Professional Woman,* edited by Athena Theodore, pp. 93-102. Cambridge, Massachusetts: Schenkman.

Blau, Judith R. 1979. Expertise and power in professional organizations. *Sociology of Work and Occupations* 6 (1, February): 103-23.

Bledstein, Burton J. 1978. *The Culture of Professionalism*. New York: W.W. Norton.

Blumstein, Philip, and Peppen Schwartz. 1983. *American Couples*. New York: Morrow.

Bock, E. Wilbur. 1971. The Female Clergy: A Case of Professional Marginality. In *The Professional Woman*, edited by Athena Theodore, pp. 599-611. Cambridge, Massachusetts: Schenkman.

Bodine, Laurence. 1983. Sandra Day O'Connor. *American Bar Association Journal* (October): 1394-98.

Bolt, Richard H. 1965. The Present Situation of Women Scientists and Engineers in Industry and Government. In *Women and the Scientific Professions*, edited by Jacquelyn A. Mattfeld and Carol G. Van Aken, pp. 139-62. Cambridge, Massachusetts: The M.I.T. Press.

Boquist, Constance, and Jeannette V. Haase. 1972. *A Historical Review of Women in Dentistry*. Washington, D.C.: U.S. Department of Health, Education and Welfare.

Brief, Arthur P., and Ramon J. Aldag. 1980. Antecedents of organizational commitment among hospital nurses. *Sociology of Work and Occupations* 7 (2, May): 210-21.

Brine, Pauline, and Patricia Peterson Rossman. 1979. Can Dental hygiene become a developing profession? *Dental Hygiene* 53 (May): 218-20.

Brown, George H. 1978a. *Doctoral Degree Awards to Women*. Washington, D.C.: U.S. Department of Health, Education and Welfare. National Center for Education Statistics NCES 78-336 A.

_____. 1978b. *Bachelor's Degree Awards to Women*. Washington, D.C.: U.S. Department of Health, Education and Welfare. National Center for Education Statistics NCES 78-336 B.

_____. 1978c. *Master's Degree Awards to Women*. Washington, D.C.: U.S. Department of Health, Education and Welfare. National Center for Education Statistics NCES 78-336 C.

Bruck, Connie. 1983. Hishon v. King and Spalding: The case no one will win. *The American Lawyer* (November): 101-6.

Bucher, Rue, and Joan G. Stelling. 1977. *Becoming Professional*. Beverly Hills, California: Sage Publications. Vol. 46 Sage Library of Social Research.

Bucher, Rue, and A. Strauss. 1961. Professions in process. *American Journal of Sociology* 66: 325-35.

Bucklew, Reba, and Vernon Parenton. 1971. Occupational Aspects of Social Work. In *The Professional Woman*, edited by Athena Theodore, pp. 173-81. Cambridge, Massachusetts: Schenkman.

Bullough, Bonnie. 1978. Barriers to the nurse practitioner movement: Problems of women in a woman's field. *Nursing Digest* 6 (3, Fall): 49-54.

Bullough, Bonnie, and Vern Bullough. 1978. The Causes and Consequences of the Differentiation of the Nursing Role. In *Varieties of Work Experience*, edited by Phyllis L. Stewart and Muriel G. Cantor, pp. 292-300. New York: John Wiley and Sons.

Burlew, Ann Kathleen. 1982. The experiences of black females in traditional and nontraditional professions. *Psychology of Women Quarterly* 6 (3, Spring): 312-26.

Burnham, John C. 1982. American medicine's golden age: What happened to it? *Science* 215 (19, March): 1474-79.

Burromeo, ed. 1968. *The New Nuns.* New York: *NAL* Signet.

Burton, Doris-Jean. 1979. Ten years of affirmative action and the changing status of women in political science. *Political Science* (Winter): 18-22.

Caroll, Jackson W., Barbara Hargrove, and Adair T. Lummis. 1981. *Women of the Cloth: A New Opportunity for the Churches.* New York: Harper & Row.

Carter, Michael J., and Susan Boslego Carter. 1981. Women's recent progress in the professions, or women get a ticket to ride after the gravy train has left the station. *Feminist Studies* 7 (3, Fall): 477-504.

Cartwright, Lillian Kaufman. 1978. Career satisfaction and role harmony of young women physicians. *Journal of Vocational Behavior* 12: 184-96.

————. 1977. Personality changes in a sample of women physicians. *Journal of Medical Education* 52 (June): 467-74.

Cavan, Ruth Shonle. 1956-57. The status of women in the professions relative to the status of men. *The Quarterly of the American Inter-professional Institute* 31, (2, Winter).

Cawsey, T. F. 1980. Why line managers don't listen to their personnel departments. AMACOM (January/February): 11-20.

Centra, John A. 1975. Women, Marriage and the Doctorate: Findings. ETS (Educational Testing Service) II (4): 1-5.

Chapman, David W., and Malcolm A. Lowther. 1982. Teachers' satisfaction with teaching. *Journal of Educational Research* 75 (4, March/April): 241-47.

Chicago, Judy. 1977. *Through the Flower: My Struggle as a Woman Artist.* Garden City, New York: Anchor Books, Doubleday.

Chicago Tribune (editorial). 1983. "More Wives Deciding Where Couples Live: For Some Spouses, Egos and Economics can Balance Out." (September 26) Section 3:3.

Child, John, and Janet Fulk. 1982. Maintenance of occupational control. *Work and Occupations* 9 (2, May): 155-92.

Clark, Donald. 1980. Physician assistants: When there's no doctor in the house. *Occupational Outlook Quarterly* (Summer): 20-23.

Cole, Jonathan R. 1979. *Fair Science: Women in the Scientific Community.* New York: The Free Press.

Cole, Roger B., and Lois K. Cohen. 1971. Dental Manpower. In *Toward a Sociology of Dentistry*, edited by Robert M. O'Shae and Lois K. Cohen, pp. 29-62. *The Milbank Memorial Fund Quarterly*, Vol. XLIX (3 July) Part 2.

Conrad, Peter. 1975. The discovery of hyperkinesis: Note on the medicalization of deviant behavior. *Social Problems* 23 (1, October): 12-21.

Converse, Philip E., and Jean M. Converse. 1971. The status of women as students and professionals in political science. *Political Science* (Summer): 328-48.

Cope, Zachary. 1958. *Florence Nightingale and the Doctors*. Philadelphia: J.B. Lippincott.

Corwin, Ronald J. 1961. The professional employee: A study of conflict in nursing roles. *American Journal of Sociology* 66 (May): 610-15.

Coser, Lewis A. 1974. *Greedy Institutions: Patterns of Undivided Commitment*. New York: The Free Press.

Coser, Rose. 1975. Stay home little Sheba: On placement, displacement and social change. *Social Problems* 22 (4, April): 470-80.

Coser, Rose L., and Gerald Rokoff. 1971. Women in the occupational world: Social disruption and conflict. *Social Problems* 18 (4, Spring): 535-54.

Davis, Anne J. 1971a. Self-concept, Occupational Role Expectations, and Occupational Choice in Nursing and Social Work. In *The Professional Woman*, edited by Athena Theodore, pp. 365-452. Cambridge, Massachusetts: Schenkman.

————. 1971b. Women as a Minority Group in Higher Academics. In *The Professional Woman*, edited by Athena Theodore, pp. 587-98. Cambridge, Massachusetts: Schenkman.

Davis, Fred. 1966. *The Nursing Profession: Five Sociological Essays*. John Wiley.

Davis, Fred, Virginia Olesen, and Elvi Waik Whittaker. 1966. Problems and Issues in Collegiate Nursing Education. In *The Nursing Profession*, edited by Fred Davis, pp. 138-75. New York: John Wiley.

Davis, Kingsley, and W. E. Moore. 1945. Some principles of stratification. *American Sociological Review*: 242-49.

Davis, Nancy J., and Larry L. Bumpass. 1976. The continuation of education after marriage among women in the United States: 1970. *Demography* 13 (2, May): 161-74.

Denzin, Norman K. 1973. Children and Their Caretakers. In *Marriages and Families*, edited by Helena Z. Lopata, pp. 247-54. New York: D. Van Nostrand.

Deutsch, Helene. 1944. *The Psychology of Women*. New York: Grune and Stratton.

Devereux, George, and Florence R. Weiner. 1962. The Occupational Status of Nurses. In *Man, Work, and Society*, edited by Sigmund Nosow and William H. Form, pp. 486-93. New York: Basic Books.

Dingwall, Robert. 1977. 'Atrocity stories' and professional relationships. *Sociology of Work and Occupations* 4 (4, November): 371-96.

Dolan, Carrie. 1983. "Success Stories: How Four Women are Prospering in Jobs Usually Held by Men." *Wall Street Journal* (June 29): 1 and 6.

Dolan, Josephine. 1973. *Nursing in Society: A Historical Perspective*. Philadelphia: W.B. Saunders.

Douglas, Ann. 1977. *The Feminization of American Culture*. New York: Avon Books.

Ebaugh, Helen Rose Fuchs. 1977. *Out of the Cloister: A Study of Organizational Dilemmas*. Austin: University of Texas Press.

Ehrenreich, Barbara, and Deirdre English. 1979. *For Her Own Good*. Garden City, New York: Anchor Books, Doubleday.

Ehrenreich, Barbara, and Deirdre English. 1973. *Witches, Midwives and Nurses—A History of Women Healers*. Old Westbury, New York: Feminist Press.

Epstein, Cynthia Fuchs. 1983. *Women in Law*. Garden City, New York: Anchor Press, Doubleday, 2nd edition.

―――. 1979. "Women on Wall Street: Encountering the Male Establishment, Ten Years Later." Paper presented at the Boston meetings of the American Sociological Association, August 29.

―――. 1978. The Women's Movement and the Women's Pages: Separate, Unequal and Unspectacular. In *Hearth and Home: Images of Women in the Mass Media*, edited by Gaye Tuchman, Arlene Kaplan Daniels, and James Benet, pp. 216-21. New York: Oxford University Press.

―――. 1971. Encountering the Male Establishment: Sex-status Limits on Women's Careers in the Professions. In *The Professional Woman*, edited by Athena Theodore, pp. 52-73. Cambridge, Massachusetts: Schenkman.

―――. 1970. *Women's Place: Options and Limits in Professional Careers*. Berkeley, California: University of California Press.

Erikson, Eric. 1965. Concluding Remarks. In *Women and the Scientific Professions*, edited by Jacquelyn Mattfeld and Carol G. Van Aken, pp. 232-45. Cambridge, Massachusetts: The M.I.T. Press.

Etzioni, Amitai. 1969. *The Semi-Professions and Their Organization*. New York: The Free Press.

Farmer, Helen S., and Martin J. Bohn, Jr. 1970. Home-career conflict reduction and the level of career interest in women. *Journal of Counseling Psychology* 17 (3, May): 228-32.

Fava, Sylvia, and Rosalie G. Genovese. 1983. Family, Work and Individual Development in Dual-career Marriages: Issues for Research. In *Research in the Interweave of Social Roles: Families and Jobs*, Vol. 3, edited by Helena Z. Lopata and Joseph H. Pleck, pp. 163-85. Greenwich, Connecticut: JAI Press.

Ferber, Marianne, and Jane Loeb. 1973. Performance, reward and perception of sex discrimination among male and female faculty. *American Journal of Sociology* 78 (January): 995-1002.

Finifter, Ada W. 1973. The professional status of women political scientists. Some current data. *Political Science* (Fall): 406-19.

Fink, Arthur. 1974a. The Development of Social Services: European Background. In *The Field of Social Work*, edited by Arthur E. Fink et al., pp. 18-34. New York: Holt, Rinehart and Winston, 6th ed.

―――. 1974b. The Social Services in America: Early growth of Voluntary Social Services. In *The Field of Social Work*, edited by Arthur E. Fink et al., pp. 35-48. New York: Holt, Rinehart and Winston, 6th ed.

―――. 1974c. The Social Services in America: From the Almshouse to Social Security. In *The Field of Social Work*, edited by Arthur E. Fink et al., pp. 49-68. New York: Holt, Rinehart and Winston, 6th ed.

Fink, Arthur E., et al. 1974. *The Field of Social Work*. New York: Holt, Rinehart and Winston, 6th ed.

Florman, Samuel C. 1978. Engineering and the female mind. *Harpers* (February): 57-63.

Fogarty, M., Rhona Rapoport, and Robert N. Rapoport. 1971. *Sex, Career and Family*. Beverly Hills, California: Sage.

Fossum, Donna. 1983. Women in the law: A reflection on Portia. *American Bar Association Journal* 69 (October): 1389-93.

Freidson, Eliot. 1960. Client control and medical practice. *American Journal of Sociology* 65: 374-82.

Friedan, Betty. 1963. *The Feminine Mystique*. New York: W. W. Norton.

Gardiner, Anne Marie (ed.). 1976. *Women and Catholic Priesthood: An Expanded Vision: Proceedings of the Detroit Ordination Conference*. New York: Paulist Press.

Garson, Barbara. 1975. *All the Lifelong Day: The Meaning and Demeaning of Routine Work*. New York: Doubleday.

Geer, Blance. 1968. Teaching. In *International Encyclopedia of the Social Sciences*, edited by David Sills, pp. 560-65. New York: The MacMillan Co. and Free Press, Vol. 15.

Gibbons, Kathleen, and Clare Grosgebauer. 1976. New health practitioneers. *Women's Work* 2 (1, January-February): 8-15.

Ginzberg, Eli, Iver Berg, Carol Brown, John Herma, Alice Yohalem, and Sherry Gorelick. 1966. *Life Styles of Educated Women*. New York: Columbia University Press.

Ginzberg, Eli, and Alice M. Yohalem. 1966. *Educated American Women: Self-Portraits*. New York: Columbia University Press.

Glenwick, David S., Sandra L. Johansson, and Jeffrey Bondy. 1978. A comparison of the self-images of female and male assistant professors. *Sex Roles* 4 (4): 513-24.

Goffman, Erving. 1956. The nature of deference and demeanor. *The American Anthropologist* 58: 473-502.

Goldstein, Frances. 1983. Let's get our act together: Symbiosis vs. discord. *Journal of Practical Nursing*, July/August 14.

Goode, William. 1960. A theory of role strain. *American Sociological Review* 25 (4, August): 483-96.

_____. 1956. Community within a community: the professions. *American Sociological Review* 22: 194-200.

Gouldner, Alvin W. 1957. Cosmopolitans and locals. *Administrative Science Quarterly* (December): 281-306, and (March, 1958): 444-80.

Grace, Helen. 1981. Unification, Reunification: Reconciliation or Collaboration —Bridging the Education-Service Gap. In *Current Issues in Nursing*, edited by J. McCloskey and H. Grace, pp. 626-43. Boston: Blackwell Scientific.

Grandjean, Burke D., and Helen Hazunda Bernal. 1979. Sex and Centralization in a semi-profession. *Sociology of Work and Occupation* 6 (1, February): 84-102.

Green, Anne E., and Anthony Jong. 1980. The role and responsibility of hygienists and their association. *Dental Hygiene* (August): 377-82.

Greer, Germaine. 1979. *The Obstacle Race*. New York: Farrar, Straus and Giroux.

Grimm, James W. 1978. Women in Female-dominated Professions. In *Women Working*, edited by A. H. Stromberg and S. Harkess, pp. 293-315. Palo Alto, California: Mayfield.

Gross, Edward. 1971. *Plus ca change . . .?* The Sexual Structure of Occupations Over Time. In *The Professional Woman*, edited by Athena Theodore, pp. 39-51. Cambridge, Massachusetts: Schenkman.

———. 1958. *Work and Society*. New York: Thomas Y. Crowell.

Gurin, Arnold, and David Williams. 1973. Social Work Education. In *Education for the Professions of Medicine, Law, Theology and Social Work*, edited by Everett C. Hughes et al., pp. 201-47. New York: McGraw-Hill.

Haas, Jack, and William Shaffir. 1982. Ritual evaluation of competence. *Work and Occupations* 9 (2, May): 131-54.

Habenstein, Robert W. 1970. Occupational Uptake: Professionalizing. In *Pathways to Data*, pp. 99-121. Chicago: Aldine.

Habenstein, Robert A., and Edwin A. Christ. 1955. *Professionalizer, Traditionalizer, and Utilizer*. Columbia, Missouri: University of Missouri Press.

Hall, Douglas T., and Francine E. Gordon. 1973. Career choices of married women: effects on conflict, role behavior, and satisfaction. *Journal of Applied Psychology* 58, 1: 42-48.

Hall, David. 1948. The stages of a medical career. The *American Journal of Sociology* LIII (March): 327-36.

Hall, Richard. 1983. "The Professions, Employed Professionals and the Professional Organization." Paper presented at the annual meetings of the Midwest Sociological Society, Kansas City.

Hall, Richard H. 1975. *Occupations and the Social Structure*. Englewood Cliffs, New Jersey: Prentice-Hall.

Handel, Gerald. 1982. *Social Welfare in Western Society*. New York: Random House.

Hansen, Sunny, and Rita S. Rapoza, (eds.). 1978. *Career Development and Counseling of Women*. Springfield, Il.: St. Thomas.

Haug, Marie R., and Marvin B. Sussman. 1968. Professional autonomy and the revolt of the client. *Social Problems* 17: 153-61.

Helfrich, Margaret L. 1975. Paths into professional school. *Sociology of Work and Occupations* 2 (2, May): 169-81.

Helson, Ravenna. 1972. The changing image of the career woman. *Journal of Social Issues* 28 (2): 33-46.

Heyrman, Karole. 1982. "Reunification on nursing: A matter of institutional realignment." Unpublished dissertation proposal, Department of Sociology, Loyola University of Chicago.

Higdon, Hal. 1969. *The Business Healers*. New York: Random House.

Hill, W. Scott. 1965. Women Engineers in Industry. In *Women and the Scientific Professions*, edited by Jacquelyn A. Mattfeld and Carol G. Van Aken, pp. 195-200. Cambridge, Massachusetts: The M.I.T. Press.

Hoffman, Leonore, and Gloria DeSole. (eds.). 1976. *Careers and Couples: An Academic Question*. New York: Modern Language Association of America.

Hoffman, Lois Wladis, and F. Ivan Nye. 1974. *Working Mothers: An Evaluative Review of the Consequences for Wife, Husband, and Child*. San Francisco: Jossey-Bass.

Holmstrom, Lynda Lytle. 1973. *The Two-Career Family*. Cambridge, Massachusetts: Schenkman.

Horner, Matina S. 1972. Towards an understanding of achievement-related conflicts in women. *Journal of Social Issues* 28 (2): 157-76.

Hornig, Lilli S. 1982. The Education and Employment of Women Scientists and Engineers in the United States. In *Women and the World of Work*, edited by Anne Holberg, pp. 35-53. New York: Plenum Press.

Hudson-Rosen, R. A., et al. 1974. Health professional attitudes toward abortion. *Public Opinion Quarterly* 38 (Summer): 171.

Hughes, Everett C. 1971a. The Study of Occupations. In *The Sociological Eye: Selected Papers on Work, Self and the Study of Society*, edited by Everett C. Hughes, pp. 283-97. Chicago: Aldine.

_____. 1971b. The Humble and the Proud: The Comparative Study of Occupations. In *The Sociological Eye: Selected Papers on Work, Self and the Study of Society*, edited by Everett C. Hughes, pp. 417-27. Chicago: Aldine.

_____. 1971c. Professions. In *The Sociological Eye: Selected Papers on Work, Self and the Study of Society*. Chicago: Aldine.

_____. 1971d. *The Sociological Eye*. Chicago: Aldine, edited by Everett C. Hughes. pp. 374-386.

Hughes, Everett C., Helen MacGill Hughes, and Irwin Deutscher. 1958. *Twenty Thousand Nurses Tell Their Story*. Philadelphia: J.B. Lippincott.

Hughes, Helen MacGill. 1977. Wasp/woman/sociologist. *Society/Transaction* (August): 69-80.

Hunt, Janet G., and Larry L. Hunt. 1977. Dilemmas and contradictions of status: The case of the dual-career family. *Social Problems* 24 (4, April): 407-16.

Jones, Arthur R., and Lee Taylor. 1971. Differential Recruitment of Female Professionals: A Case Study of Clergywomen. In *The Professional Woman*, edited by Athena Theodore, pp. 355-62. Cambridge, Massachusetts: Schenkman.

Kahn, Alfred J., and Sheila B. Kamerman. 1975. *Not for the Poor Alone*. New York: Harper Colophon.

Kahne, Hilda. 1976. The women in professional occupations: New complexities for chosen roles. *Journal of the American Medical Women's Association* (Summer): 179-85.

Kanter, Rosebeth Moss. 1977. *Men and Women of the Corporation*. New York: Basic Books.

Katz, Fred E. 1969. Nurses. In *The Semi-Professions and their Organization*, edited by Amitai Etzioni, pp. 54-81. New York: The Free Press.

Kennedy, Luella M. 1974. Social Services in the Schools. In *The Field of Social Work*, edited by Arthur E. Fink, pp. 174-95. New York: Holt, Rinehart and Winston, 6th ed.

Kirkpatrick, Martha J. 1975. A report on a consciousness raising group for women psychiatrists. *Journal of the American Medical Women's Association* 30 (5, May): 206-12.

Kleiman, Carol. 1983. "Public Relations Can Boast of Jobs: Markets Open Up: Executive Sees Opportunity for Young People." *Chicago Tribune* (Sunday, November 27) Section 8: 1.

_____. 1980. *Women's Networks.* New York: Lippincott and Crowell.

Koch, James L. 1974. Technicians: Need-environment congruity and self-investment in organizational roles. *Sociology of Work and Occupations* 1 (2, May): 175-96.

Komarovsky, Mirra. 1953. *Women in the Modern World: Their Education and Their Dilemmas.* Boston: Little, Brown.

Kosa, John, and Robert E. Coker, Jr. 1971. The Female Physician in Public Health: Conflict and Reconciliation of the Sex and Professional Roles. In *The Professional Woman,* edited by Athena Theodore, pp. 196-206. Cambridge, Massachusetts: Schenkman.

Kraft, Philip. 1977. *Programmers and Managers: The Routinization of Computer Programming in the United States.* New York: Springer-Verlag.

Kramer, M. 1976. *Reality Shock.* St. Louis: Mosby.

Kronus, Carol. 1975. Occupational values, role orientations and work settings: The case of pharmacy. *Sociological Quarterly:* 173-83.

Krueger, Cynthia, 1971. Do "Bad Girls" Become Good Nurses? In *The Professional Woman,* edited by Athena Theodore, pp. 685-96. Cambridge, Massachusetts: Schenkman.

Larson, Magali Sarfatti. 1977. *The Rise of Professionalism: A Sociological Analysis.* Berkeley: University of California Press.

Lemkau, Jeanne Parr. 1979. Personality and background characteristics of women in male-dominated occupations: A review. *Psychology of Women Quarterly* 4 (2, Winter): 221-40.

Lewis, Lionel, Richard Wanner, and David Gregorio. 1979. Performance and salary attainment in academia. *American Sociologist* (August): 157-69.

Linn, Erwin L. 1971. Women Dental Students: Women in a Man's World. In *Toward a Sociology of Dentistry,* edited by Robert M. O'Shae and Lois K. Cohen, pp. 63-76. *The Millbank Memorial Fund Quarterly,* Vol. XLIX (3, July): Part 2.

Lipman-Blumen, Jean. 1976. Toward a Homosocial Theory of Sex Roles: An Explanation of the Sex-Segregation of Social Institutions. In *Women and the Workplace: The Implications of Occupational Segregation,* edited by Martha Blaxall and Barbara Reagan, pp. 15-31. Chicago: University of Chicago Press.

Lopata, Helena Z. 1984. Social construction of social problems over time. *Social Problems* (February): 249-72.

_____. 1976. Expertization of everyone and the revolt of the client. *The Sociological Quarterly* 17 (Autumn): 435-47.

_____. 1978. Work and social policy. *Alternative Lifestyles: Changing Patterns in Marriage, Family and Intimacy* 1 (4, November): 416-22.

Lopata-Hayes, Theodora. 1983. "Understanding teacher 'burnout.'" Unpublished paper, University of Wisconsin, Whitewater.

Lopata, Helena Z., Debra Barnewolt, and Kathleen Norr. 1980. Spouses Contributions to Each Other's Roles. In *Dual Career Couples*, edited by Fran Pepitone-Rockwell, pp. 111-41. Beverly Hills, California: Sage.

Lorber, Judith. 1982. How physician spouses influence each other's careers. *Journal of American Medical Women's Association* 37 (1, January): 21-26.

———. 1979. Loyalty and the Place of Women in the Informal Organization of Work. In *Women: A Feminist Perspective*, edited by Jo Freeman, pp. 371-81. Palo Alto, California: Mayfield. 2nd ed.

———. 1975. Women and Medical Sociology: Invisible Professionals and Ubiquitous Patients. In *Another Voice: Feminist Perspectives on Social Life and Social Science*, edited by Marcia Millman and Rosabeth Moss Kanter, pp. 75-105. Garden City, New York: Anchor Books, Doubleday.

Lortie, Dan C. 1975. *Schoolteacher*. Chicago: University of Chicago Press.

———. 1969. The Balance of Control and Autonomy in Elementary School Teaching. In *The Semi-Professions and their Organization*, edited by Amitai Etzioni, pp. 1-53. New York: The Free Press.

Loseke, Donileen R., and John A. Sonquist. 1979. The computer workers in the labor force: New occupations and old problems. *Sociology of Work and Occupations* 6 (2, May): 156-83.

Lundberg, Ferdinand, and Marynia F. Farnham. 1947. *Modern Woman: The Lost Sex*. New York: Harper and Bros.

McAdams, Wanda Jean Coggins. 1976. Reasons dental hygienists dislike their practice. *Dental Hygiene* 50 (December): 563-71.

MacPhail, J. 1975. Promoting Collaboration between Education and Service. *The Canadian Nurse* 71: 32-34.

Macke, Anne Statham. 1981. Token men and women: A note on the salience of sex and occupation among professionals and semi-professionals. *Sociology of Work and Occupations* 8 (1, February): 25-38.

Malveaux, Julianne M. 1980. Moving Forward, Standing Still: Women in White Collar Jobs. In *Women and the Workplace*, edited by Phyllis Wallace, pp. 101-29. Boston: Auburn.

Mandelbaum, Dorothy Rosenthal. 1976. Toward an understanding of the career persistence of women physicians. *Journal of the American Medical Women's Association* 31 (8, August): 314-21.

Marieskind, Helen I. 1980. *Women in the Health System: Patients, Providers, and Programs*. St. Louis: Mosby.

Mayer, John E., and Aaron Rosenblatt. 1975. Encounters with danger. *Sociology of Work and Occupations* 2 (3, August): 227-45.

Merton, Robert. 1968. *Social Theory and Social Structure*. Glencoe, Illinois: Free Press.

de Mille, Agnes. 1958. Artist or wife. *Atlantic Monthly* 202 (September): 52-58.

Michener, James A. 1982. *Space*. New York: Fawcett Crest.

Montagna, Paul D. 1977. *Occupations and Society: Toward a Sociology of the Labor Market*. New York: John Wiley and Sons.

Morain, Thomas. 1980. The departure of males from the teaching profession in nineteenth-century Iowa. *Civil War History* XXVI (2): 161-70.

Morrisey, Elizabeth, and David F. Gillespie. 1975. Technology and conflict of professionals in bureaucratic organizations. *Sociological Quarterly* 16 (3, Summer): 319-32.

Myrdal, Gunnar. 1944. *An American Dilemma.* New York: Harper and Bros.

Novak, Michael. 1968. The New Nuns. In *The New Nuns*, edited by Sister M. Charles Borromeo, pp. 19-32. New York: A Signet Book, The New American Library.

Nye, F. Ivan, and Lois W. Hoffman. 1963. *The Employed Mother in America.* Chicago: Rand McNally.

Olesen, V. L., and E. W. Whittaker. 1969. *The Silent Dialogue: A Study in the Social Psychology of Professional Socialization.* San Francisco: Jossey-Bass.

Olson, Jon, and Jon Miller. 1983. Gender and Interaction in the Workplace. In *Research in the Interweave of Social Roles: Families and Jobs*, Vol. 3, edited by Helena Z. Lopata and Joseph H. Pleck, pp. 35-87. Greenwich, Connecticut: JAI Press.

Oppenheimer, Valarie Kincade. 1973. Demographic Influence on Female Employment and the Status of Women. In *Changing Women in a Changing Society*, edited by Joan Huber, Chicago: University of Chicago Press, pp. 184-99.

_____. 1970. *The Female Labor Force in the United States.* Westport, Connecticut: Greenwood.

Ortiz, Flora Ida. 1975. Women and medicine: The process of professional incorporation. *Journal of American Medical Women's Association* 30 (1, January): 18-30.

Orzack, Louis H. 1971. Professionalization and prestige deficits *Sociological Focus* 4 (Spring): 63-71.

Otten, Alan L. 1976. "Two-Career Couples." *The Wall Street Journal*, (Thursday, July 29): 1.

Otto, Luther B., Denneth I. Spenner, and Vaughn R. A. Call. 1980. *Career Line Prototypes.* Omaha, Nebraska: Boys Town Center for the Study of Youth Development.

Patterson, Michelle. 1971. Alice in wonderland: A study of women faculty in graduate departments of sociology. *American Sociologist* 6 (August): 226-34.

Patterson, Michelle, and Laurie Engelberg. 1978. Women in Male-Dominated Professions. In *Women Working: Theories and Facts in Perspective*, edited by Ann H. Stromberg and Shirley Harkess, pp. 266-92. Palo Alto, California: Mayfield.

Pennell, Maryland, and Shirlene Showell. 1975. *Women in Health Careers.* Washington, D.C.: The American Public Health Association.

Pepitone-Rockwell, Fran. (ed.). 1980. *Dual-Career Couples.* Beverly Hills, California: Sage.

Pleck, Joseph H. 1983. Husbands' Paid Work and Family Roles: Current Research Issues. In *Research in the Interweave of Social Roles: Families and Jobs*,

Vol. 3, edited by Helena Z. Lopata and Joseph H. Pleck, pp. 251-333. Greenwich, Connecticut: JAI Press.

Poloma, Margaret M. 1972. Role Conflict and the Married Professional Woman. In *Toward a Sociology of Women*, edited by C. Safilios-Rothchild. Lexington, Massachusetts: Zerox.

Poloma, M. M. and N. Garland. 1971. The married professional woman: A study of tolerance of domestication. *Journal of Marriage and the Family* 33: 531-40.

Poloma, Margaret, and Neil Garland. 1970. "The myth of the egalitarian family: Familial roles and the professionally employed wife." Paper presented at the 65th annual meeting of the American Sociological Association.

Pressley, Beatrice. 1974. Survey of Guidance and Counseling Divisions of State Departments of Education and Resolutions with Women Adopted by the Senate of the American Personnel and Guidance Association at its meeting in San Diego, California. (No publisher) flyer.

Prather, Jane. 1971. Why Can't Women Be More Like Men: A Summary of the Sociopsychological Factors Hindering Women's Advancement in the Professions. In *Women in the Professions: What's all the Fuss About?*, edited by Linda S. Fidell and John DeLamater, pp. 14-24. Beverly Hills, California: Sage.

Psathas, George. 1968. The fate of idealism in nursing school. *Journal of Health and Social Behavior* 9: 52-65.

Purik, M. 1973. Joint appointments: Collaboration for better patient care. *Nursing Outlook* 73: 576-79.

Quadagno, Jill S. 1978. Career Continuity and Retirement Plans of Men and Women Physicians. *Sociology of Work and Occupations* 5 (1, February): 55-73.

Quade, Vicki. 1983. Twelve success stories. *American Bar Association Journal* 69 (October): 1400-12.

Rapoport, Robert, and Rhona Rapoport, with Janice Bumstead. 1978. *Working Couples*. New York: Harper Colophon Books.

Rapoport, Robert and Rhona Rapoport. 1976. *Dual-Career Families Re-examined: New Integrations of Work and Family*. London: Martin Robertson.

Rapoport, Rhona, and Robert N. Rapoport. 1972. The Dual-Career Family: A Variant Pattern and Social Change. In *Toward a Sociology of Women*, edited by Constantina Safilios-Rothchild, pp. 216-44. Lexington, Massachusetts: Xerox.

Reuther, Rosemary Radford. 1976. Ordination: What Is the Problem? In *Women and the Catholic Priesthood: An Expanded Vision*, edited by Anne Marie Gardiner, pp. 30-34. Proceedings of the Detroit Ordination Conference. New York: Paulist Press.

Richardson, John G., and Brenda Wooden Hatcher. 1983. The feminization of public school teaching. *Work and Occupations* 10 (1, February): 81-99.

Ritzer, George. 1977. *Working: Conflict and Change*. Englewood Cliffs, New Jersey: Prentice Hall, 2nd ed.

Robin, Stanley S. 1971. The Female in Engineering. In *The Professional Woman*, edited by Athena Theodore, pp. 397-413. Cambridge, Massachusetts: Schenkman.

Roby, Pamela, (ed.). 1973. *Child Care. Who Cares?* New York: Basic Books.

Rosenberg, Bernard, and Norris Fliegel. 1971. Prejudice Against Female Artists. In *The Professional Woman*, edited by Athena Theodore, pp. 660-65. Cambridge, Massachusetts: Schenkman.

Rossi, Alice. 1965a. Barriers to the Career Choice of Engineering, Medicine or Science Among American Women. In *Women and the Scientific Professions*, edited by Jacquelyn A. Mattfelt and Carol G. Van Aken, pp. 55-127. Cambridge, Massachusetts: The M.I.T. Press.

_____. 1965b. Women in science: Why so few? *Science* 148 (3674): 1196-1202.

Rossi, Alice, and Ann Calderwood, (eds.). 1973. *Academic Women on the Move*. New York: Russell Sage Foundation.

Rowland, H. (ed.). 1978. *The Nurses Almanac*. Germantown, Md.: Aspen.

Rushing, William A. 1971. Social Influence and the Social Psychological Function of Deference: A Study of Psychiatric Nursing. In *The Professional Woman*, edited by Athena Theodore, pp. 182-94. Cambridge, Massachusetts: Schenkman.

Russman, Leonard. 1949. A study of role conceptions on bureaucracy. *Social Forces* 27 (March): 305-10.

Saleh, Shoukry D., Robert J. Lee and Erich P. Prien. 1965. Why nurses leave their jobs—an analysis of female turnover. *Personnel Administration* 28 (January/February): 25-28.

SanGiovanni, Lucinda. 1978. *Ex-Nuns: A Study of Emergent Role Passage*. Norwood, New Jersey: Ablex.

Schwartz, Neena B. 1973. Why women form their own professional organizations. *Journal of the American Medical Women's Association* 28 (1, January): 12-15.

Scott, W. Richard. 1969. Employees in a Bureaucratic Structure: Social Work. In *The Semi-Professions and their Organization*, edited by Amitai Etzioni, pp. 82-140. New York: The Free Press.

Sexton, Patricia Cayo. 1982. *The New Nightingales: Hospital Workers, Unions, New Women's Issues*. New York: Enquiry Press.

Simon, Rita James, Shirley Merritt Clark, and Kathleen Galway. 1967. The woman Ph.D.: A recent profile. *Social Problems* 15: 221-36.

Simpson, Ida Harper. 1967. Patterns of socialization into professions: The case of student nurses. *Sociological Inquiry* 37: 47-54.

Simpson, Richard, and Ida Harper Simpson. 1969. Women and Bureaucracy in the Semi-Professions. In *The Semi-Professions and their Organization*, edited by Amitai Etzioni, pp. 196-265. New York: The Free Press.

Singleton, Loy A., and Stephanie L. Cook. 1982. Television network news reporting by female correspondents: An update. *JOB* 26 (1, Winter): 487-91.

Sloan, Frank A., and Somchai Richupan. 1975. Short-run supply responses of professional nurses: A micro-analysis. *Journal of Human Resources* IX, 2: 241-57.

Smock, Sue Marx, Margaret Stein, and Marilyn Heins. 1980. Parental influence on female career achievement: the case of the female physician. *International Journal of Women's Studies* 3 (5): 466-78.

Sokolowska, Magdalena. 1965. Some reflections on the different attitudes of men and women toward work. *International Labor Review* 92 (July).

Sorenson, Laurel. 1983. A woman's unwritten code for success. *American Bar Association Journal* 69 (October): 1414-19.

Sorkin, Alan L. 1977. *Health Manpower*. Lexington, Massachusetts: D.C. Heath.

Spangler, Eve, Marsha A. Gordon, and Ronald M. Pipkin. 1978. Token women: An empirical test of Kanter's hypothesis. *American Journal of Sociology* 84 (1, July): 160-70.

Spender, Dale. 1980. *Man Made Language*. London: Routledge and Kegan Paul.

Starr, Paul. 1982. *The Social Transformation of American Medicine*. New York: Basic Books.

Stolte-Heiskanen, Veronica. 1983. The Role and Status of Women Scientific Workers in Research Groups. In *Research in the Interweave of Social Roles: Families and Jobs*, Vol. 3, edited by Helena Z. Lopata and Joseph H. Pleck, pp. 59-87. Greenwich, Connecticut: JAI Press.

Swindler, Leonard. 1976. Sisterhood: Model of Future Priesthood. In *Women and Catholic Priesthood: An Expanded Vision*, edited by Anne Marie Gardiner, pp. 132-34. New York: Paulist Press.

Taber, Lois R. 1974. Social Casework—A Basic Service. In *The Field of Social Work*, edited by Arthur E. Fink et al., pp. 119-39. New York: Holt, Rinehart and Winston, 6th ed.

Tinto, Vincent. 1980. College origins and patterns of status attainment: Schooling among professional and business-managerial occupations. *Sociology of Work and Occupations* 7 (4, November): 457-86.

Toren, Nina 1972. *Social Work: The Case of a Semi-Profession*. Beverly Hills: California: Sage.

———. 1969. Semi-professionalism and Social Work: A Theoretical Perspective. In *The Semi-Professions and their Organization*, edited by Amitai Etzioni, pp. 141-95. New York: The Free Press.

Trigg, Linda J., and Daniel Perlman. 1976. Social influences on women's pursuit of a nontraditional career. *Psychology of Women Quarterly* 1 (2, Winter): 138-50.

Tropman, John E. 1971. The Married Professional Social Worker. In *The Professional Woman*, edited by Athena Theodore, pp. 525-35. Cambridge, Massachusetts: Schenkman.

Tuckman, Gaye. 1978. *Making News: A Study in the Construction of Reality*. New York: The Free Press.

U.S. Department of Labor. 1982. *Labor Force Statistics Derived from the Current Population Survey: A Databook*, Vol. I. Washington, D.C.: U.S. Government Printing Office.

————. 1982. *Occupational Outlook Handbook*. Washington, D.C.: U.S. Government Printing Office.

U.S. Department of Labor. 1975a. *Dictionary of Occupational Titles, Vol. 1: Definitions of Titles*. Washington, D.C.: U.S. Government Printing Office.

————. 1966. Fact Sheet on Women in Professional and Technical Positions. (November) WB 67-164.

U.S. Department of Labor–Women's Bureau. 1966 (Bulletin 190), 1969 (Bulletin 294), 1975b (Bulletin 297). *Handbook on Women Workers*. Washington, D.C.: U.S. Government Printing Office.

Vachon, M. L. S., W. A. L. Wyall, and J. Rogers. 1976. The Nurse in Thanologology: What She Can Learn from the Women's Liberation Movement. In *The Nurse as Caregiver for the Terminal Patient and his Family*, edited by A. M. Earle, N. T. Argondizzo, and A. H. Kutscher. New York: Columbia University Press.

Vachon, M. L. S., W. A. L. Lyall, and S. J. J. Freeman. 1978. Measurement and management of stress in health professionals working with advanced cancer patients. *Death Education* 1: 365-75.

Vetter, Betty M. 1981. Women scientists and engineers: trends in participation. *Science* 214 (December 18): 1313-21.

————. 1980. Working women scientists and engineers. *Science* 207, 28.

Vollmer, Howard M., and Donald L. Mills, (eds.). 1966. *Professionalization*. Englewood Cliffs, New Jersey: Prentice-Hall.

Walsh, Edward J. 1982. Prestige, work satisfaction and alienation: Comparisons among garbagemen, professors, and other work groups. *Work and Occupations* 9 (4, November): 475-96.

Walshok, Mary. 1981. *Blue Collar Women*. Garden City, New York: Anchor Books, Anchor, Doubleday.

Wermiel, Stephen. 1983. "Lawyer's Public Image is Dreadful, Spurring Concern by Attorney: Devious Tactics, High Fees, Big Damage Suits Hurt: But They Defend System. *Wall Street Journal*, October 11, pp. 1, 20.

Widom, Cathy Spatz, and Barbara W. Burke. 1978. Performance, attitudes, and professional socialization of women in academia. *Sex Roles* 4 (4): 549-61.

Wildman, Wesley A. 1971. Teachers and Collective Negotiations. In *White Collar Workers*, edited by Albert A. Blum et al., pp. 126-65. New York: Random House.

Wilensky, Harold L. 1964. The professionalization of everyone. *American Journal of Sociology* 70 (2, September): 137-58.

————. 1961. Orderly careers and social participation: The impact of work history on social integration in the middle mass. *American Sociological Review* 26 (August): 521-39.

Williams, Robin, Jr. 1970. *American Society: A Sociological Interpretation*. New York: Alfred A. Knopf, 3rd edition.

Wilson, Margaret A. 1976. Basic principles of credentialing health practitioners. *Respiratory Care* 21 (10 October): 954-59.

Wilson, Victoria. 1971. An Analysis of Femininity in Nursing. In *Women in the Professions: What's All the Fuss About?*, edited by Linda S. Fidell and John DeLamater, pp. 55-62. Beverly Hills, California: Sage.

Wilson, William Juluns. 1978. *The Declining Significance of Race: Blacks and Changing American Institutions*. Chicago: University of Chicago Press.

Wiltse, Kermit. 1974. The Field of Social Work: An Overview. In *The Field of Social Work*, edited by Arthur E. Fink, et al., pp. 1-17. New York: Holt, Rinehart and Winston, 6th ed.

Winter, Bill. 1983. Survey: Women lawyers work harder, are paid less, but they're happy. The *American Bar Association Journal* 69 (October): 1384-88.

Wittner, Judith. 1978. "Households of strangers: Career patterns of foster children and other wards of the state." Unpublished dissertation, Department of Sociology, Northwestern University.

Wolfe, Tom. 1979. *The Right Stuff*. New York: Farrar, Straus, and Giroux.

Wright, Benjamin, and Shirley A. Tuska. 1971. Career dreams of teachers. In *The Professional Woman*, edited by Athena Theodore, pp. 334-45. Cambridge, Massachusetts: Schenkman.

Yogev, Sara. 1983. Judging the professional women: Changing research, changing values. *Psychology of Women Quarterly* 7 (3, Spring): 219-33.

_____. 1981. Do professional women have egalitarian marital relationships? *Journal of Marriage and the Family* (November): 865-71.

Yogev, Sara, and Andrea Vierra. 1983. The state of motherhood among professional women. *Sex Roles* 9 (3): 391-96.

Ziegler, Harmon. 1971. Male and Female: Differing Perceptions of the Teaching Experience. In *The Professional Woman*, edited by Athena Theodore, pp. 74-92. Cambridge, Massachusetts: Schenkman.

Znaniecki, Florian W. 1940. *The Social Role of the Man of Knowledge*. New York: Columbia University Press.

10

SUMMARY AND
IMPLICATIONS

The purpose of *City Women: Work, Jobs, Occupations, Careers* is to examine the literature produced by social scientists and other observers of the American scene focused on women in the major urban occupations and then to analyze the background and histories, the constructions of reality, and the role clusters of women in one American metropolitan center. Accepting one of the definitions of work in *The Random House Dictionary of the English Language*, namely, that it is "exertion of effort directed to produce or accomplish something; labor; toil," we see how it is woven into jobs, or sets of mutually interdependent relations forming social roles. Refraining from the view that work must be rewarded directly by earnings, we are able to include the role of full-time homemaker in the occupational structure, placing it between the occupations involving sales and management in organizations outside of the home. A homemaker is a manager of a home of various complexity and resources. Jobs are thus social roles which encompass more than sets of tasks; they include all the relations between the social person and the social circle which make possible the accomplishment of their goals and the functioning of society. Observers of workers often forget how complex the system of negotiation and rights-duties exchanges is without which the tasks can not be carried forth. It is interesting to note that the awareness of relational complexities and strains on the part of observers increases as the status and other rewards of the job increase. The scientist in an organization like a university or a profit-making firm can have the same tasks, perform the same work, but have completely different jobs because their relations are different. It is this reason that we would favor, for example, the placement of service occupations ahead of blue-collar or manual ones in the organization of occupations on the typical ladder which governmental and private agencies use to examine the American structure. Service occupations usually involve more complex social roles.

In this, Volume I of *City Women*, we have examined the available literature concerning women's occupations in the history of America and the present time. We proceeded from the least prestigious occupational category into which the numerous occupations are lumped by governmental and other social scientists for brevity's sake, breaking them into smaller units represented by the women in the Chicago area sample. Volume II then focuses on the backgrounds and schooling, employment, and occupational histories of Chicago area women aged 25 to 54, their construction of reality as far as the job and the self goes, and their role clusters. In both volumes, we find incongruities, role strain, and role conflict, as well as sources of pleasure, commitments, and changes in the lives of women in modern urban America.

There are several common threads woven through the literature on women in the world of work inside and outside of the home, as well as historical shifts in what is seen, studied, and commented upon. At first glance, we can easily repeat Edward Gross's (1971) question "Plus ca change?" or the more common "The more things change, the more they stay the same." In spite of the anti-discrimination laws and policies of the federal government—which have been extremely important for both blue-collar and white-collar women in opening up schooling, job training, and jobs—the distribution of women in various occupations has not changed as much as the mass media lead us to believe. Those people aiming toward greater equality are concerned with the possibility that pressure for "equal pay" or "open jobs" may decrease in the future on the assumption that change has already occurred across the board. On the other hand, change is taking place, even since our study of the Chicago area women, especially on the professional level and in the educational system. Women are entering many previously restricted professions and, in lesser numbers, skilled blue-collar jobs as their first choice rather than in the middle years of life as they see the advantages. Simultaneously, the educational institution has opened to people of all ages, enabling "older" women to start second careers. The secretarial or homemaking ghettos no longer have tight boundaries, ladders out of them are evident. Secretaries in organizations providing real estate, insurance, and related services are becoming agents, making much more money and being quite independent in organizing their work. Women who were full-time homemakers during the growing years of their children can go back to school and aim for clergy, technical, or professional jobs. Job-training programs are accepting women, although outward prejudice on the job is frequently mentioned. Bias in management of large corporations and in many high status occupations is more subtle, as in the failure to cooperate fully with a "token" woman by withholding necessary information. It tends to increase when the male establishment becomes concerned with the growing numbers of women successfully functioning in their roles.

The decrystallization of life courses, that is, in the sequencing of entrance and exits of social roles, is also evident in the literature and, as we shall see in Volume II, among the Chicago area women. This applies not only to school and work sequences, but also to the way women combine marriage, motherhood, homemaking, and related roles with those outside of the home. Women in highly demanding, "greedy" occupations no longer have to sacrifice marriage and motherhood, much as previous professionals or managers did without even the religious commitment of Catholic nuns. Role conflict is apparent, and the subject of much of the literature, but the comments are a result of actual combinations rather than as warnings to those not yet involved. One of the reasons role conflict forms a constant refrain is that each woman must work out her personal solution to being involved in more than one demanding social role, with little help from the employing agency or society at large, and often with little cooperation from a traditional husband and children. Much of the literature deals with the problems of the "returnee," the woman who stayed out of the labor force when the children were little, who then has to change her relations, her whole roles, established when she could give full-time energy and attention to the roles of wife, mother, homemaker. Many demanding jobs in management and professional occupations were created for men, on the assumption that they could be carried out in a two-person career fashion with a back-up person at home. When a former full-time homemaker returns to a demanding job, or to school in order to prepare for one, she usually does not drop the other roles in her cluster. In addition, she lacks a back-up person at home. At least, not all divorce or wait till the children are all out of the house or have mothers who take over the major work of these roles. Thus, role conflict and strain within each role are easily the effects of such dramatic change. Of course, not all women return to the labor force and not all take demanding jobs. Part-time work, although low in pay and other benefits, is preferred by many women who have children but still want to retain their knowledge, skills and social contacts.

What is new is the situation of women who start their marriages and even motherhood after having committed themselves to a career, or at least to a demanding job, having prepared themselves for it and delayed home roles in order to establish themselves outside of the home. Their marriages and roles as mothers are apt to be very different from those of women who stayed home and then enter jobs. It is difficult, if not useless, to speculate on the extent to which the society will respond to the pressures of women, and some men, to modify the work schedules and career lines to such an extent that couples can work out complex role clusters without sacrificing whole areas of life. Will the "greedy institutions" become less greedy?

The effect of the "true womanhood" culture can still be found in the literature dealing with occupational distributions by gender. Forgetting the history of each occupation and the way it became closed to, or a funnel for entrance into, one gender or the other, much psychological and related research has focused on the alleged match between the characteristics of the social person desired for such a job and those of candidates or incumbants. It is "natural" that women, who are the carers and healers, should become doctors in Poland; it is "natural" that objective men, able to control their emotions and be scientifically oriented, be doctors in America. A great deal of attention has been directed toward the first woman astronaut, with gender linked explanations of why she can contribute to orbiting the earth. Thus, affirmative action or Vatican II do not necessarily change the basic imagery of an occupation's social person—they only provide legitimization for entry by tokens who lack the necessary gender identity. A society which still sees women as primarily sex objects and future or current mothers does not want to encourage them to take on occupations which might interfere with such involvements, prefering them to hold in a circling pattern for at least the first half of their life course. The view of them in the second half is tinged by agism. At least, this is the conclusion one draws from the abundance of literature on role conflict of women, in contrast to that of men. Even descriptions of role strain within an occupation tend to be gender focused, either in jobs modeled after male social persons or in relations with higher status men, as in the case of nurses and doctors, nuns and priests.

We are left with relatively little literature on women workers outside of the home that is gender-free. Much of what is available about *Man and his Work*, as Ritzer (1972) named his textbook in the sociology of occupations (it was changed to *Working* in a latter edition after someone pointed out the sexism), has the underlying assumption contained in that early title—the world of work outside the home is the province of men. As Spender (1982) points out, most public language is male. This is the overwhelming image which emerges when we read the sociology or psychology of occupations.

Turning now to specific occupational categories for implications drawn from the literature, we start with the services. Increased attempts at improving the status of such workers as in protective and health services through organization and certification will undoubtedly increase strain in relations with established professions and bureaucracies. Although building and personal maintenance personnel continue to exist in the form of cleaning workers and beauticians who operate individually or in small units, these activities are increasingly standardized through organized services or chains who do their own recruiting, training, placement, and supervision. The service economy will undoubtedly continue growing and will draw to it in most jobs only temporary workers, unless we import enough uneducated foreign people willing to accept the constraints surrounding such jobs.

Implications from knowledge about blue-collar worlds can lead to paradoxical predictions. The continued demise of smoke stack industries and the number of strictly manual jobs will probably lead male workers to increase attempts to protect themselves through the removal, or blocking of entrance, of women, who ironically can more easily move to other types of jobs anyway.

The literature focusing on de-skilling of clerical jobs often ignores the internal heterogeneity of office work. It is quite possible that the field will become polarized through the use of the computer and word processor into jobs requiring greater skill and better pay and the routine ones requiring more easily learned "on the job" training. Once some of the gender based boundaries are loosened, we can expect many women now actually working as managers and semi-professional staff to be taken out of the clerical ghetto and moved up the line into management. It appears that the line between clerical and managerial positions, so clearly described by Kanter (1977) in *Men and Women of the Corporation* may be penetrated even more in the future than the current situation indicates.

The sales field is also experiencing change with the following implications: women are entering as sales agents, mobile representatives of product or service companies, with commissions contributing to better pay and independence from supervision providing greater rewards than available to sales clerks. The job of sales clerk, in any but expensive establishments, is becoming increasingly de-skilled. Customers are more knowledgeable and accustomed to making individual decisions. Retail stores wish to cut down expenses so that the sales clerk becomes mainly a ticket writer and cashier. The personal appearance and demeanor of the traditional "saleslady" are characteristics no longer required of such sales personnel so that working class and minority women are able to move into these jobs, much as they have into the lower status clerical and health services occupations.

Homemaking as a full-time occupation is increasingly a matter of choice. The expanding flexibility of the world of school and work enables women to move in and out of it as demands from other roles and personal preferences change. One of the areas in which there is a growing, albeit still limited, literature concerns the two-person career. Margolis (1979), Vandervelde (1979), Fawlkes (1980), and the new Finch (1983) *Married to the Job: Wives Incorporation in Men's Work* explain both the complexity of being a part of such a two-person career and the frequent revolt of the "new wife" against its confinement. A number of social scientists have begun to study the consequence of this revolt upon the careers of the husband. We can expect the future to hold both patterns of homemaking: full-time involvement by choice, and in-and-out movement during different stages of the family life course. Still problematic is the consequence upon external career of voluntary withdrawal into full-time homemaking as long as career lines are drawn so tightly. Of course, some women may never become full-time homemakers, regardless of the composition of their role cluster.

Although many of the women managers still manage only women, especially in retail trade and health professions, the beginning movement of women into "management" of large work organizations may have some implications on how these roles are performed. At least, there is a great debate over whether women will adopt the male model of management, create a parallel track, or convert the roles into more androgynous ones. The new styles of management require greater flexibility in work environments, which we can expect to influence the whole organizational atmosphere. Little is actually known about this subject, since so few women are as yet in management positions to change the flavor of things.

The same decision as to style of carrying out a social role faces women and men who enter professional and technical jobs previously (and still) dominated by the other gender. The dramatic increase of women in professional and scientific schools and fields can lead us to expect geometric progress of involvement in the future. Thus, the decrease of the proportions of women in highly placed, extensive education and commitment, professions in the past 50 years or so has been due mainly to the rapid increase of men in these types of jobs. We can now expect the proportions to change as men remain relatively constant in getting degrees while women expand their schooling and job training in demanding occupations.

Of course, the current swing to conservatism and to limiting governmental pressure toward equality in the world of work may make the changes which we note more difficult to achieve. However, it is doubtful whether they can stop the movement since the ideological base of restricting women's involvement in public life has been removed. As we noted in previous chapters, entrance into male-intensive occupations in the past has often been almost coincidental or in second career fashion. Now the young women appear to be directly headed for the more lucrative and less traditional jobs.

REFERENCES

Gross, Edward. 1971. Plus ca change. . .? The Sexual Structure of Occupations Over Time. In *The Professional Woman*, edited by Athena Theodore, pp. 39-51. Cambridge, Massachusetts: Schenkman.

Fawlkes, Martha. 1980. *Behind Every Successful Man: Wives of Medicine and Academia*. New York: Columbia University Press.

Finch, Janet. 1983. *Married to the Job: Wives Incorporation in Men's Work*. Boston: George Allen and Unwin.

Kanter, Rosebeth Moss. 1977. *Men and Women of the Corporation*. New York: Basic Books.

Margolis, Diane Rothbard. 1979. *The Managers: Corporate Life in America*. New York: William Morrow.

Random House Dictionary of the English Language. 1966. New York: Random House.

Ritzer, George. 1972. *Man and His Work*. Englewood Cliffs, New Jersey: Prentice-Hall.

Spender, Dale. 1980. *Man Made Language*. London: Routledge and Kegan Paul.

Vandervelde, Maryanne. 1979. *The Changing Life of the Corporation Wife*. New York: Mecox.

Index

Abbott, Edith, 31, 32, 47, 49
accounting, women in, 222
alienation, blue-collar workers, 111-113
America: employment and occupational trends of women, 49-57; reform movements, 46-47; servants, 40-41; unmarried women, 47; widows, status of, 48-49; women and work, 35-43; and women's sphere, 43-45
American Couples (Blumstein and Schwartz), 202-203
American Dilemma, An (Myrdal), 215
American Woman: An Historical Study, The (Digwall), 160
Amoskeag (Hareven and Langenbach), 47
Anderson, Michael, 154
Andre, Rae, 158, 160
Andrisani, Paul J., 112
Antos, Joseph R., 109
Aries, Phillippe, 22, 27, 30, 33-34, 45
Armstrong, Peter, 112, 115

Baker, Elizabeth Faulkner, 39, 40, 58
Baker, Sally Hillsman, 103
Banner, Lois
Barker, Diana Leonard, 61
Barnewolt, Debra, 24, 61, 157, 161
Barrett, Nancy, 64
Baruch, Grace, 167
beauticians, 94-95
Belasco, James A., 143
Bell, Carolyn Shaw, 63

Bell, Daniel, 36, 50, 77
Bemis, Stephen E., 50, 77
Benet, Mary Kathleen, 122, 128
Benston, Margaret, 169
Bergquist, Virginia A., 110
Berk, Sarah Fenstermaker, 61, 157, 161; *Women and Household Labor*, 161
Berk, Richard A., 61, 161
Bernard, Jessie: *Academic Women*, 54, 229, 232, 233; *The Female World*, 35, 40, 44, 45, 82; on homemakers, 155, 156, 157; on professionals, 218
Bielby, Denise, 203
Bird, Caroline, 43, 57, 161, 181, 215; *Two-Paycheck Marriage*, 202
Bjorn, Lars, 104, 106
Blackburn, R. M., 185
Blau, Francine D., 57, 58, 60, 111
Bledstein, Burton J., 195, 196-97, 214
Block, Marc, 21
Blood, Robert O. Jr., 160, 164
Bloomfield, Robert M., 128, 129
Blue-Collar Women (Walshok), 105, 200
blue-collar workers: alienation, 111-113; barriers to entry, 106-107; characteristics of, 102, 105-106; in Chicago area, 113-115; distribution of, 103-108; levels of complexity, 113-115; protective legislation, 108-109; union membership, 109-111; women and male-dominated jobs, 104-105

291

Reich, Micahel, 60
religious organizations, role of women in, 258-262
Reubens, Beatrice G., 104, 105, 106, 107
Reubens, Edwin P., 104, 105, 106, 107
Reymont, Ladislas, 27
Riegel, Robert E., 37
Riemer, Jeffrey W., 106
Riesman, David, 157, 160
Right Stuff, The, (Wolfe), 194
Ritzer, George, 2, 10, 14; on blue-collar workers, 111; on professionals, 195, 198, 199, 250; on sales workers, 140, 143
Robinson, John P., 157
Robinston, P. J., 144
Roby, Pamela, 59, 106, 107, 109, 202
Roethisberger, F. J., 112
role ambiguity, 10
role clusters, 11-14
role conflict, 11-14; reduction of, 203-204
role strain, 9-11; in clergy, 259-260; in communications media field, 253, 254; in direct selling, 143; inter-sender, 10; in legal profession, 256-257; in librarians, 250; in nursing, 237-237; in personnel work, 251-252; role person, 10; in social work, 247-248; in teaching, 225-227; in waitresses, 89-90
Rosaldo, Michelle Zimbalist, 27, 43, 154
Ross, H. L., 160
Ross, Jane L., 105, 108, 176
Rossi, Alice, 14, 159, 213, 214, 218
Rothman, Sheila M., 30, 33, 34, 35, 40, 45; on homemakers, 156, 161
Rubin, Lillian Breslow, 160
Rustad, Michael, 107
Ryan, Mary P., 3, 20, 35, 37, 38, 156

Sacks, Karen, 21
sales agents: defined, 141; direct selling, 142-143; recruitment, 144-146; training, 146-148
sales clerks, 140-141; limitations of role of, 140
sales workers: in Chicago area, 148; classification of, 138; literature on, 137-140; sales agents, 141-148; sales clerks, 140-141
Salmon, Lucy Maynard, 40-41
Sawhill, I. V., 160
school crossing guards, 94
Schooler, Carmi, 112
Schrank, Robert, 112
Schwartz, Eleanor Brantley, 178, 183-184
Schwartz, Neena B., 216
Schwartz, Peter, 202-203
Scott, Joan W., 24, 35, 154
Seccombe, Wally, 162
Secretarial Ghetto, The (Benet), 122
secretaries, 128-129; role of, 128; two types of, 129. *See also* clerical workers
security guards, 95
segregation, occupational, *see* occupational segregation
Seifer, Nancy, 115, 131
self-confidence, 107
semi-professions, 198, 205
Semi-Professions and Their Organization (Etzioni), 198, 205, 247
servants: defined as "help," 41; in pre-industrial Western Europe, 24; work history, 40-41
service sector, 77-96; building maintenance services, 81-84; in Chicago area, 95-96; defined, 78; food services, 84-92; jobs in, 79-80; nonprofessional health services, 93-94; occupations, 80; personal maintenance, 94-95; protective services, 95; types, 79, 81